HERO

HERO

volume 1
THE SILENT ERA TO DILIP KUMAR

ASHOK RAJ

HAY HOUSE
Australia • Canada • Hong Kong • India
South Africa • United Kingdom • United States

Published and distributed in the United Kingdom by:
Hay House UK Ltd, 292B Kensal Rd, London W10 5BE. Tel.: (44) 20 8962 1230;
Fax: (44) 20 8962 1239. www.hayhouse.co.uk

Published and distributed in the United States of America by:
Hay House, Inc., PO Box 5100, Carlsbad, CA 92018-5100. Tel.: (1) 760 431 7695 or (800) 654 5126;
Fax: (1) 760 431 6948 or (800) 650 5115. www.hayhouse.com

Published and distributed in Australia by:
Hay House Australia Ltd, 18/36 Ralph St, Alexandria NSW 2015. Tel.: (61) 2 9669 4299;
Fax: (61) 2 9669 4144. www.hayhouse.com.au

Published and distributed in the Republic of South Africa by:
Hay House SA (Pty), Ltd, PO Box 990, Witkoppen 2068. Tel./Fax: (27) 11 467 8904.
www.hayhouse.co.za

Published and distributed in India by:
Hay House Publishers India, Muskaan Complex, Plot No.3, B-2, Vasant Kunj,
New Delhi – 110 070. Tel.: (91) 11 4176 1620; Fax: (91) 11 4176 1630. www.hayhouse.co.in

Distributed in Canada by:
Raincoast, 9050 Shaughnessy St, Vancouver, BC V6P 6E5. Tel.: (1) 604 323 7100;
Fax: (1) 604 323 2600

A catalogue record for this book is available from the British Library.

ISBN 978-1-84850-152-2

Printed and bound at
Thomson Press (India) Ltd.

In memory of my uncle
Shri B. S. Hoogan
one of the founders of Hindi film music

Preface

In my family tradition, made up of the ennobling elements of both the Hindu and Sikh heritage, fine arts such as music, theatre and cinema have received a great deal of critical attention. Sometimes, adulation has been expressed and sometimes criticism.

My grandfather, Shri Ishwar Das, although an engineer by profession was an accomplished singer from Ferozepur (Punjab), specializing in rendering the Gurbani. His eldest son, the late Shri B. S. Hoogan, was one of the leading composers in the Bombay film world of the 1930s. The second son, my father, the late Shri B. R. Hoogan, too was a shabd (devotional hymn) singer and often performed popular musical plays based on Hindu mythological tales. For the last two generations, the youngsters in the family have been trained to appreciate the finer points of the aforementioned art forms.

Even as children, we were taken to musical concerts, drama events and cinema halls. We saw many film classics. Later on, there were heated but well-informed discussions and debates on the merits of the cinema of the older generation vis-à-vis ours. Invariably, these discussions and debates – after a thorough dissection of a film (based on its artistic and emotional appeal, directorial treatment, storyline, characterizations, cinematic merits and music) – would finally get focused on the performance of its hero as the prime mover of the venture. As the lead actor's role was subjected to a critical appraisal, he was also judged in comparison with his seniors and contemporaries, with the representatives of the two generations arguing passionately in favour of the acting icons of their respective eras: K. L. Saigal-Chandramohan-Prithviraj Kapoor-Ashok Kumar-Motilal-Surendra vis-à-vis Dilip Kumar-Shyam-Raj Kapoor-Dev Anand-Raaj Kumar and later Amitabh Bachchan-Rajesh Khanna-Sanjeev Kumar-Vinod Khanna and the new-age heroes of the 1990s and the new millennium.

As exemplified by the discussions in my family, the popular discourse on cinema and its impact on society have been largely centred around the hero figure – his style, mannerisms, histrionics and the roles he has played in his career. The dynamics of such a discourse and its idiom have also been expressed formally in film reviews (both in the print and electronic media), gossip columns, publicity material, biographies/autobiographies of the heroes, interviews and fan-club hagiographies. In this way, these popular expressions represent a significant part of our cinema's oral, visual as well as written history. Yet, in the amalgamation of these intertextual expressions, which manifests itself as a rereading of the cinema in the public sphere, the very essence of the making of the Indian film hero's persona and the changes it undergoes in different historical points of reference are often lost.

This work, a kind of tribute to my family's film-appreciation tradition, seeks to 'recast' the aforementioned popular discourse on the Indian film hero by retracing and mapping the historic journey of this pivotal figure through different eras of cinema to present the socio-cultural history of the Indian film and also its cinematic context. The first volume covers the silent era as well as Dilip Kumar and his contemporaries. The second volume starts with Amitabh Bachchan and his contemporaries and goes on to highlight the heroes of the 1980s, 1990s and the new millennium.

Given the large canvas and the encyclopedic nature of this work, its publication would never have been possible without the blessings and assistance of a number of people within and outside cinema. I salute these highly knowledgeable and respected individuals who were willing to share their cine-enthusiast spirit (and their inputs) to enlighten me on diverse aspects of what turned out to be a highly challenging task. I am extremely grateful to the following:

- The late B. K. Karanjia, former editor of *Screen*,
- the late Raghava Menon, music critic and writer,
- Firoze Rangoonwalla, a veteran in the field of film writing,
- the late Mohammed Shamim, film critic,
- Geeti Sen, former editor, the India International Centre (New Delhi) journal,
- Ravi Vasudevan, the renowned cinema scholar, associated with the Centre for Study on Developing Societies, New Delhi,
- Har Mandir Singh Hamraaz, the author of the monumental work *Hindi Film Geet Kosh*,
- K. L. Arora, the fabulous one-man encyclopedia and film critic,
- A. K. Balakrishnan, the late Mohan Hari and Pradeep Huda, all film makers,
- Ashok Chopra, CEO and managing director of Hay House Publishers India, for his incredible passion for this work that helped me in developing its perspective and in widening its canvas and thus enabling me to pen the grand saga of four generations of cinema and
- K. J. Ravinder (Ravi), the editor of Hay House, who lent very valuable scholarly and moral support.

My effort was guided by several path-breaking works, which have sought to address Indian cinema as an alternative expression of the wider socio-cultural processes in Indian society. A wealth of information, both hard facts and views on films and heroes, was gleaned from available sources. I specially thank Ashish Rajadhyaksha and Paul Willemen, the compilers of the classic *Encyclopedia of Indian Cinema*, as I gathered a host of insights from their highly fascinating and scholarly compendium.

This work has also made use of film reviews/articles published in the *Hindustan Times*, *The Times of India*, *Screen*, *Filmfare*, *The Indian Express*, *The Statesman* and *Jansatta* over past decades. I, therefore, convey my gratitude to the film critics K. M. Amladi, Khalid Mohammed, Amita Malik, Kavita Nagpal and Nikhat Kazmi, who have been associated with these publications (not necessarily in that order).

In formulating the perspective for this book, I received valuable insights from my cousins Pradyuman, the renowned painter, poster designer and film publicity expert, and Puran Chandra Hoogan, who has been associated with the banners of Rajshree, Rajender Singh Bedi and Mahesh Bhatt. I thank the other film lovers in my family: younger brother Ashwini Kumar, doctor by profession and star of Doordarshan's early serials like *Hum Log* and *Phir Wahi Talash*, and his wife Vibha and her film maker sister, my sister Kusum Sood and her husband Colonel R. N. Sood, Aruna Mahendru (another sister of mine) and of course my mother, the late Sushila Devi, for sharing their views and convictions about cinema.

I also thank several film-loving couples for offering their considered views on our films and heroes: Poonam and Mohan Kudesiya, Manju and S. K. Sharma, Shradha and Ravi Kashyap, Apoorva and Biswajit Dhar, Aditi and Rakesh Kapoor, Rumjhum and Girish Kumar (and their children Charu Kartikeya and Sukriti Vinayak), Kanti and Aman Baluni and Seema and Sudhir Sagar. My other friends – Surendra Prakash, Pradeep Biswas, Sangeeta, Abhay Sinha, Satya Prakash, Rahul Kashyap, Shankar Jha and two *bindaas* (happy-go-lucky) pals Rishi Kohli and Himmat Singh – too contributed towards building the information bank for this work.

Thanks also to the library staff of the Film and Television Institute of India, Pune, the Nehru Memorial Museum and Library, New Delhi, Jawaharlal Nehru University, New Delhi, the National Centre for Performing Arts, Bombay, Sangeet Natak Akademi, New Delhi, Chitrabani, Calcutta, the Centre for Study on Developing Societies, the Indian Institute of Mass Communication and the Jamia Millia Islamia University, the last three located in New Delhi.

And, finally, a sentimental hug to my wife Madhu Kumari, who, while bearing the brunt of my uninterruptible involvement in this work and the ensuing anarchy all around, kept inspiring this obstinate dullard with her soulful love and care, sharing along the way the joy of rediscovering and enjoying the romance of cinema. Our son, Pallav, also deserves a pat on his back for stealing my writing sheets and pens and for disturbing my computer work schedule.

– Ashok Raj

Contents

Preface   vii

Chapter 1
The Curtain Begins to Lift ...   1

Chapter 2
The Formative Phase of Indian Cinema   7

Chapter 3
K. L. Saigal and Other Early Heroes   37

Chapter 4
The Arrival of Dilip Kumar   119

Chapter 5
Dilip Kumar as Numero Uno   131

Chapter 6
Dilip Kumar and the Indian School of Method Acting   235

Chapter 7
Film and Portrayal Diversity in Dilip Kumar's Cinema   245

Chapter 8
Two Other Indigenous Heroes: Guru Dutt and Sanjeev Kumar   257

Chapter 9
'Disciples' of Dilip Kumar and 'The Phenomenon'   271

Chapter 10
Heroes' Gallery: Dilip Kumar's Contemporaries   283

Appendix 1
K. L. Saigal: Select Filmography   369

Appendix 2
Dilip Kumar: Filmography   375

Index   393

Chapter 1

The Curtain Begins to Lift ...

Our film heritage is a virtual treasure trove containing many valuable gems. This legacy depicts a nostalgic flashback that throws up images of the evolution of the Indian motion picture over the years and highlights the invaluable contributions of several creative talents. The magic of cinema continues to cast its spell far and wide and will do so in the future as well.

The study of Indian cinema can be slotted into various categories.

The *first* relates to the chronological documentation of its history, detailing basic information on films (banner, director, cast and other credits), major trends, the contributions of the film makers and the composers of film music.[1]

The *second* focuses on the oeuvres on individual film makers, analysing their career paths, bringing to the fore the trends set by them and projecting their overall vision.[2]

The *third* refers to a small set of autobiographies written by a few film personalities, which provide rare insights into their professional and personal experiences and the times they had lived through. These personalities include actresses Leela Chitnis, Kanan Devi, Shanta Apte, Vyjayanthimala and Durga Khote, actors Balraj Sahni and Dev Anand, film makers J. B. H. Wadia and V. Shantaram and composer C. Ramchandra.[3]

The *fourth* category covers biographical works on film celebrities such as Kundan Lal Saigal, Raj Kapoor, Nargis and Sunil Dutt, Meena Kumari, Guru Dutt, Madhubala, Ashok Kumar, Dilip Kumar, Pran, Lata Mangeshkar, Rajesh Khanna, Amitabh

Bachchan, Kishore Kumar and Shahrukh Khan.[4] However, most of these works seem to be unofficial biographies (not formally approved by their subjects) and are generally written with a sense of adoration and praise.

Into the last category fall books on particular films, which are of two types: those providing an analysis of the content and impact of a chosen film and those describing the making of a film (*Sholay*, *Dilwale Dulhaniya Le Jaayenge*, *Lagaan* and *Ashoka*, for instance) with details on the processes of its conceptualization, script writing, casting, shooting and release.

The present work revisits the history of Hindi mainstream cinema on a large canvas, placing the trends and the personalities in their specific time and cinematic contexts. It attempts to break new ground by taking up the study of Indian cinema from an unexplored perspective – that of the 'indigenous film hero'.

As the frontal figure in the sphere of cinema, *the hero* predominantly reflects the socio-cultural and, sometimes, the political basis of the film structure and content. He expresses in an indigenous idiom the people's aspirations, dreams, their links with the past and their inner turmoil, thus unleashing in them a surge of mass empathy and idolization. And as this basis changes with time, this hero's persona also begins to articulate new cinematic concerns, which result from these changes. Thus, the indigenous hero, in his evolution, development and mass acceptance, traces the history of cinema itself. Imbued with a distinct Indian ethos, this frontal figure also provides to cinema its true national identity. In the absence of such a national figure, cinema in many countries like Pakistan, Bangladesh, Sri Lanka and Egypt has failed to grow and acquire a distinct national identity in the global arena.

Amidst the galaxy of film stars, the three artistes mainly responsible for the creation of this hero image during different periods of Indian cinema were Kundan Lal Saigal, Dilip Kumar and Amitabh Bachchan. In the *formative period* of the 1930s and 1940s, the cinematic persona of K. L. Saigal, the legendary singer-actor, became the central figure for the design of the indigenous film hero prototype. As the first true 'cult figure' of the Indian screen, he not only brought about the very first revolutionary change in the image of the Indian hero, but also had a profound influence on the structure of the Indian film.

In the *classical period* of the late 1940s, the 1950s and the early 1960s, Dilip Kumar took the tradition of the cult-hero developed by Saigal to an entirely new domain. Building on the highly successful Saigal prototype, he depicted the indigenous hero in his finest form by using to maximum effect his vast repertoire of histrionics.

Given the wide spectrum of talent that flourished during the early period of classical cinema, Dilip Kumar soon distinguished himself as the architect of what came to be referred as the 'school of method acting'. The impact of this school has been so very phenomenal that no new incumbent into the field of film acting could succeed unless he is an ardent student and is able to build up his skills by borrowing some of the elements from the inventory of the master. Dilip Kumar, in fact, soon became the country's first 'professor of cinematic acting', setting the national standards for this art. Indeed, while Saigal gave his soul to film music, Dilip Kumar did the same to acting. The hero personified by him came to represent our nation the same way as Humphrey Bogart, Clark Gable, Cary Grant and later Harrison Ford in Hollywood epitomized America's national personality.

A highly commendable continuity to the long journey of the second indigenous hero was provided by Indian cinema's secondmost formidable actor, Amitabh Bachchan. Amidst the turbulent socio-political conditions prevailing in the 1970s, this actor carved a niche for himself as the third-generation indigenous film hero. By rebuilding, modifying and rejuvenating the Dilip Kumar model, Bachchan, like his senior, captured the nation's imagination on the strength of his portrayal of various characters, thus providing to Indian cinema the much-needed reaffirmation of its national identity in tune with the changing socio-political milieu. In the process, he shattered all the alien images of the film hero, validating, at least for the time being, the critical importance of an indigenous model in driving cinema in a creative and self-fulfilling direction.

For the purpose of analysis, this study divides the development of Indian cinema since its inception in 1913 into four distinct phases:

(1)   Formative phase: 1913–48.
(2)   Classical phase: 1949–65.
(3)   Post-classical phase: 1966–90.
(4)   Modern phase: 1991 onwards.

By locating the three indigenous heroes in the intellectual as well as the artistic and technological phases of Indian cinema, this work scans the various creative trends and studies the contribution of these artistes in the making of the indigenous film hero over three generations. It also examines the coming into being of the 'global Indian film' and the arrival of the 'new-age hero' during the post-Bachchan modern period of cinema characterized by a general decline in the quality of films and unprecedented changes in the audience profile.

Notes and References

1   Firoze Rangoonwalla, *Seventy-Five Years of Indian Cinema*, New Delhi: Indian Book Company, 1975.
Firoze Rangoonwalla, *Indian Cinema*, New Delhi: Clarion Books, 1983.
Ashish Rajadhyaksha and Paul Willemen, *Encyclopedia of Indian Cinema*, London: British Film Institute, New Delhi: Oxford University Press, 1994.
Sanjit Narwekar (ed.), *Directory of Indian Film-makers and Films*, London: Flicks Books, 1994.
T. M. Ramachandran (ed.), *70 Years of Indian Cinema, 1913–1983*, Bombay: Cinema India-International, 1981.

Rajendra Ojha (ed.), *75 Glorious Years of Indian Cinema: Complete Filmography of All Films Produced between 1913 and 1988*, Bombay: Screen World, 1988.
Har Mandir Singh 'Hamraaz', *Hindi Film Geet Kosh* (Vols. I to IV), Kanpur: published by Satinder Kaur, 1980.

2.   Bageshwar Jha, *B. N. Sircar: A Monograph*, Pune: The National Film Association of India and Calcutta: Seagull Books, 1990.
Rinki Bhattacharya, *Bimal Roy*, Bhopal: Madhya Pradesh Film Development Corporation, 1989.
Ritu Nanda, *Raj Kapoor: His Life and His Films*, Bombay: R. K. Films, 1991.
Bunny Reuben, *Raj Kapoor: The Fabulous Showman – An Intimate Biography*, Bombay: National Film Development Corporation (NFDC), 1988.
Bunny Reuben, *Mehboob: India's DeMille – The First Biography*, New Delhi: Indus, 1994.

3.   V. Shantaram, *Shantarama: The Autobiography of V. Shantaram* (as told to Madhura Jasraj), Bombay: Rajkamal Kalamandir, 1986 (Marathi/Hindi).
J. B. H. Wadia, *Looking Back on My 'Romance' with Films*, Bombay: Jayant Art Printers, 1955.
Durga Khote, *Mee Durga Khote*, Bombay: Majestic Book Stall, 1982 (Marathi).
Shanta Apte, *Jau Mi Cinemaat?* Bombay: B. Govind, 1940 (Marathi).
Leela Chitnis, *Chanderi Duniyat*, Pune: Srividya Prakashan, 1981 (Marathi).
Balraj Sahni, *Balraj Sahni – An Autobiography*, New Delhi: Hind Pocket Books, 1979.
Vyjayanthimala (co-author Jyoti Sabarwal), *Bonding ... A Memoir*, New Delhi: Stellar Publishers, 2007.
C. Ramchandra, *Majhya Jeevanacha Sargam*, Pune: Inamdar Bandhu Prakashan, 1977 (Marathi).
Kanan Devi, *Shobarey Aami Nomay* (I Bow before Everyone), Calcutta: undated (Bengali).
Dev Anand, *Romancing with Life: An Autobiography*, New Delhi: Penguin, 2007.

4.   Raghava R. Menon, *K. L. Saigal: The Pilgrim of the Swara*, New Delhi: Clarion Books, 1978, and New Delhi: Hind Pocket Books, 1989.
Rani Burra (ed.), *Ashok Kumar: Green to Evergreen*, New Delhi: Directorate of Film Festivals, 1990.
Nabendu Ghosh, *Ashok Kumar: His Life and Times*, New Delhi: Indus, 1995.
Devdutt Shastri (ed.), *Prithviraj Kapoor Abhinandan Granth*, Allahabad: Vishal Manch, 1963 (Hindi).
Anjan Kumar, *Shayara/Amain*, two booklets on the lives of Meena Kumari and Guru Dutt, Delhi: Raj Kamal, 1988 (Hindi).
Nasreen Munni Kabir, *Guru Dutt: A Life in Cinema*, New Delhi: Oxford University Press, 2005.
Vinod Mehta, *Meena Kumari*, Bombay: Jaico Books, 1972.
T. J. S. George, *The Life and Times of Nargis*, New Delhi: Indus, 1994.

Khatija Akbar, *Madhubala: Her Life and Films*, New Delhi: UBS Publishers' Distributors, 1997.

Isak Mujawar, *Dev Anand*, Bombay: Priya Prakashan, 1977.

Kishore Valicha, *Kishore Kumar – The Definitive Biography*, New Delhi: Viking/Penguin, 1998.

Girija Pandit, *Rajesh Khanna: Ek Abhineta*, New Delhi: Star Publications, 1973 (Hindi).

Bhawana Somaaya, *Amitabh Bachchan – The Legend*, New Delhi: Macmillan India, 1999.

Saumya Bandhopadaya, *Amitabh Bachchan* (translated into Hindi from Bengali by Amar Goswami), New Delhi: Vaani, 2000.

Khalid Mohamed, *To Be and Not to Be – Amitabh Bachchan*, Mumbai: Saraswati Creations, 2001.

Urmila Lamba, *The Thespian: The Life of Dilip Kumar*, Delhi: Vision Books, 2002.

Sanjit, Narwekar, *Dilip Kumar – The Last Emperor*, New Delhi: Rupa, 2004.

Bunny Reuben, *Dilip Kumar: Star Legend of Indian Cinema – The Definitive Biography*, New Delhi: HarperCollins, 2004.

Meghnad Desai, *Nehru's Hero: Dilip Kumar in the Life of India*, New Delhi: Roli Books, 2004.

Ashok Raj, 'K. L. Saigal: Cinema's First Indigenous Hero', *IIC Quarterly*, New Delhi: India International Centre: Summer 2004.

Alpana Chowdhury, *Dev Anand – Dashing Debonair*, New Delhi: Rupa, 2004.

Bunny Reuben, *...and Pran: A Biography*, New Delhi: HarperCollins, 2004.

Raju Bharatan, *Lata Mangeshkar: A Biography*, New Delhi: UBS Publishers' Distributors, 1995.

Kishwar Desai, *Darlingji: The True Love Story of Nargis and Sunil Dutt*, New Delhi: HarperCollins, 2007.

Namrata Dutt and Priya Dutt, *Mr. and Mrs. Dutt*, New Delhi: Roli Books, 2007.

Chapter 2

The Formative Phase of Indian Cinema

Introduction

India's experience with the film medium has been unique. Considered by many as the most powerful art form, Indian cinema has no equal the world over in terms of output, the variety of its genres, its multilingual character, the infrastructure for the dissemination of films and, most significantly, its impact on society as a determinant of lifestyle apart from reflecting socio-cultural and political realities as perceived by the film makers.

A never-ending mega-show whose seeds were sown about a century ago by Dhundiraj Govind Phalke (popularly known as Dadasaheb Phalke) in his small house in Bombay, cinema has become one of the country's most complex and largest enterprises. The diversity of its resources is indeed unique: the intellectual geniuses (directors, writers, musicians and lyricists), the vast reservoir of acting talent, the 'behind-the-camera' expertise (cinematographers, editors, sound recordists, laboratory technicians) and monetary inputs from big financiers.

Dadasaheb Phalke

The almost century-old history of Indian cinema as a popular cultural heritage evokes many nostalgic responses not only from the people belonging to the film world but also from the vast audience. This history shows how the unending experiments in creative inventiveness in order to master the technology and the creative medium led to the development of an indigenous cinematic expression, which has made India one of the world leaders in the field of mass entertainment. Indeed, the masterpieces of the pioneers and the later visionaries have created a grand spectacle, perfecting the popular Indian film genre through a synthesis of traditional cultural forms and the modern cinematic craft.

Cinema represents a modern technology acting as a mediator between popular culture (inclusive of diverse art forms) and the people. In India, in the wake of gradual disintegration of the indigenous social, cultural and political milieu during the British rule, cinema as the mass medium began the process of evolving a common aesthetic identity and soon started depicting on screen, in a larger-than-life format, the cultural expressions of a host of creative artistes. Cinema soon became the dominant channel, incorporating a wide variety of creative output including classical and folk drama, apart from dance and music. In fact, the amazing appeal of the new mass medium gradually led to the traditional cultural practices being marginalized.

The Two Founding Fathers: A Printer and a Painter

Indian cinema came into existence with the release of *Raja Harishchandra*, the first full-length silent film made in 1913 by the legendary Dadasaheb Phalke. His name has been immortalized in the chronicles of Indian cinema. Phalke, along with his equally illustrious companions – Baburao Painter, Jamshedji Framji Madan, Ardeshir Irani, B. N. Sircar, Sohrab Modi, Mohan Bhavnani, Chandulal Shah, Himanshu Rai and V. Shantaram among others – consolidated the foundation (both creative and technological) of Indian cinema in the silent era and introduced a whole range of socio-cultural themes. However, credit also goes to a group of early innovators who were the first to unravel the magic of celluloid images through their deep intuitive sense of experimentation and self-acquired technical expertise (see pp.11-12).

Phalke was born on 30 April 1870 at Nasik (now in Maharashtra) and was committed by family tradition to become a 'Shastri', the traditional Indian scholar. He eventually became a trained still photographer, painter and art printer. Inspired by *Life of Christ*, an English film that he saw after a brief spell of blindness, he got obsessed with the idea of making a film all by himself. After studying film making, through the few books he managed to acquire after a long and arduous search in Bombay bookshops, he went to England in 1912 and bought a Williamson cine camera, a printing machine and a perforator. Amazingly, his first creation was *The Growth of a Plant*, in which he filmed the growth of beans in a pot hour by hour. This experiment is accredited to be the first Indian science education film.

Soon, Phalke launched *Raja Harishchandra* in a makeshift studio at his house (located on the road now named after him) in Bombay. This 370-foot-long film was completed in eight months. However, owing to stiff competition from theatre troupes, the film failed to collect even Rs 3 on its first day. Undaunted, Phalke employed a curious publicity strategy: he popularized a new slogan: '*See Fifty Thousand Pictures in Two Annas, Don't Miss Your Chance to See the Wonderful Pictures which Are Two Miles by Three-Quarters of an Inch Size.*' No wonder, the idea of highlighting the picture length clicked and collections soon rose to Rs 300 a day.

Raja Harishchandra was soon followed by *Krishna Janam, Savitri, Kaliya Murdan* and Phalke's first hit, *Lanka Dahan*. A unique contribution of Phalke's mythological films was that they gave to the Indian public their own culture-specific cinema in sharp contrast to the prevailing foreign films, which, though wonderful, were alien to them.

Phalke made a staggering 175 films during his lifetime. When he exhibited his films in the UK, the British film industry was stunned by the content, the fine pictorial sense and the technical resourcefulness of his work. Phalke was a multifaceted personality: he was also a professional magician, a wizard in trick photography and a special-effects genius. An obsessive experimenter, his ventures ranged from filming in colour through tanning and toning, by using scenic models, to discovering a new formula for making toilet soap.

***

During this period, another visionary, Baburao Painter, who made a living by painting the sets of theatrical productions in Kolhapur, Maharashtra, emerged on the scene in a big way. He accomplished the gigantic task of developing Phalke's cinema into a full-fledged art form and laid the foundation of the great Marathi tradition of film making. Revered as 'Kala Maharishi', he soon began making films by converting a second-hand projector into a camera with the help of his cousin Anant Rao. Under the banner of the Kolhapur Film Company, he produced, in 1919, his first film, Sairandhri (based on a play, Keechak Vadh, banned by the British Government), which was followed by fifteen more films, the last one being released in 1930. Notable among these are Sinhagad, Savkari Pash (a superhit) and Netaji Palkar.

Painter was the first to organize indoor shooting using artificial lights and predesigned sets. He introduced many optical effects such as fade-in and fade-out. He also was the first to evolve the idea of a publicity campaign, such as designing and distributing of pamphlets and displaying film posters. Besides, he employed the technique of sketching the basic visual composition of a scene before shooting, a method later followed by Satyajit Ray among others. Although he trained a whole generation of film makers, his main protégé was V. Shantaram (1901–90), who was later to emerge as one of the first movie moghuls of Indian cinema.

The Early Innovators

The revelation of the moving picture in Bombay was part of a worldwide campaign launched by the Lumière Brothers (Auguste Marie Louis Nicholas and Louis Jean) to create markets for the new media technology. As the peepshow, the 'Kinetoscope' invented by Thomas Edison, was not internationally patented, many enterprising inventors had rushed to convert the peep-in machine to a projecting kinetoscope to hit quick gold. The Lumière Brothers were the first to win the free-for-all race. Their system was truly a marvel of ingenuity – a three-in-one gadget, which could serve as camera, projector or printing machine, with slight adjustments.

A very significant outcome of the arrival of foreign films during the inaugural period of Indian cinema (1896–1913) was the emergence of indigenous innovators in the technology of film making. For instance, Sakharam Bhatawadekar was the first to build a movie camera by himself and he tested its performance by filming a wrestling bout. In 1901, he shot what should be considered as the first newsreel made in India – the felicitation ceremony of R. P. Paranjpye who had returned to Bombay after obtaining a special distinction in mathematics at Cambridge.

Using Bhatawadekar's camera, a group of three enthusiasts – A. P. Karandikar, S. N. Patankar and V. P. Divakar – filmed the Imperial Durbar of 1911 and the funeral of the renowned freedom fighter Lokmanya Tilak in 1920. In between, in 1912, they produced a 100-foot-long film, *Savitri*. Around 1909, two other creative minds, N. G. Chitre and Dadasaheb Torne, made a 800-foot-long film, *Pundalik*. In Calcutta, Heeralal Sen built a camera himself in 1900 and made a film, *Indian Life Science*, in 1903. He also filmed the

Delhi Durbar of 1911. In the same period, Jyotish Sarkar shot a documentary on the big rallies held to protest against the partition of Bengal.

The Magicians Who Made Images Talk

In the wake of the rapidly growing popularity of the Indian film, the development of cinema into an all-encompassing industry was natural. Two top-notch entrepreneurs who blended business with creativity and built the most powerful film production-distribution-exhibition empires of that time were Ardeshir Irani and J. F. Madan. They were the first to introduce the talkie era in Indian cinema.

Ardeshir Irani

Born on 10 December 1885 in Poona (now spelt as Pune), Irani, like Phalke, was a multifaceted genius who went on to eventually become a film maker and, in 1905, an exhibitor. The highly intuitive Irani sensed the vast potential of cinema. Soon, he became the distributor of nearly all the Hollywood films released in India.

Irani formed Imperial Theatres in 1926, a banner that was to introduce to Indian cinema all genres, ranging from mythologicals, historicals and love legends to socials and comedies. After making a phenomenal number of silent films (130 in all), Irani became obsessed with the idea of making the country's first talkie. It was a time when even the film makers in the West were sceptical about a complete switchover to films with inbuilt sound in the form of dialogues and music. Within a short span of one month, as a result of intense efforts, Irani mastered the technology of sound and brought forth his masterpiece *Alam Ara* on 14 March 1931. Made at a cost of Rs 40,000 (a huge amount at that time), this film, 10,500 feet in length, also presented the first glimpse of the basic song-based structure, which was to remain the dominant form of the average Indian film.

Irani perhaps was the world's greatest multilingual film maker, having made forays into English, Bengali, Marathi, Tamil, Persian, Burmese, Indonesian and Pushto. He is credited with launching the talkie era in different countries such as Burma, Indonesia and Iran. He made nearly 120 talkies in a span of eight years. He was also the first film maker to establish a colour laboratory based on Cinecolour technology, which was imported from Hollywood.

J. F. Madan, a leading importer of beverages, food and pharmaceutical products and a dealer in insurance and real estate, had become a showbiz magnate as early as 1902. By 1910, he was the first to run a chain of cinema houses throughout the country. In Calcutta where he owned all the theatres except one, he laid the foundation of the Bengal film industry with his Madan Theatres. The first movie produced under this banner was *Bilwamangal* in 1918, followed by many films in quick successsion. After the death of the senior Madan, his son J. J. Madan, took over and expanded the empire.

With the advent of the sound era, Madan Theatres entered the race, competing with Irani's Imperial Theatres to make the first talkie. The Madan team not only provided to the audience the first thrills of synchronized sound added to a silent movie, *Melody of Love*, but also produced a one-reeler talkie *one month before* the release of *Alam Ara*. However, the Madans were pipped to the post by just one day when they released a full-length talkie miscellany consisting of live scenes from various stage plays and concerts, and also included a speech of the Nobel Laureate, Sir C. V. Raman. The Madan stable released its first feature talkie, *Shirin Farhad*, on 19 April 1931. Both Imperial Theatres and Madan Theatres provided a lot of creative space to many famous directors of the period such as Izra Mir, R. S. Choudhary, Moti Gidwani, Paysi Karani, Homi Master, Jyotish Bannerji and Fardoon Irani.[1]

The Blowing of Prabhat's Trumpet

The ingenuity and creative upsurge provided by Phalke and Painter as a result of their technological innovations in film making became the springboard for the Marathi school at Kolhapur. Five disciples of Painter, under the leadership of V. Shantaram (the other four being Vishnupant Damle, K. R. Dhaibar, S. Fatehlal and Sitarambapu Kulkarni), launched the Prabhat Film Company in 1929. In contrast to New Theatres in Calcutta and later Bombay Talkies, which attracted the educated elite, Prabhat's founders had no formal education.

Like his mentor, Shantaram too came from a humble background. At the age of sixteen, he became a railroad repair mechanic and also took up a part-time job as a gatekeeper in a cinema house. Soon he was employed by Painter in the Maharashtra Film Company to do all kinds of jobs, from carrying the camera to painting the sets. Thus, he was gradually getting trained in

V. Shantaram

various aspects of film making. After making his directorial debut with *Netaji Palkar* in 1927, on the basis of his amazing ingenuity and resourcefulness, he was instrumental in projecting Prabhat as one of the leading studios of that period.

The first talkie produced by Prabhat was *Ayodhyecha Raja* (1932) starring Shantaram himself, along with Durga Khote, Govindrao Tembe and Master Vinayak in the role of Narad. (Narad, a key character in many mythologies, is portrayed as mischief maker who creates discord between various gods and goddesses. He is also considered a great musician.) The second venture, *Sairandhri* (1933) was made in colour and it was to become the country's first such film (it was processed in Germany), but the experiment ended in a failure and the film was released in the black and white version. Other successful films of Prabhat included Shantaram's *Singagad* (1933), *Amrit Manthan* (1935, which had zoom shots for the first time) and the memorable *Ram Shastri*

(1947). It is said that Satyajit Ray was inspired to make films after seeing the last-mentioned film.

Prabhat also made many biographical films on Marathi saints, which won wide acclaim: *Sant Gyaneshwar* (1940), *Sant Sakhu* (1941), *Sant Tukaram* (1948), directed by Master V. Damle and S. Fatehlal and *Dharmatma* (1948, on the life of Saint Eknath) directed by Shantaram. *Sant Tukaram* immortalized the actor Vishnupant Pagnis in the lead role. Frank Capra, in fact, wrote an article in the *American Cinematographer* on *Sant Gyaneshwar* praising its technique and applauding the quality achieved without access to up-to-date equipment.

Although the main forte of Prabhat, like all its contemporaries, was mythological and devotional films and films based on Maratha history, Shantaram began to experiment with the social genre, laying greater emphasis on Hindi remakes and directed three Marathi classics in a row: *Kunku* (*Duniya Na Mane* in Hindi, 1937), *Manus* (*Admi* in Hindi, 1939) and *Shejari* (*Padosi* in Hindi, 1941).

Prabhat was a launching pad for nearly all the top Marathi film personalities who made a variety of movies under different banners. Master Vinayak, the counterpoint to Shantaram's serious cinema, was the pioneer of social and comedy films in Marathi/Hindi cinema. He made his first film, *Vilasi Ishwar* at Kolhapur Cinetone (1933), followed by films like *Ardhangi/Ghar Ki Raani* (1940) and *Jeevan Yaatra* (1946). In collaboration with famous avant garde writers such as Mama Warerkar, P. K. Atre and V. S. Khandekar, he pioneered the making of hilarious political satires (*Brahmachari*, 1938, *Lagna Pahave Karun*, 1940, and *Sarkari Pahune*, 1942), taking them beyond the dominant social reform genre prevalent at that time.

Bhalji Pendharkar, Baburao Pendharkar, Gajanan Jagirdar, Parshwanath Yeshwant Altekar, Baburao Apte, Vishram Bedekar and Raja Paranjape were other veterans of the era. A unique feature of the Marathi school of film making was that nearly all the directors and writers were also successful actors. *Shyamsunder*

(1932), directed by Bhalji Pendharkar, was the first movie to celebrate its silver jubilee in a single theatre in India. Bhalji Pendharkar also made remarkable films such as *Raja Gopichand* (1938), *Thoratanchi Kamala* (1941) and the controversial *Vande Mataram Ashram* (1938), a spoof on political opportunism in the garb of the nationalist movement.

Altekar, the famous actor-film maker, specialized largely in depicting the lives of heroes of Maratha history and portraying mythological legends on screen. He also carried out some seminal experiments in realistic cinema; for instance, in Narayanrao Sarpotdar's *Maharachi Por* (1925). He also acted in this movie besides providing directional inputs. This experiment was the first of its kind, blending film making, journalism and the avant garde theatre movement, a mix that culminated in the famous work of the Natyamanwantar group in Marathi theatre. This group specialized in sharp-witted social criticism. Jagirdar, famed actor-scenarist-director, made his mark as a director with *Begunaah* (1937), *Vasantsena* (1942) and Prabhat's *Ram Shastri* (1947).

Shantaram left Prabhat in 1942 and launched his own studio, Rajkamal Kalamandir, dedicated solely to the production of Hindi films. His memorable films under the Rajkamal banner were: *Shakuntala* (1943), *Parbat Pe Apna Dera* (1944) and *Dr Kotnis Ki Amar Kahani* (1946).

The Inventors of the Grand Spectacle

As cinema started becoming a huge commercial enterprise and the availability of the requisite finance and technology was fairly assured, the quest to do something spectacular led to the emergence of the movie moghuls on the scene. Working nearly on the same pattern as that of their contemporary big banners in Hollywood, these film makers brought to Indian cinema the genre of historical films.

Most of these spectacles were based on popular historical tales or semi-historical situations. But the magnificent re-creation of an era was carried out with the utmost emphasis on the authenticity of the period under depiction, many a time in consultation with historians and experts on art and culture. The narrative style, however, largely remained theatrical, governed by the characteristic feature of point–counterpoint verbal discourse of the Parsi stage. While V. Shantaram and Mehboob Khan should also be considered as movie moghuls in their own right, the real contenders were Sohrab Modi, S. S. Vasan (from South India) and later K. Asif (of *Mughal-e-Azam* fame) and Kamal Amrohi (of *Pakeezah* fame).

Sohrab Modi, like Mehoob Khan and V. Shantaram, was the main architect of indigenous cinema during the formative period. A renowned Parsi theatre personality, he established Minerva Movietone, which became a house of indigenous cinema after the advent of the talkie. He was perhaps the only film maker who had a highly successful career in theatre and an equally impressive record in the world of cinema. Born into a family of civil servants, and after pursuing his education, initially at Rampur (then in United Provinces) and later completing it in Bombay, he started as a travelling exhibitor in Gwalior in 1914 with his younger brother K. M. Modi. Later, in 1923, he set up a theatre group, the Arya Subodh Natya Mandali, jointly with his elder brother Rustam Modi. This group staged a series of highly successful plays.

Sohrab Modi's oeuvre was truly multifaceted, encompassing a range of genres in both theatre and cinema. He introduced William Shakespeare's plays in India in a big way through Urdu adaptations. The play, *Khoon Ka Khoon*, in which he played Hamlet opposite Naseem Banu (as Ophelia), was one of the biggest Urdu stage hits of the 1920s. (Naseem Banu was the mother of Saira Banu, the wife of Dilip Kumar, who was popular in the 1960s and 1970s.) With Rustam Modi, he started Stage Films in 1935, mainly to adapt their plays to the cinema. The film version of *Khoon Ka Khoon* (1935) was followed by Aga Hashr Kashmiri's Shakespearean adaptation, *Sayeed-e-Havas* (1936).

Soon Sohrab Modi, under his new banner, Minerva Movietone, began producing contemporary psychodramas that often dealt with marital problems from a misogynist viewpoint (Meetha Zaher, 1938, Jailor, 1938, and Bharosa, 1940). And finally he brought on the Indian screen lavishly mounted historical spectacles (Pukar, 1939, Sikandar, 1941, Prithvi Vallabh, 1943, and Jhansi Ki Rani, 1953). Modi's creations were invariably message oriented, often taking up the cause of the oppressed people (or nation-states) struggling to safeguard their sovereignty and freedom. His cinema centred around an overpowering theme in which all events, including the love affair of the lead pair, were subordinated to serve the main thrust of the film.

S. S. Vasan, the movie moghul from South India, also called the Cecil B. DeMille of India, came from humble origins. He arrived in the celluloid world after establishing himself as a print media magnate. He set up his own banner Gemini named after his zodiac sign. The early films of this banner (in Tamil) were Madanakamarajan (1941), Mangamma Sapatham (1943) and Kannamma En Kadhali (1945). However, it was Chandralekha (1948), the four-million-rupee extravaganza directed by him, which stands out as his unique contribution to the genre of Indian spectacles. Other big-budget costume dramas produced by Gemini were Apoorva Sahodarargul (Nishan in Hindi, 1949), Mangla (1949) and later the classic Avvaiyyar (1953).

The other two top-notch directors, K. Asif and Kamal Amrohi, who were to reach moghul status later in the classical period, found their foothold in cinema during the last years of the formative period.

The Bengal School: Towards Cinematic Language

Among the five centres of Indian cinema in the formative period – Bombay, Kolhapur, Calcutta, Lahore (which went to Pakistan after Partition in August 1947) and Madras – the eastern centre made a far-reaching contribution not only in getting rid of the effects of theatre on cinema but also in evolving its own language. This centre also introduced a gradual movement towards socially relevant as well as literature-based cinema.

The harbingers of the Bengal style were Dhiren Ganguly (popularly known as DG), Debaki Bose, Nitin Bose, P. C. Barua (a great romantic adventurer), and last but not the least, Bimal Roy. They were all 'graduates' of New Theatres, an institution built by another patriarch, B. N. Sircar. Sircar, who had studied engineering at the University of London, began his impressive film career by floating his company, International Filmcraft, which later grew to become New Theatres in 1930. Drawing heavily from Bengali literature for his themes, this engineer became the main architect of the Bengal school of film making. *Dena Pauna* (1931) was the first film made by New Theatres, based on the renowned writer Saratchandra Chatterjee's novel. (Saratchandra's most famous literary work is *Devdas*, which has been depicted on screen several times in different languages. Over the years, the very name Devdas has come to be associated with an agonized lover who has drowned his life in alcohol.)

Debaki Bose, born in 1898, was greatly influenced by Mahatma Gandhi's Non-cooperation Movement. He produced for New Theatres three of its early milestone films in the 1930s: *Chandidas, Meerabai* and *Puran Bhagat*. These films introduced lyricism in cinema and created a breakthrough in form and technique. Frame cutting, superimposition of images to highlight the drama and background music were tried out for the first time in these films. Debaki Bose's *Vidyapati* (1937) marked yet another qualitative leap and established the use of songs in a film, a trend that still continues. *Seeta* (1934), another classic that he directed for the East India Film Company, was widely acclaimed for its 'lyrical quality'.

P. C. Barua, the master of the romantic-tragic drama, which was epitomized in his immortal *Devdas* (with himself in the title role in the first version and with K. L. Saigal in the lead in the second version), was the son of the raja of Gauripur, Assam. An ace hunter, dancer, horseman and tennis player, he became interested in film making during his frequent European tours. Mainly financed by his father, albeit reluctantly, he set up Barua Pictures and produced *Apradhi*. Soon, he joined New Theatres and under the patronage of B. N. Sircar made a few remarkable films such as his masterpiece *Devdas* (1935), *Mukti* (1937) on social reforms, *Adhikar* (1938) on class distinction in society and *Rajat Jayanti* (1939), a social comedy. He died prematurely in 1951 at the age of 48.

Nitin Bose joined New Theatres as a cinematographer, making his debut with *Punarjanama* (1932). This film, directed by Jai Gopal Pillai, stood out in that it represented the first example of the medium having a control over the narrative. Later, as a director with the same company, Nitin Bose came up with many socially progressive themes as in *Didi* (1937), *Deshar Mati/Bharat Mata* (1938) and *Jiban Maran/Dushman* (1938). He left New Theatres in 1941 and went over to Bombay, where he became an important director under major banners such as Bombay Talkies, Minerva Movietone and Filmistan Studio.

Premankur Atorthy was another famous associate of New Theatres. He directed *Zindaa Laash* (1932), *Yahoodi Ki Ladki* (1933), *Kaarwaan-e-Hayaat* (1935) and *Bharat Ki Beti* (1935). Phani Majumdar made his mark with *Street Singer* (1938) and *Kapaal Kundala* (1939), Hemchandra Chunder with *Jeevan Ki Reet* (1939), *Wapas* (1943) and *Meri Bahen* (1944) and Amar Mullick with *Badi Didi* (1939) and *Abhinetri/Haar Jeet* (1940).

New Theatres' *Udayer Pathey* (1944) witnessed the directorial debut of Bimal Roy, a film maker who was to influence greatly the development of socially important cinema in the coming two decades. For New Theatres he also directed *Anjangarh* (1948) and *Pehla Admi* (1950), depicting the liberation struggle launched by Subhash Chandra Bose's Indian National Army (INA).

The Famous Runners-Up

Mohan Bhavnani, an engineer-turned-film maker, was among the early founders of Indian cinema. Along with Ardeshir Irani, J. F. Madan, B. N. Sircar, Himanshu Rai, V. Shantaram and Sohrab Modi, he facilitated the grand transition from the silent era to the talkie era. He had studied engineering at the College of Technology, Manchester, UK (1921–24), but after completing his degree, the young movie enthusiast went to Germany, to study film making at Universum Film AG (UFA). In 1927, Bhavnani joined Imperial Theatres and directed *Vasantsena* (1930), the first Hindi film to have Kannada intertitles.

In the wake of the arrival of the talkie, this master innovator again went to Germany to study sound-related film techniques. After his return home, he became an independent producer with Indian Art Production (1931–32), and made his first talkie *Shakuntala* (1931). (The cinematographer was Nitin Bose.) In 1933, he launched Ajanta Movietone and produced several films in quick succession.[2] Among these movies, *The Mill* (1934), scripted by the celebrated Hindi writer Munshi Premchand (whose real name was Dhanpat Rai), presented, perhaps for the first time, a realistic treatment of industrial working-class conditions in Indian cinema. Bhavnani is also accredited with making the country's first full-length colour film, *Rangeen Zamana* (aka *Ajit*, 1948) shot on 16 mm Kodachrome and blown up to 35 mm. After independence, he became the first chief producer with the Films Division, a body set up by the Government of India.

Bhavnani, who was an ace talent scout, introduced as well as promoted many artistes including Durga Khote, Bibbo, Master Nissar, P. Jairaj, S. B. Nayampalli, A. P. Kapoor, comedian Bhudo Advani, composers B. S. Hoogan, Badri Prasad and Naushad Ali (in *Prem Nagar*, 1940), lyricist-writer Mukand Lal 'Seemaab' and the renowned author Munshi Premchand.

Chandulal Shah was another stalwart who lived through the silent movie to the talkie transition period. He entered films after quitting a lucrative stock exchange business, and set up Ranjit Studio in 1929 in collaboration with Gohar, one of the most famous leading ladies of the era. His first major work was *Gun Sundari* (1925), based on the novel by Dayaram Shah. Ranjit entered the talkie era with *Pardesi Pritam* (1932), directed by Nandlal Jaswantlal. This studio soon became famous for mid-budget socials, satires and mythologicals and contributed to the consolidation of these genres, which were to shape the early cinema of the classical period in the late 1940s. With an assembly-line approach to production, this studio remained the country's biggest producer until the early 1950s.

Ranjit Studio made its presence felt with classics such as *Gun Sundari* (1925), *Achhut* (1940), *Aaj Ka Hindustan* (1940), *Tansen* (1943), *Pardesi* (1941), *Bhakta Surdas* (1942) and *Anarkali* (1935). The four most prolific directors of Ranjit were: Shah himself, Jayant Desai, Chaturbhuj Doshi and R. S. Choudhary. Others such as Nandlal Jaswantlal, Aspi Irani, Dinanath Madhok and later Abul Rashid Kardar and Kidar Sharma also directed important films for this studio. The success of Ranjit's films was attributed to famous authors including Dayaram Shah, Gunwantrai Acharya, playwright Narayan Prasad 'Betaab' and scenarist-film maker Chaturbhuj Doshi.

Wadia Movietone, set up by J. B .H. Wadia and Homi Wadia in 1933 in association with none other than the Tatas, was the production house for Hindi cinema's stunt genre. Inspired by the westerns starring Douglas Fairbanks, the Wadia productions often starred Fearless Nadia (real name Mary Evans Wadia), representing in Indian cinema the first-ever persona of a liberated, 'machismo' woman who would settle scores with the wrong-doers through physical combat (some of her films were *Hunterwali*, 1935, *Miss Frontier Mail*, 1936, and *Luteri Lalna*, 1938). J. B. H. Wadia, an erudite scholar and a keen follower of M. N. Roy (a philosopher and humanist), directed some of the early films. Homi Wadia expanded the 'family' genre with *Veer Bharat* (1934) and the Nadia films, among others. Shortly before closing, Wadia Movietone produced Madhu Bose's bilingual *Raj Nartaki* (1941), with the English version aimed at exploring the US market.

Sagar Movietone was set up in 1930 by Chimanlal Desai and Ambalal Patel. Soon it started churning out Parsi theatre-based films, mythologicals and stunt movies. This company supported the efforts of a host of early film makers such as Prafulla Ghosh, Sarvotam Badami, Izra Mir and Nanu Bhai Vakil.[3] Sagar also made documentaries on Jawaharlal Nehru and Subhash Chandra Bose with the active collaboration of these leaders.

However, the most important alumnus of Sagar Movietone was Mehboob Khan, one of the country's most influential film makers. This studio influenced his early works, such as *Judgement of Allah* (1935), *Manmohan* (1936), *Jagirdar* (1937), *Hum, Tum Aur Woh* (1938), *Vatan* (1938) and the all-time classic *Aurat* (1940). (He remade *Aurat* in 1957 as *Mother India*, which went on to become one of the all-time great movies that won international acclaim.) With the release of *Aurat*, *Bahen* (1941) and *Roti* (1943), Mehboob emerged as one of Indian cinema's foremost film makers, who took up, highly successfully, socio-political themes within the popular film genre. He, thus, further explored the political dimension in cinema, which had been initiated by Mohan Bhavnani in *The Mill* (1934). Mehboob's creations authentically reflected the social conditions perpetuated by the age-old feudal patriarchy. In 1942, he announced the setting up of Mehboob Productions, which was to have a far-reaching influence on the cinema of the classical period.

Apart from Mehboob, Sagar Movietone was also instrumental in launching the careers of Zia Sarhadi (*Bhole Bhale*, 1938) and Ramchandra Thakur (*Kasauti*, 1941, and *Garib*, 1942). In 1939, Sagar Movietone was reconstituted as the National Studio (in fact, Mehboob's *Aurat* was made at Sagar but released by the new company). R. S. Choudhary, whom Mehboob regarded as a teacher, also directed many memorable films for

Imperial and Sagar such as *Madhuri* (1932), *Piya Pyare* (1935), *Hamari Betiyaan* (1936), *Sach Hai* (1939) and *Gaali* (1944).

A. R. Kardar was a towering figure in the formative and classical periods of Hindi cinema. Born in a landed family of Lahore, he started his career as a painter and still photographer. He got his break as a director in the 1930s while working in the East Indian Film Company, Calcutta, and at the Ranjit and National Studios, Bombay. Later, he set up his own unit, the famous Kardar Studio. Kardar's oeuvre encompasses a wide range from the intense psychodramas, evoking the realism of Urdu literature (*Thokar*, 1939, *Pagal*, *Holi* and *Pooja*, all released in 1940), to musicals featuring his regular composer Naushad.

Prakash Pictures, under the leadership of Balwant Bhatt and Vijay Bhatt, kicked off with stunt movies, but later switched over successfully to high-quality social, mythological and period films such as *Nai Duniya* (1934), *Poornima* (1938), *Ek Hi Bhool* (1940), *Narasi Bhagat* (1940), *Samaj Ko Badal Dalo* (1947), *Bharat Milap* (1942) and the classic *Ram Rajya* (1943).

Pancholi Art Pictures, founded by Dalsukh M. Pancholi at Lahore, brought in the Punjabi influence on Bombay's Hindi cinema in a big way. Pancholi studied scriptwriting and cinematography in New York. His early productions *Gul-e-Bakawali* (1939), *Yamla Jat* (1940, in which Pran made his debut) in Punjabi and the superhit, *Khazanchi* (1941) in Hindi, paved the way for bringing Lahore's film industry into the national mainstream. This development brought into Hindi cinema Punjab's folk culture, songs, dance, music and lifestyle and helped a great deal in shaping the mass cultural film formula, which soon became one of the essential ingredients of the 'all-India film'. The creative individuals who took this cinema to the forefront were Pancholi's two main directors Moti Gidwani and Ravindra Dave, music directors Ghulam Haider, Shyam Sunder and later O. P. Nayyar, singers Shamshad Begum and Mohammed Rafi, actresses Noorjehan, Ramola and Smriti Biswas and actors Pran and Om Prakash. Shaukat Hussain Rizvi was another important alumnus of this studio who made his mark with *Khandaan* (1942), *Naukar* (1943), a realistic tragedy (based on a short story by the inimitable Sadat Hasan Manto), *Dost* (1944), *Zeenat* (1945) and *Jugnu* (1947) produced under his own banner.

The Legacy of Bombay Talkies and the Entry of Filmistan

In the annals of Indian cinema, the very mention of Bombay Talkies evokes memories of a rollicking past in the minds of many erudite film luminaries as well as among the lay audience. Marking a watershed in creativity, this studio brought into being many outstanding films having a pan-Indian outlook. Bombay Talkies can be considered a seminal institution that groomed several noteworthy individuals who took film making to new heights in the following decades.

Bombay Talkies captured on celluloid features such as simplicity in presentation, a breezy romantic charm and meaningful dialogues, with a distinct emphasis on socially relevant themes put across with technical virtuosity. A highly organized public limited company, which was a forerunner in adding prestige to the medium, Bombay Talkies was the only unit in the film industry during that period functioning on the basis of modern concepts of corporate management.

The builder of this institution was Himanshu Rai, ironically a Bengal-born aristocrat who chose Bombay as the centre for his project. After studying initially at Rabindranath Tagore's Shantiniketan and later in England, he ventured into film making with an Indo–German co-production venture as his springboard. His very first film, *The Light of Asia*, based on the life of Gautam Buddha, co-produced in 1924 with Emelka Film Corporation of Munich, received worldwide recognition. This movie was screened in nearly every city of Europe. It was followed by *Shiraz* (1928), *Throw of Dice* (*Prapancha Pash*, 1929) and the first Anglo–Indian venture in Indian cinema, *Karma* (1933) made in English and Hindi. While *Karma* had its premiere in London, its screening in Bombay was inaugurated by the eminent freedom fighter and poetess Sarojini Naidu. The following year, Himanshu Rai launched Bombay Talkies along with his wife, Devika Rani, who was soon to become the first symbol of glamour on the Indian screen. The first film under the Bombay Talkies banner was *Jawani Ki Hawa* (1935).

Achchut Kanya (1936), directed by Franz Osten and one of the early Bombay Talkies masterpieces, depicted on screen a love story whose main characters were a Brahmin boy and a Harijan girl. This was a bold theme considering the social milieu of that period. This film brought into the limelight the Ashok Kumar–Devika Rani pair, which inspired a whole generation. Even Jawaharlal Nehru is reported to have written a fan letter to Devika Rani. Osten, a German film maker and a lifelong associate of Himanshu Rai, was the most prolific director of Bombay Talkies, being involved in as many as twelve of its films including *Shiraz, Throw of Dice, Mamta & Miya-Beewee* (1936, a unique experiment of showing two films in one show), *Izzat* (1937), *Jeewan Prabhaat* (1937), *Saavitri* (1937), *Dukhiari* (1937), *Nirmala* (1938), *Vachan* (1938) and *Durga* (1939). However, after the outbreak of the Second World War in 1939, Osten and the other German film technicians working in India were deported by the Britsh Government.

Work, nevertheless, did not come to a standstill. *Kismet*, released in 1943, pioneered the much exploited lost-and-found genre in Indian cinema. It was the first super box-office hit, and ran for three years at a cinema hall in Calcutta. The director was Gyan Mukerjee, who was a science lecturer and the editor of the reputed journal, *Science and Culture*, before he moved over to the world of cinema. Other prominent directors from Bombay Talkies were Amiya Chakravarty (*Anjaan*, 1941, *Basant*, 1942, and *Jwar Bhata*, 1944, the last being Dilip Kumar's first movie), N. R. Acharaya (*Naya Sansar*, 1941) and M. I. Dharmsey (*Hamari Baat*, 1943).

Bombay Talkies made thirty-eight films in its eighteen years of existence. After the death of Himanshu Rai in 1940, when he was merely 48, the differences among the top brass of the company grew rapidly, leading to two factions headed, respectively, by Devika Rani and Rai Bahadur Chunnilal. This bitter rivalry between the two factions almost led to the untimely demise of this grand institution. However, at this stage, the studio was taken over by Ashok Kumar and Savak Vacha, the sound engineer. Soon the studio workers too stepped in to form a cooperative in a final bid to save Bombay Talkies from collapsing altogether. They kept the torch lit and soon several films hit the screen, such as *Majboor* (1948), *Ziddi* (1948) and Kamal Amrohi's masterpiece, *Mahal* (1949). In addition to Nitin Bose's *Mashaal* (1950), Bimal Roy's *Maa* (1952) and Phani Majumdar's *Tamasha* (1952), this cooperative also produced *Badbaan* (1952) also directed by Majumdar, for which Ashok Kumar, Dev Anand, Meena Kumari and others volunteered to work free.

Filmistan Studios, a breakaway group from Bombay Talkies, emerged as the major second-generation institution that was to have a far-reaching influence on the making of the classical era of Hindi cinema of the 1950s. It was set up by Rai Bahadur Chunnilal and Shashdhar Mukerji as part of their efforts to reorganize the talents dislocated by the decline of the parent studio. This banner set in motion a fascinating trend of film making beginning with Gyan Mukerjee's *Chal Chal Re Naujawan* in 1944. Soon Filmistan became known for producing mid-budget films and as the workplace of a flock of talented directors such as Nitin Bose, Pyare Lal Santoshi, Kishore Sahu, Bibhuti Mitra, Munshi Dil, Ramesh Sehgal and Najam Naqvi.[4]

By the end of 1940s, cinema occupied the eighth position among the top Indian industries. It ranked fourth in world cinema.

The Pen and the Camera: The Influence of Literature on Cinema

The link between cinema and literature was established from the very inception of the film medium. The immense potential offered by this medium to transfer a tale in print into a living visual experience had long tempted film makers and authors alike. The prospects of reaching a much wider audience with cinema as the most popular mass medium inspired many literary figures to seek a full-fledged film career. This particularly was the trend in the 1940s and 1950s when many writers and poets entered the Bombay and the Madras film world in a big way. However, in Hindi cinema, it was the leading personalities from Urdu literature rather than their Hindi counterparts who came forward in larger numbers to offer their services to the new medium.

Some of the Urdu writers who made the interaction between the pen and the camera a success were Aga Hashr Kashmiri, Narayan Prasad 'Betaab', Wali Mohammed Wali, Sadat Hasan Manto, Krishan Chander, Rajender Singh Bedi, Akhtar-ul Iman, Wajahat Mirza, Khwaja Ahmad Abbas, Abrar Alvi and Ismat Chugtai. The renowned short-story writer Manto scripted a string of movies such as Moti Gidwani's *Kisan Kanya* (1937), Dada Gunjal's *Apni Nagariya* (1940), Ramesh Sehgal's *Ghar Ki Shobha* (1944) and *Eight Days* (1946), J. K. Nanda's *Thumke* (1946) and later Sohrab Modi's *Mirza Ghalib* (1954).

Among the Urdu poets who streamed into Bombay and soon became successful film lyricists were Nakshab, Ehsan Rizvi, Arzoo Lukhnavi, Munshi A. Shah 'Aziz', Munshi Shams, Munshi Dil, Kamal Amrohi, Kaifi Azmi, Majrooh Sultanpuri and Raja Mehdi Ali Khan. There were also many poets known for their works in both Hindi and Urdu who made a name in films. Notable among them were Mukand Lal 'Seemab', Gauri Shankarlal 'Akhtar' and Pandit 'Phani'.

As compared with the Urdu stalwarts, the response of the mainstream Hindi literary luminaries to the clarion call of cinema was only marginal. Some of the distinguished Hindi writers and poets who did become successful during this period were Pandit Indra, Pandit Sudarshan (of Minerva Movietone), Pandit Shiv Kumar, Pandit Narotam Vyas, Narendra, Pandit Bhushan,

Sambhal Lal Shrivastava 'Anuj', Dr Dhaniram 'Prem', Pradeep (real name Ramachandra Narayanji Dwivedi), Bharat Vyas, Pandit Mukhram Sharma 'Ashant', J. S. Kashyap (the early script writer of Bombay Talkies) and Gopal Singh Nepali.

The acclaimed Hindi writer, Munshi Premchand, went to Bombay in 1934 in the hope of earning enough money to cover the debt incurred by his Sarasvati Press. On an invitation extended by Mohan Bhavnani, he worked for one year as scriptwriter for Ajanta Movietone. Apart from *The Mill* (1934), Munshiji also scripted *Sherdil Aurat* (1935) and *Navjeevan* (1935) for Bhavnani. But soon he got disgusted with the highly commercial milieu and, in 1935, left Bombay for good. Bhagwati Charan Verma and Amritlal Nagar, other famous writers of the renaissance period, also underwent similar experiences.

Among the five early regional centres of film making in the country – Bombay, Calcutta, Kolhapur, Lahore and Madras – the Bengal and Kolhapur schools were in the forefront in going in for literature-based cinema. The popularity of the works of Saratchandra, Rabindranath Tagore, Bankimchandra Chatterjee and Qazi Nazrul Islam inspired many Bengali film makers of the 1930s and 1940s to mount those works on celluloid. In Kolhapur, many noted Marathi writers, such as Mama Warerkar, P. K. Atre and V. S. Khandekar and playwrights Keshav Narayan Kale and Narayanrao Damodar Sarpotdar, influenced a great deal the evolution of Marathi/Hindi films of this period. The legendary Gujarati writer K. M. Munshi was an important literary resource for many film makers.

The unique contributions of the literature–celluloid interaction were that it boosted the trends of good cinema in the commercial film world and greatly helped the development of a true cinematic language and style. A significant part of the latter-day new-wave cinema, in fact, owes its origin to great literary works, and most often the new-wave writer-film maker is well rooted in the literary tradition of his or her region.

Early International Recognition for Indian Cinema

Since its formative period, the twin aspects of the linkage of Indian cinema with world cinema have been the joint ventures in film making and India's participation in international film festivals. The intrinsic 'Orientalism' of the themes not only inspired many ambitious joint ventures, which began as early as the silent era, but also promoted the pan-Indian outlook of the cinema. The major partners in the co-production activity in the early period were the film makers from Germany, Italy and the UK. The Indian film industry, significantly, too had a large foreign presence, particularly of German directors, cinematographers and technicians. After independence, joint ventures were few and far between and got a boost only in the 1980s with the UK, the Soviet Union and, to a lesser extent, the USA, emerging as the main partners.

The cinematic ingenuity of the early masters also won instant international recognition. Not only were their works widely shown abroad, but also many of them began to make their presence felt in most international film festivals. At Venice, Indian films were indeed hot favourites, and won several prestigious awards.

Important Landmarks in the Internationalization of Indian Films

- Dadasaheb Phalke's films were widely appreciated in the UK and the USA. The Warner Brothers, in fact, placed an order of 200 prints for worldwide distribution. The master, however, could not supply the requisite prints due to lack of financial and technical resources.
- Baburao Painter's *Sati Padmini* was shown at the Wembley Film Exhibition in the UK and was awarded a special certificate.

- India's first foreign joint venture, Himanshu Rai's *The Light of Asia*, an Indo–German production of 1924, was shown in all major European cities. Declared as one of the best films of the year, it was seen by a number of European monarchs.
- *Savitri* made by Madan Theatres was yet another maiden venture in collaboration with the Union Cinematographical Italiana of Rome. It was directed by the famous Italian director Arturo Ambrosio and boasted of a fully Italian cast.
- The earliest example of making a film on India by a foreign company was *Emerald of the East* by the British International Studio in the 1920s.
- A fascinating figure of this period was an American film maker, Ellis R. Dungan. He came to India to sell film equipment but settled in Madras to make a series of Tamil movies (the most famous being *Meera*, starring the legendary M. S. Subbulakshmi), amazingly, without understanding the language.
- *Pamposh*, directed by Izra Mir, was a trilingual film made in Hindi, English and German.
- J. B. H. Wadia's *Raj Nartaki*, another trilingual film in English, Hindi and Bengali, was acquired by Columbia Pictures for worldwide distribution. Interestingly, the songs for the English version were written by Verrier Elwin, the reputed anthropologist.
- The early films to earn the honour of participating in the Venice Cinematograph Exhibition were Debaki Bose's *Seeta* in 1933, Prabhat's *Amrit Manthan* in 1934 and *Amar Jyoti* in 1936.
- *Sant Tukaram* was declared as one of the best three films of the world in 1937 at Venice's Fifth Exhibition and brought to India its first international award. A print was also acquired by Cambridge University because the students of film art were interested in studying a film that had run for 58 weeks in a single cinema hall.

- Chetan Anand's *Neecha Nagar* bagged the best film award at the Cannes Film Festival in 1946. In fact, all entries that year were given awards as a post-World War goodwill gesture of international understanding.

Indigenous Cinema Shows the Way

Once cinema acquired a worldwide presence in the early part of the twentieth century, it became a very powerful mass medium. However, its impact on society was not fully understood. Broadly, it was observed at that time that the greatest impact of cinema could be on thought processes, perceptions and ideas as many films, even in the early period, seemed to have helped alter longstanding social and ideological leanings and the views on social issues such as devastation caused by wars, tyranny, inequality, injustice, communal intolerance, the caste system and cruelty against women and children.

In the realm of world cinema, film historians have studied the social impact of some early landmark films. For instance: D. W. Griffith's masterpiece, *Intolerance* (1916), a saga about prejudice during four historical periods, was hailed as the first important film having distinct social overtones. When Vladimir Lenin saw this film, he asserted: 'This is the medium for the masses.' Sergei Eisenstein's world classic, *The Battleship Potemkin* (1925), about a mutiny by Russian sailors aboard a czarist navy vessel in the Black Sea and has been regarded as a pioneering film for the innovative use of film technology, inspired people throughout the world over many decades. Charlie Chaplin's classic, *The Great Dictator* (1940), a spoof on Adolf Hitler, laid the foundation of the anti-fascist stance among American people at a time when the country had isolated itself from world events, when the Second World War was raging, and uncertainty and danger were the dominant features. (The US entered the war only in December 1941 after Pearl Harbor in Hawaii was attacked by the Japanese.) The impact of such films in the early years of world cinema influenced the orientation of cinema in many developing countries.

In India too, cinema played an important role during the colonial period in articulating the nationalist sentiments and promoting awareness about various social issues among people. Mohan Bhavnani's *The Mill* (1934), discussed earlier, was perhaps the first film to have serious political connotations. The story goes that the president of the Mill Owners' Association was a member of the Censor Board in Bombay and tried to get the film banned. The Punjab Censor Board cleared the film initially, but as a near-riot situation was caused by jubilant workers after its release in Lahore, banned it. The subsequent Delhi ban was followed by a Central Government decree that the film had an 'inflammatory influence' on workers.

Achchut Kanya (1936) from Bombay Talkies, set in the Gandhian mould, took up the sensitive issue of untouchability. Prabhat's masterpiece, *Padosi* (1941), focused the nation's attention on Hindu–Muslim unity. Many historical films of the Marathi school made during this period celebrated implicitly the spirit of nationalism through the deeds of great Maratha heroes, including Chatrapati Shivaji. Many films belonging to different genres, such as *Kismet* (1943), were imbued with distinct overtones of nationalist sentiment. Sohrab Modi's *Sikandar* (1941), although a historical movie, carried the anti-imperialist message by depicting the struggle of the people for safeguarding their national sovereignty. Mehboob Khan in *Aurat* (1940) and *Roti* (1943) pinpointed for the first time, poignantly and forcefully, the problems resulting from feudal exploitation of the masses in rural India.

Meanwhile, a flurry of mythologicals heralded a wave of religious revivalism, and, as a corollary, another genre came into existence that showcased the country's spiritual traditions through the lives of the saints and other mystics. Apart from Ramayana and Mahabharata, other tales from popular mythologies were also dramatized using fascinating narrative and cinematic techniques. While films of this genre contributed substantially towards reinforcing the popular religious beliefs and attitudes, they conveyed very effectively the traditionally applauded victory of good over evil (this, in fact, invariably formed the basic theme of films belonging to all other genres as well). From a broader perspective, these films also instilled a sense of pride among the people about the nation's spiritual and cultural heritage and thus inadvertently propagated the swadeshi (indigenous) ideology.

Cinema also began to perform the broader (and nobler) function of serving as a medium for education. It emerged as the main channel that enabled the poorer sections of the population to get a glimpse of a world beyond their reach (however unreal and subjective it may have been) and gain a vivid and intimate exposure to the cultural heritage of different communities, apart from providing a peephole into history. Cinema attempted to portray the realities of contemporary society. This audio-visual medium helped to overcome the barriers of mass illiteracy and lack of awareness about the state of society. Even for many urbanites, who had never seen a village closely, many films set in a rural backdrop, provided the first-ever exposure to them to the realities of rural life and its culture. Many of the meaningful films made in this period and later as well became the medium of learning for those among the audience who were not particularly knowledgeable about mythology and literature, not to mention other areas such as politics and current affairs.

In spite of its immense mass appeal, cinema, for many decades, could not obtain approval as a source of entertainment and education among all sections of Indian society. Many felt that the vulgar interpretation of sensuality was the main agenda of cinema, which was, in their view, devoid of refinement or any worthwhile cultural content. A large section of older people (even in the 1960s) discouraged youngsters from seeing most films; the oldies allowed only those that they rated 'morally safe' as 'watchable'. Dreaming about a career in cinema was frowned upon and the film people in general were considered morally corrupt and professionally worthless. Many social reformers and enlightened writers, including Mahatma Gandhi (who had seen only one film in his life: Vijay Bhatt's *Ram Rajya*), Munshi Premchand and Bhagwati Charan Verma, held strong views against the new mass medium. For them cinema was a grave social evil, and being a product of Western culture, they felt it would be highly detrimental to the moral fabric and the aesthetic sensibilities of the Indian people.

However, such informed criticism was largely countered by the dominant trends of indigenous cinema during the formative period and later in the classical period. The celebrated works of Sohrab Modi, V. Shantaram, Mehboob Khan, Nitin Bose, Debaki Bose, Zia Sarhadi, Amiya Chakravarty, A. R. Kardar and later Bimal Roy and K. A. Abbas (in the 1940s) had bestowed upon Indian cinema its distinct identity. One significant outcome of this development was that cinema, soon after independence (on 15 August 1947), began to receive extensive patronage from the state and thus acquired a renewed respectability. Soon, increasing numbers of film personalities were being included in the top echelons of decision-making bodies at the national level. Droves of political leaders, bureaucrats, academicians, corporate managers and celebrities from other fields vied to be photographed with the luminaries from the film world at state-sponsored cultural festivals, sports meets and other events. Jawaharlal Nehru, a great admirer of cinema (in contrast with his mentor, Mahatma Gandhi), patronized film makers and stars with a great deal of fanfare. He took a personal initiative in organizing the country's first International Film Festival in Delhi in 1952.

Cinema also began to tackle, in its own way, the growing alienation of people, particularly the burgeoning immigrant populations, which were reaching the urban centres as part of the modernization processes (the result of rapid industrialization) and thus had got delinked from their social, cultural and linguistic roots. The wholesome entertainment strategy inbuilt in the celebrated 'all-India film' format and based on a viable integration of various hues of life and encompassing virtually all the ingredients of local cultures began to represent a kind of monolith, in which the people now obtained a new sense of identity. In this process, the film stars became nationally so very alluring and powerful that they soon displaced the traditional *nautanki*/theatre artistes and singers, who were commonly patronized at the *mohalla* (locality or colony) level rendering them increasingly redundant.

Notes and References

1. Major films of these directors were: Izra Mir (*Noorjehaan*, 1931, *Parivartan*, 1936 and *Struggle*, 1936); R. S. Choudhary (*Maadhuri*, 1932 and *Anarkali*, 1935); Moti Gidwani (*Daakoo Ki Ladki*, 1933 and *Kisan Kanya*, 1937, the first Indian colour film in Cinecolour); Paysi Karani (*Bhaarati Maata*, 1932 and *Dorangi Duniya*, 1933); Homi Master (*Samaaj Ki Bhool*, 1934 and *Do Ghadi Ki Mauj*, 1935); Jyotish Bannerji (*Aankh Ka Tara*, 1932, and *Dhruva Charitra*, 1933) and Fardoon Irani (*Anokha Prem*, 1934 and *Jahanara*, 1935).
2. Bhavnani's other noteworthy films were: *Afzal* (1933), *Rangeela Rajpoot* (1933), *Dard-e-Dil* (1934), *The Mill* (1934), *Vasvadatta* (1934) and *Sherdil Aurat* (1935).
3. The major films of these directors are now listed. Prafulla Ghosh: *Veer Abhimanyu*, 1931, and *Subhadra Haran*, 1932; Sarvotam Badami: *Chadrahaas*, 1933, *Dr Madhurika*, 1935, and *300 Days and After*, 1938; Izra Mir: *Zarina*, 1932, and *Premi Pagal*, 1933; and Nanu Bhai Vakil: *Maya Bazaar*, 1932, and *Mahabharat*, 1933.
4. Important films of these directors were as follows: Nitin Bose (*Mazdoor*, 1945); Pyare Lal Santoshi (*Shehnai*, 1947); Kishore Sahu (*Saajan*, *Sindoor* both in 1947 and *Nadiya Ke Paar*, 1948); B. Mitra (*Safar*, 1946), Munshi Dil (*Do Bhai*, 1947); Ramesh Sehgal (*Shaheed*, 1948); and Najam Naqvi (*Actress*, 1948).

Chapter 3

K. L. Saigal and Other Early Heroes

For the success of their cinematic creativity and output, keeping in view the vast heterogeneous audience, the founders of Indian cinema, during its formative period, worked out a common denominator of emotional gratification. The totality of the instantaneous film experience (the story/ characterizations/treatment/music) obtained from the images on the screen held the viewers spellbound, activating dramatically each individual's emotional responses. Cinema soon became an inseparable part of the viewer's memory and he or she would use the images seen on screen to relate them to his or her own circumstances, both consciously and subconsciously. Thus, cinema formed (and continues to form) an important element in virtually everybody's life.

As cinema proceeded rapidly along its destined path, its relationship with the viewers soon became collective, but yet it was personal. Gradually, the highly entertaining cinematic experience began to be built around the screen persona of its protagonist, the hero (and far less around that of the heroine). This protagonist, who began to be idolized and even revered, provided to the film enthusiasts a common pivotal point for sharing their appreciation of the entire cinematic experience and also for realizing the gamut of emotions displayed. The medium acquired its universal appeal primarily because this protagonist offered to the viewers the distinct possibility of complete empathy and identification with the character and situations being portrayed on screen, although such empathy and identification were not always rooted in reality. In fact, bestowing on the persona of the protagonist a set of socially and culturally acceptable attributes considered ideal and perfect has remained the most crucial aspect for ensuring the success of the Indian film. (Of late, the norms have changed, as we shall see later.) By simply visualizing the images of the hero or listening to a recorded melody 'sung' (actually lip-synched) by him in a film, a viewer could easily interpret and express his or her own state of mind perfectly.

Given such persuasive mass idolization, even in the silent movie era, the new medium virtually became a new religion, propelling many youngsters to reach out to their idols and become a part of their world. Through an initial process of self-grooming and then by performing a rigorous imitation exercise, they would view themselves as the true mirror image of their idol. Next, they would launch themselves into a seemingly unending struggle to make a place for themselves in cinema either substituting for their idol or attempting to come on par with him.

After the arrival of the talkies, which was almost magical, the enthralling impact of the celluloid images along with dialogue (mostly powerful) and the music (invariably melodious), not to mention the prospects of obtaining creative satisfaction, fame and wealth, became so enticing and irresistible that droves of people from all walks of life began to be attracted by the lodestone of cinema, aspiring to make a career.

During this period, many adventurous people broke away from their social, cultural and geographical moorings and reached the film world. Indeed, they were truly rebels who left the safety and comfort of their homes and began to knock at the doors of film studios in Bombay, Calcutta, Madras, Lahore and Hyderabad.

The Early Entrants

The phenomenal impact of the talkies completely transformed the Indian film scene. (The first talkie, it may be recalled, was

Alam Ara, released in March 1931.) The dimensions of cinema greatly increased. The sudden expansion of the film industry created a huge demand for human resources in diverse fields. As already mentioned, large swarms of creative, talented and enterprising people from various professions and different social backgrounds arrived to take on the challenges being offered by the young medium and to find a place in the sun.

This vast sea of humanity was made up of producers, directors, music directors, lyricists, script and dialogue writers, singers, photographers, sound recordists, technicians and, of course, actors and actresses. Why such a huge phalanx of highly diversified talent reached the film world during the formative and later periods cannot be explained easily. Perhaps as a large section of people during this period were rapidly getting uprooted from their traditional occupations and delinked from their cultural moorings, they began looking for a new identity in the enchanting environs of moving and talking images. Cinema of course readily provided, at least in the initial periods, far-ranging opportunities for creative individuals, with assured highly lucrative financial returns in almost all categories of film making.

The domain of the Indian film hero too witnessed a tremendous expansion and an impressive array of new faces made their way to the silver screen through a wide range of talent-scouting procedures. A motley band of inspired youngsters, with differing screen personas, diverse acting skills and dissimilar personalities trooped in, in rapid succession. Among the first generation of heroes, Khalil, Raja Sandow, Sohrab Modi, Master Nissar, Master Vithal, Jal Merchant, Dinshaw Billimoria, Eddie Billimoria, Chandramohan, Prithviraj Kapoor, Motilal, Ashok Kumar and K. L. Saigal emerged as the main players, each creating a niche of his own in the field of acting. Apart from these big stars, this period also saw the emergence of several other second-rung heroes: P. Jairaj, Gul Hamid, Najmal Hassan, Kumar, Ishwarlal, Shahu Modak, Madhav Kale, Prem Adib, Pahari Sanyal and Surendra, among others.

The heroine slots were also rapidly being filled up by women from diverse backgrounds. The prominent leading ladies of the pioneering era were: Mehtab, Bibbo, Gohar, Patience Cooper, Seeta Devi, Sabita Devi, Zubeida, Devika Rani, Leela Chitnis, Hansa Wadkar, Durga Khote, Naseem Banu, Jamna, Kanan Devi, Shobhna Samarth, Sadhana Bose, Sitara and Raj Kumari. Their talent and screen presence matched those of their male counterparts. With the growing popularity of cine artistes and their relatively high value at the box office, Indian cinema too started adopting the star system, which was being evolved in Hollywood.

Khalil, the First Star, and Raja Sandow

Khalil could be said to be the first-ever star of Hindi cinema who reigned in the silent era as well as the talkie era from 1920 to 1937. He was the first macho hero, acting opposite all the top-notch heroines of the period. A product of Kohinoor Films, he made his debut as hero in 1924 in Kanjibhai Rathor's silent movie *Gul-e-Bakavali*, a popular Persian fable of love (opposite the celebrated actress of the time, Zubeida). He also appeared in a supporting role in *Kaala Nag* released in the same year. He then featured in two silent films of Homi Master: first in *Kulin Kanta* (1925) as the lecherous hot-headed maharaja who gets the lover of his heartthrob, a dancing girl, killed and second in *Lanka Ni Laadi* (1925, opposite Gohar) as the brave shepherd sent by his king on several dangerous missions before he could marry his daughter. Khalil came to prominence with Mohan Bhavnani's first directorial venture at Kohinoor, *Cinema Queen* (1925, opposite Sulochana). (Sulochana's real name was Ruby Myers.) He appeared in this film as a poor and frustrated painter who regains his love with creative zeal through the love and support of a film actress when he is about to commit suicide.

Khalil entered the talkie era with Imperial's *Draupadi* based on a tale from the Mahabharata epic and directed by B. P. Mishra. The heroine was Ermeline (considered to be Hindi cinema's prototype of Hollywood's most famous silent movie star Clara Bow) and Pesi Karani's *Daulat Ka Nasha*, both released in 1931. These ventures were followed by Karani's two films – *Bharat Maata* (1932) and *Dorangi Duniya* (1933) – and Moti Gidwani's *Niti Vijay* (1932). Khalil then moved from Bombay to Calcutta and made his mark with yet another Karani project, *Qismat Ki Kasauti* (1934) produced under the East India Films banner and with Tollywood Studio's (Madan Theatres) three major films: Fardoon Irani's *Miss Manorma* (1935) and *Bulbul-e-Iran* (1936) and Izra Mir's *Parivartan* (1936). Dhirubhai Desai's *Pyar* (1940) was his last important film.

***

Khalil's equally famous contemporary, Raja Sandow, was also cast in the same mould, a wrestler-turned-actor. He essayed a variety of portrayals, donning weird get-ups and even played a villain with considerable success. A Tamilian by birth, he was born in 1894 as P. K. Nagalingam in Pudukottai, now in Tamil Nadu. Sandow made his screen debut in 1922 with S. N. Patankar's *Bhakta Bodona* produced under the National Film company banner. He continued as a stunt actor in several films such as National Film's *Vratasur Vaddha* (1924) and *Veer Bhimsen* (1924). Soon he emerged as the top star of Kohinoor Studio. In Manilal Joshi's *Prithivi Vallabh* (1924), a historical based on K. M. Munshi's novel, Sandow portrayed the brave Munja king captured by his own beloved, the arrogant princess of the rival Tailanga kingdom.

Homi Master's directorial debut at Kohinoor, *Bisvin Sadi* (1924), a strong critique of the neo-rich industrial class, has been credited with starting the realist-reformist genre in Indian cinema. This film presented Sandow in his first anti-hero role of a hawker-turned-cotton mill magnate who exploits his workers and also makes his wife and daughter suffer. Manilal Joshi's *Mojili Mumbai* (1925), also about the murky lifestyle of the city's rich, presented Sandow as a lecherous rich man duped by a dancer and his pimp. This film raised a storm about the meaning of morality and realism in cinema. In *Veer Kunal* (1925) also directed by Joshi, Sandow played Emperor Asoka's son Kunal, a victim of the emperor's young queen's lust. She plots to have him blinded and Kunal, after wandering for years as a blind bard, reaches his father's court to tell the truth.

Homi Master's *The Telephone Girl* (1926) cast Sandow as the lawyer whose love affair with his Anglo-Indian telephone operator (Sulochana) is marred by family opposition to the intercommunity marriage. Khalil also appeared in this film in the role of a committed rural activist. In R. S. Choudhary's directorial debut *Neera* (1926, opposite Zubeida), Sandow essayed an offbeat anti-hero role as a wicked *kapalik* (a devotee of the fierce Goddess Kali), who proclaims that he has mystical powers, which he uses to acquire the lands of innocent and gullible tribals. Homi Master's *Bhaneli Bhamini* (1927, opposite Gohar) highlighted the dangers of sexually transmitted diseases. Both Sandow and Gohar became famous after the release of this message-oriented social.

Sandow, with Chandulal Shah's classic *Gunsundari* (1927), became a champion of reformist melodramas, playing complex psychological characters with his equally illustrious screen partners – actor Eddie Billimoria and actress Gohar. In this movie, he portrayed the archetype of an Indian husband who refuses to bear his share of domestic responsibility along with his dutiful wife. When he starts flirting with a dancing girl, the wife moves out of his domestic trap and finds a new purpose for herself through social work. His other silent movies included *Indrasabha* (1925), *Samrat Shiladitya* (1926) and *Punjab Kesari* (1929). In 1928, Sandow formed the Jagdish Film Company in collaboration with Chandulal Shah and Gohar, which was soon renamed as Ranjit Films. He also directed *Sneh Jyoti* (1928) for Love Films.

In the talkie era, Sandow kept playing both hero and anti-hero roles with remarkable ingenuity. Nandlal Jaswantlal's *Indira MA* (1934), a powerful saga on the East–West conflicting viewpoints, presented him as the dullard whom the Oxford-returned heroine rejects in an arranged marriage, whereas in Shah's *Desh Daasi* (1935), he appeared as the committed Gandhian social worker who converts the heroine and his doctor suitor, both sick of their rich lifestyle, into full-fledged social activists. Nandlal Jaswantlal's *Pardesi Pritam* (1933) and *Kashmeera* (1934), as also *Ratan Manjri* (1935) and *Vishnu Leela* (1938), were his other releases during this period.

Apart from his association with the Bombay movie industry, Sandow kept his contact alive with his native Tamil film world, directing and often acting in a series of reformist socials (silent movies) such as *Anadhai Penn* (1929), *Nandanar* (1929, based on the life of an untouchable Hindu saint), *Peyum Pennum* (1930) and *Bhaktavasala* (1931) and talkies such as *Vasantsena* (1935), *Chandrakantha* (1935) and *Choodamani* (1941). These films greatly influenced the making of Tamil legendary film maker K. Subramanyam's nationalist melodramas exemplified by the classic *Thyagabhoomi* (1939).

By the early 1940s, this formidable actor lost his foothold, appearing only in supporting roles as seen in Homi Wadia's *Dhoomketu* (1949), *Alladdin and Wonderful Lamp* (1952), *Nav Durga* (1953) and *Husn Ka Chor* (1953, released after his death). He died in 1952 at the age of 58.

Master Nissar and Master Vithal

The two actors who were pioneers in developing the cinematic personality of the Indian film hero in the talkie era were Master Nissar and Master Vithal. They were the first to capture the people's imagination and thus become Hindi cinema's first 'matinee idols'. Master Nissar was the first superstar of the talkies era, as the term is understood today. A product of the Madan Theatres, Calcutta, Nissar came into films when the company built its first studio. Because of his ability to speak fluent Urdu and sing fairly well, he proved to be an instant success. However, as an actor, Nissar's style was highly theatrical.

Nissar appeared in the first talkie of Madan Theatres, *Shirin Farhad* (1931), a tragic Persian love legend, in the role of sculptor Farhad, who, to win the hand of his beloved, had to dig a canal to bring milk from a mountain. In two other releases in the same year, he appeared as the legendary lover Majnu in *Laila Majnu* and as King Dushyant in *Shankuntala*, based on the play by the renowned poet Kalidas. In Madan Theatres's *Indrasabha* (1932), he portrayed Lord Indra (considered the king of gods), always surrounded by nymphs. He persecutes his favorite nymph for falling in love with a mortal on earth. The film was based on Agha Hasan Amanat's play, which he wrote for the court of Nawab Wajid Ali Shah of Avadh. Nissar's yet another film at Madan Theatres was *Bilwamangal* (1932).

In Bombay, Nissar became Mohan Bhavnani's favourite 'co-passenger' appearing in a string of talkies by the master. In *Rangeela Rajpoot* (1933), he featured as the brave soldier who rescues a princess being killed by a wily minister with the help of gypsies. *Afzal* (1933), an Arabian Nights-kind of fable, cast him as the poor vengeful youth whose beloved is kidnapped and made a slave. With the help of a good-hearted sweetmeat seller Afzal, he saves the life of the sultan from the designs of his ambitious prime minister. *Sair-e-Paristan* (1934), also a fantasy film, presented him as one of three love-lorn princes who succeeds in tracing a missing damsel (whom all three desire to marry) held in captivity by a fearsome ogre.

Nissar also featured in three costume dramas with J. P. Advani: *Johar-e-Shamsheer* (1934), *Shah Behram* (1935) and *Bahaar-e-Sulemaani* (1935). Nissar's last important movie was Moti B. Gidwani's *Kisan Kanya* (1937) in which he acted as a poor peasant accused of murdering his landlord. His decline was sudden in the wake of the Ashok Kumar–Saigal wave of the mid-1930s.

***

In contrast with Nissar's, Vithal's career was far more remarkable. He projected the persona of the first archetypal action hero (à la

Robin Hood): brave, dashing, strong and clever, ever ready to ensure social justice by destroying the evil anti-people forces through his miraculous deeds. Often referred to as the Douglas Fairbanks of Indian cinema, Vithal would launch crusades for safeguarding the rights of the oppressed and the poor. In these roles, he indirectly performed a political function: his roles stirred the people's feelings against colonial rule. His excellence in sword play would often be a major highlight of his films.

Vithal entered the film world in 1924 in Baburao Painter's *Kaliyan Khajina*, curiously in the role of a dancing girl. He was launched as hero by Bhalji Pendharkar in 1924 in *Bajirao Mastani*, a love tale about the eighteenth-century Maratha Peshwa's obsession for the court dancer Mastani. In K. P. Bhave's *Suvarna Kamal* (1926), he played a masked adventurer in quest of a golden lotus that he needed to win over the heroine. Naval Gandhi's *Balidan* (1927), based on Rabindranath Tagore's play, established him as a serious actor. In this powerful reformist drama, he portrayed an enlightened king who bans animal sacrifice in his kingdom but the head priest revolts and calls for the king's head to appease the angry Goddess Kali.

Apart from the first talkie *Alam Ara* (1931), Vithal also acted in a string of films such as *Zaalim Jawaani* (1932, directed by B. R. Mishra), *Raj Tarang* (1935), *Asiai Sitara* (1937) and *Netaji Palkar* (1939), the last film being based on the life of the Maratha king Shivaji's brave general.

The Billimoria Brothers

The trend of brothers becoming heroes in Hindi cinema was initiated by Dinshaw Billimoria and Eddie Billimoria. The former, pairing with the top heroine of the era, Sulochana, was not only highly popular but also sensational. As the most preferred star of Imperial Theatres, his main forte was his convincing portrayal of characters in elaborate costume fantasies carved in Hollywood's

John Barrymore style. He was the highest paid star during the silent era.

Born in 1904 at Kirkee (now a locality in Pune, Maharashtra), Dinshaw made his debut with N. D. Sarpotdar's 1925 silent movie *Chhatrapati Sambhaji*, a biographical depiction of Shivaji's valorous son. He rose to fame with Mohan Bhavnani's *Wildcat of Bombay* (1927) in the role of a police inspector in pursuit of a mysterious female criminal who masquerades as a medical student and falls in love with him. *Prem Jogan*, the silent film released in 1931, was a love triangle. He was one of the suitors of the disgruntled heroine who prefers to become an ascetic after his rival is killed in war. His other significant silent films were *Umaji Naik* (1926), *Madhuri* (1928), *Rajrang* (1928), *Rajputani* (1929), *Punjab Mail* (1929) and *Pahadi Kanya* (1930).

Dinshaw's first talkie was Chandulal Shah's *Devi Devyani* (1931), produced under the Ranjit banner. A Puranic tale about the conflict between gods and demons, he appeared as Yayati who was chosen as a husband by Lord Krishna for the daughter of the sage of demons. *Gul Sanobar* (1934), based on a Persian legend, cast him in the role of a brave prince who overcomes many hurdles to bring a flower from the mouth of a mysterious princess to cure his paralytic father. In *Indira MA* (1934, with Sandow in the second lead), he appears as the philanderer and playboy whose marriage with his educated wife ends in divorce. In R. S. Choudhary's *Anarkali* (1935) he brought to life the popular Prince Salim–Anarkali legend, with Sulochana in the title role. *Piya Pyare* (1934), also directed by R. S. Choudhary, was a fantasy adventure presenting Dinshaw performing his swashbuckling antics as the romantic outlaw who saves his sweetheart's kingdom from the designs of an evil and nasty general.

Homi Master's *Do Ghadi Ki Mauj* (1936) cast Dinshaw as an upright engineer, a family man, who gambles away his marital happiness. Nandlal Jaswantlal's *Bambai Ki Billi* (1936) was a remake of *Wildcat of Bombay*, casting him in the same role. In *Jawani Ki Pukar* (1942), directed by Dinshaw himself, the hero and his friend set out to seek their fortune in Bombay but get involved in rescuing the heroine from the clutches of the villain. *Shaan-e-Hind* (1936), *Jungle Queen* (1936), *Wah Ri Duniya* (1937) and *Pyar Ki Jyot* (1939) were his other noticeable films before the star went into oblivion in the 1940s.

***

Like his flamboyant brother, Eddie Billimoria too reached the peak of popularity in the early talkie era. A hot favourite of Chandulal Shah's Ranjit Movietone, his pairing with Gohar was greatly appreciated by audiences. He rose to fame with two roles in stark contrast to each other: first in Shah's *Miss* (1933) as the upright lover of a girl who asserts her freedom to choose her husband amid the male-dominated world and secondly in *Gunsundari* (1934, a remake of the 1927 version with Sandow in the lead role) also by Shah, as the wayward husband of a beautiful wife.

In Jayant Desai's fantasy, *Sitamgar* (1934), he appeared as a tyrannical, self-proclaimed religious fanatic who is finally reformed by the heroine belonging to the true believers. *Veer Babruwahan* (1934), also directed by Desai and set against the backdrop of the epic Mahabharata, featured him as the disgruntled son of Arjuna. In Chandulal Shah's *Desh Dasi* (1935) he appeared as a rich man, who, fed up with his affluence, leisure and purposeless life, chooses to become a Gandhian. *Keemti Aansoo* (1935), also directed by Shah, he portrayed a weak husband who is unable to save his wife from the cruelty inflicted by his parents. Finally, she becomes an ascetic after she is thrown out of the house. In *Barrister's Wife* (1935), a tragic tale about the agonies of love, Eddie came up with an engaging performance as the suffering lover whose sweetheart fails to uphold their suicide pact and marries a rich barrister. In the end, when they meet during their old age, the lover dies while the girl is prosecuted for murdering him. In this film, Sandow made a powerful impact as the public prosecutor.

Prabhu Ka Pyara (1936), Shah's critique of atheism, cast Eddie as the lover of an actress whose atheist father prostrates before god to save his daughter who has been seriously injured in a fire. In *Sipahi Ki Sajni* (1936), an adventure drama directed by Shah again, he appeared as the king's misogynist son, who gets back a treasure map stolen by a rival princess. Together they are caught by the outlaw Vijay (Ishwarlal), who also wants the treasure. Eddie's last important films were J. P. Advani's *Sneh Bandhan* (1940) and V. M. Vyas's *Niraali Duniya* (1940).

Jal Merchant and P. Jairaj

Jal Merchant, one of the most handsome heroes of the 1930s, was a serious actor and appeared in several highly appealing mythological as well as social films opposite stars such as Zubeida, Sabita Devi, Bibbo and Kanan Devi. He worked with nearly all the top directors of the period such as Prafulla Ghosh, Sarvotam Badami, Dada Gunjal, Izra Mir, A. P. Kapoor, R. S. Choudhary, Nanu Bhai Vakil, Homi Master and Balwant Bhatt. His first talkie was Prafulla Ghosh's *Veer Abhimanyu* (1931), followed by other two mythologicals, *Subhadra Haran* (1932) and *Mahabharat* (1933), and the historical *Meerabaai* (1932). He appeared in two films made under the Ajanta Movietone banner. In A. P. Kappor's *Registan Ki Rani* (1935), he appeared as a foreign-returned prince, who with the help of his fiancée, uncovers a prostitution racket run by his minister and his evil friend. *Sone Ka Shehar*, also released in the same year, was about the adventures of a prince in search of his beloved who has been kidnapped by an evil magician who has vowed to kill all human beings. His socials as hero included *Grahalaxmi* (1934), *Maa* (1936), *Mr. & Mrs. Bombay* (1936), *Punarjanam* (1938) and *Kalakar* (1942).

***

P. Jairaj was another veteran from the early era of Hindi cinema, who featured in as many as 40 films during this period as the hero. In the 1930s and 1940s, he acted in a slew of hit films in which he worked with some of the top directors of the day: Mohan Bhavnani's *The Mill* (1934), A. P. Kapoor's *Sherdil Aurat* (1935), Debaki Bose's *Jeewan Natak* (1935), Franz Osten's *Bhabhi* (1938), Zia Sarhadi's *Madhur Milan* (1938), Vijay Bhatt's *Leather Face* (1939) and *Ek Hi Bhool* (1940), Phani Majumdar's *Tamanna* (1942), Sarvotam Badami's *Khilauna* (1942), Dada Gunjal's *Kirti* (1942), Nazim Naqvi's *Naya Tarana* (1943) and *Panna* (1944), M. I. Dharamsey's *Hamari Baat* (1943), V. M. Vyas's *Dhanwan* (1946), D. N. Madhok's *Nao* (1948), Ramchandra Thakur's *Gharibi* (1949) and J. P. Advani's *Ladli* (1949).

Among these works, *The Mill*, *Sherdil Aurat* and *Leather Face* established Jairaj's screen persona in all its diversity. In *The Mill*, he appeared as a trade union leader who helps his humanitarian lady boss to lead a strike against her brother's exploitative management of their textile mill. In *Leather Face* an adventure film, he featured as the leather-masked crusader who launches a revolution against the oppressive warlord with ample support from his handful of adventurers, apart from his faithful horse and dog.

Jairaj starred opposite the top actresses of the day: Madhuri (*Raseeli Rani*, 1930), Durga Khote (*Patit Pawan*, 1933), Bibbo (*The Mill*, 1934), Khurshid and Zebunissa (*Madhur Milan*, 1938), Mehtab (*Leather Face*, 1939), Devika Rani (*Hamari Baat*, 1943), Leela Chitnis (*Berozgaar*, 1936, and *Char Ankhen*, 1944), Nargis (*Anjuman*, 1948), Suraiya (*Singaar*, 1949, and *Amar Kahani*, 1949) and Nigar Sultana (*Magroor*, 1950). His pairing with Zebunissa (especially in *Madhur Milan*) was very popular and the two were known as India's Gilbert and Garbo (after the famous Hollywood pair of John Gilbert and Greta Garbo).

Jairaj, the son of a government employee, was born on 28 September 1909 in Karimnagar (then in the Nizam of Hyderabad's princely state and now in Andhra Pradesh). He did his schooling in Hyderabad and joined the BSc course at the Nizam College in the same city. But he soon quit his studies and ran away to Bombay, where he started working as a dockyard worker. A fellow-student and friend, Rangayya, who was the manager of Mahavir Photoplays, a film distribution company, arranged his entry into films. Jairaj's first film was Nagendra Majumdar's silent film *Jagmagati Jawani* (1929), in which he not only played the side kick of the hero, Madhav Kale, but also performed the stunt scenes for him. The aspiring actor then appeared in Young India Pictures' *Raseeli Rani* (1930), based on Anthony Hope's novel *The Prisoner of Zenda.*

By the mid-1950s, the top league of film makers began to sideline Jairaj, forcing him to appear only in low-budget costume dramas and historicals. He starred in *Amarsinh Rathod* (1956), *Hatimtai* (1956), *Veer Durgadas* (1960), *Jai Chitor* (1961), *Razia Sultan* (1961), *Aalha Udal* (1962), *Kala Samundar* (1962), *Gul-e-Bakavali* (1963), *Maharani Padmini* (1964) and *Hamir Hath* (1964). *Chandrashekhar Azad* (1963), a biographical on the life of legendary revolutionary, was his only important film during his later years. He also acted in Mark Robson's controversial film *Nine Hours to Rama* (1963), which was banned in India. His other foreign ventures were MGM's *Maya* (1966), starring Clint Walker and I. S. Johar. Jairaj also produced and directed *Sagar* (1951), based on Lord Alfred Tennyson's poem *Enoch Arden,* starring Nargis and Bharat Bhushan.

Jairaj also gained distinction as a highly durable character artiste even during his best years as seen in *Shahjehan* (1946), *Badbaan* (1954), *Munna* (1954), *Pardesi* (1957), *Char Dil Char Raahein* (1959) and *Baharon Ke Sapne* (1967). He continued acting through the 1970s and 1980s and was seen in films like *Don* (1978), *Masoom* (1983) and *Khoon Bhari Mang* (1988) before finally retiring in 1994.

Jairaj bagged the Dadasaheb Phalke Award in 1981 for his contribution to Indian cinema. The legendary actor passed away on 11 August 2000. Ironically, he died a day before his biography *Jeevanachi Bharati Ohoti* (in Marathi) penned by Shashikant Kinikar (a well-known film scholar) was to be released.

Chandramohan and Govindrao Tembe

Chandramohan and Govindrao Tembe, formidable actors in their own right, were the products of the Maratha school of film making.

Chandramohan (1905–49), a distinguished alumnus of Prabhat and one of the most powerful actors of the 1930s and 1940s, is easily identifiable in the old classics because of his unusually large and piercing grey eyes. Born in Narasingpur (now in Madhya Pradesh), he started his career as an employee of Famous Pictures, the distributors of Prabhat's films. He made his debut in 1934 in Shantaram's classic *Amritmanthan* in the role of a fanatical priest of the Chandika cult who revolts against the king for his decree banning human and animal sacrifices to appease Goddess Kali. Soon Chandramohan became a forerunner in portraying mythological and historical characters in films such as Sohrab Modi's *Pukar* (1939, in the role of the Mughal Emperor Jehangir), V. Shantaram's *Shakuntala* (1943, as King Dushyant) and Kidar Sharma's *Mumtaz Mahal* (1944, as Emperor Shahjehan).

Apart from the foregoing films, Chandramohan also has several other memorable films to his credit. In K. Narayan Kale's period film *Wahan* (1937), set against the backdrop of Aryan–aboriginal conflict, Chandramohan appeared as the Aryan king committed to the ideals of Aryan justice. In the Macbethian costume drama *Jwala* (1938) directed by Master Vinayak, Chandramohan won kudos for his role as the good-hearted army general who is corrupted by ambition and wants to become the king. Next, in Shaukat Hussain Rizvi's *Naukar* (1943), written by the celebrated Urdu writer Sadat Hasan Manto, he essayed the role of a household servant, who faces lifelong guilt and persecution. His portrayal of the rebel Rajput prince Randhir Singh in Mehboob Khan's *Humayun* (1945), who challenges the mighty Mughal empire, is still remembered by old film lovers.

Chandramohan was also a rare breed of actor, who like Premnath later, specialized both in lead as well as villainous roles. He was cast as villain by his mentor Shantaram in *Dharmatma* (1935). Here, the played the role of the priest who opposes Saint Eknath's crusade against untouchability (Eknath's role was played by the Marathi stage legend Bal Gandharva; curiously this was the only male role he played during his career). Also, in the master's *Amar Jyoti* (1936) he was the tyrannical minister of the queen (played by Dhurga Khote in one of her most memorable roles). Chandramohan further elaborated his villainous streak as the lecherous industrialist in Mehboob's *Roti* (1942) and in P. Y. Altekar's masterpiece *Geeta* (1940). In *Geeta* he played a double role as the criminal father and son who are persecuted by the younger lawyer son of the family. Debaki Bose's offbeat film *Apna Ghar* (1942), highlighting the need for safeguarding tribals' forest rights (a very important topic even today), presented Chandramohan in the role of a business-minded forest contractor who disowns his social activist wife working among the forest dwellers. He also played Ravana in Vijay Bhatt's *Rambaan* (1948), based on the epic Ramayana.

Like actor Sanjeev Kumar in the 1970s and 1980s, Chandramohan had no qualms about taking up elderly roles. In Mehboob's *Taqdeer* (1943), he portrayed the feudal lord who raises the hero (Motilal) as his foster son, and in Ramesh Sehgal's *Shaheed* (1948), his commanding portrayal of the pro-establishment father on the side of the British, who condemns and persecutes his revolutionary son (Dilip Kumar), was a major highlight of the film. His other important films included *Fashion* (1943), *Bade Nawab Saheb* (1944), *Pannadai* (1945), *Meghraj* (1946) and *Dukhiari* (1948). His last appearance was in *Bal Ramayan* (1956), released several years after his death.

Chandramohan died in 1949, when he was merely forty-four years old.

***

Govindrao Tembe (1881–1955), actor, composer, playwright, theatre personality and music theorist all rolled into one single persona, was born in Kolhapur, Maharashtra. He rose to fame as hero in his very first film *Ayodhyecha Raja/Ayodhya Ka Raja* (1932), a mythological directed by V. Shantaram. He played the role of Harishchandra, the king of Ayodhya, who always spoke the truth. Another movie, *Maya Machhindra*, a classic directed by his mentor (Shantaram) and released in the same year, featured him as Guru Machhindranath who is rescued from spiritual downfall by his ardent disciple Gorakhnath. In Baburao Painter's *Usha* (1935), he was seen in the role of Lord Krishna who nullifies the designs of the demon king Banasur to eliminate Vishnu and other gods. His other films were *Manjari* (1934), *Seeta* (1934), his own directorial venture, *Raj Mukut* (1935) and *Nandakumar* (1937). As a music director, Tembe composed the music for Painter's films and some early Prabhat movies. This genius was the first to introduce the *khayal* (a singing style in classical music) in concerts and during recording when the legendary Bal Gandharva's think tank was recasting the classical-popular musical idiom. Tembe's publications include *Mazha Sangeet Vyasanga* (1939) and *Jeevan Vihar* (1948).

Mazhar Khan, Ishwarlal and Ghulam Mohammed

Mazhar Khan, an artiste known for his intense but natural performances, won kudos for his outstanding performance in Shantaram's classic *Padosi* (1941). He very ably portrayed Thakur, an upper-caste Hindu, who is hot-headed, irritable and easily susceptible to suspicion and anger. His friendship with Mirza (played equally well by Gajanan Jagirdar), his Muslim neighbour, has become legendary in their village. Every morning they seek each other's friendly company through their daily routine of playing chess with great fervour. Both are poor, living at subsistence levels by working as labourers at the dam being built on a river flowing close to their village. Their friendship comes under a cloud when the builders of the dam who want to acquire their village for the expansion of the dam (à la Narmada Sardar Sarovar Project in our times). Certain events create a rift between the two friends and by extension the two communities. In the end, both die holding each other's hands as they are swept away by the gushing water from the dam that has been dynamited by Thakur's son. In this movie, a Hindu played the role of a Muslim and vice versa.

Mazhar Khan, a talent scouted by Mohan Bhavnani, made his debut in Imperial's silent film *Gamdani Gori* (1927) in the role of a film star who falls in love with an innocent village girl (Sulochana) who is being forced into prostitution by some lustful and avaricious men. With the advent of the talkies, he moved to Calcutta and appeared as hero in several East India Films' ventures: *Nal Damyanti* (1933), *Sultaana* (1934), *Selima* (1935) and *Noor-e-Wahdut* (1936). He also became a major star of Ranjit Studio as a result of three releases: Chaturbhuj Doshi's *Gorakh Aaya* (1938), Manibhai Vyas's *Professor Waman MSc* (1938) and Izra Mir's *Rickshawala* (1938). In *Gorakh Aaya* (à la Prabhat's *Maya Machhindra*), he portrayed Guru Machhindranath, who is brought back to the spiritual path by his own disciple Gorakhnath, when the teacher starts indulging in carnal pleasures. Mazhar Khan's other works include Dwarka Khosla's *Meri Aankhen* (1939), Pesi Karani's *Akela* (1941) and A. R. Kardar's *Nai Duniya* (1942). The actor also turned producer-director with *Yaad* (1942).

***

Ishawarlal was a leading star of the 1930s and 1940s but by the early 1950s he, all of a sudden, went into oblivion. A talent scouted by the film maker Jayant Desai, his first film was *Bhola Shikar* (1933) with Eddie Billimoria in the lead. He held a lifelong association with his mentor Desai, appearing largely only in his films such as *Noor-e-Vatan* (1935), *Raj Ramani* (1936) and *Rangeela Raaja* (1936) in the second lead with Eddie Billimoria as the hero. He played the second lead in *Aaj Ka Hindustan* (1940, directed again by Jayant Desai) with Prithiviraj Kapoor in the top slot. He also featured in his mentor's *Chandni* (1942) and *Maharana Pratap* (1946). In Master Vinayak's *Badi Maa* (1945), set against the backdrop of the Second World War, he portrayed a London-returned youth who joins, along with spy-turned-patriot brother (Yakub), the Allied forces to repulse the Japanese attack on their village.

Ishawarlal was also among the few actors of his times who started directing their own films and appearing in the lead. He made his directorial debut with *Bansari* (1943), followed by *Lalkar* (1944), both produced under Jayant Desai's banner, apart from *Sohni Mahiwal* (1946), *Heera* (1947) and *Matrubhoomi* (1949). His other films included D. N. Madhok's *Jwalamukhi* (1936) and *Shama Parvana* (1937), Chandulal Shah's *Pardesi Pankhi* (1937), D. N. Madhok's *Dil Farosh* (1937), V. M. Vyas's *Sanskar* (1952) and B. Shukla and H. Bhatt's *Naulakha Haar* (1953).

***

Ghulam Mohammed, a sensitive actor who specalized in portraying a disillusioned lover, was an alumnus of Imperial Theatres. He made his debut as hero in R. S. Choudhary's *Maadhuri* (1932), an adventure spectacle set in the fourth-century (A. D.) Gupta period. Mohammed played the timorous prince of Malwa who is constantly harassed by his evil and scheming chief minister. The princess (Sulochana) disguising herself as a male soldier finally kills the minister in a sword duel. Mohammed continued his innings at Imperial with films such as R. S. Choudhary's *Shaan-e-Hind* (1936), Moti B. Gidwani's *Kisan Kanya* (1937, in a supporting role), I. A. Hafis's *Gaazi Salauddin* (1939), Dada Gunjal's *Mahamaya* (1936), Rustam Modi's *Paak Daman* (1940) and Premankur Atorthy's *Kalyani* (1940).

In the early 1940s Mohammed joined Pancholi Pictures (headed by Dalsukh Pancholi) in Lahore and made his mark with powerful performances in Shaukat Hussain Rizvi's *Khandan* (opposite Noorjehan) and Moti B. Gidwani's *Zamindar* both released in 1942. In the first film, he portrayed an overindulgent lover who is prevented from killing his beloved by his household servant since the latter, in his younger days, had been jailed for a similar crime. *Zamindar*, depicting the fall of feudal patriarchy, presented him in the role of a tyrannical landlord who plays havoc with the lives of his tenants. His noble son sides with the oppressed lot and, as the story reveals, he is arrested for killing his father.

On his return to the Bombay cine world, Mohammed appeared in Sohrab Modi's *Ek Din Ka Sultan* (1945), a story about the boat man who saves the Mughal Emperor Humayun from drowning. Humayun crowns him as the ruler for one day. Mohammed's oeuvre also includes A. R. Kardar's *Sanyasi* (1945), Aspi Irani's *Chhin Le Azadi* (1947) and Wali Saheb's *Heer Ranjha* (1948) in the role of the legendary lover Ranjha (opposite Mumtaz Shanti as Heer).

Master Vinayak and Gajanan Jagirdar

Master Vinayak (1906–47), probably Indian cinema's first avant-garde actor-director, was one of the few educated men to join the film industry. Born as Vinayak Damodar Karnataki, he studied at Kolhapur (now in Maharashtra). His father Vasudev Karnataki was a well-known cinematographer. The veteran Baburao Pendharkar (from the Marathi school of film making) was his cousin.

Vinayak started as a teacher and also acted in Marathi theatre. Soon he was picked up by V. Shantaram, who turned him into a celebrated actor, making his mark in the early Prabhat films with his powerful singing and acrobatic acting style. He played the role of Narad in his first-ever film *Ayodhyecha Raja* (1932) under this banner, followed immediately by *Jalti Nishani/*

Agnikankan (1932), *Maya Machhindra* (1932), *Sairandhri* (1933) and *Sinhagad* (1933).

Vinayak's first film as hero was Bhalji Pendharkar's *Akashwani*, released in 1934. An allegory highlighting the anti-imperialist stance of that period, the film narrated Lord Krishna's crusade against his evil maternal uncle Kansa. Vinayak appeared in the role of Vasudev, the father of Krishna dethroned by Kansa. In Premankur Atorthy's *Bhikharan* (1935), he was featured as a painter who falls in love with a destitute woman thrown out by her lustful husband (the hero). The hero ditches her because he wants to marry another wealthy woman. The disowned wife earns money by singing in the streets. She finds true love in the form of the painter. In his first directorial venture *Vilasi Ishwar/ Nigah-e-Nafrat* (1936), Vinayak appeared as the brother of a disgruntled girl abandoned by her rich boyfriend, who starts courting a rich princess (Shobhna Samarth), who is also being sought by the villain. *Chhaya* (1936) was a tragic tale about the suffering of the urban middle class and the inhuman attitude of some members of the medical fraternity. Here, Vinayak essayed a memorable role as an ordinary youth whose father, a bank employee, is jailed for stealing money to buy medicine for his sick wife. Vinayak's poem, which he wrote to describe his father's plight, is published in the same newspaper that highlighted his father's theft and wins a prize. The judge who convicted his father is the one who gives him the prize. The judge's daughter falls in love with Vinayak. But when she comes to know about his family's history, she ditches him and accuses him of molesting her and he is sent to prison. The disillusioned lover escapes from jail and manages to publish his autobiographical novel. The police then rearrest him and he is sent back to jail.

In the superhit *Dharmaveer* (1938), Vinayak appeared as a gullible dullard who is ridiculed by one and all for failing the matriculation examination eight times. He, nevertheless, leads a crusade to expose a so-called philanthropist who otherwise is a drunkard, a womanizer and also a swindler. *Brahmachari* (1938) again cast him in a comic role. This time he plays a sex-smitten commoner, who, inspired by the propaganda of Hindu nationalism, adopts celibacy and starts body building, but all his attempts go haywire in the presence of the girl he adores.

Ardhangi (1940), in contrast with Vinayak's usual radical stance, denigrated the making of the modern 'Westernized' Indian woman and advocated her dutiful return to her traditional role. The hero, a married college teacher, gets infatuated with the Anglicized wife of a colleague. After he is able to hook her, she starts treating him like a servant and in the end elopes with another rich man. *Lapandav* (1940), a comedy about the liberation from the feudal mindset, cast Vinayak and Baburao Pendharkar as the lovers of the two daughters of a feudul patriarch, who refuses to accept them as sons-in-law because of their lowly status.

Vinayak appeared in *Amrit* (1941) as the son of the village patriarch, who in his pursuit of a shoemaker's wife (to satisfy his carnal desires) becomes her slave. Her husband (a drunkard) has been arrested for killing his daughter. *Mazhe Bal* (1943) portrayed Vinayak as a nationalist, but a Westernized youth, who makes his sweetheart pregnant. She eventually marries the idealist public prosecutor who is responsible for her former lover's death sentence.

Vinayak's biography was written by his chief disciple, Dinkar D. Patil, and published in 1971. Vinayak's daughter, Nanda, who became one of the most celebrated actresses of Hindi cinema, began her career in the 1950s. After a long spell as a heroine, she went on to play character roles.

***

Gajanan Jagirdar (1907–88), the legendary actor-scenarist-director in Marathi and Hindi cinema, was acclaimed as the first major freelance director. He was a teacher before joining the film industry. Born in Amravati (now in Maharashtra), he started as a child actor in the amateur stage. Later, he set up a theatre group called Arun Players and staged Anton Chekhov's masterpiece *The Cherry Orchard* and Harindranath Chattopadhyay's play *Returned from Abroad*. Ernst Lubitsch's powerful film, *The Patriot* (1928), had a major influence on Jagirdar's work.

Jagirdar entered cinema as a writer of English intertitles at Prabhat and also taught Urdu dialogue delivery to the Marathi artistes. He became an assistant to Bhalji Pendharkar and then directed some films for Master Vinayak's Huns Pictures (*Begunah*, 1937, for example). He then worked briefly at Minerva Movietone as a scenarist for Sohrab Modi (*Meetha Zaher*, 1938, and *Talaaq*, 1938) and for P. K. Atre's company. During the shooting of *Jalti Nishani* (1932), the actor D. D. Mane could not deliver the Urdu dialogues flawlessly. Shantaram, the director, therefore selected Jagirdar for the role. He thus became an actor by playing the role of a seventy-five-year-old man at the age of twenty-five.

Jagirdar's best-known films of this era were Shantaram's *Shejari/Padosi* (1941) in the role of the Muslim neighbour of the Hindu Thakur (played by Mazhar Khan) and *Ramshastri* (1944), which he directed and in which he also played the lead role. His other works as actor include *Honhaar* (1936), *Aseer-e-Hawas* (1936), *Talaaq* (1938), *Payachi Dasi/Charnon Ki Dasi* (1941), *Vasantsena* (1942), *Kiran* (1944), *Behram Khan* (1946) and *Jail Yatra* (1947).

In his later years Jagirdar became an important character artiste, giving memorable performances in films such as *Armaan* (1953), *Chhoo Mantar* (1956), *Paying Guest* (1957), *Chacha Zindabad* (1959), *Babar* (1960), *Shahir Parashuram* (1961), *Hum Dono* (1961), *Aarti* (1962), *Guide* (1965), *Aadmi Aur Insaan* (1969), *Donhi Gharcha Pahuna* (1971), *Mandir Masjid* (1977), *Des Pardes* (1978) and *Umrao Jaan* (1981). The Bengal Film Journalists' Association bestowed upon him the best actor award for his performances in *Padosi* and also in *Ramshastri*. The Government of Maharashtra too gave him the best actor award for his role in *Shahir Parashuram*. The *Rasarang* (a weekly Marathi magazine) presented him the Vasantrao Pechelvan Shield for the best character actor in the same film.

Jagirdar was also a well-known teacher of film acting. He basically applied the Russian genius Konstantin Stanislavsky's theories to local conditions. In fact, this was the theme of a book he published in 1983. He was appointed as the first principal of the Film Institute of Poona in 1960, but he resigned from the post after serving for just one year. He published two autobiographies (in 1971 and 1986). He also produced a TV serial *Swami*, which was based on the life of the Maratha king Madhavrao Peshwa.

Shahu Modak and Prem Adib

Shahu Modak, the main icon of mythological and devotional films, that too for several decades, was one of the most long-serving actors of Indian cinema. It is an irony that a figure whose name is synonymous with the Hindu mythological film was born in a Christian family in 1918. He was introduced into films by Bhalji Pendharkar together with actress Shanta Apte as a child artiste as the young Krishna in the 1932 superhit *Shyam Sundar*. This film was followed by a double role in his second film *Aut Ghatkecha Raja*, released in 1933. He became a top-level star with his role as the upright policeman Ganpat in V. Shantaram's *Manoos/Aadmi* (1939), who saves a prostitute from a police raid on a brothel and they fall in love. But he is unable to rehabilitate her because his own reputation is at stake. He then acted in many contemporary Marathi socials such as *Mazha Mulga* (1938) and *Pahili Mangalagaur* (1942). In *Begunah* (1937), a classic directed by Gajanan Jagirdar, he portrayed an upright youth, who, in a moment of weakness, rapes a troubled girl thrown out of the house by her stepmother. As he suffers from this guilt all by himself, his relationship with his fiancée turns sour. Mehboob Khan's *Amar* (1954, starring Dilip Kumar, Nimmi and Madhubala) also had a similar plot.

After the tremendous success of *Sant Dnyaneshwar* (1940), in which he played the role of the famous Marathi saint-poet and author of *Dnyaneshwari* (a commentary on the Bhagavad Gita),

Modak appeared in a number of devotional films both in Marathi and Hindi. Over the decades Modak appeared in a stream of films produced by V. M. Vyas, Dhirubhai Desai and Vijay Bhatt among others. These films include *Sant Namdev* (1949), *Shiv Bhakt* (1955), *Aastik* (1956), *Narsi Bhagat* (1957), *Gopichand* (1958), *Gaja Gauri* (1958), *Sant Gyaneshwar* (1964), *Tere Dwar Khada Bhagwan* (1964), *Sant Tukaram* (1965) and *Sant Tulsidas* (1972). Modak is credited with having played Lord Krishna in twenty-nine mythologicals in Marathi, Hindi and Bhojpuri. His important mythologicals were *Bharat Milap* (1942), *Maya Bazaar* (1949), *Veer Ghatotkach* (1949), *Bhakta Dhruva* (1957) and *Har Har Mahadev* (1974). His last screen presence was in *Krishna Krishna* (1986). He died in 1993.

***

Like Shahu Modak, Prem Adib, another highly durable actor in Hindi cinema, specialized in mythologicals and historicals, although he did appear in several films with contemporary themes. He made his debut in 1937 with Minerva Movietone's *Khan Bahadur*, directed by Sohrab Modi. He soon found a foothold in the film world through several mythological films: Vijay Bhatt's two superhits – *Bharat Milap* (1942) and *Ram Rajya* (1943) – apart from Master Vinayak's *Subhadra* (1946), *Raja Harishchandra* (1952), *Hanuman Janam* (1955), *Ram Hanuman Yuddh* (1957), *Krishna Sudama* (1957) and *Ram Bhakta Vibhishan* (1958).

Subhadra was about the differences between Lord Krishna (Prem Adib) and his brother Balram regarding the marriage of their sister Subhadra. His noteworthy historicals were *Amrapali* (1945) and *Samrat Prithviraj Chauhan* (1959).

In social melodramas, Adib worked with famous directors in films like Mohan Sinha's *Industrial India* (1938), Virendra Desai and Mahendra Thakur's *Sadhana* (1939), Chimanlal Lohar's *Darshan* (1941) and *Station Master* (1942), D. D. Kashyap's *Chand* (1944), Mehboob Khan's *Anokhi Ada* (1948), Najam Naqvi's *Actress* (1948), O. P. Dutta's *Hamari Manzil* (1949) and Hemchandra Chunder's *Teen Bhai* (1955). *Anokhi Ada* was his most memorable

social, which featured him as a crazy adventurer who becomes
the lover of the heroine before she starts suffering from amnesia.

Other (Almost Forgotten) Heroes

Madhav Kale was a fairly well-known actor during the 1930s and
1940s. He was among the few young cine artistes who had a good
educational background. Along with S. B. Nayampalli and P. Y.
Altekar, he was a member of the creative team led by the legendary
Marathi writer Mama Warerkar. This team was to have a far-
reaching influence on the course of Marathi cinema. His first
talkie was *Malti Madhav* directed by A. P. Kapoor and released in
1933. Although he did work with some of the top directors of the
era, such as Dada Gunjal (*Aparadhi*, 1935), D. N. Madhok
(*Khoobsoorat Bala*, 1933), G. P. Pawar (*Duniya Kya Hai*, 1938) and
Bapurao Apte (*Parakh*, 1937), he could not become a top-rung star.
His other noteworthy films are *Vishnu Bhakti* (1934), *Prem Bandhan*
(1936), *Sansar Saagar* (1939), *Sachcha Sapna* (1942), *Swadesh Sewa*
(1946) and *Amar Prem* (1948). Later on, he appeared as a character
actor in *Phoolon Ka Haar* (1951), *Rangila* (1953), *Bahadur* (1958),
Gokul Ka Chor (1959), *Kangan* (1959), and *Chand Mere Aaja* (1960).

 Navin Yagnik, an important alumnus of Ajanta Cinetone, was
one of the most versatile second-rung artistes during the 1930s
and 1940s. He was a constant companion of his mentor, Mohan
Bhavnani, appearing in many films produced by him. His notable
films as hero are Bhavnani's *Jaagran* (1936), *Dilaawar* (1936), *Vijay
Marg* (1938) and *Rangbhoomi* (1946), J. P. Advani's *Farebi Duniya*
(1935), Gajanan Jagirdar's *Main Haari* (1940), Nariman Ghariali's
Safed Sawar (1941), Nanu Bhai Vakil's *Kismatwala* (1944) and Phani
Majumdar's *Insaan* (1946). In supporting roles he appeared in
Suhana Geet (1941), *Raja Rani* (1942), *Vasantsena* (1942), *Prithvi
Vallabh* (1943), *Tasveer* (1943) and *Chal Chal Re Naujawan* (1944).

 Another durable star of the 1930s was *Navin Chandra*, who
specialized largely in historicals and fantasies. His major films
included *Kaala Pahaad* (1933), *Nav Bharat* (1934), *Woh Kaun* (1935),

Baaz Bahaadur (1936), *Guru Ghantaal* (1937), *Prithviraj Sanyogita* (1933), *Lehari Jawaan* (1935) and *Banke Sawaria* (1938).

Gul Hamid was an actor with immense possibilities, but, unfortunately, he failed to find a firm foothold in the film world. His important films were A. R. Kardar's *Baaghi Sipahi* (1936) and *Khyber Pass* (1936) and Debaki Bose's *Sunehra Sansaar* (1936).

Najmul Hussain was a formidable actor who appeared in several widely acclaimed films of Bombay Talkies and New Theatres. These films include Franz Osten's *Jawani Ki Hawa* (1935, opposite Devika Rani), Hemchandra Chunder's *Anaath Ashram* (1937), Phani Majumdar's *Kapaal Kundala* (1939) and Madhu Bose's *Meenakshi* (1942).

Master Mohammed, a hot favourite of the Wadias (J. B. H. and Homi), made his mark in films such as *Harishchandra* (1931), *Vaaman Avtar* (1934), *Desh Deepak* (1935) and *Hind Kesari* (1935).

Arun, another fairly durable star of the 1940s, had several important films to his credit: *Kanchan* (1941), *Holiday in Bombay* (1941), *Savera* (1942), *Andhera* (1943), *Nurse* (1943), *Carvaan* (1944), *Chalis Karod* (1945), *Ghunghat* (1946), *Samaj Ko Badal Dalo* (1947), *Sehra* (1948) and *Sudhar* (1949).

From Heroes to Character Actors

Several character actors of the 1950s and beyond had appeared in lead roles during their younger days.

Jayant (real name Zakaria Khan; the father of Amjad Khan or Gabbar Singh of *Sholay*, 1975) was a much-sought-after actor soon after the advent of the talkies. His robust physique and deep voice were his plus points. His impressive filmography as hero included *Laal Chitthi* (1935), *Bombay Mail* (1935), *Azaad Veer* (1936), *Snehlata* (1936), besides Vijay Bhatt's *Khwaab Ki Duniya* (1937). As hero he also appeared in *Challenge* (1937), *His Highness* (1937), *Mr X* (1938), *Hero No. 1* (1939), *Apni Nagaria* (1940) and *Poonji* (1943).

Ulhas, with his huge build, typical brand of melodramatic histrionics and a sonorous voice, appeared as hero in *Mera Ladka*

(1938), *Basant* (1942), *Angoori* (1943), *Parbat Pe Apna Dera* (1944), *Suno Sunata Hoon* (1944), *Dev Kanya* (1946) and *Kaajal* (1948). He left a lasting impression in several films. For instance: in K. Narayan Kale's *Mera Ladka* in the role of a radical newspaper editor; in Amiya Chakravarty's *Basant* as the spoilt and envious youth who sets out to make his own fortune, leaving his wife and their newborn to starve; and as an ascetic-turned-playboy in V. Shantaram's *Parbat Pe Apna Dera*. Ulhas later played a prominent role in Shantaram's internationally acclaimed masterpiece *Do Aankhen Barah Haath* (1957).

Kumar (who was very impressive as the sculptor in K. Asif's magnificent spectacle *Mughal-e-Azam*, 1960) was another veteran who had played the lead in Mehboob Khan's *Judgement of Allah* (1935) and *Vatan* (1938), besides *Hamari Betiyan* (1936), *Postman* (1938), *Nadi Kinaare* (1939), *Madhusudan* (1941), *Kalyug* (1942), *Shahenshah Akbar* (1943), *Doosri Shadi* (1947) and *Abidah* (1947).

Mubarak, the famous blue-eyed character actor and villain of the 1950s, played lead roles in the beginning of his career in films such as *Baala Joban* (1934), *Tilasmi Heera* (1934), *Pardesi Sayiaan* (1935) and *Sarojini* (1937).

Nazir, another noteworthy actor of the era, was a prominent hero of his times as seen in *Pratima* (1936), *Prem Raatri* (1936), *Shokh Dilruba* (1936), *Zamana* (1938), *Sandesha* (1940), *Chhed Chhad* (1943), *Maa Baap* (1944) and *Village Girl* (1945).

Kishore Sahu, the well-known actor, writer and director, was a product of Bombay Talkies and Filmistan. After his debut in Franz Osten's *Jeevan Prabhat* (1937) opposite Devika Rani, he appeared in the lead in several films of well-known directors: Najam Naqvi's *Punar Milan* (1940), Ramesh Gupta's *Rimjhim* (1949), Shahid Lateef's *Buzdil* (1951) and Kidar Sharma's *Sapna* (1953). He also featured in his own ventures, such as *Kunwara Baap* (1942), *Sindoor* (1947), *Sawan Aya Re* (1949), *Kali Ghata* (1951), *Mayur Pankh* (1954), *Hamlet* (1954) and *Bade Sarkar* (1957). From the mid-1950s onwards, he shifted to playing negative roles, particularly in some Dev Anand films: *Kala Pani* (1958), *Kala Bazaar* (1960), *Guide* (1965) and *Hare Rama Hare Krishna* (1971).

Actor-director Trilok Kapoor, the younger brother of Prithviraj Kapoor, remained on the lower rungs of stardom, specializing in mythological and period films as seen in Prafulla Ghosh's *Char Darvesh* (1932), *The Secretary* (1938), Mohan Bhavnani's *Jhoothi Sharam* (1940), *Anuradha* (1940), *Suhana Geet* (1941), *Raja Rani* (1942), *Mirza Sahiban* (1947) opposite Noorjehan, *Shri Rambhakta Hanuman* (1948), *Bhimsen* (1950), *Har Har Mahadev* (1950), *Maya Machhindra* (1951) and *Chakradhari* (1954).

The First Four Icons: Sohrab Modi, Prithviraj Kapoor, Motilal and Ashok Kumar

In the cinema of the formative period, Sohrab Modi, as an actor, commanded great respect and gained a lot of admiration for his magnetic screen presence. He very ably transformed the basic conventions of the Parsi theatre style then in vogue into precise cinematic expressions, thus building up a highly powerful and an awe-inspiring screen persona. In this process of transformation, he got rid of the thematic obstacles of the theatre and took up new stories and sketched out roles that were later improvised by his own scripts. Yet his style remained theatrical, relying heavily on well-timed spatial movements

Sohrab Modi

and frontal positions. Other features included a highly dramatic point–counterpoint verbal oratory in chaste Urdu, which was used in copious measures. In most films, Modi appeared in the role of a humanizing patriarch except in *Jailor* (1938). He wrote, directed and acted in nearly all his films. He rarely acted in movies under a banner other than his own.

* * *

In Indian cinema, the credit for the creation of the image of a truly handsome hero, tall and robust, with sculpted Grecian features, must go to Prithviraj Kapoor (1906–72). A celebrated stage actor committed to the cause of theatre from his younger days, Kapoor's popularity in cinema skyrocketed in no time. There was a time when he has worshipped like a deity, and fans vied with one another to touch his feet. Although his style bordered on the theatrical, he brought in the tradition of speaking a rich, refined language.

Prithviraj, the son of a police officer, was born near Lyallpur (now in Pakistan). As a student of law, he made his name as an amateur drama artiste in Lyallpur and later in Peshawar (also now in Pakistan). In the late 1920s, he quit law studies and came to Bombay to join Imperial Theatres. He made his debut in 1929 in the silent movie *Do Dhari Talwar*, directed by B. P. Mishra. He, however, gained popularity with his second release *Cinema Girl* (1930) opposite Ermeline. This was perhaps the first Indian film to depict the functioning of the film industry as it then existed through the eyes of a disgruntled director. Prithviraj also appeared in the first talkie *Alam Ara* (released in 1931) in a supporting role. In Imperial's second talkie *Draupadi* (1932), he was cast in the role of Arjuna, one of the five Pandava brothers. Meanwhile, he joined the Grant Anderson Theatre, where he acted in William Shakespeare's plays in English.

In 1933, Prithviraj arrived with a bang in the Calcutta film world and became the favourite hero of Debaki Bose, who paired him with Durga Khote in several classics. He rose to fame with the master's *Rajrani Meera* (1933) in the role of the husband of the saint-poetess, followed by the same director's *Seeta* (1934, as Lord Rama), *After the Earthquake* (1935) and the classic *Vidyapati* (1937). *Vidyapati* emerged as one of the most profound cinematic interpretations in Indian cinema of the spirituality of love as envisioned in the Bhakti tradition. The narrative contended that a complete immersion of one's soul in the longing for love is the only true manifestation of human existence for all human beings:

be it the king, the queen or the common people. The broad-minded and enlightened king (Prithviraj) refuses to be troubled by his queen's platonic love for the popular saint-poet Vidyapati, who has instilled deep spiritual contentment in the masses through his songs. In Prafulla Roy's *Abhagin* (1938), the young actor appeared as the saviour of the runaway daughter-in-law of a conservative family and in Madhu Bose's *Raj Nartaki* (1941), the actor donned the mantle of a benevolent prince who has to forego his love for the court dancer to save his kingdom from disgrace.

Prithviraj's career in Bombay was equally impressive with several outstanding portrayals. Chaturbhuj Doshi's *Adhuri Kahani* (1939) presented him as the son of the woman protagonist oppressed by her conservative husband, who, along with her sister, commits suicide after their mother kills herself. In A. R. Kardar's classic *Pagal* (1940), Prithviraj probably essayed Hindi cinema's most sadistic and brutish anti-hero role. He plays a sexually obsessive maniac and a psychiarist by profession who turns his former sweetheart insane by injecting her with a drug. The doctor had turned vengeful because he was deceived into marrying the heroine's less beautiful sister.

In Sohrab Modi's *Sikandar* (1941), Prithviraj in the title role won wide acclaim for his towering performance. *Phool* (1944), K. Asif's directorial debut, was about the struggle of a devout Muslim family to build a mosque against innumerable odds. In Bhalji Pendharkar's *Valmiki* (1946), the film set in the Vedic period, he portrayed the powerful low-caste rebel who sets out to destroy the highly tyrannical and mighty Aryans and their priests. In the end, a repentant Valmiki becomes a great rishi through his spiritual enlightenment. Prithviraj also made his mark in several mythological and historical films: Bhalji Pendharkar's *Maharathi Karna* (1944), Vijay Bhatt's *Vikramaditya* (1945), Mohan Sinha's *Shri Krishan Arjun Yuddha* (1945), Kumarsen Samarth's *Nal Damayanti* (1945), Najam Naqvi's *Prithviraj Samyogita* (1946) and Ramnik Desai's *Parsuram* (1947).

His other major films in this period were: A. R. Kardar's

Milaap (1937), Sarvotam Badami's *Chingari* (1940), Dwarka Khosla's *Deepak* (1940), W. Z. Ahmed's *Ek Raat* (1942), Kidar Sharma's *Gauri* (1943), J. K. Nanda's *Ishara* (1943), Balwant Bhatt's *Ankh Ki Sharm* (1943) and Paul Zils's *Hindustan Hamara* (1950).

Apart from the lead roles, Prithviraj also played stellar supporting roles with equal fervour in Debaki Bose's *Inquilab* (1935), P. C. Barua's *Manzil* (1936), Debaki Bose's *Sapera* (1939) and Nitin Bose's *President* (1937) during his stint at New Theatres. In Bombay, he appeared in V. Shantaram's *Dahej* (1950) as the tormented father who is unable to arrange dowry for his daughter's marriage; in his son Raj Kapoor's *Awara* (1951) as his estranged biological father; in Hemen Gupta's *Anand Math* (1952) as the senior revolutionary priest; and in Bhalji Pendharkar's *Chhatrapati Shivaji* (1952) as Raja Jai Singh, one of the commanders of the Mughal Emperor Aurangzeb's vast army.

In K. Asif's magnum opus *Mughal-e-Azam* (1960), Prithviraj's powerful portrayal as the Mughal Emperor Akbar immortalized both him and the film. He carried forward his image in *Mughal-e-Azam* (as the patriarch holding on to the family honour) in films like *Rajkumar*, *Ghazal* and *Zindagi*, all released in 1964. He also appeared as Emperor Shahjehan in *Jahanara* (1964). In K. A. Abbas's *Aasman Mahal* (1965), he lent authenticity to his role as an old-fashioned nawab, who refuses to sell his dilapidated palace to a hotelier.

In the late 1960s and early 1970s, despite his failing health, Prithviraj appeared in a few Hindi films (Chetan Anand's *Heer Ranjha*, 1970, and *Kal, Aaj Aur Kal*, 1971, directed by his grandson Randhir Kapoor) and Punjabi mythologicals. In Ram Maheshwari's *Nanak Naam Jahaaz Hai* (1969), the film credited with bringing about a revival of the Punjabi film industry, he appeared in the role of a devout Sikh patriarch.

Prithviraj set up Prithvi Theatres in 1944, funded by his earnings from films. This grand institution specialized in staging secular plays such as Inder Raj Anand's *Deewar* (1945), *Gaddar* (1947) and *Pathan* (1948). Prithviraj faced death threats from

Islamic fundamentalists for *Deewar*, an offbeat play against Partition. Prithvi Theatres soon became the launch pad for a host of film celebrities including writer-film maker Ramanand Sagar, film maker Ramesh Sehgal, music directors Ram Ganguly and Shankar Jaikishan and his sons Raj, Shammi and Shashi. While directing *Paisa*, a film adapted from a Prithvi Theatres' play, Prithviraj partially lost his voice, which he could never regain fully. He then closed down his theatre, which has recently been revived by his youngest son Shashi Kapoor. Prithviraj died of cancer on 29 May 1972.

***

Motilal (1910–65), whom none other than Dilip Kumar has acclaimed as a noteworthy predecessor, can be considered a pathbreaking genius with regard to naturalistic cinematic acting. He was the first to put in place the flamboyant, happy-go-lucky, unpretentious and glamourized image of the Hindi film hero cast in the Hollywood mould of that era. He was the first product of the Mehboob school of film making in the 1930s, when the legendary director himself had merely managed to get a foothold in Hindi cinema,

Motilal

Motilal was born in 1910 in Shimla in a Rajvansh family. He made his debut Kaliprasad Ghosh's *Shaher Ka Jadoo* (1934), produced by Sagar Movietone. The film, a scathing critique of the decadent urban milieu, had Motilal in the role of a drunkard millionaire. He is made to give up this vice by a poor village girl, who is exposed to the ugly aspects of city life as she desperately launches a search for her lost father. Sarvotam Badami's *Dr Madhurika* (1935) was about the conflict between modern and traditional values. The hero marries a lady doctor girl on the precondition that she will not bear any children and he should not interfere with her practice. Such a situation leads to serious marital discord. In *Silver King* (1935), a costume drama directed by Chimanlal Lohar, he appeared as the people's leader who frees the king kidnapped by his wily commander and, in the process, falls in love with the princess.

In Kaliprasad Ghosh's period drama *Lagna Bandhan* (1936), Motilal appeared in a rare double role. The good prince impersonates his debauched twin brother to get married to the latter's sweetheart. Chimanlal Lohar's *Do Diwane* (1936), based on the noted Gujarati writer K. M. Munshi's acclaimed comedy, cast him as a doctor who along with his sweetheart (Shobhna Samarth) wants to become committed revolutionaries but are hindered by their conservative family background. In Sarvotam Badami's *Three Hundred Days and After* (1938), Motilal appeared in an offbeat role as a young bored millionaire who takes a bet with his doctor that he will go out into the world without taking any money and survive for 300 days. In R. S. Choudhary's *Such Hai* (1939) he was featured as the benevolent son of an influential priest, who rebels against the caste system and falls in love with an untouchable girl.

In *Jagirdar* (1937), Motilal won kudos for portraying the agony of a disillusioned son of the landlord protagonist who is taken to be dead, while his mother gets married to a caring man. When the son grows up, he refuses to accept his father after his sudden entry into their happy family life. *Hum Tum Aur Woh* (1938) was about a passionate man–woman relationship in which a woman acknowledges her desire for a man and bears a child by him without feeling guilty about it and even releases him from his promise (he need not shoulder any responsibility vis-à-vis the child). The actor once again proved his mettle in the role of the charming seducer-turned-sufferer. A. R. Kardar's *Holi* (1940) cast him in a powerful anti-hero role as a criminal-minded but suave youth who kidnaps the heroine who eventually succumbs to his charms and reforms him. In some of these films, his pairing with Sabita Devi became very popular.

In Chandulal Shah's *Achhut* (1940), Motilal pitched in with a portrayal par excellence. He appears as a youth, who is the childhood friend of an untouchable girl (adopted by a rich businessman). The youth joins hands with her to organize a revolt by Harijans against the oppression perpetuated by the upper castes. The Harijans also seek social equality. The hero dies while pursuing his goal and the girl is jailed, but eventually the village temple is opened to all castes. The film was promoted as part of Mahatma Gandhi's anti-untouchability campaign and it obtained the approval of both Gandhiji and Vallabhbhai Patel (another intrepid freedom fighter known as the 'Iron Man') even before it was made. Kidar Sharma's *Armaan* (1942) was set in an entirely different setting. In this rare sc-fi film, Motilal is a crazy scientist who invents a ray that can record pain and pleasure photographically. As his experiments render him blind, a poor village belle starts taking care of him and soon they fall in love. Driven by her obsessive love, the girl kills a sage to obtain a medicine that he has developed for curing blindness. As she returns, she is surrounded by a powerful storm as if nature is protesting against the loss of social morality triggered by her wilful desire.

In Mehboob Khan's *Taqdeer* released in 1943, Motilal was in his finest element as the debonair playboy indulging in antics with a dancer (Nargis), the foster daughter of his rich father. With this superhit, he attained celebrity status as a result of his suave, urbane and sophisticated image. Najmal Hussain's *Tasveer* (1943) presented him as a lovelorn photographer who pursues a haughty girl using his camera skills. When he gets disillusioned, he thinks of committing suicide. Roop K. Shorey's hit comedy *Ek Thi Ladki* (1949), penned by I. S. Johar (who went on to become a multifaceted artiste), cast him in an absolutely comic role. He made a great impression as a jovial but crazy manager who employs the runaway heroine (Meena, who is a witness to a murder but on the run), as his stenographer. As they fall in love, his boss's haughty daughter (Kuldip Kaur) schemes to separate them. Motilal's other important films during this period were: Chimanlal Lohar's *Captain Kirti Kumar* (1937), Sarvotam Badami's *Kokila* (1937), Jayant Desai's *Diwali* (1940), Chaturbhuj Doshi's *Pardesi* (1941), N. R. Acharya's *Aage Kadam* (1943), Mohan Bhavnani's *Biswin Sadi* (1945), Chaturbhuj Doshi's *Phulwari* (1946) and D. D. Kashyap's *Aaj Ki Raat* (1948).

With *Mr Sampat* (1952), directed by S. S. Vasan and based on the renowned writer R. K. Narayan's famous novel of the same name, Motilal paid a befitting tribute to his classic image of a polished and utterly charming man who cares two hoots for the world around him. He portrayed the archetype of a gentleman crook involved in a series of dubious acts (managing the election campaign of a shady businessman, setting up a bank and then a theatre, both of which fail) to impress his love interest, the heroine (Padmini). In H. S. Rawail's *Mastana* (1954), his last important film as hero, he virtually replayed the role of Charlie Chaplin in his 1921 classic *The Kid*.

In the second half of the 1950s, Motilal emerged as a consummate character artiste. He appeared in Bimal Roy's *Devdas* (1955) as Chunnilal, the drunken friend of the tragic hero Dilip Kumar (Jackie Shroff played this character in the 2002 version of the film, directed by Sanjay Leela Bhansali). In Sombhu Mitra and Amit Moitra's *Jagte Raho* (1956; Raj Kapoor was the hero) he plays a drunkard who torments his wife. He appears as a sophisticated yet cunning business magnate in Hrishikesh Mukherjee's *Anari* (1959) and S. S. Vasan's *Paigham* (1958). In Bimal Roy's *Parakh* (1960), Motilal pitched in with a lively performance as the industrialist who promises to finance his native village's development, leading to sharpening of social contradictions within the rural milieu caused by the influx of money from outside. In this way the film sought to highlight the influence of external capital on social relations. The legendary actor also specialized in lawyer roles, in which he would appear in court scenes (usually during the climax), adding a zing to the proceedings with his mesmerizing performance as seen in R. K.

Nayyar's *Yeh Raaste Hain Pyar Ke* (1963) and B. R. Chopra's *Waqt* (1965).

Motilal, with his characteristic spontaneity, coupled with breezy dialogue delivery, presented the image of a romantic who seemed to be playing with life and therefore looked extremely at ease with his environment. No other actor till date has matched his histrionics and his ability to turn acting into a way of life. His last impressive performance was in *Chhoti Chhoti Baatein* (1965), the only film that he produced and directed.

***

Ashok Kumar represented Indian cinema's first typical middle-class hero: a nice, lovable, non-vagrant and rather timid youth

who would uphold the spirit of tradition, ensure good family ties and thus maintain the status quo. Along with Motilal, he brought about a refreshing change in the portrayal of the film hero, but unlike the latter's elitist image, he came close to representing the common man per se. Very unassuming, with a subtle spontaneity and a charming smile, which would suddenly light up his face, he always appeared to be floating through the narrative of a film.

Ashok Kumar

Ashok Kumar was born on 13 October 1911 as Kumudlal Kunjilal Ganguly in Bhagalpur (now in Bihar). He spent his childhood in Khandwa (now in Madhya Pradesh) where his father was a renowned lawyer. After studying law in Calcutta, he joined Bombay Talkies as laboratory assistant in a film-processing unit and became a disciple of his future brother-in-law Shashdhar Mukerji. He made his screen debut in 1936 with *Jeevan Naiya*, directed by Frank Osten, opposite Devika Rani. It is said that on the first day of the shooting of the film, the actor who was supposed to play the hero did not turn up and Devika Rani asked a shy Ashok to put on the make-up and face the camera. In this film, he appeared as a rich, puzzled youth, who is engaged to a *tawaif*'s (courtesan) daughter raised by a social worker, but he is not sure of himself and what course of action he should adopt.

In the coming years, Ashok Kumar's films with Devika Rani became vehicles for delineating the ideas and thought processes for modernizing society vis-à-vis the prevailing oppressive parochial-feudal structure. The narrative would intermingle the issues of social morality, traditional beliefs as well as caste- and class-ridden tensions.

Achhut Kanya (1936), directed by Frank Osten, presented Ashok Kumar as a rich Brahmin youth desperately in love with a Harijan girl (Devika Rani). But their affair triggers a massive upheaval, leading to large-scale mob violence and suffering for the lovers. The same director's *Kangan* (1939) cast him as the son of the village zamindar, a budding writer who falls in love with a village belle (Leela Chitnis). When the hero moves over to the city and becomes a famous novelist, his father persecutes the girl, forcing her to leave the village in search of her lover.

In the 1940s, Ashok Kumar kept up his momentum as the proponent of social change in several memorable films. In N. R. Acharya's *Azad* (1940), he is featured as the socially conscious youth who rescues a damsel (Leela Chitnis) in distress and marries her. In the same director's *Bandhan* (1940), he appears as the humble teacher in a village school who is in love with the daughter (Leela Chitnis) of the zamindar, but is framed in a murder case by the villain. In Gyan Mukerjee's *Jhoola* (1941), he appears as a postman who is disinherited from his right to his ancestral property and who loves the same woman (Leela Chitnis) sought by his wily half-brother. N. R. Acharya's *Naya Sansar* (1941) was based on the celebrated work of the Leftist K. A. Abbas. A love triangle built within the framework of the inspiring journalism of the pre-independence era, Ashok Kumar portrays a cynical journalist working for a radical newspaper *Sansar*, run by a fearless editor. When the editor dilutes his radicalism and starts negotiating with a corrupt businessman, he resigns and starts publishing a broadsheet called *Naya Sansar* (new world) to uphold the freedom of the press. In the end, the editor realizes his mistake and opts out to let his junior marry the girl with whom he was also in love.

With the superhit *Kismet* (1943) directed by Gyan Mukerjee, Ashok Kumar went in for an image changeover and established the evergreen anti-hero persona in Hindi cinema. The smooth talking, chain-smoking conman of *Kismet*, who was assertive and ruthless, sought to conduct his affairs on his own terms (this image was taken up later by Raaj Kumar in B. R. Chopra's 1965 blockbuster *Waqt*). According to film historian Ravi S. Vasudevan, '*this new character shifted the emphasis* [during the 1930s and the 1940s] *from revolting against the British to conning them. He seemed to appeal more to a new generation of audience. He was not a freedom fighter but the one who broke the law and fooled the police. And they* [the viewers] *loved him even as a thief* [italics added].

In another venture of Gyan Mukerjee, *Chal Chal Re Naujawan* (1944), a tale about friendship and betrayal spanning more than two generations, the young actor made his mark as the nationalist son of a musician who falls in love with a haughty girl (Naseem Banu), the daughter of his father's estranged friend. Dattaram Pai's *Eight Days* (1946) featured him as a discharged military officer-turned-farmer, whom the heroine first rejects and then marries when she learns that she stands to inherit a fortune if she gets married within eight days. In Kamal Amrohi's ethereally seductive film *Mahal* (1949), Ashok Kumar posted a memorable performance as the obsessive lover falling prey to an exquisitely beautiful 'ghost' in the form of Madhubala who flits around in an abandoned mansion he has purchased, singing the haunting melody *Aayega, Aayega, Aayega ... Aanewala ...*

Nitin Bose's *Mashaal* (1950), based on Bankimchandra Chatterjee's novel *Rajani*, presented Ashok Kumar as a disgruntled childhood lover, who in vengeance, marries a blind flower girl when his beloved marries a wealthy zamindar. In Ramesh Sehgal's *Samadhi* (1950), a patriotic drama, he appeared as a wealthy Indian youth who joins Subhash Chandra Bose's Indian National Army, thus coming in conflict with his brother (Shyam), a captain in the British army. Gyan Mukerjee's *Sangram* (1950) featured him as a suave criminal pursued by his own father, who is a policeman.

Ashok Kumar also made his mark in Mehboob Khan's two films: in *Najma* (1943), as a young doctor who cannot marry the daughter of a nawab (Veena) because his family is not aristocratic, and in *Humayun* (1945) in the title role.

In the 1950s and the decades that followed, Ashok Kumar maintained his well-established image, embarking upon a series of lead roles as seen in B. R. Chopra's *Afsana* (1951), Anand Kumar's *Naubahar* (1952), Bimal Roy's *Parineeta* (1953), M. V. Raman's *Bhai Bhai* (1956), Satyen Bose's *Bandi* (1957), Shakti Samanta's *Howrah Bridge* (1958), Satyen Bose's *Sitaron Se Aage* (1958), Bimal Roy's *Bandini* (1963) and Asit Sen's *Mamta* (1966). The seasoned actor appeared in the second lead in several movies such as: Nitin Bose's *Deedar* (1951; hero Dilip Kumar), M. L. Anand's *Bewafa* (1952; hero Raj Kapoor), Phani Majumdar's *Baadbaan* (1954; hero Dev Anand), B. R. Chopra's *Ek Hi Raasta* (1956; hero Sunil Dutt), H. S. Rawail's *Mere Mehboob* (1963; hero Rajendra Kumar), B. R. Chopra's *Gumrah* (1963; hero Sunil Dutt) and Vijay Anand's *Jewel Thief* (1967; hero Dev Anand).

He also featured in a string of movies with Pradeep Kumar and Meena Kumari such as Phani Majumdar's *Aarti* (1962), Kidar Sharma's *Chitralekha* (1964), Kalidas's *Bheegi Raat* (1965) and M. Sadiq's *Bahu Begum* (1967).

In his later career, mostly as a father figure, his screen persona was so enduring that he would often become the common denominator to a narrative connecting various characters caught up in their individual fantasies and conflicts. The movies in this category are numerous and would need a separate book! One superlative performance of Ashok Kumar was in Hrishikesh Mukherjee's 1968 film *Aashirwad*, for which he won the *Filmfare* best actor award. In the 1980s, he also played the title role in a

TV serial based on the last Mughal, Bahadur Shah Zafar. This legendary actor died on 10 December 2001 at the ripe old age of 90.

Select Filmography of the Four Icons as Heroes (till 1950)

Sohrab Modi

Khoon Ka Khoon (1935), Saeed-e-Havas (1936), Atma Tarang (1937), Khan Bhadur (1937), Jailor (1938), Meetha Zaher (1938), Pukar (1939), Sikandar (1941) and Prithvi Vallabh (1943).

Prithviraj Kapoor

Be-dhari Talwar (1929), Cinema Girl (1929), Prince Vijaykumar (1929), Sher-e-Arab (1930), Namak Haram Kaun (1931), Bur Ke Pobar (1931), Golibar (1931) and Toofan (1931) (all silent). Alam Ara (1931), Draupadi (1931), Dagabaaz Ashiq (1932), Rajrani Meera (1933), Daku Mansoor (1934), Ramayan (1934), Seeta (1934), Inquilab (1935), Josh-e-Inteqam (1935), Swarg Ki Sidhi (1935), Grihadah/Manzil (1936), Milap (1937), President (1937), Vidyapati (1937), Jeevan Prabhat (1937), Anath Ashram (1937), Abhagin (1938), Dushman (1938), Adhuri Kahani (1939), Sapera (1939), Aaj Ka Hindustan (1940), Deepak (1940), Chingari (1940), Pagal (1940), Sajani (1940), Raj Nartaki/Court Dancer (1941), Sikandar (1941), Ujala (1942), Ek Raat (1942), Aankh Ki Sharam (1943), Bhalai (1943), Gauri (1943), Ishara (1943), Vish Kanya (1943), Maharathi Karna (1944), Phool (1944), Devadasi (1945), Nala Damyanti (1945), Shri Krishna Arjun Yuddha (1945), Vikramaditya (1945), Prithviraj Samyogita (1946), Valmiki (1946), Parashuram (1947), Azadi Ki Raah Par (1948), Dahej (1950) and Hindustan Hamara (1950).

Motilal

Shaher Ka Jadoo (1934), Silver King (1935), Dr Madhurika (1935), Jeevan Lata (1936), Lagna Bandhan (1936), Do Diwane (1936),

Captain Kirti Kumar (1937), *Jagirdar* (1937), *Kokila* (1937), *Kulavadhu* (1937), *300 Days and After* (1938), *Hum Tum Aur Woh* (1938), *Aap Ki Marzi* (1938), *Sach Hai* (1939), *Achhut* (1940), *Diwali* (1940), *Holi* (1940), *Pardesi* (1941), *Sasural* (1941), *Shadi* (1941), *Armaan* (1942), *Iqraar* (1942), *Muskurahat* (1943), *Prarthana* (1943), *Pratigya* (1943), *Taqdeer* (1943), *Tasveer* (1943), *Vijay Lakshmi* (1943), *Aage Kadam* (1943), *Dost* (1944), *Kaliyan* (1944), *Mujrim* (1944), *Pagli Duniya* (1944), *Raunaq* (1944), *Umang* (1944), *Biswin Sadi* (1945), *Murti* (1945), *Pehli Nazar* (1945), *Piya Milan* (1945), *Sawan* (1945), *Phulwari* (1946), *Beete Din* (1947), *Do Dil* (1947), *Aaj Ki Raat* (1948), *Gajre* (1948), *Mera Munna* (1948), *Ek Thi Ladki* (1949), *Lekh* (1949), *Parivartan* (1949), *Hanste Aansoo* (1950), *Hamari Beti* (1950) and *Sartaj* (1950).

Ashok Kumar

Jeevan Naiya (1936), *Acchut Kanya* (1936), *Janambhoomi* (1936), *Izzat* (1937), *Prem Kahani* (1937), *Savitri* (1937), *Nirmala* (1938), *Vachan* (1938), *Kangan* (1939), *Azad* (1940), *Bandhan* (1940), *Anjaan* (1941), *Jhoola* (1941), *Naya Sansar* (1941), *Angoothi* (1943), *Kismet* (1943), *Najma* (1943), *Chal Chal Re Naujawan* (1944), *Kiran* (1944), *Begum* (1945), *Humayun* (1945), *Eight Days* (1946), *Shikari* (1946), *Saajan* (1947), *Chandrashekhar* (1947), *Padmini* (1948), *Mahal* (1949), *Adhi Raat* (1950), *Khiladi* (1950), *Mashaal* (1950), *Nishana* (1950), *Samadhi* (1950) and *Sangram* (1950).

Kundan Lal Saigal: The Hero Prototype

The first revolutionary change in the image of the film hero was brought about by K. L. Saigal, the legendary singer-actor. He had a considerable influence on the constitution of the Hindi film and far more on its music. This immortal singer-actor not only changed the standards for defining the film hero, but also cultivated the cinematic style of singing in Indian cinema. He elevated his audience to a new plane of sensuous experience.

Born on 11 April 1904 into a Punjabi
Khatri family of Jammu, Saigal was a
child prodigy, a compulsive singer from
boyhood. His mother Kesar was also an
accomplished singer, famous for singing
bhajans, Heer*and other varieties of
Punjabi folk songs at the local
gatherings. While the patriarch of the
family disapproved of his introvert son's
curious passion for singing, the mother
provided all the care and support to
nurture the lad's hidden talent. The first

K. L. Saigal

taste of fame that the young Kundan got was for his role as Seeta
in the local Ramlila held every year in the *tehsil* (district) under
the jurisdiction of his father, Amar Chand Saigal.

Legend has it that when Kundan was about 12 years old, his
voice began to show the first signs of breaking. As he tried to
sing the well-known favourites of his childhood, the boy was
shocked to realize that he could no longer do so. The worried
mother took him to a local Sufi saint, Salman Yussuf. This Pir, it
was believed, was a direct descendant of Serajuddin, a Sufi
belonging to the venerated Yesevi sect. In those days, in Jammu,
many Sufis and Pirs lived outwardly ordinary lives as beggars,
artisans (specializing in the manufacture of copper items and
brassware) and weavers of carpets and silks; they practised their
faith somewhat secretly. They used music not as a means to
becoming performers, but to acquire spiritual enlightenment
through a transformation of their inner self and thus attaining an
everlasting connection with the divine. The Yesevis, like the
Naqshbandis and the Suharwardis, can be found even to this day.

The Pir, who had blessed Kundan soon after he was born,
embraced the lad within his mystical fold, and, as per the rituals
of his order, bestowed upon him a *zikr* (invocation of god) and a

---

*A soulful and pathos-filled form of singing.

riaz (the art of practising music). As per the Sufi tradition of achieving fulfilment though music, the bestowing of the *zikr* and the *riaz* by a Sufi upon on a disciple seeking revelation has been stipulated as an essential pathway for ensuring his entry into the mystical world. This ritual forms part of the secret discipline, which enables a disciple to explore and attain, within the notes of particular scales, those inaudible emotional responses that conventional musical training completely fails to develop.

The Pir now enlightened young Kundan on the code of music learning and how to engage in an inner exploration of the eternal music: *'Do not sing for two years. Practise the* zikr *and the* riaz *I have given you all the time. Waking and sleeping, keep your mind upon it, and keep your voice silently and softly aimed at it. Let no one hear it. If at some later stage you want to practise it on your singing pitch, go out into some lonely place where no one will hear you ... and remember this is a secret practice. Like the darkness that a seed needs to sprout, this* zikr *and this* riaz *need a secret place to sprout. As you grow in this practice you will have made the* swaras *of your music all by yourself and since these are your own* swaras, *the songs you will sing with them will also be yours, your own songs, no matter whose they might have been, before you sang them. Speech and song will become one for you.'*

For years Kundan Lal remained engrossed in the spiritual silence of this music, practising with complete dedication the discipline of the *zikr* and the *riaz* bestowed upon him. In his later years, when he attained fame as K. L. Saigal, he often used to say to his close friend Ali Bokhari, who worked in those days in All India Radio, 'I was "born" at the age of about 12, in a Pir's hut one windy evening in Jammu.'

After his father's retirement, the family shifted to Jullundur (now spelt Jalandar) in Punjab and settled in an area near the Panj Pir gate, which is now famous as the Saigal *mohalla*. After he grew up, his father forced him to join the North-Western Railway as a clerk. Then he became a salesman with the Remington Typewriter Company earning Rs 80 per month, exercising his voice to persuade hard-headed customers to buy the product, rather than enjoy the melody. But, all this while, deep down in his soul, music stirred, yearning to be expressed through full-throated songs. This keen desire often found an outlet at the small parties where the humble salesman and his friends assembled.

The irresistible longing to rise above the mundane and enter a higher plane, where he would be able to create and bring forth his own music, finally compelled Saigal to leave home and his mother, whom he loved and cared for a lot. When he reached his late twenties, this lanky and balding runaway made desperate stopovers at Moradabad, Lucknow, Kanpur, Bareilly (all in present-day Uttar Pradesh) and other places in the hope of eking out a livelihood. In 1932 he reached Calcutta, the high seat of film making and music. (Saigal was soon to make the prevalent music systems obsolete and introduce an entirely new idiom in film music, but more on that later.) On his arrival in Calcutta, the enterprising singer persuaded his would-be mentor, the reigning music monarch Rai Chand Boral of New Theatres, to listen to his rendition. Boral was thunderstruck by the timbre of this voice, which seemed to fill the whole space around him. On Boral's recommendation, the patriarch of Bengali cinema and owner of New Theatres, B. N. Sircar, immediately recruited Saigal as the new singer-actor for the studio.

Saigal's first screen appearance was in a Bengali film, in which he played a small role. He very soon rose to fame as a result of the two Bengali songs he rendered in the version of *Devdas* starring P. C. Barua (who was also the director). In this film, as one of the visitors to a *kotha* (a brothel), he entertains the gathering, singing *Kaharey Je Jodathey Chai* and *Goalab Huey Uthuk Phutey*. Since this was his initiation into Bengali films as a singer-actor, the film company was unsure of his accent and had doubts whether or not a non-Bengali singing Bengali songs would be acceptable to the audience. Fortunately, Saigal's singing got the personal approval of the author Saratchandra himself. The argument was fairly simple – it was not only Bengalis but also people from other parts of the country who visited the *kotha*.

Saigal made his debut as hero in New Theatres' *Mohabbat Ke Ansu* (1932), directed by Premankur Atorthy, which did not make much of an impact. After a few more insignificant films, he eventually announced his arrival with the phenomenal success of Nitin Bose's *Chandidas* in 1934. In *Devdas* (1935), a remake in Hindi and directed by the same P. C. Barua, he played the title role. Here Saigal established the new persona of the film hero, introducing a complete change in acting, demeanour, style and characterization. This persona not only freed film acting from the morass of typical theatricality, but also completely deglamourized the film hero image. He managed to release this image, trapped in a heavily ornate style and verbosity (as far as dialogues were concerned) and ensconsed amidst ostentatious sets, and brought it down to earth by imbuing it with simplicity and naturalness. Later, this style was substantially shaped by other luminaries such as directors Nitin Bose and Phani Majumdar and music directors R. C. Boral, Timir Baran and Pankaj Mullick. The new hero soon zoomed to the zenith of popularity with films such as *Didi/President* (1937), *Desher Mati/ Dharti Mata* (1938), *Jiban Maran/Dushman* (1938), *Saathi/Street Singer* (1938), *Parichay/Lagan* (1940) and *Meri Bahen* (1944).

In the early 1940s, Saigal made a phenomenal entry into the Bombay film world. Here, a string of films – Chaturbhuj Doshi's *Bhakta Surdas* (1942), Jayant Desai's *Tansen* (1943), Kidar Sharma's *Bhanwra* (1944), all for Ranjit Studios, Jayant Desai's *Tadbir* (1945), A. R. Kardar's *Shahjehan* (1946) and his last film J. K. Nanda's *Parwana* (1947) – added more substance, not to mention colour and verve, to his powerful screen persona and singing.

Saigal acted in thirty films over a short career span of sixteen years, appearing, on an average, in two films per year. His oeuvre covered several languages, such as Hindi, Urdu, Bengali (haunting solos in Rabindra Sangeet), Punjabi, Persian and even Tamil. His vast corpus of non-film songs constitutes a highly valuable part of his repertoire. These songs were of his own choosing and often his own compositions. These creations sprang from the legacy

Jamuna and K. L. Saigal in *Devdas* (1935).

Jayashri and Chandramohan in V. Shantaram's *Shakuntala* (1943).

Prithviraj Kapoor sitting on the throne in *Sikandar* (1941).

he had inherited during his childhood in Jammu and later during his youth in Punjab. Some of them were inspired by his wandering in different parts of the country, whose origins were varied – from bhajan singers, beggars, Sufi minstrels, the dancing girls and the numerous *baithaks* (sessions) and music conferences he attended.

The Genesis of the Saigal Phenomenon

As discussed in the last chapter, during the formative period of Indian cinema, three fundamental socio-cultural constructs informed the new vision of the founders. The early pioneers concentrated all their creative efforts towards evolving a new popular culture through a series of measures: by reconstructing the traditional themes and metaphors; by using Western narrative forms; and by positioning implicitly in the narrative many contemporary 'burning issues' and encoded messages of social change. This form of cinema soon began to define and project recognizable facets of the pan-Indian identity, encompassing its sentiments, outlook and diversity.

   These three constructs, which defined the overall cinematic purpose and vision of Indian cinema in the 1930s and 1940s and which were mutually linked and reinforced each other, can be identified as follows:

(1) the spiritual basis of cinematic themes;
(2) the evolution of the film song as an intimate personal expression of human emotions, shared through the cinematic experience; and
(3) the creation of the persona of the indigenous film hero as the frontal figure in the narrative.

   Saigal, immediately after this arrival in the film world, became the powerful (and identifiable) manifestation of these constructs on celluloid. As already mentioned, although four other icons of Indian cinema in this period – Sohrab Modi, Prithviraj Kapoor,

Ashok Kumar and Motilal – were also in the forefront, influencing the cinematic trends with their distinct styles, yet it was Saigal, who, with the natural advantage of being a great singer, became the numero uno in forcefully expressing the various moods, aspirations and concerns of indigenous cinema.

The Spiritual Basis of Cinematic Themes

Since its inception, Indian cinema has built its narrative around the notion of spiritual enlightenment, focusing on cogent themes relating to the human connection with the divine and metaphysical. At the same time, this cinema has, at times, presented an incisive critique of the age-old pernicious orthodox practices besides bringing alive on screen the prevalent social tensions and turmoil and the ensuing agony and suffering. In a very significant way, the films of this era systematically broke down the narrow, biased and inward-looking Indian cultural and religious customs and practices and instead sought the reawakening of humanitarian compassion and the assurance of justice for all strata of society. During this formative time, film makers such as Debaki Bose, V. Shantaram, Fatehlal Damle, Nitin Bose, Amar Mullick, Kidar Sharma, Dhirubhai Desai, Jayant Desai, Gajanan Jagirdar, V. M. Vyas, Vijay Bhatt and later Raja Nawathe and S. N. Tripathi contributed towards creating the classic narrative in its *indigenous* form as an enlightened interpretation of tradition and faith vis-à-vis an individual's predicament in a decaying socio-cultural milieu.

Two main trends were Prabhat's highly acclaimed 'saint' films and the devotional films made by New Theatres, Calcutta. These films concretized on the Indian screen the aura of the Bhakti cults of the medieval times – in the form of biographies on celluloid. These movies represented the nationally familiar stock of religious figures and legends, which could be easily employed to articulate social concerns and highlight societal ferment through the prism of history and mythology. They also underlined the development of the religious or linguistic cults such as the Nathas, Kabirpanthis, Shaivites, Lingayats and Mahanbhavas in various parts of the subcontinent. Through easily understood and widely disseminated renditions that reached the masses, they, in fact, challenged the dominant position of Brahmins in the religious hierarchy. Notable films of this genre were: *Bhakta Vidur* (1921), *Puran Bhagat* (1933), *Chandidas* (1934), *Surdas* (1936), *Sant Janabai* (1938), *Sant Gnyaneshwar* (1940), *Narsi Bhagat* (1940), *Sant Sakhu* (1941), *Bhakta Kabir* (1942), *Ram Shastri* (1944), *Vidyapati* (1937), Kidar Sharma's *Chitralekha* (1941), V. Shantaram's *Parbat Par Apna Dera* (1944), apart from *Meera* (1945, starring the legendary classical singer M. S. Subbulakshmi), *Sant Tukaram* (1948) and *Dharmatma* (1948).

These films also carried encoded messages of national resurgence, attempting to merge the symbolism of religious awakening with the emerging thrust of the nationalist movement and the Gandhian forms of non-cooperation. For instance, *Bhakta Vidur* was banned by the British Government for its nationalistic overtones; *Dharmatma* drew an obvious parallel between Mahatma Gandhi and the eleventh-century saint Eknath; and *Sant Gnyaneshwar* echoed a call for peace during the Second World War period.

The basic tenets of devotional films were further reinforced by certain committed film makers to evolve a powerful spiritual discourse besides laying stress on the value of suffering resulting from separation from the beloved (a euphemism for god), leading to the final emancipation. In many of these films, the Oriental concept of willingly sacrificing one's mortal frame for a noble cause was also used to emphasize the concept of the immortality of the soul.

The contribution of New Theatres in establishing the spiritual foundation of cinema was not only unique but also far-reaching. Built largely around the cinematic persona of Saigal, the films made by New Theatres resulted in a forceful cultural revival, using the iconography from tradition and mythology.

More significantly, they sought to blend rather subtly the spiritual and social content of devotional films with socially relevant cinema. Sometimes, they used literature-based cinema to drive home their point. These films (mostly in Hindi), like their Marathi devotional counterparts, attempted to constantly highlight human protest against social and religious authority, against the orthodox schools of thought and against the clergy. With such a 'mission' in mind, these movies ensured mass mobilization to overcome evils such as social inequality, untouchability, gender inequality and other forms of injustice. With soul-searching music as its forte, coupled with a clutch of innovations in film making, the New Theatres' banner introduced a new kind of lyricism in cinema. In the process, this banner came up with a series of film classics that stood on a far higher spiritual and musical plane than those made under other banners.

In these films, Saigal's own personality and his ability to make singing the main focus of his cinematic input also helped in capturing, with amazing accuracy, the widespread spiritual appeal inherent in the Bhakti tradition. His initiation into the mystical tradition right from his younger days and the *zikr* and the incessant *riaz* resulted in a gradual revealing of the artiste's inner being, layer by layer, which began to be manifested through his art. According to Kanan Devi, the famous co-star of the singer-actor in many films, Saigal was always tuning his *swara*, sitting or standing. It was in such a spiritual ambience of sustained self-discovery that this now-immortal singer directed his entire self towards mastering the *swara* and immersed himself in the depths of its magical relationship with singing.

Through his soulful renditions, Saigal was indeed sharing his inner self with his listeners. That was probably the reason why when his voice rode over the rudiments of raga, it was filled with wonder, pathos and a kind of abstract intrinsic beauty. In this context, Raghava R. Menon observes: 'So when you heard him sing, the power and the enchantment of his music was not because he knew raga or the complexities of classical music as taught by the *gharanas* [schools of music associated with particular places, e.g., the Patiala *gharana* or the Jaipur *gharana*]. It was the inaudible emotional attraction of highly perfected *swaras* that had been ruthlessly cleansed and purified to such a degree that they gleamed with the meaning and significance of Saigal's inner being.'[2]

Saigal's singing evoked a deep sense of spirituality, as if one was in harmony with a mystic, deeply experiencing the feelings of eternal love despite suffering the agony of separation. Even in his films set in contemporary times, he would look far removed from the materiality of the world around him and would resort to a rather tragic idiom in an endeavour to enrich his life experiences. He displayed the aloofness of a roaming bard but his persona reflected an uneasy sense of melancholy. He would often smile wistfully at his plight, but at the same time, try to hide his anguish from the world. And the sadness of this smile was truly touching. The lifelong inner exploration through music and the constant, silent devotion to the *zikr* and *riaz* made singing for Saigal an obsession, a way of life, no matter whether he was singing to himself, or in a *mehfil* (gathering) or in front of a mike. It is doubtful whether New Theatres could have reached its glory as one of greatest banners that not only influenced but also shaped Indian cinema without Saigal's powerful screen persona.

In real life this remarkable artiste was a true *bairagi* (an ascetic), in spite of being a part of the highly glamorous and competitive film world. He forgave all those who hurt him or slighted him; he was generous and compassionate, without rancour or pride whatsoever. He cared little for pelf and power and was indifferent towards material possessions. Jamini Roy, the painter, who knew Saigal from his early days in New Theatres, once said: 'He was such a pure character, so simple, that it is hard to describe him in simple words. He was like somebody who had stepped out of an icon [sic], so unaffected, totally oblivious of himself, like a line drawing.'

Like a true people's singer, Saigal rarely moved around or travelled without his grand old harmonium, a plain-looking instrument and black in colour bereft of the usual ornamentations used to make musical instruments attractive. According to maestro Naushad Ali, even when Saigal was positioned in front of the playback microphone, he needed a dummy harmonium (with dummy keys) so that he could get the feel of things and get going. The songs of the film *Shahjehan* were recorded by Naushad in this manner.

A Rare Interview with Saigal

In a rare interview with Kirit Ghosh, the editor of *Jayathi*, a monthly cultural magazine published from Calcutta those days, Saigal talked in detail about his singing style and its place in classical music: 'I am not a singer, not really. I can only be called a "phraser". I have had *no true classical training* except what I have heard and remembered ... I do not think of a song in terms of its notes, at least not exclusively ... I think of the meaning of the words and wrap the tune around the words. I have no clear understanding of the grammar of music. I manage to sing because of a strong feeling about how certain sounds should feel in a given raga. I have a certain feeling how the *dhaivat* [one of the higher notes] should feel in [the raga] Malkaus, and the *madhyama* [the middle note] and also the nature of the *nishad* [again, one of the higher notes], in its relationship with the *shadj* [this name is for both the lowest and the highest notes] ... I do not know whether this feeling is right to have for I have never been taught Malkaus by a musician .... People who learn to sing with the help of their ears alone cannot explain how they do it. All I can say about my own singing is that I do not use ten notes if I can manage to do the same with one .... This is because I know very little.'[3]

'Anything for a Song'[4]

In his endeavours to comprehend the spiritual connection of the self with the soul, Saigal influenced the evolution of the film song. In the melodious company of the trio of composers in Calcutta – R. C. Boral, Timir Baran and Pankaj Mullick – Saigal laid the foundation of light classical music, on which arose the magnificent structure of the golden era of film melody in the 1950s.

Saigal's music, in fact, became the finest and most evocative expression of the musical experimentation started by the founders of film music in the 1930s in their pursuit to evolve the Indian film song into a separate genre of music distinct from the other forms. In their quest for a universally appealing film song, the composer and the lyricist 'extracted' the relevant ingredients from classical, folk and, later, Western music traditions and mellifluously blended them into their own compositions.

This evolution of the film song was facilitated by two major developments that had taken place in the realm of Indian music during that time: first, the setting up of the grand institution of Gandharva Mahavidyalaya by the legendary musician and visionary D. V. Paluskar in Lahore in 1901 and, second, the new music genre innovated by the Nobel Laureate Rabindranath Tagore. The Gandharva Mahavidyalaya was the first of its kind in the country to offer formal educational courses in music to young aspirants. This institution came into being as part of Paluskar's vision to reconstitute the traditional Indian music system and bring about structural changes in it. His pioneering effort stemmed from a countrywide dissatisfaction (and at times even disgust) with the feudal *gharana* system, which was then patronized exclusively by the aristocracy and kept its repertory restricted to the guru's kinsmen. Paluskar thus achieved a complete democratization of the Indian music system vis-à-vis learning, teaching and sponsorship.

This new institution soon acquired immense respectability in the music world. In view of the growing demand for learning music among common people, a dozen similar schools were set up in northern and western India over the next thirty years. For example, the Saraswati Sangeet Vidyalaya at Karachi (1916), the Gopal Gayan Dutt Samaj at Poona (1918), the Gandharva Mahavidyalaya at Kolhapur (1920) and the School of Indian Music at Bombay (1925). The alumni of these music schools soon found their way into the recording industries of Lahore, Kolhapur, Bombay, Karachi and Calcutta, and into the Sangeet Natak and Company Natak troupes. After the advent of the talkies in the early 1930s, many of these musically knowledgeable aspirants moved into films. They included composers such as Master Krishnarao, Saraswati Devi, B. S. Hoogan,[5] Rafiq Ghaznavi and actress Shanta Apte.

In Bombay, Poona, Kolhapur and Lahore, during this period, many music directors evolved their own distinct styles – Ustad Zande Khan, Saraswati Devi, Mir Sahib, B. S. Hoogan, Govindrao Tembe, Keshavrao Bhole, Master Krishnarao, Anil Biswas and Khemchand Prakash. These styles led to the eventual evolution of the film melody in the next decade. The film song, which finally took proper shape in the 1940s, emerged as a compact socio-cultural product, which proved to be a highly valuable link between the people and the diverse music traditions of the land.

In Calcutta, the visionary composer Rai Chand Boral laid the foundation of the eastern school of film music. With his eminent companions at New Theatres – composers Timir Baran, Pankaj Mullick, Pahari Sanyal and singers K. L. Saigal and Kanan Devi – Boral ushered in a music renaissance by combining various forms such as *thumri*, *keertan*, *akhrai* and *kabigaan* as well as the dominant Rabindra Sangeet. The music that emerged thus represented a new cultural fusion of various forms of the north and the east, brought in by the immigrants to Calcutta.

The essence of this music tradition could be found in the mystical tenor of Saigal's singing persona. His phenomenal ability and his unique style of singing became a kind of an a priori condition for the development of this form of music. These qualities offered to his composers unforeseen opportunities to experiment and innovate. In a way, their compositions became mere vehicles through which this singer from the 'other world' would precipitate the phenomenal release of mystical energies. Saigal indeed became the ultimate metaphor of this form of music. By making singing the main focus of his cinematic discourse, he seemed to be emphasizing that the only way to interpret life was through song. As the noted writer on film music Bhaskar Chandravarkar observed, with respect to Saigal, that nothing like the Bhakti movement has had such impact on the life of the common man. For the first time, film songs, which came to be surrounded by an aura of classical music and the simplicity of folk tunes, began to be greatly appreciated and enjoyed by the common people.

The sophistication and subtlety in Saigal's renditions prompted many innovations in film music. This singer was responsible for the eventual liberation of classical music from its elitist captivity. Yet he was successful in capturing its spirit in a form and idiom easily understood by the common people. He was also the first to exemplify a unique blending of syllables into musical contours in forms such as the *thumri* and the *ghazal* (a genre of Persian/Urdu poetry that can be easily set to music), thus providing a wholly new interpretation to the lyrics. Saigal achieved the true amalgamation of words with music in the film song, making it virtually impossible for the listeners to remember the voice of the singer without the accompanying words. And then he had the remarkable aptitude to lend his own inimitable touch to a song, as, for instance, in *Devdas*, the melancholy-tinged laughter in *Dukh Ke Ab Din Beetat Naahin*.

Saigal was also the first Indian singer to introduce his own innovations in the technique of *ghazal* singing. With his musical interpretation of the *ghazal*, he not only enriched its resonance but also brought the words alive. He blended the rhythm of the *ghazal*'s exquisite metres with the poet's pathos and agony. Without any mediation, he lent form and content to mere words.

For example, no other singer has possibly sung the distinguished poet Mirza Ghalib's poetry and brought out its symbiosis with life as endearingly and as effectively as Saigal. Saigal's rendition made Ghalib's *ghazals* so alluring musically that suddenly people began understanding the poet's works much better than by merely reading them. Apart from Ghalib, he also sang, and splendidly at that, the immortal poems of Mukund Lal Semaab, Arzoo Lucknavi, Hafiz Jullunduri, Rabindranath Tagore and Nazrul Islam.

Saigal, though a Punjabi by birth, also contributed towards a subtle blending of the northern and eastern music streams both in film music and in popular music. He not only mastered the nuances of Bengali but he also further enriched his singing style by blending it with Rabindra Sangeet. As described by Raghava Menon in his intimate biography of the artiste, Saigal even drove to Shantiniketan from Calcutta on his old motorcycle with his harmonium tagged on the back seat to sing in front of Gurudev Rabindranath Tagore. Initially, Tagore was reluctant to hear Saigal sing, but when he was persuaded to listen to this stranger, he was deeply impressed. While blessing Saigal, Tagore asserted that this was the way in which his music was to be interpreted.

Saigal as the Indigenous Film Hero Prototype

Although Saigal is remembered for his unique and trendsetting influence on film music, his contribution towards the development of Indian cinema's first indigenous hero is less appreciated. In the dominant cinematic genre, his hero became the main expression of a human being's search for his destiny in an alien world. On the basis of his compelling screen persona, he redirected the Indian film onto a truly indigenous path. His cinema drove home the point that it was the acquisition of an inner strength drawn from an affinity with the divine that made the sufferer an icon in his or her own right. Accompanying this hero in his attempts to overcome suffering and despair was the woman figure, the suffering womanhood, exemplified by the screen personas of Kanan Devi, Jamuna, Uma Shashi, Leela Desai, Rattanbai, Raj Kumari, Khurshid, Shamali and Suraiya.

Saigal's hero manifested himself in many ways: as a poet and musician seeking a way out to express his creativity; as a rebellious prince in pursuit of his ideals and his love through his songs; as an aristocratic zamindar trying to resolve the dichotomy between his feudal past and the socialist present; as a ruralist waking up to combat the oppressive realities of his life; as an industrial worker struggling to find equality in society; and as a social activist in search of his identity in the contemporary world.

For the first time in Indian cinema (and for that matter, even as far as Hollywood was concerned), Saigal defied all the generic stereotypes of a film hero – handsome, macho and dashing, with women swooning at his sight. In his presentations of the 'real man', Saigal displayed both spontaneity and simplicity, depicting a curious kind of realism, which was both disturbing as well as fascinating. Saigal's presence on the screen, in fact, reflected his own lifestyle – marked by a holistic contentment and tranquillity. His gait was easygoing and natural and he maintained his poise. In acting, he was the least theatrical of his contemporaries; his face remained mostly composed and he never resorted to facial contortions such as the twisting of the eyebrows and grimacing. In his portrayals, which were mostly low key, he played his roles with conviction and integrity, supplementing his acting with the natural pathos of his singing. Overall, he appeared genuine.

Saigal's Films

Saigal's first three films as hero – *Mohabbat Ke Ansu, Zinda Lash, Subah Ka Sitara* – all released in 1932 were tragic love stories and represented his apprenticeship in cinema (this author has not been able to find any information on the storylines or songs of these films). *Yahoodi Ki Ladki*, released in 1933, formally announced the arrival of Saigal as the new hero. The film was a screen adaptation of the Bengali stage version [Baradaprasanna Dasgupta's *Misarkumari* (1919)], which was itself based on the well-known Parsi theatre classic written by Agha Hashr Kashmiri in 1915. A saga of the Roman–Jew conflict, it presented the new hero in the role of a Roman prince in love with a Jewish girl.[6] Saigal as Prince Marcus enlivened the dilemma of a lover trying to transcend the historical conflict between the two communities through his love for Hannah. As one of the early New Theatres' spectacular productions, the film was packed with as many as nineteen songs including Saigal's powerful rendering of Ghalib's famous *ghazal*, *Nuktanchi Hai Gham-e-Dil Usko Sunaye Na Bane*. Among the other songs were *Lag Gai Chot Karejwa Mein Hai Rama*, *Lakh Sahi Ab Pi Ki Batiyan* and *Ye Tasarruf Allah-Allah Tere Maykhane Mein Hai*.

In *Puran Bhagat* (1933), Saigal did not have a full-fledged role and appeared only as a guest bhajan singer rendering three devotional songs: *Bhaju Main To Bhav Se Shri Girdhari Hirday Se …. Din Nike Bite Jaat Hai*, *Avsar Bito Jai* and *Radhey Rani De Daro Na Bansari Mori Re*.

As a singer-actor, Saigal made his mark with his role in the highly popular devotional film *Chandidas* (1934), the Hindi remake of Debaki Bose's 1932 film and directed by its cameraman, Nitin Bose. A biographical depiction of the legendary poet-saint Chandidas, the film revolved around the popular tale of his love for a low-caste washerwoman, Rami Dhobin (played by Uma Shashi). The movie presented a powerful narrative focusing on socially forbidden love and made a fervent plea against the age-old evil of untouchability. In this film, the lovers rebel against the social taboos and religious orthodoxy and thus achieve a deep sense of spiritual fulfilment. The film had a highly engaging musical score by R. C. Boral and was studded with several popular duets by Saigal and Uma Shashi such as *Prem Nagar Mein Basaoongi Ghar Main …*. The film was New Theatre's first success in Hindi and established Nitin Bose as an outstanding craftsman and a highly skilled director.

P. C. Barua's *Rooplekha* (1934) was based on a well-known Buddhist fable. Saigal played Emperor Asoka, the repentant Mauryan king who suffers pangs of agony because of the devastation and carnage he has caused in the Kalinga war. He decides to embrace Buddhism and dedicates his life to the cause of *dhamma*. He goes in for an unusual experiment in public governance by making an ordinary honest monk the ruler of his kingdom for a year.

Kaarwaan-e-Hayat (1935), directed jointly by Premankur Atorthy and Hemchandra Chunder for New Theatres, is the only important adventure film of Saigal. It is a musical tale about a wild rebellious prince in quest for love amidst long-drawn-out palace intrigues.[7] Saigal rendered three popular songs in this film: *Koi Preet Ki Reet Bata De Hamen, Hairat-e-Nazara Aakhir Ban Gai Ranayian* and *Dil Se Teri Nigaah Jigar Tak Utar Gai*.

It was *Devdas* (1935), the Hindi version directed by P. C. Barua with Saigal in the lead role, which helped the actor-singer to establish the new persona of the film hero, introducing a complete change in acting style and characterization. This new image not only helped in moving film acting from its theatrical overtones to a semblance of reality but also completely deglamourized the film hero. Saigal thus released the hero's image from the heavily ornate style and verbosity, carried amidst ostentatious sets, and brought in a down-to-earth simplicity and naturalness. In this film, the young actor lent such a kind of popular image to the film hero, with his natural acting style and singing, that it turned this character as well as its player into an idol (writer Saratchandra, in fact, lauded Saigal's depiction of the character sculpted by him). Actress Jamuna played the role of Parvati (or Paru) and Raj Kumari portrayed the singing courtesan Chandramukhi. The songs like *Balam Aaye Baso More Man Mein, Dukh Ke Din Ab Beetat Nahi* and *Piya Bin Aavat Nahi Chhein* composed by Timir Baran and penned by Kidar Sharma soon echoed throughout the country (according to Kidar Sharma, the first two songs were composed by Saigal himself).

Apart from the songs, *Devdas* also won critical acclaim for a series of innovations in film-making techniques. Photographed by none other than Bimal Roy, the movie incorporated features such as the parallel cutting of the shots and sound effects, making way for further exploiting the potential of the film medium to lend power to a narrative. The montages of Devdas crying out in delirium, Paru stumbling upon seeing him and then Devdas falling from his berth in the train, apart from the climax depicting a long journey and the hero's death on reaching the beloved's doorstep, indeed, had a stunning impact on the audience. (It is said that the renowned director Ritwik Ghatak admired the film greatly and often used some of the scenes to teach film students about cinematography.)

Devdas proved to be a path-breaking venture in the annals of film making. The film also had an everlasting influence on the persona of the Indian film hero. Saigal, the new hero, was to be soon further shaped by luminaries such as directors Nitin Bose and Phani Majumdar, and his singing was moulded by music directors R. C. Boral, Timir Baran and Pankaj Mullick. Soon the artiste attained the zenith of popularity with a series of socials released in quick succession.

P. C. Barua's *Pujarin* (1936), like *Devdas*, was also based on Saratchandra's story. It was the Hindi remake of Atorthy's *Dena Paona* (1933); it was New Theatres' first sound film. It presented Saigal in the role of an anti-hero – a good-for-nothing youth Jibananda who initially marries Alaknanda (Chandra) for her money, but eventually falls in love with her. After committing a crime, he is forced to abandon her only to reappear years later as a wealthy man. He soon turns into an oppressive landlord and comes into conflict with the *pujarin* (priestess) of the local temple who leads a popular revolt against him. She turns out to be his wife. Eventually, Jibananda undergoes a change of heart and the couple is reunited. The singer-composer K. C. Dey played his usual role of a blind beggar. In this film Saigal sang two songs: *Piyeja Aur Piyeja Zindagi Ka Hai Yahi Mudda* and *Jo Beet Chuki So Beet Chuki.*

Crorepati/Millionaire (1936), directed by Hemchandra Chunder, brought Saigal into an entirely different genre, strangely in a comic role, the only one in his career. He plays a star-crazy youth carried away by the magic and glamour of cinema. He wins a big amount in a lottery and wants to experience the film world first-hand. The film presented a delightful farce about the workings of a film company and the eccentricities of those connected with it. The film was hailed for its probing, yet sympathetic, caricature of the industry and for drawing humour out of commonplace situations. Saigal's songs in this film were *Jagat Mein Prem Hi Prem Bhara Hai, Kisse Kahe Ki Kaun Hai Dil Mein Sama Raha* and *Oh Dilruba Kahan Tak Zulm-o-Sitam Sahenge.*

President (1937), directed by Nitin Bose, dealt with workers' participation in factory management and perhaps was inspired by *The Mill* (1934), the first-ever political film in Indian cinema directed by Mohan Bhavnani and scripted by Munshi Premchand. A famous musical, *President* presented Saigal in the role of a highly innovative textile mill worker (Prakash), who develops more efficient machines to help the young lady owner Prabhavati (Kamlesh Kumari) to turn the factory into an extremely profitable enterprise. Initially, his ideas are rejected and he is sacked. But soon he is re-employed and the lady mill owner starts loving him. But the hero now falls in love with Prabhavati's younger sister Sheila (Leela Desai), who later makes way for her elder sister. Pained by her withdrawal, Prakash starts bullying the workers to go on strike. Prabhavati realizes the problem and presumably commits suicide (she disappears into an office room and locks the door from inside) for the benefit of her sister and of the factory. The film thus highlighted the importance of sound owner–worker relations as the key to economic growth and social good and the film further suggested that personality problems should not be allowed to undermine the functioning of industry.[8] S. S. Vasan's classic, *Paigham* (1958), starring Dilip Kumar in the role of a talented mill worker, seemed to have been inspired by this film, as also Guru Dutt's *Baharen Phir Bhi Ayengi*, the film which the master could not complete, due to his untimely death in 1964. (The film was later released in 1966 with Dharmendra as the hero.) Saigal sang some unforgettable songs like *Hello Bachon, Aao Mein Tumhe ..., Ek Raje Ka Beta, Rahegi Na Badaria Chai, Ek Bangla Bane Nyara* and *Na Koi Prem Ka Rog Lagaye*.

Like *President*, *Dharti Mata/Deshar Mati* (1938) depicted a love story set in a down-to-earth socio-economic context. Inspired apparently by the Soviet film makers of that era (Sergei Eisenstein and Alexander Dovzhenko, for example), the film was a great saga on agrarian reforms through technological modernization and collective farming to ameliorate rural poverty and prevent migration from villages to cities. It presented Saigal in an unusual role of a social activist who leaves the city's comforts to work among the rural poor. Ashok (Saigal) mobilizes the peasantry into a collective, disseminates new agricultural techniques and fights the oppression of the village headman and thus helps the farmers achieve not only their rights but also bumper crops.

The film then builds up the conflict between the two radically different approaches to development – the people-centred agrarian reforms and industrialization. Ashok's childhood friend Ajoy (Jagdish Sethi), who had studied mining engineering in England, decides to launch a mining project in the rural area where Ashok is working. The area has the most productive coalfields. Ajoy's sister Protibha (Kumari), who loves Ashok, secretly finances his rural modernization endeavours. Ajoy, unaware of these facts, falls in love with Gauri (Uma Shashi), daughter of the social outcast Kunja (K. C. Dey). The crisis is manifested through a drought that threatens to destroy Ashok's work and prove Ajoy's contentions right. Ajoy starts buying up the land from the farmers but the rains arrive just in time to resurrect Ashok's rural socialist dreams. Saigal came up with a memorable performance in capturing the agony of an idealist caught in the turmoil of an unequal world. He completely dominates the film, in spite of singing only three songs: *Kisne Yeh*

Sab Khel Rachaya and *Ab Main Ka Karun Kit Jaoon* and *Duniya Rang Rangili Baba* (with Pankaj Mullick and Uma Shashi).

Another masterpiece of Nitin Bose, *Dushman/Jiban Maran* (1939) was, curiously, a venture sponsored by the British Government. It was specially produced by the New Theatres at the request of the Tuberculosis Fund set up under Lady Linlithgow's (the viceroy's wife) Immunization Programme. The film sought to promote people's awareness about the scourge of the disease and the measures to fight it and also sought their participation in strengthening the public health system.

The film presented Saigal in the role of Mohan, a radio singer, who becomes a dedicated health worker providing support to people suffering from tuberculosis. He falls in love with Geeta (Leela Desai), who is also pursued by his friend Kedar (Najam), a doctor. When Mohan comes to know that he is a TB patient, he makes way for Kedar, who eventually marries the girl. In a state of delirium, he wanders in the streets and when he falls on the roadside, he is taken to a sanatorium. After he is cured of TB, he joins the same hospital as a worker, providing love and care to the patients. He now starts singing on the radio to raise funds for the campaign launched by the government to set up more sanatoria. The film was a major hit, followed by a remake in Bengali. The songs rendered by Saigal were: *Karun Kya Aas Niras Bhaee, Sitam The Julam The, Aafat The Intzaar Ke Din, Preet Mein Hai Jiwan Jokho Ke Jaise Kolhu Mein Sarso* and *Pyari Pyari Suraton.*

Street Singer/Saathi (1938), Phani Majumdar's directorial debut and one of Saigal's most famous films, virtually immortalized the artiste as a true people's singer. This classic musical was about two destitutes, childhood friends, Bhulwa (Saigal) and Manju (Kanan Devi), who grow up to become street singers in Calcutta. Bhulwa constantly dreams of becoming a singing star on stage, but it is Manju who succeeds in the fickle theatre world. At the height of her fame, Manju almost forgets Bhulwa until at the end – in an obviously symbolic landscape (literally showing a boat washed ashore in a storm) the two are united. Among the songs, the haunting piece, *Babul Mora ...,* has almost become synonymous with the memory of Saigal as an eternal singer. Since hand-held cameras, trolleys, booms and hidden microphones were not available for film shooting in those days, Saigal sang this immortal song into a microphone that was held by hand just out of camera range. A wind-blowing machine was also needed to create the effect of a breeze flitting by. Unfortunately, the force of the blast sent the famous Saigal wig flying, interrupting the song midway. His other song in the film was *Jeevan Been Madhur Na Baaje Jhude Par Gaye Taar.*

K. L. Saigal in *Street Singer*

P. C. Barua's *Zindagi* (1940) was based on Probodh Sanyal's famous short story, *Priya Bandhavi.* It can be regarded as one of the most offbeat films in Indian cinema as it made a daring attempt to show on celluloid the live-in relationship of an unmarried couple, considered one of the most scandalous acts during that period (and even today by a large part of Indian society). Saigal appeared in a Chaplinesque role, as a tramp named Rattan, who makes a living by resorting to small-time gambling. He encounters Shrimati (Jamuna) who has left home to escape the atrocities of her brutal husband. The duo joins hands and begins collecting donations by pretending to belong to a charitable religious trust. With money made by defrauding rich people, they buy a flat and live together.

Soon the girl's rich father dies and she inherits his wealth. Renouncing her earlier life, she devotes herself and her wealth for the uplift of the poor and employs Rattan to tutor an adopted orphan, Lakhia. When the lovelorn hero approaches her again, she, feeling she must pay for her past immoral life, rejects him. Rattan returns to his earlier life of a tramp and she bequeathes her fortune to Lakhia and withdraws to a lonely dwelling, awaiting death. The film ends with the two lovers meeting again on the threshold of a new afterlife. Saigal rendered several songs penned by Kidar Sharma, including the famous *lori* (lullaby) *So Ja Rajkumari So Ja*, besides *Jiwan Aasha Yeh Hai Meri Jiwan Aasha*, *Mein Kya Jaanu Kya Jaadu Hain In Do Matvale Naino Mein* and *Diwana Hoon Diwana Hoon*.

Nitin Bose's *Lagan/Parichay* (1941) made an important contribution to Saigal's screen persona, helping to define the Indian cinema's anti-hero stereotype who destroys his life in pursuit of unfulfilled love. The protagonist is a poet from a lower middle-class family, who makes a living by giving tuitions. In a college concert, his student Kusum Kumari (Kanan Devi) wins all the applause from the audience, while her tutor who has put his heart and soul to train her is ignored. While the poet leaves the city, the girl marries the benevolent rich publisher Deendayal (Nawab). Her husband tries to please her by bringing the poet back to the city and publishes his work, making him famous. The hero, now an obsessed man, wants to possess her but when Kusum rejects him, he, in a fit of desperation, kills himself by deliberately falling in front of a running car. Guru Dutt reworked this theme in his classic *Pyaasa* (1957), adding far more refined social and political dimensions to the narrative. The popular songs of *Lagan* rendered by Saigal were *Kahe Ko Raar Machai*, *Ye Kaisa Anyay Data* and *Main Sote Bhag Jaga Doonga*.

Bhakta Surdas (1942), directed by Chaturbhuj Doshi for Ranjit Studio, was the first film Saigal did in Bombay. The film offered him another very powerful devotional role, some ten years after he appeared in *Chandidas*. On the basis of a role virtually carved out for the singer-actor, the film beautifully sketched the spiritual journey of Surdas (1479–1583), the blind Vaishnavaite saint. In his powerful portrayal, Saigal very ably captured the devotion of this poet-saint to his personal god, Lord Krishna, and sang soulfully a number of bhajans: *Nain Heen Ko Raah Dikha Prabhu, Madhukar Shyam Hamare Chor, Manuwa Krishan Naam Rate Ja, Rein Bhayee Ab Hua Savera, Kadam Chale Aage Man Pichhe Bhage, Jis Jogi Ka Jog Liya* (with Khurshid) and *Sar Pe Kadam Ki Chhaya Muraliya Baaji Ri* (with Raj Kumari).

The popularity of our indigenous hero was further enhanced by the historical classic *Tansen* (1943). (Tansen, an accomplished musician, was one of the *navratnas*, nine gems, of Akbar's durbar.) One of the greatest musicals of Indian cinema, *Tansen* was the first film to celebrate the beauty of India's composite culture built around the liberal worldview of the torchbearers for Hindu–Muslim unity during the medieval period. This film paved the way for other musicals such as *Baiju Bawra* (1952), *Basant Bahar* (1956), *Sangeet Samrat Tansen* (1959), *Rani Roopmati* (1960) and *Meera* (1979), which are still remembered for their strong presentation of the Indian cultural ethos during the fifteenth to the seventeenth centuries, especially during reign of the Mughal Emperor Akbar, when the state consciously promoted intercommunity cultural assimilation in fields such as literature, classical music and dance.

Directed by Jayant Desai, the movie presented Saigal in the celebrated role of Tansen. Based on the theme of how music can beautify life, the film weaved into the narrative the love fantasy involving Tansen and a shepherdess, Tani (Khurshid), and presented several legends highlighting the spiritual powers of Indian classical ragas, including their ability to calm animals, cause trees to flower, affect the weather and cure the seriously ill.

As the lovers wander amidst nature seeking a spiritual bliss through music, Raja Ramachandra Baghela of Rewa happens to listen to Tansen's renditions, and after much cajoling, brings him to his court. Emperor Akbar (Mubarak), on hearing about the musical genius of Tansen, requests Raja Baghela to spare this great musician for the imperial court. Tansen enters the service of Akbar and attains fame and distinction as one of the *navratnas* of the Mughal court. This shifting of the artiste to the royal ambience separates the lovers and Tani for years keeps waiting for her lover to return. Meanwhile, Akbar's daughter falls seriously sick and Tansen has to sing the Raga Deepak to cure her. Since this raga is supposed to have the power to create fire, it almost consumes the singer. However, Tani's singing of the rain-bringing Raga Megh Malhar eventually saves her lover.

All the thirteen songs of *Tansen*, composed by Khemchand Prakash, were big hits and took the country by storm. Saigal in this film fully revealed the mystical contours of his singing in *Kare Guman Kahe Ri Gori, Bag Laga Doon Sajni, Tore Nainan Mein He Ri, Sapat Suran Teen Gram, Bina Pankh Ka Panchi Hoon Main* and *Diya Jalao Jagmag Jagmag*. About Saigal's portrayal of Tansen, Raghava Menon writes, 'there was a good bit of mystery and wonder in the singing Saigal .... Doubtless the original Tansen who sang in the court of the emperor had this same mystery and this wonder a millionfold more. But the people who flocked to see the film knew this [and] were convinced that it was the same stuff, the same order of strangeness, admittedly attenuated in degree but of the same fire and so were able to go home after the movie ... impassioned'.

Apart from music, *Tansen* also won critical acclaim for its narrative as well as technical quality. As Partho Chatterjee (a well-known writer on films) observes, '*in its lighting, composition, camera movement, set design mise-en-scène, cutting and music, Tansen is a truly sophisticated achievement. The film wears its years lightly and still enthralls the viewer. K. L. Saigal's superb singing, very well supported by Khurshid's, the charisma of their individual presence, and of them together easily cuts through the barriers of race, language, culture and time.* Tansen *is a film of its time and for times to come'* [italics added]. Interestingly, director Jayant Desai made a worthwhile innovation: he himself appeared in person after the credits, surrounded by camera equipment, and introduced the theme of the film and the way the legend of Tansen had been interpreted.

In this film, Khurshid, with her breezy and yet intense singing (*Aao Gauri Aao Shyama Aao, Ho Dukhia Jiyara Rote Naina* and *Barso Re*) stood out on her own as the female singer icon alongside Saigal.

Bhanwra (1944), a romantic tale directed by Kidar Sharma, Saigal's most prolific dialogue writer and lyricist, presented the actor in the role of a passionate man in pursuit of fulfilment through platonic love. The film was studded with a variety of Saigal's songs: the typical melancholic renditions *Hum Apna Unhen Bana Na Sake* and *Yeh Woh Jagah Hai Jahan Ghar Lutaye Jate Hain*; the romantic numbers *Kya Humne Bigara Hai Kyoon Humko Satate Ho* and *Muskurate Huye Yun Aankh Churaya Na Karo*; and the dulcet *Diya Jisne Dil Lut Gaya Woh Bechara* sung in chorus in an extremely light and free-flowing vein.

New Theatres' *My Sister/Meri Bahen* (1944), set against the backdrop of the Second World War, recounted a touching tale of a brother's sacrifices for his sister. Ramesh (Saigal) is a poor but upright schoolteacher who adores his adolescent sister Bimala (Akhtar Jehan). He falls in love with Krishna (Sumitra Devi), the village zamindar's daughter. In spite of the class difference, the zamindar agrees to accept him as his son-in-law on the condition that, after marriage, he lives in his household. But Ramesh declines to marry Krishna because this arrangement would make his sister unhappy. The brother and sister then move to Calcutta where Ramesh becomes a singer in the Great Metropolitan Theatre Company. Soon he attains popularity and the famous female star Miss Rekha of the company (Chandrbati Devi) falls for him.

Meanwhile, Calcutta comes under air attack by the Japanese.

Ramesh gets seriously injured and is hospitalized. His beloved sister is separated from him. Rekha dies in the same hospital, unknown to Ramesh.

Like all Saigal films, this movie too relied heavily on his songs: *Do Naina Matware Tiharey Hum Par Julm Karen*, *Chupo Na O Pyari Sajaniya*, and the most famous *Ai Qatib-e-Taqdeer Mujhe Itna Batade*. Director Hemchandra Chunder very effectively employed some quasi-documentary scenes showing life during the Japanese bombardment, the functioning of a blood donation programme and the destruction of the theatre (where the hero performs) as the result of an air raid.

Kurukshetra (1945), made by a relatively less known director (Rameshwar Sharma), was a truly offbeat film, an interesting forerunner to the art cinema, which was to take shape much later in the late 1950s. This unique, but less-known film of Saigal, was a pioneering effort at blending mythological fables with the discomforting aspects of contemporary life vis-à-vis the social, political and economical realities. The film opens with a scene showing a director shooting the *swyamvara* scene for his film on the Mahabharata. (*Swyamvara* is a ceremony in which a woman chooses her own husband from several suitors.) The actress Swarna Rekha, who plays Draupadi in this film, is so overwhelmed by her own character that she goes beyond the written script and she vehemently deplores the Pandavas for their passive attitude – a reflection of the contemporary society's own quiet resignation to the prevalent evils. The film now reverses the Mahabharata narrative as both the Pandavas and Kauravas, who are mortal enemies, inspired by Draupadi's call, now unite to face a common foe in the person of Gandharva Raj, symbolizing the colonial rule.

In another scene being shot by the director of Mahabharata, Draupadi is seen feeding the now-united cousins in a poor locality in Calcutta. A hungry boy among the crowd, watching the shooting, rushes to her and Swarna Rekha, the actress, is so moved by his plight that she starts feeding him. She then attempts to collect funds for feeding the city's poor but fails. Consequently, she offers her own body in an auction to the highest bidder and money starts pouring in.

This unique step is noticed by a demented, suffering poet (Saigal) who starts worshipping her – through his songs – as a goddess for whom he has been eagerly waiting throughout his life. Thus, he symbolizes the Indian people thirsting for freedom, metaphorically represented by Swarna Rekha, the goddess of liberty. The poet eventually dies in his worship of his goddess, emphasizing the ultimate sacrifice required for getting freedom.

Kurukshetra was greatly appreciated by Sarojini Naidu (the highly respected poetess and freedom fighter): '*It is a novel venture to adopt the Puranic stories to interpret political and social problems of the country – a pointer to the necessity of a united front to free the society from ignorance, poverty and aggression.*' Saigal enhanced the pathos of his role by singing his heart out to the illusive 'people's goddess': *Kidhar Tu Hai Meri Tamanna, Mohabbat Ke Hay Taar Goondhta Hoon, Aayi Hai Tu To Kaise Dil Apna Dikhaun Main* and *Tu Aa Gai Dil Ki Tamanna Jaag Uthi.*

Tadbir (1945), directed by Jayant Desai, was another extremely offbeat film of Saigal. This film sought to examine the role of destiny in human affairs and how astrological predictions stand transformed vis-à-vis the happenings in real life. When Kanhaiyalal (Saigal) is born, an astrologer predicts that upon growing up he shall follow a prostitute, learn to wield a knife and be sentenced to the gallows. The predictions come true but destiny shows its own ways of interpretation. The hero and his mother find shelter in the house of Saguna (Suraiya), a prostitute who eventually sacrifices her life to save the hero's. The knife-wielding prediction comes true when Kanhaiyalal becomes a surgeon. He and his mother are determined to fight poverty as well as crime. Unfortunately, the hero is framed in a murder case, but is finally acquitted, despite the astrologer's prognostications. This film was embellished with some of the most passionate renditions by Saigal: *Janam-Janam Ka Dukhiya Prani Aaya Sharan Tihari*, *Mein Panchi Azad Mera Kahin Door Thikana Re* and *Mein Kismet Ka Mara Bhagwan*.

Omar Khayyam (1946), directed by Mohan Sinha, again paired Saigal with Suraiya, the emerging new-generation singer icon. A musical saga about the legendary Persian poet, the film offered the singer-actor a rare opportunity to portray man's quest for eternal bliss through wine and worship of feminine beauty. Saigal's rendition included *Allahu Khayyam Hai Allahwala Matwala*, *Hare Bhare Bagh Ke Phoolon Pe Rijha Khayyam* and *Insaan! Kyon Rota Hai Insaan*.

A. R. Kardar's masterpiece, *Shahjehan* (1946), presented Saigal in one of the best roles of his career – an ultra-romantic, yet cynical, poet named Suhail in the court of Emperor Shahjehan. The poet catches a rare glimpse of Ruhi, the extremely beautiful ward of a Rajput noble in the royal court. From that moment onwards, she becomes the one and only object of his thoughts, his music and his poetry. This constant adulation and laudation of her beauty by the poet in his songs make her an instant celebrity in the kingdom. However, while virtually the entire populace gets carried away by this beauty queen, Shahjehan, deep in love as he is with his own queen, Mumtaz Mahal, remains aloof, lost as ever in the blissful company of his beloved.

Meanwhile, Queen Mumtaz falls seriously ill, and, on her deathbed, she asks Shahjehan to build a monument that would immortalize their love. The emperor invites Shirazi (Jairaj), the celebrated craftsman and architect of Iran, to transform this wish of the queen into a masterpiece of art. When the architect, on his way to India, hears of Ruhi's beauty, he instantaneously falls in love with her. The emperor, by mistake, promises the damsel's hand to him as well as to the poet.

Shirazi works out various extremely beautiful models of the monument but to the emperor's frustration, they fail to portray the exact imagery that he has built up in his sorrow-filled mind. The architect thus must first experience a loss as intense and devastating as that of Shahjehan's loss of Mumtaz. And so, Ruhi's father kills her; the agonized Shirazi, in this state of separation from his beloved, finally gets the grand vision of the Taj Mahal. Later, it is revealed that Ruhi is still alive as the poet Suhail has sacrificed his life to save her.

Apart from the magnificent décor and the royal ambience, the restrained yet consummate performances of Saigal and others added to the artistic content of the film. Saigal, in fact, lifted the film to a higher plane, making it a remarkably intimate musical experience. His passionate and moving renditions of some of his best songs leave one enthralled even today. The melodies (composed by Naushad and penned by Majrooh Sultanpuri) include *Mere Sapnon Ki Rani Ruhi Ruhi Ruhi*, *Chaah Barbad Karegi Humhen Maloom Na Tha*, *Gham Diye Mustaqil*, *Ai Dil-e-Beqaraar Jhoom* (in Raga Kaafi) and the timeless *Jab Dil Hi Toot Gaya* (in Raga Bhairavi). The film critic of the *Bombay Chronicle* wrote (about Saigal's portrayal in *Shahjehan*), '*it is perhaps so true to the ideal of his own life that never before in his long brilliant career can one find another instance in which he been better fitted*' [italics added].

Parwana (1947), Saigal's last film, presented him in the difficult role of an unhappy man in quest of true love without disrespecting the social milieu in which he is placed. Married to a domineering wife against his wishes, he seeks refuge in the love of a village girl (Suraiya). Though the story follows the familiar pattern of the 'love triangle', it not only lends new meaning to the love that draws the husband to the 'other woman' but it also deglorifies the highly idealized image of an Indian wife and portrays her as a realistic human character with all its weaknesses and shortcomings. All the characters eventually suffer for their deeds. While satirically commenting on the hypocrisy of the city-bred educated class, the film showed how petty jealousies and lack of moral faith in oneself lead to unwanted devastation. Released after Saigal's death, the film was a superhit throughout the country.

In 1953, R. C. Boral and Nitin Bose jointly produced *Amar*

Saigal, one of the few biographical films made on cine artistes in Indian cinema. The film was based on the songs and clippings from Saigal's films.

Saigal's Hero and the Social Realities

Saigal's screen persona and its phenomenal popular appeal were rooted in the socio-cultural milieu of his times. His ordinary looks and seemingly clumsy bearing evoked a deep sense of lost glory and pride among the common people who had been colonized and their cultural identity seriously threatened by the alien pressures. Saigal's hero also represented a forceful cultural revival using the iconography from tradition, as a counterpoint to the rapid onslaught of Western culture and the manifestations of the associated forms of modernity. His songs echoed the anguish of an enslaved nation; they were intense, pensive and self-reflective, expressing the agony of the people at large. At the same time, this music announced the spiritual and cultural superiority of the colonized culture over the colonizers, despite suffering and bondage.

Saigal's protagonist would earnestly endeavour to protect his autonomy and freedom of expression, indicating indirectly the growing social disquiet against the colonial rule. In *Tansen* (1943), for instance, he is shown as a rural rustic who had learnt singing from Mother Nature and could not be forced to sing even by a king. If he would do so, it would be only on his own terms. Even in *Street Singer* (1938), set in the modern times, the compulsive singer does not compromise his art nor does he sell his soul. This strong and self-assertive characteristic assigned to a common-looking man created a tremendous affinity in the collective consciousness of a generation, and remained intact long afterwards.

The characters delineated by Saigal reflected the growing clash between the orthodox feudal class, which was not yet fully prepared to imbibe the new values associated with the emerging social change, and the hidden conservatism of the outwardly

Westernized ruling class unable to come to terms with this change. In their own way, these characters were reflecting the growing cynicism and the deterioration of human relationships in a social set-up caught up in undue tension as seen in films like *Devdas, Pujarin, Didi/President, Desher Mati/Dharti Mata, Parichay/ Lagan* and *Kurukshetra*.

The Untimely End

Despite his outward tranquil disposition, in the final analysis, deep down, Saigal seemed to be a very sad man, wasting his valuable life by becoming a slave to alcohol. Although the source of his sadness cannot be pinpointed, it seems that the singer lived through the lifelong frustration of not being able to become a great classical musician like the renowned and respected icons of his times. In this context, Raghava Menon writes, '*unlike Tansen, who had in all likelihood received the spiritual empowerment from the Sufi saint Mohammed Ghaus, that Saigal got from ... Sheikh Salman Yousuf, he did not get a Swami Haridas later to nurture and sustain him, to provide him with the incalculable ambience of a* parampara [tradition]. *This, for a man of Saigal's sense of destiny and talent, was indeed a grievous shortcoming*' [italics added].

Saigal even went once to study music under the highly acclaimed classical musician Ustad Faiyaz Khan, but after hearing him sing a short *khayal* in Raga Darbari, which Saigal had specially learnt for the occasion, the Khan Saheb told him: 'My dear boy, there is nothing that I can teach you now that will make you a greater singer. You are ready to serve.' Later, the two became close friends.

The deep frustration that rankled within Saigal for not achieving the status of a celebrated classical singer can be seen in one of the most significant incidents in his life. In 1938, he attended with his mother and his wife, Asharani, the Annual Music Conference organized by the Prayag Sangeet Samiti. The place was the Allahabad University Senate Hall where a galaxy of Indian classical musicians were present: Pandit Onkarnath Thakur, Ustad Faiyaz Khan, D. V. Paluskar, Narayan Rao Vyas and Vinayak Rao Patwardhan.

As soon as Saigal entered the hall, the students crowding the upper galleries began shouting: 'Saigal! Saigal!! Saigal!!!' They kept on asking him to sing. He obliged them. He sang some of the favourites from his recent films such as *Devdas*, *Yahoodi Ki Ladki*, *Chandidas* and *Street Singer* and then some bhajans and *ghazals*. But the requests kept pouring in, scribbled on pieces of paper. Eventually, he had to stop as many musicians, great names of the day, were awaiting their turn on the stage. Even after he had come down from the dais, the crowd continued to shout his name and asked him to carry on. Extremely moved, Saigal held his mother by her hands and then lifting her off the floor, he began swinging her round and round in the hall against her repeated protests, exclaiming: 'Listen, mother, listen, they are shouting for me to sing. They don't want me to stop. *They think that I am a musician!*'

As Saigal could seldom reach the peak of his creative expression without the help of alcohol, heavy drinking became part of his life. Perhaps he never attained inner solace from his own soul-filling music, which enthralled audiences for at least two generations. Like Devdas, whose incarnation he appeared to be, he died prematurely of cirrhosis of the liver on 18 January 1947. With his demise, the soul-stirring quality in film music appeared to have come to an end. The article carried by the *Bombay Chronicle* on 25 May 1947 paid glowing tributes to Saigal's memory by quoting George Eliot's famous poem:

O may I join the choir invisible
Of those immortal dead who live again
In minds made better by their presence ...
To make undying music in the world
So shall I join the choir invisible
Whose music is the gladness of the world!

Towards the end of his fascinating biography of Saigal, Raghava Menon writes:

> When he died, it was a strange thing that had departed this world. The yeast was out of the bread of music. A presence of freedom and wonder, surprising ability and gift had gone out. An era had ended. A new one is yet to begin.[9]

As an institution, Saigal inspired a whole generation of singers such as C. H. Atma, Surendra (the quick-hire imitator of the icon promoted by the producers in Bombay), Kozhikode Abdul Qadir and later Mukesh, Talat Mehmood and even Kishore Kumar. Imitating this grand master of singing, in fact, had become a compulsion for everyone, both for amateurs as well as professional singers during this period and later.

P. C. Barua and Pahadi Sanyal: Saigal's Constant Companions

Celebrated director-actor P. C. Barua (1903–51) entered the film world as an actor in silent era in 1930 with Debaki Bose's *Panchasar*. This film was followed by *Aparadhi* (1931), *Nishir Dak* (1932), both directed by Bose, and Kaliprasad Ghosh's *Bhagyalakshmi* (1932). He proclaimed his highly successful entry into the talkie era as the ultimate romantic hero in 1932 with his own directorial debut *Bengal 1983* and then in the superhit Bengali version of *Devdas* (1935). In *Griadah/Manzil* (1936), he portrayed a poor youth who falls in love with a liberated girl and marries her, while his rich friend eventually elopes with her. His best-known film, *Mukti* (1937), a Tagore adaptation, was about the problems of women's liberation in a feudal milieu. He was cast in the role of a romantic artist who gets married to a rich girl, but their respective egoistic stances lead to divorce. The lady opts to get married to a rich man, while the disillusioned artist becomes a forest dweller.

In *Adhikar* (1938), a tale about inheritance and love, the hero (Barua) loves the rich heroine but the real heiress stakes her claim to the property and the hero. In *Rajat Jayanti* (1939), one of the best comedies ever made in Indian cinema, he appeared as a simple-minded youth in pursuit of a neighbourhood girl. He receives ample comical advice from his street-smart cousin and from the latter's friend. *Shesh Uttar/Jawab* (1942) featured him as a rich, self-obsessed but deranged man who prefers to opt for a down-to-earth girl than his rich fiancée. His last screen presence was in *Maya Kanan*, released in 1953.

***

Pahadi Sanyal (1906–74), along with K. L. Saigal, was the main singing star of New Theatres. His screen persona represented a highly durable romantic hero stereotype drawn from the Bengali literary ambience. Born as Narendranath Sanyal in Darjeeling, he studied music at Morris College, Lucknow. He joined New Theatres in 1931. His first film as hero was Debaki Bose's *Vidyapati* (1937) in the title role. In Amar Mullick's *Badi Didi* (1939), based on Saratchandra's novel, he appeared as a disgruntled suitor whose love is rejected by a widow. However, when he becomes a landlord, he saves her from the oppression unleashed by his staff. Debaki Bose's *Sapera* (1939) cast Sanyal in the role of the heroine's lover. The heroine is also desired by her guardian, a mystic healer of snake bites. In *Abhinetri/Haar Jeet* (1940), directed by Amar Mullick, he appeared as a stage actor who marries the actress of a rival theatre company and wants her to forego her career and become a homely wife. Apart from playing lead roles, Sanyal became a constant companion of Saigal in films such as *Yahoodi Ki Ladki*, *Rooplekha*, *Devdas* and *Zindagi* in the second lead.

In 1942, Sanyal moved to Bombay and acted in the films like Nandlal Jaswantal's *Kadambari* (1944) and Sudhir Sen's *Mahakavi Kalidas* (1944) as hero and as supporting hero in Nitin Bose's *Milan* (1946) and Ram Daryani's *Shravan Kumar* (1947). By the late 1950s, he started appearing in character roles in several Bengali films such as Asit Sen's *Deep Jweley Jai* (1959) and Sushil Majumdar's *Hospital* (1960). He continued the trend in some Hindi films as well, for instance: Shakti Samanta's *Aradhana* and Tarun Majumdar's *Rahgir*, both released in 1969. He has two Satyajit Ray's films to his credit: *Kanchanjungha* (1962), in which he portrayed an obsessive bird watcher, and *Aranyer Din Rotri* (1969), in which he appeared as a retired singer.

Surendra: The 'Other' Saigal

Surendra (or Surendra Nath), the singer-actor model launched by the Bombay film world as the prototype of New Theatre's K. L. Saigal, was a highly successful hero of the 1930s and 1940s. He was born on 11 November 1910 in Batla village, Punjab. After completing his studies in law, he started working as a lawyer. Since he was tall and handsome and a fairly good singer, peer pressure compelled him to opt for a career in cinema. He came to Bombay in 1935 and joined Sagar Movietone.

It was Mehboob Khan who introduced Surendra as the new hero of the studio in 1936, in the film *Deccan Queen*, in the role of a cop who is sought by both the heroine and her twin sister. He sang the song *Birha Ki Aag Lagi* ..., a rehash of K. L. Saigal's *Baalam Aaye* ... in *Devdas*. Soon Surendra (like Motilal) became the favourite hero of the master before his association with Dilip Kumar. He appeared in many of his mentor's films: in *Manmohan* (1936) as the obsessed painter in love with the heroine (Bibbo), who finally becomes a destitute (*Tumhi Ne Mujhko Prem Sikhaya* ..., the song he rendered with Bibbo was a hit); in *Jagirdar* (1937) as the disgruntled husband who struggles to get back his wife (Bibbo) and son (Motilal), now settled with another man; and in

Aurat (1940) as the diligent elder son of the film's woman protagonist (in *Mother India*, 1957, a remake of *Aurat*, Rajendra Kumar was cast in this role). In *Alibaba* (1940), based on the Arabian Nights fable, he was cast in the title role.

In the 1940s, Surendra added further vitality to his screen persona. In *Garib* (1942), produced by Mehboob Khan and directed by Ramachandra Thakur, Surendra appeared as an unemployed graduate who transforms the shelter built by a philanthropic industrialist for destitutes into a successful factory for their productive rehabilitation. In Mehboob Khan's *Elaan* (1947), he won acclaim for his role of a simple-hearted step-brother who is ill-treated and exploited since childhood. He loses his childhood beloved (Munawwar Sultana), who is forced to marry the villainous step-brother. In the same director's *Anmol Gadi* (1946), he again won accolades for his role as the relentless seeker of childhood love (Noorjehan). For this film, composer Naushad inspired Surendra to sing some of his most popular songs: *Aawaz De Kahan Hai* (a duet with Noorjehan), *Kyun Yaad Aa Rahe Hain Guzre Hue Zamaane* and *Ab Kaun Hai Mera* .... The film *Anokhi Ada* (1948, directed again by Mehboob Khan) presented him as a suave professor in pursuit of the heroine (Naseem Banu) who is suffering from amnesia.

Apart from Mehboob's works, Surendra also appeared in a slew of films of the top directors of the era: Sarvotam Badami's *Grama Kanya* (1936) and *Ladies Only* (1939), R. S. Choudhary's *Kal Ki Baat* (1937), Hiren Bose's *Mahageet* (1937), C. M. Lohar's *Dynamite* (1938), Ramchandra Thakur and V. C. Desai's *Gramophone Singer* (1938), Nandlal Jaswantlal's *Comrades* (1939), Kidar Sharma's *Vish Kanya* (1943) and *Chand Chakori* (1945), K. B. Lall's *Lal Haveli* (1944), Acharya Atre's *Parinde* (1945), Sohrab Modi's *Majhdhaar* (1947), Mohan Sinha's *Mere Bhagwaan* (1947), D. K. Ratan's *Dukhiyaari* (1948) and Surya Kumar's *Kamal* (1949).

In *Grama Kanya*, he appeared as Kumar, a university student supported by his poor father with the money borrowed from a rich landlord, who, in return expects Kumar to marry his daughter. Although Kumar hooks a city girl and makes her pregnant, he is forced to wed the arranged match. Like Master Nissar, Surendra formed a popular pair with Bibbo, one of the most important female stars of the 1930s and 1940s.

Surendra also made his presence felt in some costume dramas/historicals – Sultan Mirza and S. Varman's *Qazzaak Ki Ladki* (1937), Mohan Sinha's *1857* (1946) and *Chittor Vijay* (1947) – and in three films with religious themes: *Bharthari* (1944), *Gorakh Naath* (1951) and *Mahatma Kabir* (1954). In *Bharthari*, he rendered songs such as *Bhanwara Madhuban Me Jaa ...*, *Bhiksha De De Maa ...*, *Allah Naam Ras Pina Praani ...* and *Prem Bina Sab Soona*, composed by none other than veteran Khemchand Prakash. In *Gawaiya* (1954), Surendra's song *Teri Yaad Ka Deepak Jalta Hai Din Raat* was a superhit (the other faster version was rendered by Talat Mehmood). The composer was Ram Ganguly. Surendra's last lead role was in *Ram Bhakt Vibhishan* (1958).

In senior roles, Surendra appeared in the role of the musician Tansen in three films: *Baiju Bawra* (1952), *Rani Roopmati* (1957) and *Mughal-e-Azam* (1960). He also acted in films like *Dil Deke Dekho* (1959), *Haryali Aur Raasta* (1962), *Baaghi* (1964), *Geet Gaya Pattharon Ne* (1964), *Waqt* (1965), *Johar Mehmood in Goa* (1965), *Boond Jo Ban Gai Moti* (1967), *An Evening in Paris* (1967), *Milan* (1967), *Saraswatichandra* (1968) and *Kunwara Badan* (1973).

***

Dilip Kumar, like his many illustrious companions of the future, must have been sitting among the audience, observing with a great deal of excitement and adulation the grand developments taking place in Indian cinema during its formative period and the spell cast by Saigal's persona. Eventually, destiny invited him to leave his seat in the audience to preside over the classical era of Indian films. The cinema towards the end of this period had witnessed a spectacular spell of creativity and the creator of its first *true* indigenous hero was all set to arrive on the cinematic scene.

Notes and References

1. Ravi S. Vasudevan, 'Film Studies: New Cultural History and Experience of Modernity', *Economic and Political Weekly*, Bombay, Vol. XXX, No. 44, 1995.

2. Raghava R. Menon, *K. L. Saigal: The Pilgrim of the Swara*, New Delhi: Clarion Books, 1978, and New Delhi: Hind Pocket Books, 1989.

3. Ibid.

4. K. L. Saigal said this to actress Damayanti, wife of the versatile actor Balraj Sahni (whom we shall meet later), when he happened to visit the sets during the shooting of K. A. Abbas's *Dharti Ke Lal* (1946). During the conversation, Damayanti told Saigal she would exchange her fortunes for a beautiful song. Saigal, who was seriously ill at that time, smiled and said, 'yes young lady, anything for a song!'

5. B. S. Hoogan was the author's paternal uncle. Like Saigal, he also died young at the age of thirty-seven. During his merely five-year stay in Bombay, he scored music in as many as eighteen films made between 1933 and 1937.

6. The well-known story was about the rivalry between the Roman priest Brutus and the oppressed Jewish merchant, Ezra. Brutus sentences Ezra's son to death and Ezra, in turn, kidnaps and raises Brutus' only daughter, Decia. When the daughter, renamed Hannah (Rattanbai), grows up, Marcus (Saigal) falls in love with her. To court her, he disguises his Roman identity. When his religion is discovered, he is ejected from Ezra's house. Marcus then agrees to marry Princes Octavia (Tara) as arranged, but Hannah denounces him in open court and he is sentenced to death by his own father, the emperor. When Hannah and Ezra respond to Octavia's pleas and retract their accusations, they, in turn, are sentenced to death by Brutus. Ezra reveals to Brutus that Hannah, who is about to be killed, is, in fact, Brutus' own daughter.

7. The plot was that of a typical costume drama: Prince Pervez (Saigal) is the heir to the throne of Kascand. When his mother (Zutshi) and the Vizir (Hamid) insist that he marry the princess (Raj Kumari) of neighbouring Bijapore, he leaves the palace and joins a band of gypsies where Zarina (Rattanbai) falls in love with him. The villain Tikkim, who wants to marry the princess himself, has her kidnapped by the gypsies. In the gypsy camp, Pervez sees her as a dancing girl and they fall in love. Finally, the villain is defeated, while Zarina makes way for the lovers.

8. Another noteworthy aspect of *President* was Bose's innovative use of sound in the film narrative at a time when few Indian film makers had grasped its creative possibilities. By dexterously using sounds in the workplace, he was able to evoke the right mood and atmosphere, thus making the narrative more dramatic.
9. Raghava R. Menon, op. cit.

Chapter 4

The Arrival of Dilip Kumar

As discussed in the preceding chapters, during the formative phase of Indian cinema, institutions such as Bombay Talkies, New Theatres, Ajanta Movietone, Minerva Movietone, Prabhat, Ranjit Studios, Sagar and Filmistan had carried out extensive groundwork for harnessing the film technology and for establishing this cinema in its wider socio-cultural context with a strong thematic base built into a formal style and structure. Following the huge strides being made during the great period of the renaissance in Indian literature and arts in the 1930s and 1940s, the early visionaries had completed the process of using film-making technology to explore entirely new forms of cinematic expression. This exploration was soon to establish finally in the country's cultural scene one of the most powerful traditions of communication with the common man as its central concern.

By the mid-1940s, Mehboob Khan, Nitin Bose, V. Shantaram, Gyan Mukerjee, Phani Majumdar, Kidar Sharma, A. R. Kardar, Zia Sarhadi, Amiya Chakravarty, Bimal Roy and others had achieved a number of thematic breakthroughs along with innovations in characterization, narration and treatment. This achievement was evident in films like *Aurat* (1940), *Pagal* (1940), *Padosi* (1941), *Kismet* (1943), *Udayer Pathey/Humrahi* (1944) and *Dr Kotnis Ki Amar Kahani* (1946). Overall, the main cinema trends were also progressively moving away from the stunt-costume-fantasy genre and mythologicals to the more meaningful social genre (see the table on p. 121). The emergence of a new class of cinematographers and technicians during this period also facilitated rapid changes in the use of the camera, film processing, editing techniques and sound recording as well as playback singing. Not only did they follow the path-breaking developments in film technology taking place in Hollywood but they also introduced on their own many innovations in their craft. Thus, having mastered the technology and established powerful trends of indigenous cinema, the Indian film makers were gradually preparing for ushering in an era of excellence in the content, the treatment and the overall aesthetic appeal of the Indian film.

The Indian film's main protagonist, the hero, was also undergoing a rapid transformation. As film technology was reaching yet another stage of maturity, the film makers were intuitively in search of an entirely new framework in the presentation of their protagonist who would help them realize their emerging vision. In spite of the immense strength of the themes in the formative phase of cinema and the expertise acquired, there was something amiss. The days of the mythological and historical hero as a symbol of national identity and protest were coming to an end. The new hero figure was expected to act as a driving force to establish the efficacy of film technology in articulating the complexities of the Indian psyche as being reflected in the emerging reality of the post-independence period and ensuring a sense of security in the context of a painful past and an uncertain future. This protagonist, therefore, was to become the pivot around which indigenous cinema would revolve and express society's emerging concerns and anxieties. In the process, such cinema would take the audience along on a journey in tune with the changing socio-cultural and political milieu. It was anticipated that the protagonist, as the true indigenous film hero, would not only help in realizing the immense potential of creative expression inherent in celluloid, but also

Type of film	1931–35	1936–40	1941–45	1946–50
Social	148	256	325	401
Costume drama	81	125	22	31
Stunt (including suspense thrillers)	66	63	39	96
Mythological	60	14	13	43
Fantasy	32	19	12	26
Historical	17	4	17	20
Love legend	18	1	3	10
Devotional	12	8	11	11
Total number of films	434	490	442	638

Source: Compiled from Har Mandir Singh 'Hamraaz', *Hindi Film Geet Kosh* (Vols. I and II), Kanpur: published by Satinder Kaur, 1980.

in enhancing the appeal of the new medium among the already highly receptive audience.

By this time, Saigal's screen persona, built painstakingly over the whole range of film genres – devotional, historical, fantasy and social – had paved the way for the development of Indian cinema's first *true* indigenous hero. By the mid-1940s, however, this indigenous hero prototype seemed to have been fully exploited. Although his screen persona during this period was in the process of acquiring a more contemporary look (as seen in films like *Lagan, Tadbir* and *Parwana*), such a prototype could not grow beyond its original framework, remaining more or less stuck within its own stereotype. In the grand classical era – to be marked by romance, narrative beauty, glamour and melody – which was waiting to be ushered in, the legendary singer-actor's persona and the genre instituted by him, in all likelihood, might have become obsolete and out of tune with the times. Saigal, however, did not live to experience this historical shift.

The other reigning stars of the 1940s were not fully equipped to respond to the looming challenge. Other actors like Jairaj, Shahu Modak, Ishwarlal, Kishore Sahu and Ghulam Mohammed somehow seemed to lack the intensity needed for a performance par excellence. The models offered by the two reigning stars – Ashok Kumar and Motilal – did not meet the requirements, although they had overcome the hurdles of theatricality, which most early heroes could not cross. Both of them were 'modern heroes' as far as looks and persona were concerned, but too natural and unstylized to be able to depict the complexities of the socio-political milieu.

All these gentlemen inherently lacked the deep emotional appeal and the ability to generate among the audience a deep sense of empathy. Indian cinema, therefore, was waiting for a new artiste who could not only bring about a metamorphosis in the hero's persona, keeping in view the new societal realities, but also imbue it with a new aura and new dimensions to meet the emerging requirements of film aesthetics and mass appeal.

The wait did not last long as the new artiste appeared on the horizon most unexpectedly. The year was 1944, a few years before the country gained independence. The Indian film world witnessed a rare incident of talent scouting. Devika Rani, the owner of Bombay Talkies, had gone out for shopping to a local market. At one fruit shop, she looked keenly at the young man engrossed in selling his merchandise. It was by mere chance that the shy shopkeeper had only replaced his ailing father in the shop that day. Devika Rani found this young man with a sensitive face and expressive eyes quite unusual. She gave him her visiting card and asked him to meet her at the studio.

Devika Rani: The Ace Star Maker

Devika Rani (1907–94), the first 'wonder lady' of Indian cinema, was far ahead of her times. In spite of her extensive exposure to the world of art and cinema, she shared with her equally illustrious husband, Himanshu Rai, the vision of a truly indigenous Indian film. Through her screen persona, she also set the standards for the Hindi film heroines of the 1950s.

Grandniece of Rabindranath Tagore and daughter of Colonel N. Choudhury (who later became the surgeon-general of Madras), she studied at the Royal Academy of Dramatic Arts and at the Royal Academy of Music (London) and then obtained a degree in architecture and became a successful designer of paisley textiles. After her marriage to Himanshu Rai, whom she met in London, she became his constant companion in his film-making pursuits. She worked as the costume designer for *Prapahcha Pash* (1929), the first film produced by Rai and directed by Franz Osten. In Germany, where the film was made, she had the opporunity to interact with top directors like Max Reinhardt, Fritz Lang, G. W. Pabst and Josef von Sternberg. She also assisted Marlene Deitrich on the sets of *Der Blaue Engel* (1930). When co-production with Germany became difficult after 1933 (the year Adolf Hitler came to power), the couple returned to India. Devika made her debut in Rai's first sound film, *Karma* (1933), made in English. The following year the couple laid the foundation of Bombay Talkies in Bombay.

This young man was born as Yusuf Khan in Peshawar (now in Pakistan) on 11 December 1922. He was the third son in a family of twelve siblings. His father moved to Bombay in the early 1930s to set up the family's dry fruit business. Dilip Kumar graduated in the arts from Khalsa College and took up his first job, as assistant manager, in the Army Canteen in Devlali, near Nasik (now in Maharashtra). As a typical middle-class youth, he was preoccupied with making a living and taking care of his family. Interestingly, unlike many others stars in the making in those years, he had no family or other affiliations with theatre, music, cinema or other performing arts. While one brother studied medicine and eventually migrated to the USA, the other acquired a degree in management and only the youngest, Nasir Khan, joined the film line and became an actor.

The versatile
Dilip Kumar

After preliminary screen tests, Yusuf Khan was selected as an apprentice at Bombay Talkies and Devika Rani began grooming him as the company's new hero. Celebrated Hindi writer, the late Bhagwati Charan Verma (he was engaged by Bombay Talkies as scriptwriter at that time), gave him the screen name Dilip (perhaps after Raja Dilip of the Kuru dynasty of the early Vedic period). The second name Kumar seems to have been borrowed from Ashok Kumar, the reigning star at that time. According to the well-known writer, Bunny Reuben,[1] Devika Rani came up with three screen names (Dilip Kumar, Vasudev and Jehangir) and asked Yusuf Khan to choose one. We all know the name he chose.

Apart from the chance factor, the discovery of Dilip Kumar was essentially due to the sharp perceptive abilities of Devika Rani. As B. N. Sircar, the founder of New Theatres, in the 1930s sensed the immense cinematic possibilities in K. L. Saigal, she, a decade later, perceived the need for a new kind of acting talent for the further enrichment of Indian cinema. Perhaps a growing stagnation in themes and style in films, coupled with lukewarm responses to many Bombay Talkies films at the box office during this period, created this need. Such perceptive abilities of the matriarch of Hindi cinema were also due to her extensive exposure to the Western world of art and culture. In fact, Bombay Talkies was a great institution that was constantly on the lookout for new talent and offering opportunities to make a career in films. The examples are many. Ashok Kumar faced the camera for the first time in this studio's third venture, *Jeevan Nayya* (1936), in the lead role. The veteran actor Jairaj made his debut in *Bhabhi* (1938) and later appeared in the lead role with Devika Rani in *Hamari Baat* (1943) and *Char Ankhen* (1944). Legendary Hindi poet Pradeep made a highly successful debut as lyricist in *Kangan* (1939). K. A. Abbas started as a writer with Bombay Talkies, his first film being *Naya Sansar* (1941), directed by N. R. Acharya. Bimal Roy made his debut as director in the Bombay film world with *Maa* (1952).

Dilip Kumar arrived when the Saigal era was at its zenith, and, after the premature death of the legendary singer-actor in January 1947, Ashok Kumar had risen to occupy the top spot. Soon after his arrival, the young and eager-to-experiment actor engaged himself in building an entirely new cinematic identity on the basic mould set by Saigal. He began developing a new institution of a 'cult following' in Indian cinema by taking the clue from Saigal and also from his other noteworthy predecessors, namely, Ashok Kumar, Motilal and Surendra.

The Formative Phase of Self-discovery and Image Building

In spite of the seemingly dramatic talent scouting, the entry of Dilip Kumar into the film world was extremely low-key; he was just one among many faces of the new generation being experimented with by the film directors at that time. Devika Rani introduced him in *Jwar Bhata* in 1944, under the direction of the veteran Amiya Chakravarty. The heroine, Mridula, was also a new find of Bombay Talkies.

Jwar Bhata cast him in the role of a *nautanki* (equivalent to folk theatre) artiste, named Jagdish, a sensitive young man who provides support to a young girl in distress. Meanwhile, the marriage of the heroine Renu (Mridula), the younger daughter of an old patriarch, is arranged with a rich urban youth Narendra (Agha Jaan), who on a visit to the family, mistakes the elder sister Rama (Shammi) for Renu and falls in love with her and marries her (Rama). After the wedding Rama becomes supicious about her sister's evil designs to win back her fiancé. Eventually, Renu is thrown out of the house; she then meets Jagdish, and to conceal her identity, she joins his troupe. Jagdish, who is now in love with her, persuades her to go back to her family. On her return, Renu finds Rama pregnant and very ill and a choice must be made between the foetus and the mother. Renu forgives her sister and invokes god to save the lives of the mother and her child.

The general response to the film was not encouraging. The critics as well as the people in the industry felt that the new actor did not seem to have much spark in him and the quality of his voice in particular was bad, but the heroine had the potential to become a good actress. As Bombay Talkies' scenarist Inder Raj Anand wrote later, the company didn't think much of Dilip Kumar and didn't see a bright future for him. They had all their hopes pinned on Mridula. However, time proved them wrong; none of them indeed had the slightest idea that this shaky, unimpressive new talent would soon become the 'founding father' of cinematic acting, taking this art form far beyond the domain of the legendary artistes ruling the film world at that time.

The second film of Dilip Kumar, *Pratima* (1945), directed by actor-turned-director Jairaj, presented him as a seeker, who in pursuit of an idolized love, would defy every social convention to reach out to the world of eternal beauty and innocence.

In this film, Dilip Kumar (as Rajan) appeared as a persuasive lover entangled in a curious plot. He falls in love with a poor girl Pratima (Swaranlata) brought up by Parvasi (Pithawala), a curio-dealer, who had once been a notorious dacoit. Rajan's family wishes him to marry the rich Lal Sahib's spoilt daughter. In the *haveli* (mansion) of Lal Sahib, there is a female statue in the courtyard after which the heroine has been named. The very mention of this figure makes Lal Sahib shudder with fear, and he starts looking at the picture of his country house hanging on the wall.

The hero, who now has turned into a desperate lover, starts worshipping the statue, the *pratima*, and restores the shrine in the model village he has constructed for the poor. The shrine is jealously guarded by a demented looking woman. In the end, the mystery about the birth of the heroine and the statue is revealed: This woman is the mother of Pratima, the heroine, and the real owner of the estate, which was usurped by Lal Sahib by killing her husband in the country house. Parvasi had saved the girl from the evil Lal Sahib and her mother had installed the statue of her long-lost daughter to remind the world about the misdeeds of the villain.

Milan (1947) – based on Rabindranath Tagore's famous novel, *Nauka Dubi*, and which marked Nitin Bose's debut at Bombay Talkies – was a meaningful commentary on the sanctity of the institution of marriage and the role of destiny in separating and reuniting two souls in love. The film portrayed Dilip Kumar as an upright landed aristocrat, Ramesh, who upholds the dignity of a newly married woman under testing circumstances. He has had to forgo his beloved and marry, under family pressure, another woman, but loses her when the wedding party's boat is caught up in a storm while crossing a river. The bride of another wedding party hit by the same storm loses her husband but believes that it is the hero to whom she has been married off. The hero takes care of her till her groom, who is believed to have drowned in the storm, is found to be alive. *Milan* won critical acclaim for the effective treatment of the theme and for the photography of outdoor night scenes. This movie greatly helped Dilip Kumar in defining his screen persona.

Nitin Bose

Nitin Bose (1897–1986), the cameraman-turned-director, was one of the early founders of the realist genre in Bengali and Hindi cinema. A child prodigy, he learned still photography from his father, Hemendra Mohan Bose, owner of the famous Kuntalin Press and distributor of pathephone recording systems. The young Bose began making home movies, which he developed himself. In 1921–22 he even made newsreels for the International Newsreel Corporation and Fox Kinogram.

Nitin Bose joined the film world as a cinematographer for *Punarjanam* (1927). He continued camerawork with Aurora, Indian Kinema Arts, Sisir Bhaduri and International Filmcraft and shot many films for New Theatres in the 1930s. These included Debaki Bose's *Chandidas* (1932) and *Meerabai* (1933) and Premankur Atorthy's *Dena Paona* (1931).

Bose made his directorial debut with *Chandidas* and soon was among the most important directors of New Theatres, introducing a new kind of realism in Bengali cinema helping K. L. Saigal in realizing his full potential as actor-singer. He also influenced the films of his own student and cameraman Bimal Roy (*Udayer Pathey*, 1944) and also Mrinal Sen's (another to-be renowned director) early films.

After leaving New Theatres in 1941, Bose directed *Milan* (*Nauka Dubi*, 1945) for Bombay Talkies, the first commercially successful film of Dilip Kumar. The actor had great respect for his senior and thus invited him to direct his only in-house production, *Ganga Jumna* (1961).

Apart from these three films, Dilip Kumar also appeared in a family drama, *Ghar Ki Izaat* (1948) directed by Ram Daryani, an alumnus, again, of Bombay Talkies. This film was perhaps the first family drama on the conflict between orthodox parents and the noble daughter-in-law in Hindi cinema. The plot was primarily centred round the role of Mumtaz Shanti, the legendary actress of *Kismet* fame. Here, Dilip Kumar portrayed a typical upper-class youth, Chanda, who wants to be rebellious but is unable to challenge parental authority. He falls in love with a poor girl Roopa (Mumtaz Shanti) and marries her without the consent of his parents. They make Roopa's life miserable by repeatedly taunting her about her lowly background. Chanda is unable to go against his orthodox parents to ensure his wife's dignity and happiness. He leaves home and becomes a drunkard and a gambler until finally good sense prevails over his parents.

The above films had strong heroine-oriented characters, with Dilip Kumar cast as the usual romantic hero simply filling the need of the character in the overall narration (in the same way as Rajendra Kumar's roles in many such films later). For the young actor, these films constituted the period of apprenticeship and failed largely in establishing him on a sound footing. However, his potential was soon to be recognized and exploited by some of the best directors of this period.

'Those Were My Formative Years': Dilip Kumar Remembers His Days at Bombay Talkies

'Bombay Talkies was an institution the like of which I cannot sight anywhere today. It was said in those days that it had the aura of Shantiniketan [the institution near Calcutta associated with Nobel Laureate Rabindranath Tagore] ...

'I can vividly recall the mornings with Mrs Rai (Devika Rani) tending the flowering plants in the garden herself. She was so poised and dignified and elegant and very kind. She was a remarkably intelligent woman herself and was a perfectionist in her work. We were in awe of her, too. It was she who gave me my first break in films and I learned a number of useful lessons from her. She noticed that I had potential and talent and certain natural propensities and she also saw my application to my work and so she used to call me sometimes and give me very valuable advice ...

'The studio employed practically all the established writers of the time. They were not required to write regularly, but as and when their services were required they were sought and consulted ...

'I must say that Bombay Talkies produced men and women who went on to achieve great fame. If you take a count of all the men and women who emerged from Bombay Talkies you will find quite a few illustrious names of today. Later, when one went over to other studios one missed all its great qualities. To belong to Bombay Talkies in those days itself [sic] was something of an achievement .... Its board of directors was made up of eminent persons and it had a social status.'

Source: An interview with Udaya Tara Nayar, Screen, 5 October 1984.

Notes and References

1.   Bunny Reuben, *Dilip Kumar: Star Legend of Indian Cinema – The Definitive Biography*, New Delhi: HarperCollins, 2004, p. 62.

Chapter 5

Dilip Kumar as Numero Uno

By the time Indian cinema entered its classical phase in the late 1940s, Dilip Kumar had virtually completed his self-discovery as an actor. The great directors of that era soon embarked on a journey to realize their cinematic vision with the new actor as their main protagonist. In the coming years, these directors, inspired by the actor's tremendous felicity and impressive acting acumen, finally established the persona of Indian cinema's first *true* indigenous hero by using K. L. Saigal's prototype as its basis.

The Classical Phase of Indian Cinema:
Perfecting the Cinematic Expression

The emergence of Dilip Kumar as the indigenous hero happened to coincide with the arrival of the classical era of Indian cinema. Therefore, before analysing the career graph of this hero, it would be worthwhile to undertake a short overview of this period.

With the early institutions having laid the foundation and film technology having largely been mastered, Indian cinema entered a new creative phase. This phase was essentially marked by four qualitative changes: an expansion of the thematic concerns and innovations in storytelling; greater technical expertise and means for enhancing of narrative pace as well as the overall aesthetic appeal; a further refinement in the emotional content; and, finally, the evolution of the classical film melody.

These developments propelled the Indian film much further beyond the impact of theatre and the technical imperfections of the earlier period.

Mehboob Khan, V. Shantaram, Sohrab Modi, Bimal Roy, Nitin Bose and Amiya Chakravarty, among others, were the first-generation film makers who laid the foundation of what is termed as the classical period of Hindi cinema (from the late 1940s to the mid-1960s). Although they had their roots in the formative phase, these visionaries, with their trademark styles, helped in developing an indigenous form of the Indian film not only in the way a story was told, with definite socio-cultural bearings, but also by introducing a wide range of innovations in narration, treatment and film-making techniques.

Along with the continuing contributions by the aforementioned first-generation masters, entirely fresh inputs (both thematic and aesthetic) were provided by the group of second-generation directors, such as Kidar Sharma, K. A. Abbas, Chetan Anand, Raj Kapoor, Guru Dutt, Ramesh Sehgal, Raja Nawathe and Mahesh Kaul. The outcome of the efforts of these two generations of film makers was a complete mastery over the narrative as well as the elimination of earlier technical flaws. The film-making potential in the classical period indeed was at its highest artistic peak, leading to the development of many progressively refined and highly appealing genres.

The classical film genres were largely the creation of five distinct schools, each governed by the distinct style represented by its main architects.

Mehboob Khan and Bimal Roy along with their camp followers, respectively, represented the indigenous cultural format largely rooted in the backdrop of the Hindi heartland, Uttar Pradesh, and Bengal in the east.

Sohrab Modi, V. Shantaram and S. S. Vasan specialized in creating the classic, exotic Oriental narrative and also intense message-oriented melodrama revolving around a social problem.

The banners of Raj Kapoor and Dev Anand, on the other hand,

were engaged in articulating, through an elaborate entertainment mode, the problems and aspirations of the rapidly modernizing urban Indian society.

The neo-realist school, spearheaded by K. A. Abbas, Ramesh Sehgal and Zia Sarhadi, proceeded to design the popular political film largely influenced by European and Soviet cinema.

The last school – representing the cinema of despair, with Guru Dutt in the forefront – was far more intense and sharply focused in the sense that it responded to an individual's predicament in the context of the wider socio-politico-cultural reality.

***

At the level of thematic development, Indian cinema in this era began to distance itself from its earlier dedication to mythology and fairy-tale adventurism and expanded its domain to cover a vast range of genres. Some of the major concerns of Indian literature were also meticulously incorporated in cinema. In this process, it fulfilled an important social function by depicting on screen the main agenda of Indian society at that time: interpreting human suffering in an inequitable society and attempting to release the cultural traditions from the influences of the recent colonial past.

The basic emotional structure of the films in the classical era, as in the formative period, had its roots in the medieval Bhakti and Sufi traditions. Leading a life submerged in the platonic, sublime love for the soulmate through a cycle of union and separation became the main theme of the films. Therefore, the protagonist was presented essentially as an introvert, a restless soul in search of his identity through love and suffering. The intense pathos, which characterized a large part of the cinema of this period, reflected the internal suffering of a nation at large. Traumatic events, such as the Partition of 1947, the large-scale killings and the mass uprooting of people that followed, created a deep sense of insecurity. The film makers took up the task of alleviating the nation's pain and anguish through highly appealing storytelling, scene by scene and frame by frame.

The characteristic features of the films in the classical period can now be highlighted:

- locating the narrative and the ambience in a relevant social-political and historical context;
- exploiting film technology and carrying forward innovations to enhance the aesthetic appeal of the narration;
- blending a series of melodies with the narrative to enrich the appeal of a film and lending to it a distinct identity; and
- promoting compulsive repeated viewing among the audiences who would like to renew the intimate film experience again and again.

The Landmarks

During this period, Sohrab Modi's Minerva Movietone continued to churn out historicals and period films including *Jhansi Ki Rani* (1953, the first Indian film in Technicolor), *Mirza Ghalib* (1954), *Raj Hath* (1956) and *Nausherwan-e-Adil* (1957). V. Shantaram entered the highly creative second phase by enriching Indian cinema with his masterpieces – *Dr Kotnis Ki Amar Kahani* (1946), *Dahej* (1950), *Amar Bhopali* (1951), *Parchhaiyain* (1952), *Teen Batti Char Raaste* (1953), *Subah Ka Tara* (1954), *Jhanak Jhanak Payal Baje* (1955), *Do Aankhen Barah Haath* (1957) and *Navrang* (1959). In the realm of cinema and international politics in the post-Second World War period, *Dr Kotnis Ki Amar Kahani*[1] became an important document. S. S. Vasan contributed many memorable films like *Nishan* (1949), *Mangla* (1950), *Sansar* (1951), *Mr Sampat* (1952) and *Raj Tilak* (1958). As already mentioned in Chapter 3, *Mr Sampat* was based on the renowned writer R. K. Narayan's novel, and presented the suave Motilal in the memorable role of a gentleman crook.

Mehboob Khan announced his spectacular entry into the classical phase with gems such as *Anmol Ghadi* (1946), *Anokhi Ada* (1948), *Andaz* (1949), *Aan* (1952) and *Amar* (1954). And then came his magnum opus, the classic *Mother India* (1957).[2] Bimal Roy's amazing creativity during this period resulted in masterpieces such as *Do Bigha Zameen* (1953), *Devdas* (1955), *Kabuliwala* (1956),* *Madhumati* (1958), *Yahudi* (1958), *Sujata* (1959), *Parakh* (1960), *Usne Kaha Tha* (1960, based on a famous Hindi short story by Chandradhar Guleri) and *Bandini* (1963). Hemen Gupta directed the memorable *Taksak* (1956) and Nitin Bose enlarged his film portfolio with *Mashaal* (1950), *Deedar* (1951), *Waris* (1954) and *Ganga Jumna* (1961). Amiya Chakravarty made his most memorable films in this period: *Badal* (1951), *Daag* (1952), *Patita* (1953) and *Seema* (1955).

While Mehboob Khan, Bimal Roy and Shantaram were busy giving a new orientation to the mainstream cinema, a progressive neo-realist wave was also surging in Bombay, almost at the same time when it became the vogue in Europe. This early 'new wave' (though there was no concept of a parallel cinema at that time) was part of a cultural movement launched by the Indian People's Theatre Association (IPTA). Born amidst the turmoil of the Second World War and the agony of the Bengal famine of 1943 (which, according to some reports, resulted in the death of more than three million people), not only did IPTA play a unique role in the revival of the Indian theatre but it also became a springboard for new talent in journalism and films. The pioneers of the neo-realist cinema were totally committed and highly talented individuals such as K. A. Abbas, Chetan Anand, Zia Sarhadi, Balraj Sahni, Mulk Raj Anand, Rajender Singh Bedi, Joytendra Mitra, Shambhu Mitra, Uday Shankar and Ravi Shankar and his wife, Annapurna.

K. A. Abbas emerged as an important player during this period, coming up with low-budget, but purposeful, films. *Dharti*

---

* *Kabuliwala* was produced by Bimal Roy and directed by Hemen Gupta.

Ke Lal (1946) and *Munna* (1954), made under his banner Naya Sansar Productions, won international acclaim, the latter being singled out by Prime Minister Jawaharlal Nehru for praise. His other notable films were: *Rahi* (1952) based on Mulk Raj Anand's novel, *Anhoni* (1954), *Pardesi* (1957), *Char Dil Char Rahen* (1959) and *Shehar Aur Sapna* (1963).

Chetan Anand made his highly impressive debut with his memorable film *Neecha Nagar* (1946). Zia Sarhadi pitched in with three significant films of the era: *Hum Log* (1951), *Footpath* (1953) and *Awaaz* (1956).

Raj Kapoor, one of the most celebrated film makers of the classical period (and even later), set up R. K. Studios in Chembur, a suburb of Bombay, as early as in 1948, becoming perhaps the youngest actor-producer-director of the era. After his first two films, *Aag* (1948) and *Barsaat* (1949) in which he played serious roles, he went in for a complete turnaround in his screen persona. In collaboration with Abbas, he evolved his own version of an Indian Charlie Chaplin, through the amalgamation of proletarian themes (which formed the 'staple diet' for the Leftist Abbas) with his own quixotic romantic flavour.

The R. K. banner produced some landmark films during this period: *Awara* (1951), *Aah* (1953), *Boot Polish* (1955), *Jagte Raho* (1957) and *Jis Desh Mein Ganga Behti Hai* (1960). Raj Kapoor's cinema projected the attainment of political intelligence as a loss of innocence and the acquisition of excess wealth at the expense of the downtrodden as despicable. His characters were almost constantly yearning for a new idyllic world. The result was a rather socially pretentious but a highly entertaining cinematic genre. In contrast to Mehboob Khan's rural emphasis, Raj Kapoor took up the rich-versus-poor conflict in a metropolitan milieu. Yet, like Mehboob's works, Kapoor's oeuvre also performed a socio-political function by taking up many populist slogans as themes: for instance, 'houses for all' in *Shri 420*, the uplift of working children in *Boot Polish*, Sarvodya's (a Gandhian concept, literally meaning 'uplift of all') non-violent answer to the dacoit problem in *Jis Desh Mein Ganga Behti Hai* and the 'Clean Ganga' mission in *Ram Teri Ganga Maili* released much later (in 1985). But unlike Mehboob Khan and Bimal Roy, the cinema of Raj Kapoor was far less culture specific and could easily be transferred to another ambience. This factor could be one explanation for the immense popularity of Raj Kapoor's films abroad.

Like Raj Kapoor, Dev Anand also started his career with serious roles (*Ziddi* 1948, *Vidhya* 1948, *Khel* 1949, *Jeet* 1949, *Afsar* 1950, *Sanam* 1951, *Rahi* 1952 and *Aandhiyian* 1952). He unfurled his own banner, Navketan Films, in 1949, in collaboration with elder brother Chetan Anand. Younger brother Vijay Anand joined his siblings in 1953. This banner became the harbinger of a slew of films that focused on the growing complexities of life in the metropolis of Bombay. Memorable films produced under the Navketan banner were: *Baazi* (1952), *Aandhiyan* (1952), *Taxi Driver* (1955), *House Number 44* (1955), *Funtoosh* (1957), *Kala Bazaar* (1960) and the masterpiece, *Guide* (1965). Chetan Anand, apart from directing films for Navketan, also made *Anjali* (1957), a Buddhist tale, and later the classic, *Haqeeqat* (1964), one of the very few realistic Indian war films till date. His other films include *Heer Ranjha* (1970), *Hindustan Ki Kasam* (another war film) and *Hanste Zakhm* (both 1973) and *Sahib Bahadur* (1976).

The classical era is also indebted to five other masters: A. R. Kardar, Kidar Sharma, S. U. Sunny, B. R. Chopra and Guru Dutt. Kardar remained preoccupied with psycho-social melodramas and love tales in films like *Dard* (1949), *Dastaan* (1950), *Jadoo* (1951) and *Do Phool* (1958). Kidar Sharma reached the zenith of his intense creative work with *Suhaag Raat* (1948), *Jogan* (1950), *Banwre Nain* (1950), *Jaldeep* (1956) and *Hamari Yaad Aayegi* (1961). Sunny worked in a familiar love story format (*Mela* 1949, *Babul* 1950 and *Udan Khatola* 1955), but broke new ground with the rip-roaring comedy *Kohinoor* (1960).

Baldev Raj Chopra, one of the most consistent and influential film makers of Hindi cinema, heralded a wave of socially committed cinema using a highly innovative commercial format with films like *Afsana* (1951), *Ek Hi Raasta* (1956), *Naya Daur* (1957) and *Sadhana* (1958). Like Amiya Chakravarty, he would take a contemporary social problem and dissect it to the core. *Dhool Ka Phool* (1959) and *Dharmaputra* (1961) were directed by younger brother Yash Chopra under the BR banner.

Guru Dutt, the intense, hypersensitive film maker, left his indelible mark with a memorable potpourri of classics consisting of *Baazi* (1951), *Aar Paar* (1954), *CID* (1956), *Mr and Mrs 55* (1955), *Pyaasa* (1957), *Kagaz Ke Phool* (1959) and *Sahib, Bibi Aur Ghulam* (1962).

The banner of Filmistan occupied a distinguished place in the classical era. The memorable output of this studio included Ramesh Sehgal's *Shaheed* (1948), *Samadhi* (1950) and *Shikast* (1953); Kishore Sahu's *Bade Sarkar* (1954) and *Nadiya Ke Paar* (1948); B. Mitra's *Shabnam* (1949); Nandlal Jaswantlal's *Anarkali* (1953) and *Nagin* (1954); Subodh Mukerjee's *Paying Guest* (1957) and *Love Marriage* (1959); I. S. Johar's *Nastik* (1954); and Satyen Bose's *Jagriti* (1954).

Two movie 'mughals' arrived during this period in a big way, K. Asif and Kamal Amrohi. Asif's meteoric rise is all the more curious because he is associated with only four films in a career span of three decades: *Phool* (1945); *Hulchal* (1951, as producer), a social; *Mughal-e-Azam* (1960), a historical spectacle; and *Love and God*, which he could not complete during his lifetime (1924–71), but was eventually released in 1986. Kamal Amrohi directed *Mahal* (1949) for Bombay Talkies, as the country's first mystery film. He also made *Daera* (1953) on suffering womanhood and ungratified love and his classic, *Pakeezah* (1972), depicted the rupturing of values and patriarchical dominance in a feudal aristocratic milieu, portrayed through the suffering of the protagonist and her eventual emancipation. In both these movies the heroine was his wife, Meena Kumari.

Apart from the big names, many other film makers also made significant contributions to one or the other classical film genre. Notable among them were Mahesh Kaul, Vijay Bhatt, S. N. Tripathi, Raja Nawathe, M. Sadiq, R. C. Talwar, P. L. Santoshi, D. D. Kashyap, Raj Khosla, Ramanand Sagar, Nasir Hussain and Shakti Samanta.[3]

This period also launched a highly innovative and creative film maker: Hrishikesh Mukherjee. As the protégé of Bimal Roy, he enriched the classic era with his creations like *Musafir* (1957), *Anari* (1959), *Anuradha* (1960), *Chhaya* (1961) and *Asli Naqli* (1962). *Anari* was noteworthy as much for Raj Kapoor's outstanding role as a simpleton trapped amidst the intrigues of a cruel and scheming world as for Motilal's slick performance as an avaricious business magnate. *Anuradha* juxtaposed a husband's (Balraj Sahni) total devotion to medicine with his wife's (Leela Naidu) complete dedication to the purity of music – an unusual theme in Hindi cinema. Mukherjee, who had the immense ability to keep his creative zeal alive amidst changing trends, was to become a major influence in the post-classical period.

In spite of the overall serious tone and mood, the classical era also saw the maturing of comedy as a genre. Apart from the Chaplinsque Raj Kapoor, there were a set of superclowns – Gope, Bhagwan, Kishore Kumar, Johnny Walker, Dhumal, Mukhri, I. S. Johar, Anoop Kumar and Agha.[4] (Mehmood made his mark a few years later as an ace comedian.)

The technical support system played a crucial role during the classical period. Highly talented cinematographers, editors, sound recordists and set designers continued extensive research to master the film technology and to meet the changing demands of the narrative and aesthetics as being envisioned by the film makers. Many of these professionals were not formally trained, and they acquired their skills through an elaborate system of on-the-job training as assistants to a master technician who would gradually impart the inputs of the trade through the actual process of film making. Notable among these stalwarts were photographers V. Baba Saheb, Fardoon Irani, R. D. Mathur, Fali Mistry, Kamal Bose, Radhu Karmakar, Dilip Gupta, V. Ratra, V. Avadhoot, Dwarka Divecha, Jaywant Pathare, Sudhendu Roy, V. K. Murthy and M. N. Malhotra and sound recordist R. Kaushik.

International Recognition won by Mainstream Cinema during the Classical Period

- *Amar Bhopali*: Best sound recording, Cannes, 1952.
- *Do Bigha Zameen*: Cannes, 1954.
- *Aan*: Background music records issued in London, 1952.
- *Jagte Raho*: Grand Prix at Karlovy Vary (now in the Czech Republic), 1956.
- *Jaldeep* by Kidar Sharma: Best children film award, Venice, 1956.
- *Pardesi*: first Indo–Soviet co-production, co-directed by K. A. Abbas and V. Pronin, 1957.
- *Gautam The Buddha*: Special certificate of merit, Bimal Roy (shared with Rajbans Khanna), Cannes, 1958.
- *Mother India*: (i) Best foreign film nomination, Oscar, 1958, and (ii) best actress award for Nargis, Karlovy Vary, 1958.
- *Do Aankhen Barah Haath*: (i) Best foreign film, the Catholic Bureau's Prize; (ii) the Hollywood Press Association Award; (iii) Samuel Goldwyn Award; and (iv) Special Award (Silver Bear), the Berlin Film Festival, 1958.
- *Ganga Jumna*: Special honour to Dilip Kumar, Karlovy Vary, 1962.
- *Guide* (1965): (i) English version made as an Indo–US co-production, directed by Ted Danielewski; Pearl S. Buck, the famous author and Nobel Laureate, was the co-producer of the foreign version and (ii) best actress award for Waheeda Rehman, the Chicago International Film Festival.
- As an example in reverse, *Naya Daur* (1957) was banned by the French Government in Algeria.

A large number of highly talented scenarists and dialogue writers also made their contribution in the making of the classical film. The famed ones included: Inder Raj Anand, Rajender Singh Bedi, Sadat Hasan Manto, Pandit Mukhram Sharma, Ali Raza, Wajahat Mirza, R. S. Choudhary, Kamal Amrohi, Zia Sarhadi, Ramanand Sagar, Rajinder Kishen and K. A. Abbas.

The films that heralded the classical era in Hindi cinema were: *Shaheed* (1948), *Barsaat* (1949), *Mahal* (1949), *Baazi* (1951), *Aan* (1952), *Baiju Bawra* (1952), *Anarkali* (1953), *Do Bigha Zameen* (1953) and *Nagin* (1954), each representing a different genre. The golden period tapered off with *Ganga Jumna* (1961), *Ek Musafir Ek Hasina* (1962), *Mamta* (1965), *Guide* (1965) and *Pakeezah* (which was in the making for more than a decade and was ultimately released in 1972).

The 'Invention' of the Film Melody

By around 1947, when the Saigal era was about to end, the film song suddenly underwent a radical transformation. This genre of music got liberated from its classical royal court and courtesan hangover, and in this simplification, it became lighter and more melodious.[5] The quest for its melodious form can be said to have ended with Khemchand Prakash's score for *Mahal* (1949) and Shankar Jaikishan's compositions for *Barsaat* the same year. These two films announced the beginning of the famous golden age of film melody of the 1950s.

The development of the film melody was carried out by three distinct schools: the first school was represented by Anil Biswas and Khemchand Prakash (followed by Naushad, Ghulam Mohammed and S. N Tripathi); the second by Sachin Dev Burman, Salil Choudhury (as well as Hemant Kumar); and the third by Ghulam Haider and Shyam Sunder (and later by Hansraj Bahl, O. P. Nayyar and Khayyam). Broadly, these schools, respectively, introduced the folk forms of Uttar Pradesh, Bengal and Punjab to Hindi film music. The scene was further enriched by composers Husnlal Bhagatram (duo), C. Ramchandra, Sajjad Husain, Vasant Desai, Roshan, Madan Mohan, Jaidev, Shankar Jaikishan (duo), Chitragupta, Ravi, Nashaad (not to be confused with Naushad), Iqbal Qureshi and S. Mohinder. In the illustrious company of these music directors, the second-generation singers had arrived a big way to usher in the golden era of film melody of the 1950s: Shamshad Begum, Lata Mangeshkar, Suraiya, Geeta Dutt, Talat Mehmood, Mukesh (Mukesh Chand Mathur), Mohammed Rafi, Manna Dey, Kishore Kumar, Hemant Kumar and Asha Bhosle amongst others.

Anil Biswas, a revolutionary-turned-composer, came up with pathbreaking music for films like *Arzoo* (1950), *Tarana* (1951), *Rahi* (1952), *Pardesi* (1957) and *Sautela Bhai* (1962). Khemchand Prakash, the creator of the haunting melody *Aayegaa ... Aanewala* in *Mahal* was an expert classical musician from Rajasthan. His other memorable films during the classical era were: *Samaj Ko Badal Dalo* (1947), *Ziddi* (1948), *Rimjhim* (1949) and *Jaan Pehchan* (1950).

S. D. Burman (originally from Tripura) represented the Bengal school of film music where the composer quite often was also a versatile singer. A favourite of Navketan Films, Bimal Roy and Guru Dutt, he was among the first to compose film songs in tune with the demands of the narrative.

Ghulam Haider, the founder of the Lahore school of film music, was among the pioneers to define the Hindi film song with its indigenous aesthetics and appeal. Along with Shyam Sunder, Khurshid Anwar and S. D. Batish, he introduced Punjabi folk rhythms and the use of percussion instruments like the *dholak* (a kind of drum played by hand). His score for Pancholi's *Khazanchi* (1941) saw Shamshad Begum attain immense popularity. He also gave Lata Mangeshkar her first big break in *Majboor* (1948).

In the development of film music, the contribution of Naushad has been unique. At one level he was a forerunner in creating classical music-based film melodies and making them widely acceptable. At another level, as a pioneer of the use of film orchestra, he was the first to recognize the importance of background music in the real sense of the term. He composed the musical score of nearly all the films produced by the mughals Mehboob Khan, K. Asif, A. R. Kardar and S. U. Sunny.

Vasant Desai (along with Vasant Pawar) has been credited with the change in the whole complexion of the Marathi film score, particularly with the use of '*lavni*' folk music. He laid the musical foundation of many of Shantaram's classics. C. Ramchandra introduced a totally Westernized score in *Albela* (1951), an all-time hit for its music. In nearly all his films he also sang a large number of songs under his surname Chitalkar.

The score of O. P. Nayyar represented a curious mix of Punjabi folk and Latin American music. A hot favourite of the early Guru Dutt films and other banners, his enticing music never failed a film. He based many of his songs on the beat generated by horse hooves.

The music director duo that responded fully to the changing milieu was Shankar Jaikishan. Their repertoire was amazing, and their compositions spanned a wide range. An important exception in their long career was *Basant Bahar* (1956) in which their score was completely based on classical ragas.

Three films, which became important milestones for the film melody, were Vijay Bhat's *Baiju Bawra* (1952, music by Naushad), Filmistan's *Anarkali* (1953, music by C. Ramchandra) and *Nagin* (1954). The last-mentioned movie heralded the arrival of the highly accomplished singer-composer, Hemant Kumar, a rare breed in Indian films. Like his contemporary Salil Choudhury, he was a leading activist in Bengal's IPTA and composed some of the best songs for the movement. Salil Choudhury made his mark in Hindi cinema with his score for Bimal Roy's films: *Do Bigha Zameen* (1953), *Madhumati* (1958), *Parakh* (1960) and *Usne Kaha Tha* (1960).

Two outstanding composers, who took melody, particularly the *ghazal* (a form of Persian/Urdu poetry that can be easily set to music), to new heights were Roshan (Roshan Lal Nagrath) and Madan Mohan (Madan Mohan Kohli). Roshan's score in films like *Chandni Chowk* (1954), *Taj Mahal* (1963) and *Mamta* (1965) and that of Madan Mohan in *Ada* (1951), *Adalat* (1958), *Anpadh* (1962), *Ghazal* (1964) and *Jahanara* (1964) remain landmarks.

Three lyricists who revolutionized the Hindi film song, both thematically and linguistically, were Majrooh Sultanpuri (real name Asrar-ul Hassan Khan), Shailendra (full name Shankardas Kesarilal Shailendra) and Sahir Ludhianvi (real name Abdul Hayee). Majrooh was the undisputed monarch of film lyrics, whose songs have been sung by early masters like K. L. Saigal to the present-day singers like Udit Narayan and Alka Yagnik. He wrote beautiful lyrics for all kinds of situations, be it romantic, patriotic, comic or sad. Sahir, the radical poet, with Marxist leanings and owing allegiance to the Faiz Ahmed Faiz school,* was the first to popularize the new trends in Urdu poetry through the film medium. Shailendra contributed a great deal to the use of colloquial language and the progressive content in the film song. Other talents such as Pradeep, Bharat Vyas, Shakeel Badayuni, Rajinder Kishen, Raja Mehdi Ali Khan, Kaifi Azmi, Qamar Jalalabadi, Hasrat Jaipuri. Khumar Barabankavi and Prem Dhawan also made the film song not only meaningful but also immensely popular. Other meritorious lyricists who could not make it really big in the films during the classical period included Indivar, Sardar Jafri, Anjaan, Asad Bhopali, Farookh Kaiser, Akhtar Romani and Kaif Irfani.

One multifaceted genius of this era was Kishore Kumar, the yodelling expert and a great comedian. He not only pioneered the comedy song in Hindi film music but also brought on screen some of the most passionate and sensuous songs.

The Heroes Make Their Presence Felt

The 'magic' of the classical period, which began soon after

---

* Faiz was a legendary Pakistani poet whose works were thought-provoking and inspired many generations. In 1951, he was arrested on charges of 'conspiracy' by the Pakistan Government.

independence, was created by the presence of the best talent ever in Indian cinema at that point of time. A galaxy of artistes – heroes, heroines as well as supporting actors and actresses – each with his or her distinct style and screen persona helped in bringing on celluloid some of the most remarkable films in Indian cinema. However, as already said earlier, the key requirement of the cinema of this period was the creation of the persona of its indigenous hero who would help not only in channelizing the emerging thematic concerns, but also in providing to the cinema its complete national identity. This hero, in the changed milieu, was to project on screen, with profundity, spontaneity and ease, the realities of the times and thus achieve a powerful universal appeal.

Among the young heroes, apart from the trio of Dilip Kumar, Raj Kapoor and Dev Anand, other luminaries-in-the-making such as Karan Diwan, Suresh, Shekhar, Ajit and Premnath had also arrived on the scene. Raaj Kumar, Guru Dutt, Bharat Bhushan, Sunil Dutt and Pradeep Kumar constituted an impressive array. As mentioned earlier, after a few initial serious movies, Raj Kapoor opted completely for a Chaplinsque image, while Dev Anand deliberately invoked an imitation of the debonair and, at times, jaunty Hollywood giant Gregory Peck (whose major films include *Keys of the Kingdom*, *Roman Holiday*, *The Guns of Navarone* and *Mackenna's Gold* and who won the Oscar in 1963 for his role in the film *To Kill a Mockingbird*).

Raaj Kumar, an icon in film acting in his own right and a strong contender for the status of the indigenous hero, exhibited immense abilities in coming up with down-to-earth portrayals of a sufferer as in *Mother India* (1957), *Godan* (1963) and *Dil Ek Mandir* (1963). But the actor, towering, but sometimes stiff, soon got stereotyped in larger-than-life portrayals. He never really looked at ease in romantic and comic roles. Guru Dutt was also a strong contender for the aforementioned slot, considering his awe-inspiring screen persona. But he was more of a visionary film maker than a complete actor, and his priorities were thus divided.

Bharat Bhushan presented a reasonable continuity of the K. L. Saigal image in terms of screen presence and also in terms of the roles the master took up in some of his films (*Chandidas, Bhakta Surdas* and *Tansen*), but was far less intense. He lent credibility to many memorable musicals and period films of the era such as *Baiju Bawra, Shabab, Basant Bahar, Sohni Mahiwal, Mirza Ghalib* and *Jahanara*. With his natural flair for performing in historical films or those based upon mythology and folk tales, Bharat Bhushan contributed magnificently in capturing the true Indian spirit. In his characterizations, he appeared gentle, sophisticated, poet-like and projected a kind of innocence, which was to become the hallmark of classical cinema. But again his repertoire was rather limited. Other stars, such as Ajit, Suresh, Karan Diwan, Sunil Dutt, Pradeep Kumar, Shammi Kapoor and Rajendra Kumar, were durable without being spectacular.

Dilip Kumar's cinema, in contrast, set the dominant trend in Indian cinema of this period. Not only did his portrayals become predominantly the indigenous benchmarks, but they also marked an excellence in histrionics as far as range and depth were concerned. Such a calibre was not exhibited by any of his contemporaries. The hero represented by him captured the angst and the suffering of a romantic engaged in an utopian search for harmony, both spiritual and material, in a highly unequal and inequitable world. Such a world was also torn between the traditional and the modern, and between the prevalence of myths and the dynamics of the emerging social changes due to industrialization and urbanization.

Dilip Kumar's Films and Portrayals in the Classical Period

The classical phase not only encompassed some of Dilip Kumar's best films, but it also showed how cinema could create a model of the indigenous hero as inspired by the socio-politico-cultural demands of the times. In this phase, the actor's identity was characterized by a complex cultural/historical/psychological pattern displaying the anxieties of a newly independent nation. Such a pattern depicted, allegorically, the painful transition from the pre-Partition childhood to a deep sense of uprootedness and despair caused by the event. His portrayals often presented him as an innocent lover entrapped amidst, and often destroyed by, the powerful oppressive social forces.

The basic features of the Dilip Kumar 'model' were clearly identifiable: an introvert who has been greviously wronged by society, takes it to his heart and generates a complete catharsis through a whole range of emotions. He portrayed the search for an ideal self, that is, one proclaiming true emancipation through platonic love, but desires such emancipation only in a just and equitable society. Since that is not possible in reality, the self has to perish so as to validate this idealized conviction. The actor, in fact, represented the popular Saratchandra image of a vulnerable, self-destructing hero in Bengali literature. And yet, often an improvisation in the form of comedy was also built in to provide relief from the overall depressing mood of the film.

The roles portrayed by Dilip Kumar during this period can be analysed under the following four themes:

- Internalized suffering and emancipation through unfulfilled love.
- The anti-hero manifestations.
- The neo-realistic context.
- Towards the liberation of the image.

Internalized Suffering and Emancipation through Unfulfilled Love

In many early films of the classical phase, Dilip Kumar's characterizations were built around the premise of unrequited love. A string of films such as *Jugnu* (1947), *Nadiya Ke Paar* (1948), *Mela* (1948), *Anokha Pyar* (1948), *Shabnam* (1949), *Andaz* (1949), *Arzoo* (1950), *Jogan* (1950), *Deedar* (1951), *Hulchal* (1951), *Devdas*

(1955), *Insaniyat* (1955), *Udan Khatola* (1955), *Musafir* (1957), *Yahudi* (1958) and *Mughal-e-Azam* (1960) helped the actor consolidate the basic traits of his personality on celluloid. His characterizations, in fact, determined the very tenor of these films.

The plot in these movies essentially centred around a woman's love – the compulsive longing, the short-lived winning over, and the aftermath of separation, i.e., anguish and suffering. The protagonist seemed to be interpreting the larger society's suffering as a personal grief. This portrayal, in essence, represented an agonized, self-pitying and self-indulgent hero who helped the viewers in releasing their own trapped emotions of hopelessness and despair. For the viewers, the in-built metaphor of destruction of the self (often through alcohol) and a perpetual death wish (or the inevitability of overhanging death) had the same appeal as that of the sacrifice of a hero for an intimate or greater cause. All the situations in a film had the basic objective of creating a pensive and masochistic character who appeared to be enjoying his pain but, at the same time, seemed to be sinking deeper into it.

At a different level, the roots of the mass appeal of such a *tragic image* (and as in the case of K. L. Saigal too) can be traced to our folk culture. Since medieval times, the ultimate greatness of love and the inevitability of painful separation found expression in a spectrum of folk tales, songs and drama and became an important and inseparable part of the heritage of the Indian subcontinent. The basic structures of these films, despite most of them being set in contemporary times, therefore, were inspired by the innumerable love legends in which the status quo in society was challenged and provoked through the manifestation of socially forbidden love. This love was internalized by the lovers as suffering and they would often find their salvation only through the meeting of the souls in heaven after death. Thus, the Oriental concept of sacrificing one's physical form, the body, for a cause led to the immortality of the soul.

This unfulfilled love for the 'beloved' – invariably used as a euphemism for god – in fact, was a central theme of the medieval Bhakti Movement. The origins of this movement lay in the by and large passive response of the masses to feudal oppression. The ultimate emancipation was portrayed as a seemingly unending internal suffering and not as an external struggle against the oppressors. Such suffering was rationalized and even justified through a greater and nobler vision of life, in which seeking the loving attention of the 'beloved' was presented as the sole purpose of existence.

The social setting of the aforementioned films of Dilip Kumar was invariably feudal. The authenticity of the story and the period depicted in these films were of secondary importance to the main theme of unfulfilled love. As in most folk tales, the romance was invariably located at the interface between the rich and poor and the conflict arose over the social unacceptability of the love affair. This affair would not only become the central issue around which these two segments of society interacted and reaffirmed their social positions, but also emerged as the only instrument of social protest for addressing the problem of social inequality.

In these films, childhood love occupied a prominent place. Such love invariably blossomed against the backdrop of the huge chasm between the aristocracy and the common people. This aspect perhaps was a reflection of the mood of the masses in the post-independence period, when the expectations of a new life and a new social order based on equality had soon started looking gloomy. The innocent and delicate craving between two tender souls always became a victim of the tyranny of family elders and subsequently of the social inequalities. As the childhood lovers reach adulthood, they carry with them the earlier intense infatuation and undergo the agony of separation, which often finds solace in a mutual death pact. Dilip Kumar's persona in this period also projected another dimension: the 'one-way love syndrome' that soon was to become a typical feature of Indian cinema. This love was perceived by the sufferer as his only means of emancipation;

in fact, virtually the essence of his existence. And it took distinct forms in different films.

Shaukat Hussain Rizvi's *Jugnu*, a scathing attack on the decadent feudal values, can be considered the first tragedy film of Dilip Kumar. In this extremely passionate love story set amidst a university campus, the actor, for the first time, revealed his trademark ability to transform the character from a rib-tickling comedian in the first half of the narrative to a tragedian par excellence in the latter half, a trend seen in many of his subsequent films. Ashok, the hero, is a jovial, fun-loving college student belonging to a rich aristocratic family. He and his college mates (including singer Mohammed Rafi who appeared in a small role) play a prank or two with a bunch of girl students who have come to enjoy a picnic on the banks of a lake. The hero falls in love with Jugnu (Noorjehan), but she refuses to accept the overtures of this persuasive suitor. Consequently, he climbs on to a huge rock and threatens to jump into the lake and kill himself if she keeps on rejecting him. Jugnu is swayed by this antic and pleads with him to come down.

As the love affair builds up through a series of comic encounters, the hero's father, a landed aristocrat gone bankrupt, forces him to marry a girl from a rich family in order to pay off his debts, which he had incurred to maintain his feudal lifestyle. The heart-broken heroine falls seriously ill and eventually dies. Unable to bear the anguish of lost love, the hero jumps into the lake from the same spot where he had earlier threatened to commit suicide.

S. U. Sunny's *Mela* and Kishore Sahu's *Nadiya Ke Paar*, both released in 1948, celebrated the saga of unmerited love in the form of an improvised folk tale. These films established not only the dominant childhood love theme and the inevitable death syndrome in Dilip Kumar's cinema, but also his persona as a restless seeker of love.

Mela (heroine Nargis) was set against a rural backdrop, where the two adolescent lovers serenade each other, unaware of the cruel and harsh world around them. They represent their love as a pair of mud dolls, living happily in a small mud house, and enter into a pact of upholding their love at all costs. But the resourceful villain (presented as a city-returned conman) creates havoc in their innocent lives. And as the two dolls are broken, the lovers also die, thus upholding their love pact. Within this simple narrative, the director shows that life is a mere passage of time in which the only meaningful existence is to live for eternal love. Naushad's soul-stirring musical score was another highlight of this film.

Nadiya Ke Paar, in contrast, depicted the immortality of love despite the huge rich–poor divide. This time the river is the metaphor, representing not only this divide but also the only path for the emancipation of the lovers. A curious love affair between the son of a zamindar (Dilip Kumar) and a fisherwoman (Kamini Kaushal), the film takes the lovers through a journey of socially unacceptable love, and in close embrace, they drown in a whirlpool in which their boat gets caught.

In these two films, the young actor made his mark through an eloquent display of emotions: first joy and hope and then suffering and despair. They also prepared him for the series of tragedies, which he was to take up in the following years.

S. U. Sunny

S. U. Sunny, the legendary film maker who has the credit of directing the highest number of Dilip Kumar's films, was the best disciple of A. R. Kardar. He started as an assistant at Kardar Studios. The first film he directed was *Namaste* (1943, jointly with M. Sadiq), followed by *Geet* (1944). After directing *Shanti* (1947) for Firthous Art Productions and *Mela* (1948) for Wadia Movietone, Sunny set up his own banner in 1949 in collaboration with composer Naushad. The first film, *Babul* (1950), was a runaway hit, followed by *Udan Khatola* (1955). He directed his best-known work, *Kohinoor* (1960), under the Citizens' Films banner. Naushad and Shakeel Badayuni provided the musical and lyrical support for all his films except *Shanti* (1947). Like his master's, Sunny films were characterized by the use of conflicting spaces around characters in an otherwise direct narrative, neo-classical décor, heavy lighting and a haunting effect further extended by the grandeur of the musical score.

In M. I. Dharamsey's *Anokha Pyar*, Dilip Kumar found himself in the company of two heroines: Nalini Jaywant and Nargis. Ashok (Dilip Kumar) is an aspiring writer. He comes across a flower seller called Bindiya (Nalini Jaywant) but has the money to buy just one rose. One day, while protecting Bindiya from a tramp who tires to rob her, Ashok loses his eyesight. Bindiya, who falls in love with Ashok, escorts him to a doctor's clinic for treatment. There, Ashok meets Geeta (Nargis), the doctor's daughter, who takes care of him during his convalescence. He falls in love with her. In the end, Bindiya sacrifices her love to pave the way for the two lovers to unite in life.

In *Shabnam*, Filmistan's musical hit directed by Bibhuti Mitra, Dilip Kumar as the restless lover traverses an intricate path of love and hate. The plot again involves a love triangle. Heroine Shanti (Kamini Kaushal), her aged father and a young man, Manoj (Dilip Kumar), are refugees fleeing Rangoon after the 1942 Japanese bombing. They try and make their way to Bengal. Shanti initially disguises herself as a man to avoid being molested. When Manoj discovers her real identity, they fall in love, although he is ensnared by the charms of a gypsy girl (Paro). Shanti accepts shelter from a rich zamindar (Jeevan) who also falls in love with her. She next encounters the hero when the zamindar hosts a gypsy dance: Manoj is part of the troupe but misunderstands Shanti's presence in the palace; he views it as a betrayal.

However, the most powerful portrayal as a one-way love seeker by Dilip Kumar was in Kidar Sharma's *Jogan* (a female ascetic). One of the classics of the times, the film focused on the two possibilities of human emancipation: spiritual solace through *bhakti* (worship) and the realization of a blissful state through suffering in love, both having an eternal dimension of their own. In fact, in its spiritual context, this film attempts to juxtapose the two traditions represented by the Bhakti Movement and Sufism. The heroine (Nargis), deeply immersed in *bhakti*, wants to annihilate herself and become one with the creator, while the hero enjoys the agony of separation from his beloved (upon being spurned by her) so that this intense emotion itself becomes his being.

Delving deeper into the theme, Kidar Sharma builds into this conflict the spiritual transformation of the male seeker who seeks solace in pursuing the woman he desires not only by cajoling her to accept him but also through his own self-realization, which happens later. The film allegorically depicts the man–woman relationship in the context of the spiritual realm and the physical world, in which the separation between the two is represented by the banyan tree located at the final boundary of civilization (in this case the last point of the village; see the matter in screen below for details). The hero, on the other hand, becomes a saint in his own right as he accepts the pain caused by the separation from his object of adulation, while the heroine seeks absolute peace (*Om Shanti*) and finds it only in death.

The Story of *Jogan*

The heroine, Surabhi (Nargis), is a young poetess waiting for the arrival of her ideal handsome lover whom she keeps on referring to in her poetry. But when her debt-ridden father and alcoholic brother fix her marriage with an old zamindar, she runs away, becomes a *sanyasin* and thus seeks to give up her romantic dream about the ideal lover through *bhakti*. Virtually, depicting the sixteenth-century saint-poetess Meerabai incarnate, the heroine goes in quest of Lord Krishna but suppresses her desire for her real seeker in life. Vijay (Dilip Kumar), on hearing Surabhi singing bhajans in the village temple, falls in love with her. Despite her protests, he keeps following her to her *kirtan* assemblies, where she sings the poems penned by Meerabai. Once when the mendicant falls sick, she confines herself to her room in the temple and keeps the door closed. The hero places a fresh flower every day in front of the closed door. After she partially recovers, she decides to leave, unnerved by the constant seeking by the hero for an intimate interaction. Vijay asks her for the notebook in which she used to write poetry but the *jogan* refuses to give it to him. When she leaves, she prohibits the hero from crossing the banyan tree at the end of the village to again reach out to her. She goes away and takes her final refuge in the ashram of her *guru-mata*. She begins praying and fasting. She falls seriously ill because of her unending *tapasya* (penance) for self-purification, and after months when she is about to die, she tells a fellow *jogan*: 'After I die, please go in the direction of that village. When you reach the big banyan tree outside the village, you will find a man sitting there. Please give this book to him.' The *jogan* indeed finds Vijay waiting by the tree and hands over the book to him. Thus, by presenting her poetry to her seeker before dying, the *jogan* pays a tribute to her lover and finally achieves *moksha* (liberation from physical existence).

In *Jogan*, Kidar Sharma deftly employed the concept of 'space' to express his classical romantic idiom. While the heroine has defined her space of autonomy, the hero completely keeps on moving his own space in relation to hers but her rebuffs make him feel disillusioned and suffocated by the intensity of his emotions. *Jogan* enabled Dilip Kumar to further refine his ability in underplaying the character and brought to the audience an enlightening experience far more profound in content and treatment than in his other films of this period. The songs were undeniably melodious and were composed by the relatively unrecognized musician Bulo C. Rani. *Jogan* is remembered even today as a memorable saga of platonic love.

Kidar Sharma

Kidar Sharma (1910–99), the maker of some offbeat films during the classical period, was a genius par excellence. Like Mehboob Khan, he too was a young runaway lured by the magic of cinema. After seeing Debaki Bose's *Puran Bhagat* (1933), he went to Calcutta from Lahore and became an employee of New Theatres. An impressed B. N. Sircar gave him the required break. In New Theatres' *Devdas* (1935), as a scenarist, he pioneered a 'de-theatrical' style of dialogue writing.

In contrast with the realist school, Kidar Sharma's cinema largely focused on the spiritual power of eternal love and the possibility of emancipation of souls through separation and suffering, thus taking further the tradition set by New Theatres in the 1930s. His famous trilogy – *Neel Kamal* (1947), *Banwre Nain* (1950) and *Jogan* (1950) – indicates not only a complete break with the formalistic melodrama, but also his striking ability to explore complex themes, using mystical imagery and an original musical score and a sense of song picturization. With Dilip Kumar, Kidar Sharma did *Jogan*, a one-of-a-kind classic. The film contributed a great deal in projecting Dilip Kumar as a serious actor of great calibre. Towards the end of his career, Kidar Sharma made *Hamari Yaad Aayegee* (1961) introducing his son, Ashok, evoking once again his curious approach to love and suffering. He also made many films for children, including the highly acclaimed *Jaldeep* (1956).

Deedar (directed by Nitin Bose), one of Dilip Kumar's best-known tragic performances, established formally his style of acting and film persona. The film clearly evoked the Homeric legend, with blindness signifying an escape from the unbearable present and mourning for a lost innocence. (Homer, who is credited as the author of the epics *Iliad* and *Odyssey*, was a blind minstrel.) Drawn again on the rural rich–poor divide, the film tracks the painful journey of the destitute boy Shamu (who grows up to become Dilip Kumar) who is unable to forget his childhood sweetheart Mala (who grows up to become Nargis), the daughter of the landlord. The boy and his housemaid mother are thrown out of the landlord's house during a raging storm. The mother is unable to withstand nature's fury and dies and Shamu turns blind. He is rescued and brought up by poor Champa (Nimmi) and her canny guardian, Choudhury (Yakub). Champa falls in love with Shamu, but he just cannot forget Mala. He keeps wandering, singing songs in remembrance of his love, modelled perhaps on K. L. Saigal's portrayal in *Street Singer* (1939).

Dr Kishore (Ashok Kumar), an eye surgeon and the fiancé of Mala, is moved by the melancholic songs of Shamu, and succeeds in restoring his eyesight. The lover, however, blinds himself once again immediately after having a glimpse of his lost childhood sweetheart, who is now engaged to someone else. He thus avenges himself simply by slinking back into the dark alleys of lost love. The film indeed seemed to be articulating the basic premise of Sufism: at last, one glimpse of the beloved! The lover now does not want anything more and his life's mission has been fulfilled.

Hulchal, produced by K. Asif (of *Mughal-e-Azam* fame) and directed by S. K. Ojha, was yet another saga on the travails of childhood love and the tragic social persecution of the hero till his death. The film, like many others of its times, depicted the cruel exploitation of discontented rural migrants by the urban neo-rich to make quick money and alluring them to join the big crime syndicates. Shankar (Dilip Kumar) is a poor lad in love with a landlord's daughter. As the family rejects him because of his poverty, he vows that he would become rich and only then would ask for the hand of the heroine (Nargis). He goes to the city and is forced to take up the job of a 'burning man' in a circus; in every show he has douse himself with kerosene and set himself on fire and then jump from a height into the water tank below. The owner of the circus, the danseuse Sitara, falls in love with him, but he pines for his lost love. Eventually, as the film proceeds, the hero is accused of murder and jailed, while the heroine Nargis is married off to the jailer (Balraj Sahni), who develops sympathy for the young prisoner. When the desperate hero comes to know the reality he dies of shock.

K. Asif

The meteoric rise of Karimuddin Asif (1924–71) as a great director is all the more curious because he made only three and half films in a career spanning three decades. *Phool* (1945, starring Prithviraj Kapoor, Veena and Suraiya) and *Hulchal* (1950) were tragic love stories set in modern times. The magnum opus *Mughal-e-Azam* (1960), the epitome of historical spectacles in Indian cinema, was hailed as an authentic document of India's composite culture. This film (as well as also Sohrab Modi's *Sikandar*) was the final culmination of the efforts of the Indian film maker in mastering the film technology to create spectacles comparable with those mounted by Hollywood. The film is also considered as the best contribution of Urdu literature to cinema. *Love and God* (1986), the film he could not complete, was a remake of the legend of Laila Majnu.

In *Love and God*, Asif attempted an interpretation of the famous legend by locating it in the Sufi tradition. The mystical relationship between love and god was to be shown as the love between two soulmates drawn into its inherent obsession and the impending separation and pain, which alone can lead to the path for union with God. Thus, the film was not to become yet another narrative of the famous legend, but as a serious discourse on the relationship among love, god and society and how the mundane social prejudices and perceptions are unable to stop the ultimate emancipation of the souls. Unfortunately, Asif died before completing this ambitious project.

In his style, Asif was essentially a formalist, having apparent allegiance with the Sohrab Modi school of film making. Using vast horizontal spaces for the placing and movements of the characters and juxtaposing them with minutely framed middle and close shots, he would masterfully expand the frontal space as well as introduce a sense of depth, making the presentation look virtually three-dimensional. However, the progressive movement of the conflict in the narration was carried out by the conventional verbal mode: the point–counterpoint dialogues, which further strengthened the overall classical personality of the film.

Hulchal once again reaffirmed Dilip Kumar's excellence in portraying the obsessed lover who faces life's trials and tribulations with immense inner strength but finally he himself plays up his life-long obsession with the inevitable death. In the tragic climax, the heart-broken hero, after seeing that his beloved is now married, falls and rolls down a staircase in a state of shock; he gets up and climbs up the stairs, despite the unbearable pain, to go near the heroine, but rolls down the stairs again and meets his death.

In *Insaniyat*, directed by S. S. Vasan, Dilip Kumar once again appeared as a reticent lover, who this time upholds the glory of his one-sided love. He not only gives up his obsession for his heartthrob, which he has been nurturing since childhood, but transforms it into a sublimated emotion by opting for death in order to ensure the safety and well-being of the woman he loved.

Set in medieval times, the film recounts the story of a rural uprising against a tyrant ruler Zangura (Jayant; real name Zakaria Khan, the father of Amjad Khan who played Gabbar Singh in the

1975 blockbuster *Sholay*). Mangal (Dilip Kumar) is the people's leader who adores Bina (played by Bina Rai) since childhood but is unable to express his feelings. Zangura sends his general Bhanu (Dev Anand) to suppress the uprising but he (Dev Anand) falls in love with Bina who reciprocates his overtures and they get married. Mangal is shell-shocked but accepts the situation, silently suffering the loss. Then Bhanu becomes a rebel and takes up command of the villagers in their struggle against Zangura. Zangura attacks the village but is defeated. He retreats, only to attack again. He manages to capture Bhanu. Bina accuses Mangal of betraying her as he has failed in saving her husband. Deeply hurt by this unjust accusation, Mangal immediately rushes to Zangura's fort and frees Bhanu; he himself is killed in this daredevil mission. A major highlight of this film was Zippy, the acrobatic chimpanzee, who virtually stole the show from the two heroes!

Insaniyat performed a very significant function for Dilip Kumar as it provided him the basic parameters for the role of a typical rustic rural Indian youth: strong, upright and sensitive, and a victim of circumstances. The actor later employed this model more gainfully in *Ganga Jumna* (1961). Incidentally, the role of Kamalahasan in *Sagar* (1985) was modelled on Dilip Kumar's character in *Insaniyat*.

S. S. Vasan

S. S. Vasan (1903–69), the movie mughal from South India, also called the Cecil B. DeMille of India, came from a humble background. He moved to the celluloid world after becoming a print-media magnate. Vasan's maiden venture into the film world was as a storywriter in Ellis R. Dungan's *Sati Leelavathi* (1936). Soon he set up his own banner, Gemini, named after his zodiac sign.

With *Chandralekha* (1948), his magnum opus, Vasan heralded a new era of multistarrer period spectacles in Indian cinema. Together with other films that followed in quick succession – *Nishan* (1949), *Mangla* (1950), *Bahut Din Huye* (1954), *Insaniyat* (1955) and *Raj Tilak* (1958) – he showed his immense ability in blending many popular Indian folk tales and legends and projecting them on screen.

Vasan's spectacles thus involved intricate palace intrigues, people's uprisings, massive sets, elaborate song-and-dance sequences, terrific battle scenes involving thousands of people. However, beneath these spectacles was hidden Vasan's grand vision of employing cinema for a nationalist mobilization of popular culture, as reflected in his unique and honest manifesto on cinematic populism, *Pageants for our Peasants*.

Gemini's era of grand spectacles came to an end in the late 1950s and the movie mughal made a sudden shift to the contemporary milieu, making a series of family melodramas on the lines of the AVM banner.

Dilip Kumar's association with Gemini was highly benefiting for the actor. Both *Insaniyat* and *Paigham* offered to him highly valuable opportunities to further expand and enrich his screen persona in two entirely different domains: first as a melancholic rural youth and then as the people's leader.

Insaniyat: Extract from a review
The Hindustan Times, 16 October 1955

Gemini films have all that an extrovert could want but I go a step further and [assert that this film] has at least one good character role assigned to Dilip Kumar. This very popular but at the same time intelligent actor is not just a good looker as he appears in this film. Playing the role of a rugged yokel with a heart of gold, Dilip Kumar is made to dance in village lanes and sing for all his worth and of course do a good bit of fencing. All the same his character is that of an intensely sincere and selfless man which he reveals in a few characteristic words and gestures.

S. U. Sunny's *Udan Khatola* (1955), a musical hit, was yet another tribute to unfulfilled love. Visualized as a tragic love story located at the crossroads of modern life and a tribal past, the film attempts to establish the transcendental nature of the man–woman relationship. This relationship is regarded as omnipotent even as the inflicted souls move far beyond the limits of the mortal frame and are caught up in a life-long wait for the beloved. They are finally united in death. In *Udan Khatola*, as in *Kohinoor* later (1960), Dilip Kumar in the role of a singer-lover provided a beautiful interpretation to the songs filmed on him and created an enchanting aura of romance rarely witnessed on the Indian screen.

Uran Khatola was an adaptation of Frank Capra's *Lost Horizon* (1937). A single-seater aeroplane crashes in the island of Shanga, a tribal kingdom. Kashi (Dilip Kumar), the pilot, is saved by Soni (Nimmi), the daughter of the *peshwa*, the minister of the kingdom ruled by a young queen (Suryakumari). Kashi and Soni fall in love, which angers her fiancé Shangu (Jeevan). When Kashi goes to the queen to seek her permission to settle in the kingdom, she falls in love with him. The queen and Shangu conspire to make Soni sacrifice her life in order to cool the anger of the stormy sea, which has threatened all life on the island. In this unbearable separation, the lover becomes a hermit, grows old and finally follows his beloved in death. The film was produced by composer Naushad and it included some of his most melodious songs. It was dubbed in Tamil and released successfully as *Vanaratham* (1956) with new lyrics by Kambadasan.

Devdas (1955), directed by Bimal Roy, marked the crowning of Dilip Kumar as the king of tragedy in Indian cinema and also a formal recognition of his school of acting. Based on the novel by Saratchandra Chatterjee, *Devdas* in its essence mourns the inevitable self-destruction of a man in conflict with the prevailing feudal order and constantly pining for his lost love. His intensely felt emotions lead him to hit the bottle, and he tries to forget his sorrows by drowning himself in alcohol, apart from getting involved with a courtesan. In fact, the name Devdas has become symbolic of an individual who is a victim of the process of decay, both morally and physically.

The basic theme of *Devdas appears* to underline the self-inflicted agony by a man who sacrifices himself at the anvil of a woman's love. Yet, it is far more complex than the traditional view of puritan love and separation. The narrative goes beyond the superficial and interprets the deep-rooted sense of alienation and uprootedness being faced by the common people vis-à-vis the oppression by the upper classes. Devdas, a victim of the feudal society, cannot marry his childhood love, Parvati or Paro (Suchitra Sen). He rebels but meekly and leaves his village and moves to Calcutta to seek solace in city life. There, he runs into Chunilal (played delectably by none other than Motilal), who initiates him into drinking and also seeks to entertain him by taking him to a *kotha* (brothel). Here, Devdas meets the courtesan Chandramukhi (played creditably by Vyjayanthimala). They are mutually attracted to each other. He soon becomes addicted to alcohol and sinks deeper and deeper into its deadly embrace.

When he returns to his village he comes to know that his childhood sweetheart (Paro) has been married off to a much older man. He is heartbroken. An incurable restlessness grips him and compels him to embark on a seemingly unending journey on a train so as to get rid of his his intense suffering due to separation from his beloved and also to reach an idyllic place where he could just rest peacefully. He fails in his quest and finally decides to go back to his native village, and, in a dying condition, climbs on to a bullock cart to reach his destination. But his body has decayed beyond redemption and he finds his salvation from his life-long agony only in death just outside the gate of his childhood sweetheart's house.

The Hindustan Times, Sunday, 19 June 1955
(From our Bombay office)

Dilip Kumar Repeating K. L. Saigal's Role

In playing the role of *Devdas* in the film of that name now being made by Bimal Roy, Dilip Kumar has realized a long-cherished ambition. It was an education to watch him do the famous scenes of this film at Mohan studio ...

Dilip in a undershirt and Bengali-style dhoti looks quite impressive. Although he has not got Saigal's height and the seriousness of the face, his desire to excel, his understanding of the theme and his expressiveness of face should enable him put up a good show. Dilip must remember that in every scene in the film, he will be compared to Saigal and he must therefore be more than normally careful in doing this role. *Devdas* will have all the advantages of technical progress, which the country has achieved during the last two decades. The sets, lighting, décor and sound will be much better than that in the New Theatres' film ...

Put the two productions side by side and you have two examples of the film technique – as it was 20 years ago and as it stands today. The large number of Dilip Kumar's fans would, of course, be happy to see him in a favourite role.

Devdas, in his attempts to come to terms with the world's realities, proves to be a half-hearted rebel who, in the final analysis, sacrifices his life for the status quo. His rejection of the love of the dancing girl, Chandramukhi, in fact, can be viewed as an unconscious desire to get rid of his own feudal past. The character thus becomes the archetype of a disillusioned man who seeks his identity through self-inflicted suffering. He could see no other option except the inevitable self-destruction in the face of an oppressive social milieu in which true happiness could not materialize in the physical unity of the lovers. The character had a universal appeal for the Indian mindset because the theme also represented escapism, and indecisiveness, whereby the failures of the individual are attributed to the external social factors.

Bimal Roy: 'Working with Him Was Educative'
By Dilip Kumar
(Excerpts from an interview for Channel 4, London)

In my formative years it was important to work with a director who [could] lead you gently under the skin of the character. Today we have institutions, they teach cinema, acting, etc. We did not have these then. We had instead men like Bimal Roy .... Take making *Devdas*. The question often while doing my role was 'not to do' than do anything. Initially, Bimal Roy felt songs would be a distraction in this tragedy ... except songs in Chandramukhi's *kotha* portions ... this was discussed in the story conferences that were regular features of working in Bimal Roy Productions .... He used to allow free discussion on the script. At the discussion, the songs became controversial issues. Quickly, the song 'Mitua ...' [penned by Sahir Ludhianvi, set to tune by S. D. Burman and sung by Talat Mehmood] was recorded; it had the same melancholy mood:

> *Mitua ... mitua ...*
> *lagi re.*
> *Ek ek chup mein,*
> *sau sau baina,*
> *Rahe gaye ansoo,*
> *loot gaye raag ...*
> *mitua, mitua ... lagi re*

In the final decision, the song was retained ...

Bimalda's grammar was selectivity and he left room enough for the common man to react. As to acting, he largely left it to the actor to fend for himself ... the character, or the psyche of the character in a given situation, would be before us.

I place Bimal Roy head and shoulders above his contemporaries. Not yet have I come across a man with his all-round proficiency. I miss him!

Source: Rinki Bhattacharya, *Bimal Roy*, Bhopal: Madhya Pradesh Film Development Corporation, 1989. (Rinki Bhattacharya is Bimal Roy's daughter.)

With the 1955 film *Devdas*, Dilip Kumar finally established himself as the ultimate hero of the times, the same way this character had turned K. L. Saigal into an icon some two decades ago. The actor enhanced the efforts of Saigal in establishing the image of Devdas. This movie not only affirmed his status as the actor with unique abilities, but also brought his histrionics into full bloom. With discomforting ease, he 'lived' the legendary character by merely internalizing the unending agony and restlessness. The film also elevated the image of the actor as the desperate lover to far greater heights, thereby locating the character in a definite social setting and making it more identifiable.

However, the many connoisseurs of the old film school were of the view that the younger actor was no match for Saigal, whose depiction of Devdas, they asserted, was far more intense and shattering. According to them, although Bimal Roy's version was an excellent example of portraying a novel on celluloid, the film could not grow beyond its romantic flavour and therefore lacked a realistic depiction of the pain and agony as brought out in the written text. Yet, Bimal Roy created his film in a more resonant historical background, given that the original story focused almost exclusively on Devdas's physiological and psychological obsessions. He also dedicated his film to P. C. Barua and K. L. Saigal.

Devdas: A Review
The Hindustan Times, 22 January 1956

Remaking of a Classic

It is [the] desire of every director, producer and, of course, star to remake or reinterpret a great classic whether it is on stage or [on] screen .... It, therefore, appears to be the most natural thing that Bimal Roy should have thought of remaking *Devdas.* But the critic who asked Bimal Roy why it was necessary to remake the film had a good reason to do so, the reason which Dilip Kumar understood well, namely, the last Hindi production, Saigal's *Devdas,* which has been one of the most successful films during the last 20 years. Dilip Kumar was only too keen to admit that playing of the title role had been 'a perilous task'. He was only too conscious of Saigal's *Devdas* and of Saratchandra and it was not a comfortable feeling trying to surpass one and be worthy of the other ...

Anyone who goes to see Bimal Roy's *Devdas* will turn nostalgic for Saigal's voice but what the production loses by way of music and songs it gains in character development and perhaps in acting. Bimal Roy's idea of *Devdas* is not merely a story of frustration but that of conflict. That is where Dilip Kumar's acting ability comes in. He makes a fairly facile *Devdas* ...

***

Dilip Kumar's role in *Musafir* (1957), the directorial debut of Hrishikesh Mukherjee, was an obvious shadow image of Devdas. An innovative package in one film of three stories about the lives of families, which happen to reside as tenants of the same house in a metropolis one after another, the film invokes a cyclic sequence of marriage, birth, death and rebirth. Apart from the house, another common backdrop of the stories is the figure of a neighbourhood destitute and sick 'madman' (Dilip Kumar), who hangs around on the street, often playing the violin.

All the three stories are about initial desperation and then hope. The first segment is about an orphaned young woman, Shakuntala (Suchitra Sen), who desperately wants her husband Ajay (Shekhar) to make up with his estranged parents so that that she may be accepted by the family. After she leaves, the house is occupied by a family whose elder son has died and the second son, a wayward young man, Bhanu (Kishore Kumar), is desperate to find a job to support his aged father (Nazir Hussain) and his widowed sister-in-law (Nirupa Roy).

The third section is about a single mother Uma (Usha Kiran) who rents the house and finds that the madman is her ex-lover. Earlier when they were to get married, she disappears just before their wedding day. In this narration he becomes friendly with Uma's highly talkative paralytic child (Daisy Irani) and this relationship rekindles in him some sense of belonging and affection. Dilip Kumar, through his prolonged conversation with the child, expresses his agony about his lost love and the eventual futility of life communicated through the rendering of melancholic tunes from his violin. Yet, in the end, the madman's death and the miraculous recovery of Uma's paralysed son coincide, indicating the continuity of life.

Although the film presented Dilip Kumar as Devdas reincarnated, there was a difference; the lover-sufferer in this case is not restless, but in a state of chronic depression, which finds expression not in self-indulgence but in a kind of resigned sadness. He keeps on playing his violin as if announcing his inevitable death any moment. It seems that Hrishikesh Mukherjee took this idea from *Last Leaf*, the famous short story by O. Henry. In his later highly acclaimed film, *Anand* (1970), Mukherjee transformed this role of death-in-waiting to a highly spirited positive character (played by Rajesh Khanna), a cancer patient, who intends to take death merely as way of life. *Anand,* unlike *Devdas*, lives every precious moment of life with full zest before accepting an untimely death.

Musafir fulfilled Hrishikesh Mukherjee's cherished desire of doing a film with Dilip Kumar. In fact, it was the actor who encouraged Mukherjee to take up film direction. The young editor-turned-director brought together his old friends from the Bengali theatre and cinema including Ritwik Ghatak and music director Salil Choudhury, who were in Bombay mainly through Bimal Roy's patronage. Like Mehboob Khan's *Mother India* (1957) and K. A. Abbas's *Pardesi* (1957) and *Char Dil Char Rahen* (1959), *Musafir* was designed as a true multistarrer. Incidentally, *Musafir* was the only film in which Dilip Kumar has sung a duet with Lata Mangeshkar, which has been written by Shailendra and composed by Salil Choudhury.

In *Yahudi* (1958), Bimal Roy, the distinguished alumnus of New Theatres, reworked Saigal's classic, *Yahoodi Ki Ladki*, with Dilip Kumar in the lead. In this highly subdued role punctuated with interim inner conversations with the self, the actor enlivens the dilemma of a prince trying to transcend the historical conflict between the two communities (the Jews and the Romans, as the film is set in the pre-Christian era). However, for the actor, *Yahudi* was no more than a dress rehearsal for his role in *Mughal-e-Azam*, although the timing of the making of these films overlapped to some extent.

K. Asif's *Mughal-e-Azam* (1960), considered to be a masterpiece of Indian cinema and the finest example of a unique blending of the classical theatre with cinema, provided Dilip Kumar a rare opportunity to display his immense talents in the historical spectacle film genre. As Prince Salim (the heir to the Mughal throne after his father Akbar), the master actor undertook one of the more challenging roles of his career. He once again reaffirmed that the characters he had played during the last ten years or so were not 'flashes in the pan'. Salim (who later adopted the title Jehangir), a born rebel and a romantic, is apparently disenchanted with the royal milieu in which he is placed. His deep alienation is very vividly captured in a scene in which he is seen, on horseback, directing his troop movement with the swaying of his sword, but looking with forelorn eyes at the far horizon as if his mind is somewhere else and not focused on his present actions. In the following scene, the prince now in his military camp, is seen writing poetry on his sword using blood oozing from his fresh battle wounds as ink. It seems as if his restless being is in search of real soulful solace, which was to materialize in the form of his adulation and love for Anarkali (a court danseuse) when he returns to the royal capital after spending a good part of his youth on the battlefront. In fact, it is Akbar who has sent off Salim to the battlefront when he finds his teenage son falling victim to debauchery and indolence.

Mughal-e-Azam

Based on the popular legend of Anarkali, the film narrates the story of the Mughal emperor, Akbar (Prithviraj Kapoor), and his Rajput wife, Joda Bai (Durga Khote), who after many years manage to have a son. Akbar undertakes the ordeal of walking barefoot on the desert sands to seek the blessings of the Sufi saint Khwaja Salim Chisti to have his desire for offspring fulfilled. Prince Salim, much to his parents' chagrin, grows up into a weak and pleasure-loving youth. Akbar then decides to make his son strong and brave and sends him to the battlefront, where he proves himself worthy as a warrior. Having proved himself in battle, he returns to the capital and falls in love with Anarkali (Madhubala), a beautiful slave girl and wants to marry her. Anarkali too reciprocates the prince's love. Akbar pressurizes Anarkali to give up Salim by humiliating her and even imprisoning her, but to no avail. For his part, Salim remains devoted to her and disobeys his father to the point of rebelling against the emperor and challenging him to battle. The prince loses the battle and the royal court sentences him to death. Anarkali comes out of her hiding and is allowed to sacrifice her life to save Salim. However, contrary to the legend, according to which Anarkali was buried alive with four walls built around her, Akbar spares her and secretly exiles her from his kingdom, while Salim is made to believe forever that she has been put to death.

To highlight the oppressive nature of royal power, the director beautifully weaves into the narrative the character of the *sangtarash* (sculptor, played by the veteran actor Kumar), who represents the people's voice against the imperial tyranny, its indulgence in wars and suppression of freedom and free love. When the scheming emperor orders him to marry Anarkali, he defies the royal order and spurns the awards bestowed on him and the offer of royal patronage of his art and joins the camp of the prince.

In *Mughal-e-Azam*, the idea used by the sculptor to present a live Anarkali as a stone sculpture was first used by Kidar Sharma in *Neel Kamal* (1947), also starring Madhubala. The musical score by Naushad was phenomenal, and each and every song was honed to perfection, the most popular being *Pyar Kiya To Darna Kya...*

Dilip Kumar and Madhubala in a poignant scene from *Mughal-e-Azam*

Dilip Kumar drew upon his vast repertoire of histrionics to portray the agony of a prince caught in the vice symbolic of the the royalty–commoner divide. Helpless as he is against the adamant and mighty state power, which refuses gratification of his love, he frets, keeps on shouting out his frustration in the corridors of the palace and even goes down on his knees in front of his mother, imploring her to give Anarkali in charity to him and take away all the royal decorations bestowed on him. Unlike *Devdas*, the self-indulgent lover this time finally takes charge of his life and challenges the status quo. He makes his love for the court danseuse, Anarkali, an issue of social justice and freedom of individual choice.

In this complex role with several undertones, Dilip Kumar's histrionics were at their best, a unique blending of underplay with the passion of obsessed love reflected in his eyes, interrupted intermittently with explosive overplay marked by rapid body movements and forceful dialogue delivery. In spite of such a memorable performance, Dilip Kumar's role has not been given its rightful due in the discussions on *Mughal-e-Azam*, overshadowed perhaps by the powerful portrayals of Akbar by Prithviraj Kapoor and the highly sensitive presence of Anarkali, who seemed to be Madhubala's alter ego.

The Anti-Hero Manifestations

One important corollary of Dilip Kumar's obsession with the sensuous female figure was the anti-hero manifestations in his characterizations in some of his films during the classical period and later. This self-destructive syndrome was highlighted by selling one's soul to avenge unreciprocated love, by remaining captive to the dilemmas of an ugly past and often indulging in sadism, leading to distrust and hatred in his relationship with the heroine. These features became the basis of his 'negative' roles in the classical phase (*Andaz* 1949, *Arzoo* 1950, *Babul* 1950, *Sangdil* 1952 and *Amar* 1954) and later in the post-classical phase (*Dil Diya*

Dard Liya 1966 and *Aadmi* 1968). In a sense, this anti-hero stance of the protagonist was a protest, against the dominant social system, articulated by denying himself what he actually desires.

In his not-so-heroic characterizations, Dilip Kumar seems to have been greatly influenced by two classic nineteenth-century novels: *Wuthering Heights* by Emily Brontë and *Jane Eyre* by Charlotte Brontë.

Andaz, the first film Dilip Kumar did with Mehboob Khan, presented the actor in the archetype of a desperate singer-lover. Located in the affluent society setting (urban) of the post-colonial period, the film raised the issue of the modern identity of Indian women vis-à-vis the traditional values enshrined in Indian womanhood. It also attempted to examine the contradictory propositions that the newly independent India should value, i.e., capitalist modernization, while retaining feudal family and moral values.

The heroine, Neeta (Nargis), a modern young woman who dresses in the Western style, inherits the business empire of her father Sir Badriprasad (Sapru). A dashing young man Dilip (Dilip Kumar) saves her life when her horse goes amok and the two become good friends. She soon makes him a business partner. The hero, under the illusion of apparently reciprocated love gestures of the easygoing heroine, communicates his feelings through his songs so as to win her love. Meanwhile, her fiancé, Rajan (Raj Kapoor), returns from abroad, and she marries him. Dilip's managerial efficiency disintegrates under the pressure of his frustrated desires, while the infantile Rajan begins to suspect his wife's fidelity. Eventually, the tensions erupt into a violent clash between the two men in which Dilip is hurt badly. He recovers and, in his desperation, makes advances on Neeta, who shoots him and is jailed for murder. The ensuing trial establishes that the root cause of the tragedy was the excessively liberal lifestyle of Neeta, which in a male-dominated world is full of danger and a source of her family's unhappiness. The shooting, in fact, represents the stereotype, self-preserving image of the Indian woman, no matter how modern she seems to be in her conduct.

In *Andaz*, Dilip Kumar demonstrated his newly acquired style of an agonized and disillusioned lover. This film, along with *Babul* and *Udan Khatola*, also helped him in establishing the image of an intensely romantic hero who conveys to his woman his dreams through his songs. However, it was Raj Kapoor who stole the show in *Andaz* as the overtalkative, easygoing, but yet suspicious, husband trying to do a balancing act amidst the turmoil caused by a stranger in his married life.

Arzoo (directed by Shahid Lateef), inspired by *Wuthering Heights*, recounts a sad tale of childhood love turned sour due to the overobsessive attitude of the hero. Set against a rural backdrop, the film attempts to capture the contradictions in the personalities of the hero (Dilip Kumar) and the heroine (Kamini Kaushal). While the hero is a typical rustic rural youth who wants to *possess* his woman, demanding her complete attention, the heroine is far more logically inclined and tends to look at her world rationally. For the hero, nothing exists beyond the heroine but for her, in spite being a poor rural girl, she feels that life can be beautiful if one can have a respectable space of one's own. This tension-ridden and uneasy relationship between the two is further shaken when a young, city-bred zamindar pays a visit to his ancestral house in the village. Charmed by the affluent lifestyle of the zamindar, the heroine, in her innocence, tells her lover that it would be nice to be rich and poverty indeed is a curse. The hero is deeply hurt and he decides to leave the village and go elsewhere to make enough money so that he can fulfil the heroine's wish to live in luxury.

The night the hero leaves the village, his family house, in which a beggar has taken refuge, catches fire and his charred body is mistaken to be that of the hero. (Guru Dutt repeated this concept in his 1957 masterpiece, *Pyaasa*, with some variations.) The heroine's parents now convince her to marry the zamindar, who has developed a liking for her. Time rolls by. On his return to the village as a rich man, when the hero finds out that the heroine is already married, he is unable to come to terms with his misfortune, and accuses the heroine of betrayal. He seeks revenge and his mission in life is to torment the heroine. He befriends the zamindar and his younger sister (Shashikala) and begins a long-drawn-out process of cornering the heroine and raking up her past to make her confess that she still loves him. When the zamindar realizes that it is the hero who has been tormenting his wife, he shoots at him but the heroine shields him and dies. In the end, the hero-turned-villain is left repenting.

In its offbeat narrative, *Arzoo* attempted to show that childhood love, as representing the static past, cannot be easily upheld in changing times and obsession with such love can lead to much pain and devastation of the body and the soul. Through its second protagonist, the zamindar, the film also underlined the transformation of the traditionally cruel feudal elite into a more humane, pro-poor and modern class in post-independence India. But the film also glorified the suffering of women caused by the erosion of their own independent space by male dominance.

Dilip Kumar as the obsessive lover-turned-tormentor leaves the viewers spellbound with his rapid switching of emotions. At one moment, the glow of the turmoil within him is manifest in his eyes and the next moment, he conceals it with a twinkle in his eyes and a benign smile.

Babul (directed by S. U. Sunny), perhaps the most curious and tragic love triangle ever depicted in Hindi cinema, presented Dilip Kumar as the lover in pursuit of two equally demanding women, with neither of whom is he able to lead a happy life. The participants in this triangle are the new and young postman Ashok (Dilip Kumar), Bela (Nargis), the old postman's vivacious daughter, and Usha (Munawwar Sultana), the haughty daughter of the local zamindar. Ashok teaches Usha music until Bela warns her to keep away from her man.

In this unusual plot, the film attempts to locate the hero and the two heroines in three distinct spaces, where each of them becomes finally incommunicable. The hero, indecisive and confused as he is about the true love of Bela, is charmed by the aristocratic lifestyle of Usha and flirts with her. In the end, her father marries off Usha as the hero lacks conviction about his love for her and fails to win her hand. The climax unravels a quick sequence of tragedies: Bela watches the wedding procession of Usha and, in a deranged condition, falls from a tree and is fatally injured. She insists that Ashok marry her, which he does minutes before she dies. Her death scene portrays a medieval horseman descending from the skies to carry her away as the smoke from the cremation pyre merges with the clouds.

In this somewhat peculiar role, Dilip Kumar effectively juxtaposes his moments of silence with occasional outbursts of emotional articulation of his innermost feelings. Composer Naushad was in his element and came up with some fabulous melodies, sung by Shamshad Begum and Talat Mehmood.

R. C. Talwar's *Sangdil*, inspired by *Jane Eyre*, once again cast Dilip Kumar in a veritable anti-hero role. The young flamboyant aristocrat, living under the shadow of a lunatic wife (played by Kuldip Kaur), is torn between his ugly present and the promise of a bright future offered by the love of the exquisitely beautiful heroine (Madhubala). Unable to bear the aggression of his wife, he has to thrash her and lock her up. In the end, she sets the house on fire in a fit of anger.

Mehboob Khan's *Amar* provided a down-to-earth analysis of the question of morality in the man–woman relationship. The film depicted the moral crisis of an aristocrat, Amarnath, an upright lawyer, who is in love with his fiancée Anju (Madhubala), but in a moment of weakness seduces a woman Sonia (Nimmi) belonging to the lower class. The hero watches silently as Sonia suffers the consequences of their passionate moments together, while the villain, Sankat (Jayant), offers her help and comfort. When Sankat comes to know that it is the lawyer who is responsible for Sonia's suffering, he attacks Amar, but is killed in the fight by his own knife. However, Sonia is arrested for murder and, while defending her in the court, Amar reveals the truth and eventually marries her. The title of the film implies immortal love that can have its basis in sacrifice and suffering. The melodramatic theme, combined with some unusually surreal imagery, made the film an oddity in the genre. The film did not fair well at the box office as the audience refused to accept Dilip Kumar in an extremely negative role.

In *Amar*, Dilip Kumar exhibited his immense skill in underplay, living through his guilt with a chilling silence, as he is unable to express his feelings to his fiancée. In the whole film, the actor uses his intense, stark facial expressions to share his pent-up guilt with the audience, and in this discourse in silence, he enacted the dilemma of self-preservation vis-à-vis the moral position of doing justice to his own victim.

Mehboob Khan

Mehboob Khan (1907–64), born in Billimoria town of Gujarat, was among the first runaways to make it big in films. His first assignment was as a junior artiste in Imperial's *Ali Baba* (1927) as the one among the forty thieves. He was selected to play the lead role in *Alam Ara* (1931, the first talkie of India), but Master Vithal from the Sharada Studio got this part (the studio sued Vithal for breaching the contract; it was Mohammed Ali Jinnah who defended him). Mehboob also acted as hero in *Mirza Sahiban* (1933).

In the wake of the talkies when the demand for directors rapidly increased, the young Mehboob succeeded in convincing Sagar Movietone to give him a break. He made his directorial debut with *Judgement of Allah* (1935), a period film, set in the backdrop of the Roman–Arab conflict. This was followed by a stunt film *Deccan Queen* (1936) about a vengeful woman's crusade against the evildoers. His first social was *Manmohan* (1936), also a women-centred film, with

Bibbo (of *The Mill* fame) in the title role. *Jagirdar* (1937) was about a woman's social illegitimacy when she secretly marries her lover, while *Hum Tum Aur Woh* (1938) was a daring attempt to showcase a woman's refusal to feel guilty about fulfilling her sexuality and who releases her man after bearing a child by him. *Watan* (1938), a period tale set against the backdrop of Cossack oppression by the Russian tsar, echoed the sentiments for the country's independence. *Ek Hi Raasta* (1939), Mehboob's powerful exposé of the urban destitutes' struggle for survival in a ruthless city milieu, was about the lives of a coolie, a pickpocket and a rickhsawallah. *Bahen* (1941) was about an overpossessive brother who does not want his sister to get married.

With *Aurat* (1940) and *Roti* (1942), Mehboob's vision broadened and he began a search for more meaningful cinema indicating a sudden and intense intellectual awakening. *Aurat*, the powerful predecessor of *Mother India*, had his wife Sardar Akhtar in the lead role played in the latter version by Nargis (the role of Birju, the rebellious son, was played by Yakub). *Roti*, Mehboob's perhaps the most offbeat film, brought about an intense interpretation of the contradiction between the perverting capitalist mindset and the primitive tribal commune lifestyle, presented in a Brechtian (epic) framework. The late Begum Akhtar (Akhtari Faizabadi, the legendary *ghazal* singer) made a rare appearance in the role of a high-society woman who helps the tribal couple (Sheikh Mukhtar and Sitara Devi) to free themselves from the trap of the merciless urban milieu. In these works, Mehboob showed his immense ability in blending Cecil B. DeMille's cinematic approach with the conventions of Urdu theatre and thus following the basic style of Imperial Theatres.

The master unfurled his own banner in 1943 with *Najma*, a Muslim melodrama, following it up with *Taqdeer* (1943) a lighthearted comedy in the lost-and-found genre. *Humayun* (1945), Mehboob's only historical venture, advocated the need for strong Hindu–Muslim relations in the context of the contemporary Indian conditions of the 1940s by drawing his material from Indian history. The film made an attempt to reinterpret the brotherly relationship of the Mughal Emperor Humayun with a nationalist Rajput princess. *Elaan* (1947), one of the most outstanding Muslim socials till date, was about liberation of Muslim women from the feudal yoke (the heroine, after her husband, the villain, dies, refuses to marry her erstwhile lover and opts for setting up a school for poor girls in her *haveli* or mansion).

From the late 1940s onwards, Mehboob's cinema focused on two dominant genres: socially committed 'spectacles' (as evident in *Aan*, 1952, and *Mother India*, 1957) and the depiction of the theme of eternal love as in *Anmol Ghadi* (1946), *Anokhi Ada* (1948), *Andaz* (1949) and *Amar* (1954). They established some of the basic unfailing formulae for commercial cinema and since then have continued to inspire the box office. In his work on political themes, Mehboob represented a very powerful link between the early works of Mohan Bhavnani (for example, *The Mill*, 1934, and *Jaagran*, 1936) and the social critique located in the industrial commercial milieu worked out in the mainstream cinema by K. A. Abbas and Raj Kapoor in the post-independence period. This evolution as a pioneer of socially progressive cinema was totally indigenous; he never had any formal education and political grooming. (Although his banner's emblem was hammer and sickle, he was not formally associated with Left politics.)

Among anti-hero roles performed by other actors, Ashok Kumar's role in *Mahal* (1949) and Dev Anand's in *Jaal* (1954) were also well conceived. In *Mahal*, Kamal Amrohi created an illusion for the hero in the form of an ethereal female figure, with which he gets obsessed, juxtaposed with the reality represented by his newly wed wife. In his pursuit of the image, the hero oppresses his wife, who finally commits suicide and implicates her husband for poisoning her. In *Jaal*, director Guru Dutt presented his hero in a true anti-hero mould: a mercenary gangster in pursuit of lucre, who is the least bothered about the love and affection being offered to him by the heroine.

The Neo-Realistic Context

Considering the kind of films in which Dilip Kumar has acted, unlike many of his illustrious contemporaries, such as K. A. Abbas, Chetan Anand, Guru Dutt and Balraj Sahni, the actor's participation in the neo-realistic cinema was largely symbolic. And yet the undeniable Indianness of his cinematic image propelled many film makers to utilize his tremendous potential to create very effective realist cinema. Great directors like Mehboob Khan, Bimal Roy, Ramesh Sehgal, Zia Sarhadi, Amiya Chakravarty, Nitin Bose and later Tapan Sinha designed some of their films around this image. Even Guru Dutt is reported to have offered the hero's role in *Pyaasa* to Dilip Kumar, which (according to some sources) the actor declined, as it was very similar to *Devdas*.

In the potpourri of films of the actor, *Shaheed* (1948), *Daag* (1952), *Shikast* (1953), *Footpath* (1953), *Musafir* (1957), *Naya Daur* (1957), *Madhumati* (1958), *Paigham* (1959), *Ganga Jumna* (1961) and later *Sagina* (1974) in the post-classical period are the movies that had some elements of the neo-realist cinema of the times.

Ramesh Sehgal's *Shaheed*[6] (meaning martyr) was a saga of childhood love, narrated against the backdrop of the freedom struggle during the 1940s. One of the most passionate love stories ever told on the Hindi screen, with a series of highly emotionally charged sequences between Dilip Kumar and Kamini Kaushal, the film projected in detail the turmoil caused in the lives of people who have opted to sacrifice everything for achieving the freedom of their nation.

Ramesh Sehgal

Ramesh Sehgal was the first director to impart to Dilip Kumar's persona in *Shaheed* (1948) a strong anti-establishment orientation as well as that of a sufferer in troubled love. He was one of the leading proponents of the neo-realist cinema of the 1940s and 1950s. After a brief stint at Ranjit Studio and Bombay Talkies, he made his first film *Renuka* in 1947 under Jayant Desai's banner. He became one of the top directors of Filmistan with *Shaheed,* followed by *Samadhi* (1950) and *Shikast* (1953). Nalini Jaywant was a regular heroine in most of his films.

In 1954, he set up his own banner, Sehgal Productions, inaugurating it with *Railway Platform*, the film that introduced Sunil Dutt. His last important film, *Phir Subah Hogi* (1958), was a loose adapatation of Fyodor Dostoevsky's *Crime and Punishment,* built around the radical poetry of lyricist Sahir Ludhianvi.

Shaheed presented Dilip Kumar in the role of a revolutionary, Ram, who leads an armed struggle against the British. This characterization was peppered with some of the basic ingredients that were to determine the content of his roles in later films: (i) childhood love destined to remain unfulfilled; (ii) living through the contradictions between his quest for true love and the harsh realities of the external world; (iii) the vulnerability of his love caused by misunderstanding with the heroine; and (iv) the inevitability of death during the climax of the film.

Shaheed signfied the arrival of Dilip Kumar as a consummate artiste and gave the first-ever glimpse of his highly acclaimed style. It helped the actor not only in gaining a strong foothold in the film world, but also in creating the basic model of an anti-establishment hero in Hindi cinema. His performance was marked with amazing underplay. With tears glistening in his eyes and a smile on his face, he suffered without expressing his feelings and used his agony as his strength to carry out his duty towards the nationalist cause.

Shaheed also later became an important reference film for many film makers. It seems that the writers of *Mughal-e-Azam* borrowed heavily from the high-tension conflict between Ram and his father (a civil servant representing the Raj, played by Chandramohan) in sketching out the scenes involving Emperor Akbar and Prince Salim. The scene in which Emperor Akbar meets Salim in his army camp and Salim threatens to kill him if Anarkali is harmed seemed to have been inspired by the meeting of father and son in *Shaheed* in which the hero asks his father to release his senior revolutionary leader, otherwise he would shoot him.

Daag, like other films by Amiya Chakravarty (*Badal*, *Patita* and *Seema*), dealt with a burning social problem: alcoholism. Conceived as a tribute to the Gandhian theme of prohibition, the film projected an excellent narrative through its alcoholic protagonist. The film brings to light the creativity of a village artisan who seeks momentary release from the prevailing social oppression through the bottle. For Shankar, the statue-maker, alcohol is a vehicle that takes him beyond the vagaries of life to a world where he can devote time to his art. But in society he is looked down upon as a diehard drunkard beyond any redemption. He spends all his earnings and even the money for his ailing mother's medicines on drink. The bottle also separates him from his sweetheart Paro (Nimmi) when her family gains a higher status in society after inheriting a fortune.

Daag offered to Dilip Kumar the opportunity of a lifetime to demonstrate his capabilities in full measure. The artiste articulated his restlessness, caused by a perpetual deprivation, through his drinking bouts, mood swings and highly charged dialogues. He shouts out his frustrations, but his helplessness soon pushes him into deep silence as if the alcoholic is talking to his inner self. In the scene showing him in an inebriated state, when he is angry with everyone and with himself, he accuses god of being hypocritical in that he helps only the rich, but finally breaks down upon realizing his own helplessness. This scene encompasses one of the most compelling pieces of acting on Indian celluloid. In this scene, the helpless sufferer in desperation becomes an iconoclast, questioning the very existence of god; an act employed in many latter-day films (for instance: by Sheikh Mukhtar in *Do Ustad*, 1959; Raaj Kumar in *Kaajal*, 1965; and Amitabh Bachchan in *Deewar*, 1975). In appreciation of the social importance of the theme, Dilip Kumar did not charge any fee for this film.

Amiya Chakravarty

Dilip Kumar's first director, Amiya Chakravarty (1912–57), like the actor, was also one of the illustrious alumni of Bombay Talkies. Born in Bogra (now in Bangladesh), he started off as a political activist in the Gandhian movement. He was arrested during the Salt Satyagraha of 1930 and was forced to leave Bengal in 1935. He came to Bombay and joined Bombay Talkies as a scenarist and wrote Najam Naqvi's *Punarmilan* (1940) and Sushil Majumdar's *Char Ankhen* (1944). Devika Rani introduced him as director in *Anjaan* in 1941 and soon he became the company's top director. In *Girls' School* (1949), he took up a novel theme of promoting education of girls in villages. In the 1950s, he set up his own banner, Mars & Movies, and produced some of the most memorable films in that period including his famous trilogy *Daag* (1952), *Patita* (1953) and *Seema* (1955), each dealing with a specific social problem.

In his style, Chakravarty followed the typical formalistic and generic conventions of Bombay Talkies. He relied heavily on constricted spaces to develop and interpret the drama, often releasing the tension in the vast outdoors, particularly using open sky full of white clouds to symbolize freedom.

Like many of his contemporaries, Chakravarty died young. His last film *Kathputli* (1957) was completed by his senior Nitin Bose.

Chakravarty cast Dilip Kumar in his most memorable film, *Daag*, nearly a decade after he directed him for the first time. This film prepared the actor for his historic role in Bimal Roy's *Devdas* a few years later.

In *Daag*, Chakravarty, as in his other films, extensively used white clouds spread across a clear sky as a metaphor to express the hope of a beautiful world. The film, in fact, opened with the famous poem by Alexander Pope, 'Lead kindly light...' appearing on the sky with the hero standing on a rock watching the clouds. Noted film writer Partho Chatterjee observes: 'The song, *Aye Mere Dil Kahin Aur Chal* (Come let's go elsewhere dear heart), sung by the alcoholic toymaker walking briskly across an unyielding landscape, was shot in extreme long, long, mid-long and mid-shots. The spiritual despair of a good man held prisoner by an addiction could have scarcely been filmed with greater empathy. A curious dichotomy is achieved in the picturization as if to mirror ordinary people's ambivalent attitude towards helping alcoholics in a positive way. Nature, photographed in semi-silhouette, seems to embrace and reject the hapless toymaker at one and the same time.'

In *Shikast*, Ramesh Sehgal makes a purposeful attempt to extend the ambit of the famous Bengali writer Saratchandra's *Devdas* by linking the predicament of the characters with the wider social reality. Based on the famous novel, *Palli Samaj* by the same writer (though the credits did not say so), the film attempted to capture the complexities involved in promoting rural uplift in a decadent feudal environment in independent India. The narrative is built around an intricate love story involving a young zamindar Ashok (Dilip Kumar) who returns to his native village after studying medicine, and to his childhood beloved (belonging to a feudal household), whom he could not marry earlier because of the conflicts between the two families. While the hero is away pursuing his studies, the heroine is married, but later becomes a widow.

Dilip Kumar once again used his patented natural ability to underplay to portray the complex character, who wants to undo his feudal past. Transcending the agony of lost love, the protagonist interprets his pain in the wider social context, and against all odds created by his family and the heroine, he initiates a series of programmes for the uplift of the poor villagers. When plague breaks out in the village, inflicting death both on the rich and the poor alike, the young doctor organizes medical relief on a mass scale, shaking the people out of the age-old superstitions pertaining to the dreaded epidemic. Finally, he saves the life of the heroine's son with utmost devotion, indicating *shikast*, the defeat, of the old order and the arrival of a new age.

Footpath, directed by Zia Sarhadi, is the only film of Dilip Kumar that truly falls in the category of neo-realist cinema. Set during the Second World War, the film foretells the development of a new class, which is expanding its economic base at the expense of the poor and how, in this process, the educated middle class gets lured into becoming an equal partner in acquiring ill-gotten wealth. The film, therefore, took up a serious debate on the responsibility of the educated people towards society.

The film depicts the moral crisis of an upright, but poor, writer, Noshu (Dilip Kumar), who comes into contact with black marketeers hoarding medicines in a famine-stricken area and joins them in their nefarious activities. As he begins to amass wealth, he not only abandons his erstwhile principles but also his doting elder brother (Ramesh Thapar) and his love, Mala (Meena Kumari). The brother, who refuses to accept Noshu's help because his money is tainted, eventually dies a destitute. In the end, Noshu realizes that his path is wrong and comes back to his roots. *Footpath* reaffirmed the reputation of Dilip Kumar as a sensitive actor, signifying the possibility of his valuable participation in the emerging new-wave cinema, which had started taking shape at that time. But this possibility was never explored, neither by the film makers nor by the actor.

Zia Sarhadi

Zia Sarhadi (b. 1914), the writer-film maker, was another important figure of the classical period known for his strong political stances. Although he was a product of Mehboob's school of film making, he was greatly influenced by IPTA.

He was born in Peshawar (now in Pakistan). He first joined East India Films, Calcutta, in 1933 and then moved to Sagar Movietone in 1934, where Mehboob Khan included him in his core group. Mehboob cast him as hero in *Manmohan* (1936), for which Sarhadi also wrote the script and the lyrics. He scripted Mehboob's *Bahen* (1941), *Jagirdar* (1937) and *Anokha Pyar* (1948). Later he became a noted scenarist and writer at Ranjit Studio.

Sarhadi's best-known trilogy – *Hum Log* (1951), *Footpath* (1953) and *Awaaz* (1956, produced by Mehboob) – designed as part of IPTA's efforts in film making in the 1950s, established this unusual film maker among the top names of the classical era. Apart from his own films, he also scripted *Kal Ki Baat* (1937), *Jeevan Saathi* (1939), *Sajani* (1940), *Garib* (1942), *Badi Maa* (1945), *Elaan* (1947), *Dil Ki Duniya* (1949) and *Khel* (1950). He also wrote the dialogues for *Baiju Bawra* (1952). After independence, he migrated to Pakistan mostly remaining there, except for a brief period in the mid-1970s.

B. R. Chopra's *Naya Daur* was a unique film even on the broader canvas of world cinema as it took up, perhaps for the first time on celluloid, the academic debate relating to high capital-intensive technology vis-à-vis traditional technology (involving tremendous physical labour) for promoting rural development. Simply put, the theme was: man versus machine. The film also tried to show how an alien technology (useful in developed countries), when forcibly implemented, can adversely affect the socio-economic life of the downtrodden. The film validates the proposition that the threat of private ownership of means of production for the sake of modernization would play havoc with the livelihood of the poor and this threat can only be overcome by the people's collective power.

The movie starts off with a series of idyllic scenes, punctuated with songs, of a village whose people are peace loving, friendly and hard working. The real action begins begins when Kundan (Jeevan), the son of Seth Magan Lal (Nazir Hussain), first introduces an electric saw in the local mill and then a motorized bus for public transport. The saw threatens the livelihood of many woodcutters and the bus creates insecurity among the local *tonga* (horse carriage) drivers. The economic, caste and religious divisions in the rural society are woven into the main story of the rivalry between Shankar (Dilip Kumar), a *tonga* driver, and Krishna (Ajit) the village carpenter, both of whom are eagerly vying for the attention and love of the heroine Rajni (Vyjayanthimala).

The narration reaches a dramatic high point when Shankar, despite initially facing tremendous odds, mobilizes the whole village community facing the threat of mechanization to build a road through rocky and inhospitable terrain to prove the community's belief that traditional technology is no less efficient in meeting people's needs. This collective initiative by the village gets massive publicity in the media (thanks to the comedian Johnny Walker who plays a reporter in the film) as a unique experiment in harnessing people's power for the community's benefit.

A race takes place between the bus driven by Kundan on the main road and the *tonga* driven by Shankar who takes the route of the newly built road. Shankar eventually wins the race and the film finally ends when the benevolent father figure, Seth Magan Lal, hopes that a humanist attitude towards the new technologies will abolish all class divisions. The hero argues for collectivization as the proletarian way of managing the technology. One interesting aspect of the narrative is that it is the villain who advances the policy of technological modernization being pursued by the country. His clash with the hero is not over the heroine as is the case in most films, but due to differing viewpoints.

Dilip Kumar's performance was exceptional. He essayed the role of the *tonga* driver with aplomb. Some of the scenes from this movie stand indelibly etched in every aficionado's memory. *Naya Daur* stands out as an important milestone in the thespian's career.

Bimal Roy's *Madhumati*, one of the most beautiful films ever made in Hindi cinema, was a highly moving saga of immortal love. The film presented Dilip Kumar in search of his soulmate amidst a domain in which suffering and helplessness were inescapable. Deploying the whole range of his naturalist style, the actor covers a vast area in terms of acting abilities. He is seen in full form while expressing his love for Madhumati who epitomizes nature in all its beauty and innocence. In this ethereal love tale, he transcends his present life and, from the depths of his subconscious, he rediscovers the injustice done to his love in his previous birth.

In this classic, the director, Bimal Roy, and the writer, Ritwik Ghatak, etched a surrealistic plot in which the age-old feudal oppression and brutality are avenged through a transmigration of souls.

Devendra (Dilip Kumar), after his car breaks down on a rainy night, takes shelter from a raging storm in a deserted *haveli* (mansion), where he hears a woman crying. Upon exploring the mansion, he finds a painting of its former owner Raja Ugranarayan. Devendra intuitively feels he must have painted the portrait in a previous life when he was called Anand. This premonition finds expression in the form of a flashback to Anand's life when he worked as a manager on a plantation. Anand was in love with Madhumati (Vyjayanthimala), a young tribal girl from a nearby village. The girl dies while escaping from a libidinous assault by Raja Ugranarayan (Pran) by jumping off the roof of the *haveli*. The hero lays a trap for Ugranarayan by means of another woman, Madhavi (who looks exactly like the dead Madhumati). But it turns out that it is the original Madhumati's soul, which returns to take revenge.

In its texture and appeal, *Madhumati* appeared like a poem on celluloid. The photography by cinematographer Dilip Gupta created a succession of magical images. Salil Choudury's enchanting musical score and Hrishikesh Mukherjee's editing exquisitely enhanced the eerily romantic atmosphere. The film went on to bag nine *Filmfare* awards, but the hero was *not* one of the recipients despite the fact that, as the tormented lover, Dilip Kumar excelled himself.

The Genius Called Bimal Roy

Bimal Roy (1909–66), the first ever film maker who transformed cinema into poetry, was among the founders of the classical cinema of the 1950s. He was born in Dhaka and completed his education in Calcutta. Like his mentor Nitin Bose, he was a child prodigy; he became an excellent still photographer in his early years. He began his film career as an assistant cameraman to Nitin Bose. Soon he became the top cinematographer of New Theatres and shot P. C. Barua's *Devdas* (1935), *Grihadah, Maya* (both 1936) and *Mukti* (1937) and Amar Mullick's *Badi Didi* (1939) and *Abhinetri* (1940).

Bimal Roy's first film *Udayer Pathey* (1944) was about the trade union movement and it evoked a great response in Bengal. Later, it was made in Hindi titled *Humrahi*. Interestingly, this film's songs included Tagore's *Jana Gana Mana* ... which in a few years was to become the country's national anthem. Although he is accredited to have pioneered the cinema of protest with his first film, his later films remained far from radical. For New Theatres he also directed *Pehla Aadmi* (1950), depicting the liberation struggle of the Indian National Army (INA) spearheaded by Subhash Chandra Bose.

In contrast with Mehoob Khan, Bimal Roy's route to progressive cinema was fairly straight. Having been groomed in the Bengal tradition of New Theatres, he broadened its scope by refining P. C. Barua's cinema of self-indulgence, making it more socially and culturally specific, and above all, suggesting a social reconstruction devoid of the old feudal value system. Roy further modernized the Bengal genre of romantic melodrama by incorporating the realist style of Vittorio De Sica, the famous Italian film maker and actor. He experimented with new film techniques, evolved an aesthetic style and introduced simplicity and understatement, commensurate with his intellectual efforts, to reach a wider audience.

In his highly acclaimed masterpiece, produced under the aegis of the Indian People's Theatre Association (IPTA), *Do Bigha Zameen* (1953), Bimal Roy depicted the pathos of migration from rural to urban areas. This film offered Balraj Sahni the role of a lifetime. His other films dealt with conflicts between the old and new values, drifting gradually towards reformist ideals. Among his later films, *Parakh* (1960) should be considered one of the most remarkable films in Indian cinema.

A unique contribution of the Bimal Roy school was that it trained many talented directors like Hemen Gupta, Asit Sen, Hrishikesh Mukherjee, Gulzar (real name Sampooran Singh) and Bimal Dutt, who went on to create their own niches in Hindi cinema.

Bimal Roy provided a crucial turning point in the career of Dilip Kumar by casting him in *Devdas* (1955). *Madhumati* (1958) and *Yahudi* (1958) further exploited the immense collaborative talents of the two masters.

S. S. Vasan's *Paigham*, a tribute to the working class by the master, presented Dilip Kumar as a highly talented technician

(à la K. L. Saigal in *President*) in a textile mill, where he impresses
the mill owner (Motilal) and the workers by repairing state-of-
the-art machinery. However, he soon becomes a union leader and
leads the strike by the workers who are demanding their rights.
This move results in souring of his relations with the mill owner
and his (Dilip Kumar's) not-so-well-to-do elder brother (played
by Raaj Kumar), who also works in the same mill and who
opposes the strike. Meanwhile, the romantic aspect comes into
play. The mill owner's daughter (B. Saroja Devi) falls desperately
in love with Dilip Kumar even though she knows that he is in
love with a poor girl (Vyjayanthimala). Later, it is revealed that
Vyjayanthimala is also the daughter of the mill owner who, in
the past, had ditched her mother after having an affair with her.
In the end, the film, like *President*, stressed the importance of sound
owner–worker relations as the key to economic and industrial
harmony and growth.

In *Ganga Jumna*, directed by Nitin Bose and the only film
produced by Dilip Kumar, the actor made his final contribution
to the realist cinema. The film, which had a very strong social
underpinning, enforced with excellent directional and technical
support, presented the actor completely integrated with the
theme of the film and his relationship with the rest of the cast.
The film also signified a unique linguistic breakthrough: it used
the rural dialect of eastern Uttar Pradesh and neighbouring areas,
Bhojpuri, and yet had big stars and the associated large-canvas
sets and paraphernalia.

Shot in Technicolor by veteran V. Baba Saheb, the film
narrated the tale of two brothers on opposite sides of the law:
Ganga (Dilip Kumar) and Jumna (played by Dilip Kumar's
younger brother, Nasir Khan). Ganga, a farm labourer, is framed
by the zamindar (Anwar Hussain) for a crime he did not commit,
and sent to jail. After his release, he becomes the leader of the
dacoits living in the ravines. Meanwhile, he marries his childhood
beloved Dhanno (Vyjayanthimala). His brother, whom Ganga has
sent to the city for education, becomes a police officer. When

Ganga is to become a father, he decides to return to the village to ask for the people's forgiveness, but his righteous brother Jumna (who has been posted there) asks him to surrender to the police. Dhanno intervenes and tries to take him away. In the ensuing gun battle, Dhanno dies in the crossfire and Jumna shoots his rebel brother dead. This section was studded with some of the most poignant scenes ever to be filmed in Indian cinema. In fact, the 'star of the millennium', Amitabh Bachchan, considers Dilip Kumar's role in *Ganga Jumna* his career's best performance.

Ganga Jumna drew some of its inspiration from the great saga, *Mother India*. Although Mehboob Khan provided the basic model of the *baghi* (the rebel) in the form of the angry rural youth Birju (played by Sunil Dutt), it was in *Ganga Jumna* that Dilip Kumar redesigned this character with far more depth and insight. The making of this film, like the two others in this period that dealt with dacoits – Raj Kapoor's *Jis Desh Mein Ganga Behti Hai* (1960) and Sunil Dutt's *Mujhe Jeene Do* (1963) – was also influenced by the dedicated reformer Jayprakash Narayan's famous crusade for eradicating the problem of dacoity in rural India. JP's efforts sought to win over the people gone astray by peaceful Gandhian means by persuading them to return to the mainstream. This approach evidently enthused these three film makers. In *Jis Desh Mein Ganga Behti Hai*, Raj Kapoor modelled the character of the protagonist simply on Jayprakash Narayan himself. A simple-hearted activist single-handedly disseminates his peace doctrine among the dacoit community settled in the ravines of Chambal and finally brings it back to the mainstream. In *Mujhe Jeene Do*, Sunil Dutt modelled his image of a dacoit on his earlier portrayal in *Mother India*.

However, among these three films, *Ganga Jumna* was the most authentic in portraying the root of the dacoity problem: rampant exploitation of the rural poor by the zamindars and the inhuman response of the state. The failure of the law-enforcing machinery to address the grievances of the honest labourer-turned-rebel, and his eventual killing by his upright brother, showed the omnipotent nature of the state, which refuses to look into the actual causes of human suffering and exploitation and has a stock response: crush the non-conformist.

In *Ganga Jumna*, Dilip Kumar came up with some innovations: he completely changed his body language to liberate himself from his usual restrained postures, while, at the same time, he revelled in his new spontaneity. The actor totally declassified his image from his earlier characters (which were mostly set in the aristocratic or middle-class milieu) and presented on screen a typical rustic rural youth, rambunctious but down-to-earth and strongly rooted in his socio-cultural milieu. The metamorphosis of this youth into a dacoit was one of the high points of the movie. The film also depicted a distinct class attitude against which the protagonist rebelled and had to face the grim consequences. Composer Naushad was on home ground here, and came up with some memorable folk songs.

The Death Syndrome

In the classical period as well as later, the highly appreciated death scene, enacted by Dilip Kumar in the climax in as many as fourteen films, has been a singular trademark of his screen persona and one of the most compelling points of reference in his inventory of skills. Here, the protagonist, after undergoing a protracted struggle and a great deal of suffering to uphold his convictions, meets his end virtually as if on a sacrificial altar. In fact, many characters played by Dilip Kumar, at least in the classical period, tend to emphasize that irrespective of whether one is rich or poor, young or old, life is essentially futile; it has to be given up on one pretext or the other. As the character dissolves his identity in suffering and finally in death, it is as if his physical being has lost its meaning.

It seems that the death scene was a consciously designed ploy by the actor and his script writers to precipitate the release of the pent-up emotions built up during the course of the narrative and to provide the by-then already emotionally charged audience the much-needed catharsis from the intensely melancholic experience, which seemed to be unending. Moreover, through death, the artiste not only achieves a 'grand finale' to life, but also gains sanctity, according to the Indian philosophy, for sacrificing one's life for a cause. Such an act, it is believed, would eventually lead to the salvation of the soul. Thus, death becomes some sort of a celebration, which involves a prolonged ritual of departure, often in the arms of a dear one, replete with moving dialogues. At times, many relatives, friends, well-wishers and other persons from the community surround the dying man. No other artiste, except perhaps Meena Kumari, had this ability to infuse a dying character with such an intricate range of emotions.

Towards the Liberation of the 'Tragic' Image

The seemingly unending appearances of Dilip Kumar in tragedy-laden roles during the classical phase, and the possibility of the audience becoming less appreciative of such roles, were having discomforting implications for both the parties. The actor began to realize that he was becoming increasingly typecast and perhaps foresaw its negative impact on his future career. He perhaps also apprehended a gradual loss of patronage of his vast, faithful audience if he continued with his tragic image.

At the personal level, the anxiety caused by doing a series of tragedies in quick succession and a kind of acute melancholy being caused by them in his own mental make-up seemed to have created some kind of an apprehension in the actor. The problem seemed to have become so grave that Dilip Kumar had to seek treatment from an eminent psychotherapist in England. The consultant proposed one single solution: switch over to comedy roles. And it worked; the switchover brought to the fore an immense hidden talent for comedy in the actor, thereby initiating a complete transformation of his screen persona. The gains from this transformation were substantial, as the heady blending of tragedy and comedy that took place was to have far-reaching implications for his career. This change indeed resulted in his emergence as a complete actor. This switching over also led to a greater degree of spontaneity in the actor's performance.

The audience also felt equally relieved. The overwhelming sagas of suffering, pain and death depicted on screen by their favourite hero gave way to more lively, jubilant and fun-filled narratives, with the hero portraying a character with whom they could now sing and dance. The outcome was very refreshing and extremely entertaining. Another significant feature was that, with his comedies, Dilip Kumar entered the domain of well-established entertainers, including Raj Kapoor and the whole set of comedians, and even outsmarted them in many ways. The blending of tragedy with comedy by the actor, in fact, reflected the emerging 'split personality' in most characterizations in Indian cinema. A hero or heroine now had to carefully balance these two aspects in their roles (with the outstanding exception of Meena Kumari, who remained largely tied to her image of tragedy queen).

Dilip Kumar's cinema thus witnessed a unique division into two streams in response to the actor's liberation from the stereotyped image of the tragedian. This development not only led to an enrichment of his film personality, but also resulted in the 'revision of the syllabus for film acting'. The film makers immediately responded to the availability of this new combination, and soon some landmark films were on the anvil.

In the classical phase, three films *Aan* (1952), *Azaad* (1955) and *Kohinoor* (1960) were the outcome of the liberation of Dilip Kumar's image from a depressive-neurotic caught in the morbidity of pain and suffering to a dynamic and upbeat personality. The hero now appeared to be not only deriving strength from his suffering but he was also addressing wider social concerns to some extent, moving cautiously away from the narrow preoccupations with a woman's love.

Mehboob Khan's *Aan*, one of the first Technicolor spectacles in Indian cinema, provided to our hero the first-ever opportunity to move beyond his image of the besotted lover to an action hero who possessed strong convictions and resolute inner strength. Conceived as a tribute to the formation of the Republic of India, this film, a grand costume drama, captured the colourful life of Rajasthan in all its glory. The colour sequences brought alive an exceedingly beautiful countryside, the neo-classical decor, village belles and farmers dancing and singing lively songs, and warriors on horseback, who rode their steeds imperiously under fiery golden-orange skies.

The film, in a series of powerful sequences and highly charged dramatic interludes, depicted a peasant uprising against the corrupt and intrigue-ridden world of the maharajas of colonial India. The hero, Jai Tilak (Dilip Kumar), is the young chieftain of a Rajput clan, the Haraas, who by tradition are bound to serve the royal family headed by the benevolent ruler (Murad). The villain is Prince Shamsher Singh (Premnath) who tries to usurp power by killing his elder brother, the ruler. In the true spirit of liberation, the hero draws up a project to destroy the arrogance and oppression of the tyrannical usurper, even at the cost of sacrificing his childhood love Mangla (played by Nimmi).

The hero, much to the distress of Mangla, resolves to tame the proud princess (played by Nadira), the sister of the villain. For his part, Shamsher Singh kidnaps Mangla and tries to molest her, causing her to fall to her death. Jai retaliates by capturing the rajkumari (princess), forcing her to take Mangla's place. Eventually, it turns out that the senior ruler is still alive and the princess realizes she loves her suitor. Jai, with the support of the people, defeats and kills Shamsher. On the eve of the final victory of the masses over the royal tyranny, when the erstwhile king declares his real identity, the people start shouting '*Maharaj Ki Jai Ho!*' (Victory to the king.) The king stops them and declares: 'Not mine! Say *Jai Praja!*' (victory to the people), thereby indicating that royalty has to make way for a democratic republic.

Aan presented an extremely youthful Dilip Kumar, with a glowing face and a sparkle in his eyes, who projected a definite sense of dynamism in his acting style, which was greatly enhanced by sharp and witty dialogues. And yet, the character effectively concealed the lingering pain caused by his decision to abandon his childhood love so as to execute his project of transforming the arrogant princess into a humble woman. In this endeavour, he fulfilled the last wish of Mangla who wanted him to bring about a mass awakening that would establish the people's power and put an end to the atrocities committed by despots.

Three years after the colossal success of *Aan*, Pakshiraja Studio's *Azaad* provided yet another breakthrough for the actor for expanding his acting domain. It was the first film Dilip Kumar did in South India under the direction of S. M. S. Naidu. The film was about a zestful young man's heroic efforts in organizing the poor against the prevailing feudal order and creating an ideal model of a self-governed society far away from the shadow of the state. Representing liberation metaphorically, the protagonist, à la Robin Hood, is a dispenser of justice who reallocates the wealth looted from the rich among the poor. Despite the immoral stance of the hero, the conflict looked far more humane considering the violence-ridden spectacles in present-day cinema.

Azaad was a Hindi remake of Pakshiraja Studio's Tamil superhit *Malaikallan* (1954), starring M. G. Ramachandran, who, after a phenomenally successful career in films, went on to become the chief minister of Tamil Nadu in 1977. Dilip Kumar appeared in the twin roles of Khan Saheb, who is an urbane businessman by day, but becomes the urban vigilante Azaad by night (it is instructive to note that at that time not even Hollywood had the temerity to cast businessmen as vengeful superheroes). Heroine Shobha (Meena Kumari) is kidnapped by villains Sunder (Pran), Jagirdar (Murad) and Chunder (Nazir). Azaad rescues her and she falls in love with him. Various efforts by the villains to kidnap her again are foiled by Azaad, as are other crimes, while Khan Saheb takes the investigating cops (Om Prakash and Raj Mehra) on a merry ride before his identity is revealed.

Azaad was one of the early films that laid the foundation for double roles by the same character through changes in appearance and style. Dilip Kumar, in his first-ever twin role, mesmerized the audience with his acumen in depicting two highly diverse characters: Khan Saheb the elderly Muslim aristocrat, who talks in chaste Urdu, has a great sense of humour and is fond of music and Azaad, who breezes through the film as the flamboyant, dashing young crusader. The peppy musical score for the movie was the creation of C. Ramchandra, who also lent his voice to Dilip Kumar.

S. U. Sunny's *Kohinoor* was among the final tributes of our indigenous hero to the classical film era and the artiste indeed was truly in his element. The film, one of the greatest musicals ever made (again thanks to composer Naushad), in fact, represented a case study in film making, with each department perfectly in tune with the overall tenor of the film. Sunny devised a clever interweaving of diverse components: classical music and dance; the prevailing culture of the princelings; the palace life; the impending intrigues; and an extended celebration of comedy, curtailed intermittently by the designs of the villain. The climax was the fight sequence in which the patrons of love, music and dance ultimately emerge triumphant.

Kohinoor, a landmark in entertainment, was an authentic depiction of the Indian cultural ethos in which Indian music and dance flourished under the patronage of small kingdoms during the medieval and later the colonial era. Presenting Dilip Kumar as an exponent of classical music, the film builds up on the music itself and becomes a beautiful tribute of commercial cinema to the Indian classical music and dance traditions. In fact, after *Baiju Bawra* (1952) and *Shabab* (1954), it was *Kohinoor*, which marked the unique contribution of composer Naushad in continuing the trend of classical music in Hindi cinema.

Kohinoor: A Brew of Rare Vintage
The Times of India, 20 November 1960

Kohinoor is a film which revives memories of the swashbuckling hero [defying] death to get his girl.

The content of this many-hued picture is a heady brew of rare vintage. All the gags known to showmen from the early days ... duels and dances, songs and spectacle, torrid romance and ... comedy [have been included] ...

Maestro Naushad once again scores a personal triumph in this picture; though he has considerably changed his style .... Shakeel Badayuni who wrote the superb lyrics for *Mughal-e-Azam* and [Guru Dutt's] *Chaudhvin Ka Chand*, completes the hat trick with his memorable songs in this film ...

The real highlights of the film are the eye-filling dance ensembles led by vivacious Kum Kum. They have been skilfully choreographed by Hiralal, Sitara Devi, Satya Narayan and Chiman Seth. Wajahat Mirza's pithy dialogue enlivens this picture, photographed by veteran Faredoon Irani ...

Dilip Kumar, matinee idol of the Indian screen, sheds the mask of tragedy to play a flamboyant and out-and-out comedy role. He displays a flair for comedy and brings the roof down with his utterly delightful characterization ... Meena Kumari, the supreme tragedienne, joins hands with Dilip in the merry proceedings and even fights the villains single-handed. Veteran Jeevan [the villain] is his usual boisterous self and proves that the passage of time has not cramped his grand manner ... Mukhri is utterly delightful as Dilip's sidekick ...

In *Kohinoor*, Dilip Kumar plays an unusual character: a young prince, vagabondish, carefree and unconventional, pursuing music and love with great enthusiasm. As the plot develops, the prince enacts the role of Kohinoor Baba, the spiritual healer who mends broken hearts with his soul-stirring music. He also uses his singing prowess to save the rajkumari (princess), his fiancée, from the clutches of the villain. In this role, the actor seemed to be attempting a complete amalgamation of some of the elements of his earlier characters: the flamboyant, suave, sword-wielding chieftain of *Aan*, excelling in rapid-fire dialogue delivery; the comical nawab of *Azaad*; and the romantic singer of *Udan Khatola*. The liberation from his tragic image and the tremendous ease with which he performed comedy, as witnessed in *Kohinoor*, also influenced Dilip Kumar's screen persona in the coming decade, particularly in *Leader* (1964), *Ganga Jumna* and *Ram Aur Shyam* (1967). It is interesting to note that 1960 was a somewhat peculiar year for Dilip Kumar; he essayed two diametrically opposite roles in *Kohinoor* and *Mughal-e-Azam*.

The Post-Classical Period

Before we get back to Dilip Kumar, we need to take a brief diversion. The mid-1960s can be considered as the second turning point in Hindi cinema as it witnessed a qualitative change in content, texture, treatment, presentation, music and overall social appeal. Indian cinema now began to break free from its classical mould to build a modernist image, which was unfortunately not based on an enrichment of the classical format. The new trends did not enhance its scope in tune with the times; rather, what resulted was the overall decline of the Hindi film. This wonderful art form lost its inherent aura and grace. The earlier strengths of a film, namely, story, narration, characterizations and its overall emotional and cultural content, were whittled away. Hindi cinema thus began to gradually lose its intellectual basis and creative continuity. This downward spiral also marked the end of committed cinema for many celebrated film makers of the bygone era. Music, however, maintained its predominance, although the classical elements were slowly disappearing.

The changeover of celluloid technology from black-and-white to colour during this period transported the Indian film into an entirely new domain of glamour and glitz. The films became glossy with emphasis on depicting the affluent lifestyles of the traditionally wealthy as well as those of the nouveau riche. A typical film of this era resorted to elaborate indoor decor, picturesque outdoors and lavish wardrobes for the lead artistes (some of whom changed their costumes several times during a single song sequence). Even the rural settings were 'beautified' as evident from the costumes, the sets and the outdoor locales. The deficiencies in a wobbly storyline and a weak script were compensated for by an emphasis on opulence and ostentation.

The image of the lead pair also witnessed a dramatic change. In most movies, the hero of the post-classical period was far more debonair than, say, the Dev Anand of the 1950s; he was sufficiently 'Westernized', possessed oodles of charm, apart from being stylish, cocky and full of energy. Capable of doing no wrong, he emerged as the ultimate winner of both the romantic and material worlds. The heroines too underwent a complete 'remodelling'. By and large, decked up as glamorous dolls (with elaborate hairdos, which were then in vogue) and being peripheral to the theme of the film, they lost the soothing mystical beauty and the feminine sensitivities of their counterparts in the earlier periods. In fact, the heroines' sensuality became an object of perversion. Lecherous overtures, either through gestures or songs, became the order of the day. Thus, the post-classical period announced the ostensible 'liberation' not only of the Hindi film but also of the actors and actresses.

The foregoing changes made the original classical format lose its identity. The making of a film soon essentially became a piecemeal, slapdash and purely formula-oriented exercise based on certain set ingredients for ensuring success at the box office. This decline affected nearly all film makers, writers and lead artistes. K. A. Abbas was now of no use to Raj Kapoor, Chetan Anand to Dev Anand and S. Raza and Wajahat Mirza to Dilip Kumar. Mehboob Khan, Bimal Roy and Guru Dutt had already departed from the scene. Some films of this period, which had a semblance of the classical-era features, failed at the box office. The new cinema went 'pulp', and lost its earlier strong links with literature. The result of such a loss of its moorings took away the soul of the Indian film from its body.

This unfortunate deterioration can be attributed to a combination of factors: the decay of the film studio as the central institution for film making and locating and creating new talent; the arrival of a new brand of free-lance film producers; and, above all, an overriding commercial mindset, blocking the possibilities for expanding the domain of film aesthetics and for a renewed effort towards developing the next generation of quality cinema.

To come out of the shadow of the classical film, the post-classical cinema based itself on the following aspects:

(1) A complete redefinition of film aesthetics and appearance, making, in most cases, not only the heroine but also the hero pink faced, effete and namby-pamby. The heroines appeared gorgeous, alluring and mannequin-like and were more decorative than substantial. The heroes made far more provocative gestures and sported flashy, and at times, gaudy costumes. Elaborate indoor settings (sometimes garish) and extensive outdoor locales, particularly the hill stations, to create a sense of freedom and escapism were resorted to. Song sequences sometimes were thrust upon the audience rather than their blending with the narrative.

(2) A simplification of the interpretation of love, by taking away its platonic/mystical feel and touch, thereby making it look less intimate and more an externalized communication; in other words, 'an affair'.

(3) A renewed emphasis on a new genre of flashy and fast romance combined often with a crime plot (which had a secondary status in the classical period), employing in a rudimentary manner the basic model developed by Guru Dutt Films and Navketan in the early 1950s.

The three films, which bore the typical hallmarks of the post-classical period, were Subodh Mukerjee's *Junglee* (1961), Raj Kapoor's *Sangam* (1964) and B. R. Chopra's *Waqt* (1965).

Junglee, a musical comedy, transformed Shammi Kapoor completely: he emerged as the quintessential Westernized hero, an Indian version of the legendary Elvis Presley.

Sangam became a trendsetter in that it was the first Hindi film shot extensively in foreign locales, which considerably boosted its commercial value. Soon, many other film makers followed suit. Borrowing its plot from Mehboob's *Andaz* (1949), the film reworked the eternal love triangle (here made up of Raj Kapoor, Vyjayanthimala and Rajendra Kumar) in an entirely new and liberated sensuous environment.

While his films of the 1950s tended to indulge in socialist rhetoric, *Sangam* indicated a sudden intellectual decline in Raj Kapoor's film-making standards. During the post-classical period, he resorted to different tactics to reaffirm his status as show-biz's top impresario. Unable to carry his Chaplinesque image any further and finding it difficult to envision a new direction for his cinema in the changing socio-political milieu, he took the easier path of translating his obsession with the female figure into cinema. His work began to discard the earlier thematic strengths and the treatment now looked superficial with an explicit emphasis on sensuality. His next highly ambitious (ostensibly autobiographical) project *Mera Naam Joker* (1970) was again suffused with several sensuous ingredients, against all expectations. This film did not evoke much audience response and failed miserably at the box office. Raj Kapoor was soon in trouble financially. To make sure that he made up his losses and also to ensure that he was still capable of coming up with new concepts and ideas, he launched *Bobby*, which was released in 1973 and turned out to be a huge money spinner (but more on this film later). *Bobby* was followed by *Satyam Shivam Sundaram* (1978), with Zeenat Aman as the sensuous female figure.

Waqt, a remake of the lost-and-found tale (à la *Kismet*, the old-time classic), set the style of the Indian film for both indoors and outdoors in the coming years. The film was studded with decked up mansions, different shaped and highly decorated beds, lawns with fountains, slick racing cars, fancy motorboats and romantic duets amidst enchanting gardens and mountain locations, apart from dramatic court scenes.

The other luminaries of the post-classical era of the 1960s and 1970s included Dev Anand, Ramanand Sagar, J. Om Prakash, Nazir Hussain, Vijay Anand, Shakti Samanta, Raj Khosla, Arjun Hingorani, Manmohan Desai, G. P. Sippy and Manoj Kumar. Their cinema determined the making of the personae of the leading stars of this period (some of whom were active in the classical period as well): Shammi Kapoor, Rajendra Kumar, Shashi Kapoor, Dharmendra, Manoj Kumar, Biswajit, Joy Mukerji, Jeetendra, Rajesh Khanna, Feroze Khan, Sanjay Khan, Vinod Khanna and Sanjeev Kumar (among the heroes) and Meena Kumari, Nutan, Vyjayanthimala, Waheeda Rehman, Mala Sinha, Sadhana, Saira Banu, Nanda, Asha Parekh, Sharmila Tagore, Babita, Leena Chandavarkar, Raakhee, Hema Malini, Rekha, Mumtaz, Zeenat Aman, Parveen Babi and Neetu Singh (among the heroines).

The late 1960s and early 1970s indeed belonged to the highly charismatic Rajesh Khanna, who achieved dizzying heights in one film after another, beginning with Shakti Samanta's *Aradhana* and Raj Khosla's *Do Raaste*, both released in 1969. The actor soon earned the sobriquet of 'the phenomenon'.

The 1970s witnessed the gradual downfall of Dev Anand. He began to direct and write his own films, largely focusing on the disorientation of youth vis-à-vis the traditional Indian way of life, but failed largely in upholding the earlier Navketan tradition of providing engrossing cinema. On, the other hand, younger brother Vijay Anand (nicknamed Goldie), with his innovative craftsmanship, introduced many new features in the narration and treatment of the film, particularly in the dexterous use of music and dance. *Teesri Manzil* (1966), *Jewel Thief* (1967), *Johny Mera Naam* (1970) (slick, suspense-filled movies) and *Tera Mere Sapne* (1971, based on doctor-turned-writer A. J. Cronin's masterpiece *The Citadel*) directed by him, provided a new lease of life to the crime thrillers and social movies but with far more gloss and earthy sensuality.

Manoj Kumar, the actor-turned producer-director unleashed a spate of nationalistic movies, replete with melodrama and music (*Upkaar* 1967, *Purab Aur Paschsim* 1970, *Roti Kapda Aur Makaan* 1974 and *Kranti* 1981). (His cinema is discussed later in this book.)

The house of Barjatiyas introduced a new genre: the cinema of the middle class. More or less a rework of numerous family dramas churned out earlier by A. V. Meyappan Studios (of South India), this cinema championed the cause of family kinship, the importance of the joint family system and the amity and goodwill among various generations. Any deviant behaviour from the traditional set-up was appropriately corrected within this framework.

Amidst the overall decline of the film culture during the post-classical period, a small band of sensitive film makers like Hrishikesh Mukherjee, Asit Sen, Basu Bhattacharya, Basu Chatterjee and lyricist-turned-film maker Gulzar, all alumni of the old Bengal school, kept the tradition of good cinema alive.[7] Their works were marked by excellence in blending Bengal's romantic literary tradition with the undercurrents of neo-realism. Not only did they make a significant contribution by rising above the qualitative decline in Hindi films, but also they were instrumental in introducing a new idiom of cinematic expression and reviving its linkages with the earlier traditions.

This period also saw the emergence of larger-than-life anti-establishment cinema. The engine of this cinema was the new superstar, Amitabh Bachchan, who put in place his extremely popular image of the angry young man with films like *Zanjeer* (1973) and *Deewar* (1975). (His cinema is discussed in Volume 2.)

Some of the other unconventional films of this era were: Ram Sharma's *Shaheed* (1965), Rono Deb Mukerji's *Tu Hi Meri Zindagi* (1965), Sunil Dutt's *Reshma Aur Shera* (1971) and Tapan Sinha's *Sagina* (1974). M. S. Sathyu's *Garam Hawa* (1973) was a landmark film depicting the trauma of Partition meaningfully and forcefully. Among the numerous films of this period, a handful, such as *Aashirwad, Anokhi Raat, Teesri Kasam, Mamta, Dil Ek Mandir, Shaheed* and *Khamoshi* also looked more like the products of the classical period. *Teesri Kasam*, envisioned by lyricist Shailendra and based on a short story by the celebrated Hindi writer Phaneshwarnath 'Renu', was perhaps the most outstanding example of indigenous cinema during this period. Had it been made in the 1950s, it would have been a big box-office hit, but failed commercially when it was released in 1966.

In this era, comedy created a distinct niche for itself. Largely organized around the persona of Johnny Walker, Kishore Kumar, Mehmood (full name Mehmood Ali) and I. S. Johar, the films of this genre attained a fair amount of success and recognition. Other 'jesters' – Keshto Mukherjee, G. Asrani and Kawarjit Paintal – also showcased their comic antics as sidekicks of the hero in a large number of films. The domain of this genre was expanded by other traditional heroes such as Dilip Kumar, Shammi Kapoor, Dharmendra, Sanjeev Kumar and Amitabh Bachchan.

The film melody, which reigned supreme till around the mid-1960s, began losing its classical splendour. With the overall decline in music tastes and artistic standards, and large-scale plagiarizing of Western pop music, the film song started losing its original pristine musical form and content and gradually acquired a noisy, staccato and patchy structure devoid of its earlier aesthetic appeal. In the 1980s, one had to be careful while listening to film songs; most of them assaulted the eardrums. However, all hope was not lost. A few dedicated composers (especially Khayyam, Hridyanath Mangeshkar and Ravindra Jain) managed to keep the melody alive.

Dilip Kumar's Films and Portrayals in the Post-Classical Period and Beyond

Like his contemporaries, notably Raj Kapoor and Dev Anand,

Dilip Kumar failed to reverse the negative trend in Hindi cinema. Consequently, a possible second phase of classical cinema did not materialize. By the early 1960s, the name of Dilip Kumar had become synonymous with the most versatile and successful actor in this part of the world. He had indeed acquired complete mastery over capturing the nuances of his art and his portrayals had gained unusual strength and depth, apart from wide acclaim from the majority of the people. But the quality of his films began to lose the charm and the grace of the classical period. Hardly any serious breakthroughs in terms of worthwhile screenplays and characterizations were forthcoming his way. It is ironical that the actor, who had painstakingly worked to master the essence of film acting and elevated it to an art form, was unable to get roles in keeping with his capabilities and potential.

In this period, Dilip Kumar carried himself on the *basis of his talent*; the overall quality of his films became secondary. The portrayals were now largely drawn on his acting skills already acquired in the classical phase of his career, but there was a distinct shift in their execution. There was no more the typical natural softness of the singer-lover and the passive sufferer as in his earlier portrayals, but a suave and aggressive protagonist, whose attitude, even in suffering, was accompanied by a different use of body language and facial expressions.

Also, the mannerisms and style of the master now looked more pre-designed rather than spontaneous, indicating the actor's preoccupations with his own larger-than-life image. Most writers and directors conceived films according to this prerequisite. As most films had weak story formulations and lacked the required seamless integration with other areas, the actor now had to exercise his predominance on the overall nature of the film; he used his 'stamp of authority' to enhance the prospects of his films at the box office. This period, in fact, marked the final liberation of the actor from the influence of his old masters and a consolidation of his self-acquired autonomy in influencing the nature of his films.

The contribution of the master to Hindi cinema in this period was twofold. The first was the characterization in *Ganga Jumna*, which provided the highly usable blueprint for the soon-to-emerge cinema of violence, depicting the extra-constitutional fight of the wronged individual against the powerful criminal forces. The second was in developing a new image of the Indian film hero as in *Leader* (1964): extrovert, dynamic, suave and clever. Thus, *Ganga Jumna* and *Leader*, both scripted by Dilip Kumar, were to establish the two basic paradigms of Hindi cinema.

Ram Mukherji's (the father of the present-day heroine Rani Mukherji) *Leader* moved our quintessential romantic tragedian from an agonized existence, often located in a feudal setting, to a cosmopolitan milieu and infused in him new self-confidence and courage. Although Dilip Kumar in this role was articulating his newly found idealism and anti-establishment stance through an entirely new technique, the basic moral attributes of the character were the same as in the classical era: the unshakeable uprightness; a deep sense of social consciousness; and a complete dedication to the woman he loves. But, at the same time, in the new avatar, he was sometimes seen indulging in self-gratification at the expense of others. The film *Leader*, in fact, defined the deviant hero in a new setting.

For Dilip Kumar, *Leader* performed two important functions: First, it helped him to express his deep admiration for Jawharlal Nehru and the Congress ideology (perhaps as a counterpoint to Hindu fundamentalism). The character of Acharyaji, the typical Congress leader of old times, so ably played by Motilal, was structured on the Nehruvian model. Secondly, the film helped him in consolidating the gains made by him in his earlier films, adding the elements of glamour as well as humour to his screen image. A comparison with *Kohinoor* would show that the Vijay in *Leader* was essentially the same fun-loving and easygoing prince now living in the modern times.

For Hindi cinema too, *Leader*, inadvertently, contributed in two significant ways. First, it anticipated one of the forthcoming genres: the political film. This genre focused on the growing decadence in the country's political culture and its value systems and their repercussions for the individuals in particular and society in general. The film also perhaps for the first time depicted political corruption and the nexus among the various corrupt elements for seizing political power. The second contribution was its shaping the image of a new-generation hero, Rajesh Khanna, who was waiting in the wings, so to say. For this superstar-in-the making, *Leader* seemed to have provided the basic material for developing his cinematic image; in fact, it appeared as if Dilip Kumar had prepared the ground for his arrival, both at the physical level and the psychological level. The typical attire was a coloured kurta and trousers. The attitude was one of a go-getter in the romantic sphere and in the politico-social arena as well. The emerging manifestation of this superstar, however, largely rejected the previous attributes of simplicity and naturalness of the Indian film hero, and the result was a more glamorous, self-assured, stylized and dashing protagonist, who, at times, indulged in narcissism and make-believe.

Leader, however, suffered from one fundamental drawback with respect to the image of Dilip Kumar: it projected him in a role that looked far less dignified and much more emotionally deficient than his earlier portrayals. Although the actor used this film for further enlarging his screen image, the liberation of the actor from his earlier image did not find much favour with his traditional fan clubs and the movie failed at the box office. The audience was not prepared to accept their idol in the role of a leader who indulged in breaking the traditional conventions and in bending the rules (for example, organizing an escapade with his adolescent friends and, in a football match, in which his young admirers play against another team, the hero, as the referee, takes the side of his 'disciples' and even scores a goal for them).

Immediately after *Leader* flopped, A. R. Kardar's *Dil Diya Dard Liya*, released in 1966, was conceived by the actor to write off the failure of his upbeat comedy role and to resurrect his time-tested image of a tragedian: a persecuted man in pursuit of his childhood love. Deriving its basic plot from K. L. Saigal's *Lagan* and his own *Arzoo* and *Hulchal* and borrowing again the characters from *Wuthering Heights*, the film tells the story of the tyrannical Ramesh (Pran), son of the *thakur* (feudal chieftan or headman), who falls into bad company, while Shankar (Dilip Kumar), a farm hand who is constantly harassed by Ramesh, is unaware that he is the real heir to the kingdom. Shankar loves Ramesh's sister Roopa (Waheeda Rehman) and vows to earn enough money to win her hand. However, Ramesh's men beat him up and leave him for dead. But Shankar manages to survive and later returns as a rich but bitter man. He begins suspecting Roopa of betraying him and makes it his life's mission to destroy the very woman whom he loves along with the whole feudal milieu in which the heroine is placed.

In spite of the complex anti-hero characterization of Dilip Kumar (in the latter part of the movie) and the fairly impressive performances by all members of the cast, *Dil Diya Dard Liya* turned out to be a contrived melodrama with Dilip Kumar present virtually in the entire footage. Though the narrative sought to highlight the aberration in human behaviour caused by excessive harassment and a series of disappointments, the audience was hardly impressed. Moreover, the overall environment was typically feudal and the rebel hero's preoccupation with his love depicted within this framework appeared rather soulless. Dilip Kumar adopted a curious blending of underplay (with respect to the victimized hero in the first half of the film) with overplay of vengeance in the later half. But his normally reliable histrionics could not salvage the film and it was a fiasco commercially. Even veteran Naushad's fabulous musical compositions could not save the movie.

Two failures – the first in a comedy role in *Leader* and the second in a serious one in *Dil Diya Dard Liya* – in quick succession seemed to have unnerved the actor, thereby compelling him to work out a synthesis of the two genres to regain his position in the film world. And this time the strategy clicked. *Ram Aur Shyam* (directed by Chanakya), made in 1967 with Dilip Kumar in a double role, was a runaway hit. The film presented the actor in two entirely diametrically opposite characterizations, virtually at the two ends of the human personality. While the character of the introverted Ram was partly derived from that in *Hulchal*, the extrovert Shyam was based on the elements borrowed from *Kohinoor* and *Leader*. *Ram Aur Shyam* thus was essentially a 'demonstration film' by the seasoned actor; a final statement on his unquestionable supremacy in film acting.

The contrast between these two characters was indeed awe-inspiring. Ram symbolized aspects such as the growing neurosis in society, the deep insecurity caused by an oppressive environment and a negation to a rightful life. Shyam, created as an antithesis of Ram, represented the much-dreamt-about saviour: omnipotent but playful and mischievous, like Lord Krishna. (In fact, Shyam is one of Lord Krishna's names.) However, except for the magnificent performance by Dilip Kumar, the film had little else to offer. In contrast, the double roles by Nargis in *Anhoni* (1952), Raj Kapoor in *Paapi* (1953) and Dev Anand in *Hum Dono* (1961) were backed by strong storylines and were located in identifiable social settings.

H. S. Rawail's *Sunghursh* (1968), a true multistarrer, offered Dilip Kumar a rare opportunity to reaffirm his acumen in a narrative set in an authentic historical setting. Based on a story by noted novelist Mahashweta Devi (with socialist leanings), the film brought on screen the feud between two families against the backdrop of *thuggee*, a cult perpetrated by bandits from the medieval period onwards in central and northern India. For generations, these bandits have practised the tantra of Goddess Kali. They have looted the pilgrims to Kashi (also known as Banaras or Varanasi) and have also performed human sacrifice by waylaying their victims and taking them to the underground sanctum sanctorums of the temples for the rituals.

In *Sunghursh*, set in nineteenth-century Kashi, the initial focus is on Bhawani Prasad (Jayant), who heads a family of bandit

Dilip Kumar as he appeared in *Jugnu* (1947).

Nargis, Raj Kapoor and Dilip Kumar in *Andaz* (1949).

Dilip Kumar and Usha Kiran in a poignant scene from *Musafir* (1957).

Prithviraj Kapoor (with a beard) and Raj Kapoor in *Valmiki* (1946).

Raj Kapoor and Premnath in *Aag* (1948).

Ashok Kumar (sitting in front of the painting), Raj Kapoor and Nargis
in *Bewafa* (1952).

The debonair Dev Anand

priests whose own relatives have threatened to destroy him. He initiates his grandson, Kundan (Dilip Kumar), against the wishes of his wife (Durga Khote) into the ancestral profession. The boy, however, grows up into a pacifist, virtually a peace activist, whose mission is to completely replace the doctrine of hate with love and brotherhood (à la Raj Kapoor in *Jis Desh Mein Ganga Behti Hai*). When his cousins (Balraj Sahni and Sanjeev Kumar) try to kill him, a mysterious dancer (Vyjayanthimala), who was his companion during childhood, saves him. In the end, he wins the heart of his senior cousin (Balraj Sahni) by serving him in disguise as his servant and sacrificing his own love. The younger cousin becomes a victim of his own plot to poison Kundan.

Given the kind of inputs that went into the making of *Sunghursh*, the film had a great potential to emerge as a classic during a time when this genre was being not so earnestly attempted. But the film was marred by an overemphasis on the romance of the leading pair. The main beneficiary of *Sunghursh* was Sanjeev Kumar, who provided a glimpse of his formidable potential. The newcomer did give the stalwart a run for his money. Soon after this film, Sanjeev Kumar carved a niche for himself in Hindi cinema in an impressive manner.

Dilip Kumar, with his characteristic overlap of underplay and overplay, meticulously builds up an intense character who suffers due to the ancestral burden of guilt and wants peace to reign over the two families. But in the latter part of the film, the focus entirely shifts to the love triangle involving Kundan, the dancer and the senior cousin (Balraj Sahni) in which the actor (as seen in his earlier films like *Shaheed* and *Dil Diya Dard Liya*) gets obsessed with winning over his enemy, sacrificing his own love and thus perpetuating suffering on himself and his beloved. As a result, the basic spirit of the story fails to come through.

Dilip Kumar's preoccupation with the anti-hero image found expression once again in *Aadmi* (1968) directed by A. Bhimsingh. The hero, who belongs to a very affluent family, has been living with a guilty conscience for years because he has killed a friend over a toy during his childhood. He tries to assuage his guilt by helping the downtrodden financially. He falls in love with a girl (Waheeda Rehman), whose family is one of his many beneficiaries, and decides to marry her. When he comes to know that his closest friend (Manoj Kumar), whom he had supported all along financially and otherwise, is involved with his fiancée, he becomes extremely jealous and his compulsive childhood obsession of acquiring everything he desires instantly resurfaces. He begins to torment both his fiancée and his friend, but again the feeling of guilt becomes so overwhelming that he attempts suicide but finally regains his equanimity. As the film was a remake of a Tamil hit, K. Shankar's *Alayamani* (1962), starring Sivaji Ganesan, Dilip Kumar's role was packed with all the elements of a typical Tamil film: highly flashy characterization, excessive melodrama and lengthy dialogues.

In A. Bhimsingh's *Gopi* (1970), in Tapan Sinha's Bengali film *Sagina Mahato* (1970, which was titled *Sagina* in Hindi and hit the screen in 1974) and later in Asit Sen's *Bairaag* (1976), Dilip Kumar made an attempt to introduce some new elements in his acting style. His comical roles were portrayed through an impulsive, overtalkative, one-track minded and naïve simpleton who was a victim of circumstances. But, unlike in his earlier roles, he did not internalize his suffering; he responded to it with a sense of simplicity quite in the same way that Raj Kapoor did in many of his films. The actor also improvised and came up with new mannerisms to depict the character, such as repeatedly jerking his head and crinkling his eyes.

The protagonist in *Gopi* is a hot-headed, self-willed country bumpkin, brought up by a step brother (Om Prakash) and his wife (Nirupa Roy), both of whom he adores. He has the guts to raise his voice against the autocratic zamindar (Pran) of the village. The turning point in the film is when the zamindar refuses to give back the money that the elder brother had deposited with him as savings for their sister's marriage. Gopi goes over to the zamindar's mansion and robs that money from the safe at gun point. This act leads to a serious altercation between the brothers as the elder one is a strict moralist. Gopi leaves home with his sister (Farida Jalal), takes up employment elsewhere and returns home to rejoin his brother and sister-in-law whom he has been missing immensely throughout his separation from them. However, in spite of the presence of all the shades of his histrionics, Dilip Kumar's performance in *Gopi* was extremely loud and garish, again perhaps due to the influence of the Tamil film style. In this film and *Sagina*, in the company of his actress wife, Saira Banu, the actor also attempted to establish a hero–heroine relationship based on a similar pattern as in *Daag*, *Ganga Jumna* and *Leader*: a quarrelsome beginning with showdowns galore; the mellowing of the emotions; and then the final falling in love.

Sagina Mahato (1970), based on a Bengali story by Gourkishor Ghosh, was directed by Tapan Sinha with its Hindi version, *Sagina*, arriving four years later. *Sagina* was the only thematically strong film of Dilip Kumar during the post-classical phase, presenting him in a role that was located in a definite social context. The film was a critique of the extremist radical politics in the country represented here by Anirudha (played by the renowned Bengali actor Anil Chatterjee), who seeks power by manipulating oppressed people. For him, the 'wretched of the earth' are merely tools to be employed for establishing the supremacy of his ideological belief.

The story is set in the colonial period and is woven around a British-owned factory and the adjoining labourers' colony (located somewhere near Darjeeling, now in West Bengal). Sagina Mahato (Dilip Kumar) is the natural leader of the factory workers who has learnt, early in life, that an underdog has to snatch his rights in order to survive in this cruel world. A rebel, he defies the authority of the British owners and managers of the factory who are brutally exploitative. Sagina comes to the rescue of his fellow factory workers and challenges the high-handed bosses.

In Calcutta, Anirudha comes to know about this unconventional, but natural, leader of the workers. He sends two representatives of his party (Aparna Sen and Swaroop Dutt) to the labourers' colony to meet Sagina and make him a party member. They begin indoctrinating him, telling him about the fall of the Bastille and the gains of the Russian Revolution only to find the latter snoring loudly; a sarcastic comment on the lack of understanding on the part of the city-bred revolutionaries about the reality at the grassroots and the attitudes of the downtrodden about them and their viewpoints.

Anirudha, however, turns paranoid, and gets unnerved by the growing political stature of Sagina among the workers and the party members. He lays a trap and ensures that Sagina is made the welfare officer in the factory. He now has been sent to 'the other side'. The workers see him as a stooge of the management. In the end, after much intrigue and melodrama, Anirudha is exposed as a ruthless power seeker, while Sagina is rehabilitated in the colony as the symbol of hope for the working class.

In both the versions of the film, Dilip Kumar took his acting to an entirely new domain and exhibited once again his deep understanding and handling of a character through excellent intuitive gestures and his interaction with events as they unfolded. He 'lived' the character by depicting, in his typical style and through crisp dialogues, the ideological influences on his thinking and actions. The way in which he improvises his mannerisms when he is officially made the welfare officer, intoxicated with newly acquired power and status, and when he puts forth his forthright down-to-earth understanding of the class relations and the Left politics, is truly amazing. Thus the character, Sagina, in the novel gets sucked into the actor and virtually emerges as a true incarnation of the original.

And yet the complex theme of the film is largely negated by the formula packaging and overemphasis on Sagina's love affair. As in other films of this period, Dilip Kumar's histrionics overpowered everything else in the film including its political context. The political evolution of Sagina, the illiterate, unindoctrinated worker, and his subsequent disillusionment with the wider working class movement in Bengal, looked too diffused to make the film a memorable document on the struggle of the working class in the country. The Bengali version was able to attract the attention of critics as well as the audience, while the Hindi version was a complete washout at the box office. Nevertheless, *Sagina* should find a place in the study of Indian cinema.

The box-office success of *Ram Aur Shyam* and the failure of most of the films that he did afterwards seemed to have tempted Dilip Kumar to tackle the slump in his career by going in for double and triple roles. But the outcome was not very rewarding. *Dastaan* (1972), under the banner of B. R. Films, presented him in a double role. Written by I. S. Johar, and a remake of the 1951 film *Afsana*, a runaway hit starring Ashok Kumar in the main role, *Dastaan* was about a simple-hearted judge who is betrayed by his sluttish wife (Bindu) and his best friend (Prem Chopra), who are having an affair. By sheer coincidence, the lookalike of the judge, a playboy (whom the judge has befriended), gets killed in a road accident and the judge takes his place and devises a trap, which includes staging a play, to expose his two tormenters. One of the most unimaginative productions under the B. R. Films' banner, the film also contained a number of sequences that look like shoddy imitations of certain scenes from such old Hollywood masterpieces as *Spellbound* (1945, directed by Alfred Hitchcock), *The Woman in the Window* (1944) and *Random Harvest* (1942).

In *Dastaan* Dilip Kumar once again shows his innate ability to succinctly capture the distinction between the two characters. It seems that he partly designed his two roles on his resounding portrayals in *Azaad* and *Leader*, respectively, but they failed to make a much of an impact on the viewers.

Bairaag (1976) must have been taken up by Dilip Kumar out of desperation in an attempt to reap once again the gains of *Ram Aur Shyam*. This movie presented him in a triple role: a father and two sons, who are separated in childhood. Located in an affluent household, *Bairaag* had all the elements of a melodrama-in-the-making. There were three Dilip Kumars: first, the suffering father belonging to an aristocratic class; the second, the playboyish, extravagant son, whiling away his time in pursuit of the luxuries of life; and the third, blind at birth and leading a menial existence in a zamindar's household. Here was ample material for coming up with a great movie. However, the film lacked a sense of coherence in its narration and treatment.

In *Bairaag*, Dilip Kumar in his portrayals just performed a juxtaposing of the three characters designed simply to demonstrate his excellence in three entirely different kinds of roles. The storyline was so weak that the restoration of the eyesight of the blind son (who is a Shiva devotee since childhood) through the blessings of his pet snake had all the connotations of a mythological and was against the overall rationalist image of the actor. *Bairaag*, his last film as a young hero, failed to enthuse the audience. The only gain was that, by doing this film, Dilip Kumar prepared himself for his possible entry into senior roles in the near future. The magazine *Star & Style* captioned its review of *Bairaag* as RAM AUR SHYAM GET A FATHER, and went on to lampoon the movie.[8]

The box-office debacle of all these films must have been alarming for Dilip Kumar. The actor, caught up in the web of his own histrionics, failed to uplift the films as a result of his preoccupation with his screen image. The once-formidable thespian seemed to have lost his grip and magnetism and was about to go into oblivion.

The Senior Reaffirms Himself

The danger of sinking into oblivion does not affect great artistes who have made an impact in their respective fields. After *Bairaag* (1976), Dilip Kumar waited for five years in the wings to rediscover his lost space in Hindi cinema. Ironically, the shift to senior roles was facilitated by none other than his most faithful disciple, Manoj Kumar.

Kranti (1981), apart from its extensive paraphernalia and gloss, typical of a Manoj Kumar extravaganza, presented Dilip Kumar as a senior revolutionary leader in the people's struggle against British rule; predictably, Manoj Kumar, as the hero of the film, played Dilip Kumar's revolutionary son.

There seemed to be two reasons that inspired Manoj Kumar to offer the role to Dilip Kumar. Having made his place among the most successful film makers in the late 1960s and early 1970s, Manoj Kumar wanted not only to pay a tribute to the senior who had been the main inspiration for him to become an actor but also he (Manoj Kumar) had a cherished desire to match his acting style with his guru, but on his own ground. However, the result – the rapid-fire dialogue exchanges in some scenes between the two and the ponderous exchange of looks – looked rather contrived without much substance or impact.

Kranti was yet another example of the underutilization of an actor because of weak characterization, a meandering storyline and excessive melodrama. Apart from Dilip Kumar and Manoj Kumar, the cast was made up of several big-time stars (Pradeep Kumar, Shashi Kapoor, Shatrughan Sinha, Prem Chopra, Hema Malini, Sarika and Parveen Babi), all of whom had to be given their due place in the sun. It is said that the thespian's role was 'cut down to size' at the editing stage and he simply became an appendage to the entire drama. This film was also an instance wherein the film maker adopted a populist slogan-mongering approach to the theme without really understanding the socio-cultural roots of the political struggle in question.

Dilip Kumar got his real breakthrough in a senior role in Ramesh Sippy's *Shakti* (1982). A well-crafted movie on the conflict between family affinities and societal responsibilities and penned by Salim-Javed (Salim Khan and Javed Akhtar), the film offered to the actor the most valuable opportunity to validate once again his unquestionable supremacy in the field of acting.

Shakti was not an original script in terms its plot and characterizations, but a reworking of the classic, *Mughal-e-Azam*, set in the modern era (as *Deewar*, 1975, was an urban reworking of *Ganga Jumna*, 1961). Dilip Kumar's character of an upright police officer was created by combining the three most powerful characters of Hindi cinema: Akbar (Prithviraj Kapoor) in *Mughal-e-Azam*, Radha (Nargis) in *Mother India* and Jumna (Nasir Khan) in *Ganga Jumna*. The character, subscribing to the 'supremacy of the state' theory, strives to prove that the law is omnipotent and, in fact, he represents the law. The film also indicates that there is an in-built vulnerability in the state apparatus, which can be exploited by the unscrupulous evil forces in society, and its overpowering presence is made possible only by an operational cruelty in its functioning. The state builds into the mental make-up of its representatives (in this case, Dilip Kumar, the police officer) an uncompromising sense of commitment to live and die for the state even at the cost of one's personal life and emotional attachments. Therefore, Dilip Kumar becomes the patriarch representing the state apparatus whose own rigidly lawful conduct results in a greater alienation of its present victims and prospective ones.

However, the character of Dilip Kumar was far more multidimensional and complex than that of Akbar in *Mughal-e-Azam*. The police officer was not a mere symbol of the state but also a human being, who has internalized the ensuing conflict between his professional imperatives and family obligations. This makes the character not only uphold his convictions but also live through the conflict itself. The father is so sure about his doctrinal moral precepts and idealism that he expects to infuse them in his son (Amitabh Bachchan) and thus build the latter's personality on his own model. The son has his own ideas and beliefs, which run counter to his father's lofty principles. In the film, the son (as a small boy) is kidnapped by a bunch of gangsters, whose leader (Amrish Puri) threatens to kill him unless Dilip Kumar releases one of the gang members who is in police custody. The ethically minded police officer refuses to accept this demand. The son overhears his father telling the gang leader (on the phone) that protecting the law is more important than his son's life. This incident sows the seeds of antagonism in the son's mind against his father. The son manages to escape from his kidnappers, thanks to one of them who takes pity on the boy. With the passage of time, the predictable conflict between the father and the son becomes one between the older generation signifying moral uprightness and the younger generation, alienated and vulnerable, looking for security by attaining material success by any means, even at the cost of destroying delicate family relationships and giving up one's ethics and morality. While Dilip Kumar ignores personal emotions as a result of his duty-bound conduct, Bachchan plans the course of his life in response to his deep-rooted animosity for his father's idealism. He teams up with a well-known smuggler (the same kidnapper who developed sympathy for the boy and has now moved 'up' in life) and takes the short cut to earning piles of money, somewhat reminiscent of *Deewar* (1975). The film depicts very effectively the lack of communication between the two generations despite the mutual affection between the father and the son. Although they make attempts to understand each other, they only end up creating friction between themselves. It is eventually the woman (Raakhee, Dilip Kumar's wife in the film) who has to bear the brunt of the antagonism between the father and the son.

The senior actor interpreted his character through an extremely well-inducted sensitivity in his portrayal. Dilip Kumar virtually rediscovered a new reservoir of talent within himself, which helped him in re-establishing once again his indisputable status as 'numero uno', beyond the constraints of age and the changing film milieu. Through his typical sense of underplay seen in his earlier films, Dilip Kumar in *Shakti* internalizes the dilemma posed by his son and progressively builds into his character an unusual emotional intensity. In the climax, the father is compelled to shoot his son who refuses to surrender to the police and tries to flee.

The character of the rebel son, Vijay, portrayed by Amitabh Bachchan, on the other hand, was far less effective in its design and execution than of Salim in *Mughal-e-Azam*, Birju in *Mother India*, Ganga in *Ganga Jumuna* and the anti-hero character played by Ashok Kumar in *Sangram* as early as 1950 (in this film, the hero is also finally shot by his retired police officer father for his links with the city's mafia). While in the aforementioned films, the rebellion was set against a broader social oppression, in *Shakti*, Bachchan goes deviant not for a cause but due to a deep personal grudge against his father: to avenge his unprotective attitude towards him. As the character lacked strength on his own, it undermined the relative impact of Bachchan in the clash between the two titans, each representing his own generation and its value systems.

Shakti indeed should be considered as the final outstanding contribution of Dilip Kumar to Hindi cinema. The film, in fact, harks back to his portrayals of the 1950s, when his agony and the inner turmoil were expressed in his characteristic style. *Shakti*'s success at the box office, boosted by the memorable performance of the senior actor, brought him centrestage once again, thereby opening up several new avenues for him.

Having won wide critical acclaim for his roles in *Kranti* and *Shakti*, the senior actor now was all set to storm the film world in a big way. The quick succession of films that he signed up seemed to be due to a sense of urgency on the part of the thespian to resurrect his career and consolidate his position at the top. These films presented him as the patriarch, towering high over the rest of the cast. His cine persona now embarked upon two distinct tracks as influenced by the current preoccupations of cinema: the agonized man as the upholder of the law or the vengeful veteran.

In addition to *Shakti*, Dilip Kumar also appeared in this phase of his career as the upholder of the law in Subhash Ghai's *Karma* (1986), K. Raghavendra Rao's *Dharm Adhikari* (1986), B. Gopal's *Kanoon Apna Apna* (1989) and Umesh Mehra's *Qila* (1998).

Karma (1986), a rehash of *Sholay* (1975) and Hollywood's *The Dirty Dozen* (1967), presented Dilip Kumar as the upright and benevolent jail superintendent, Rana, most of whose family has been massacred by Dr Dang (Anupam Kher), the dreaded kingpin of an international terrorist organization. Only his wife, played by Nutan, who turns dumb with shock, and his youngest son are saved. Like the protagonist in V. Shantaram's classic *Do Aankhen Barah Haath*, the jailer holds the view that hardened criminals in prisons can be transformed by showing them the right direction, thus enabling them to become socially useful persons. He selects three criminals – Jackie Shroff, Naseeruddin Shah and Anil Kapoor, all condemned to death – to constitute a special anti-terrorist squad under his leadership. With his humane approach as well an aggressive stance of nationalism, the jailer transforms them into his committed allies and the quartet eventually destroys the villain's heavily guarded high-tech military hideout located in a border area.

Karma, like *Sholay*, thus justified the role of extra-constitutional interventions in the nation's affairs. Dilip Kumar, in his awe-inspiring performance, was his usual self, masterfully internalizing the agony of the victim. Using his trademark histrionics, he once again captured the undercurrents of irreparable personal loss and transformed his anguish into a posture that exuded strength. His soulful relationship with his wife was a major highlight of the film.

Dharm Adhikari was intended to project a journey back in time to depict virtues of the traditional institution of justice in Indian rural society, which is beyond the pale of the state, and to highlight its plus points over the modern system. Dilip Kumar personified the classical sage-like figure of Dharm Adhikari, the traditional dispenser of law who is revered by the people of the village for his virtually divine sense of justice. His court is a desolate ground where the poorest of the poor can get immediate access to justice.

In *Kanoon Apna Apna*, the senior actor portrayed an upright district magistrate, who has to uphold the law of the land in the face of the challenges posed by two other ideologies: first that of a mob leader, who thrives on public sentiments, and second that of a pro-people militant activist. In this film, Dilip Kumar, as in

Shakti, opted for highly sophisticated underplaying of the role. In spite of its powerful theme, the film and the thespian's noteworthy performance failed to get the appreciation they deserved.

Kanoon Apna Apna: A Review
Moving Away from Escapism

The era of escapism is temporarily dead in mainstream Hindi cinema and the new Dilip Kumar starrer *Kanoon Apna Apna* even offers a plausible solution to the problems and the confusion which have besieged the modern Indian state.

In a powerful, hard-hitting statement, the film also offers an alternative to the now-routine celluloid war for justice by the lone ranger. Director B. Gopal's film makes perhaps the most critical comment (in the Hindi cinema) on the new breed of the populist, unscrupulous, criminalized politicians we have seen emerge during the last decade ...

Kanoon Apna Apna rips through the machinations of the corrupt local politician and we have three interpretations of the law of the land: the upright administrator's understanding of the law; its manipulation by the mob leader; and the (morally justified) violation of law by a militant activist who also happens to be the collector's son.

The film quite naturally revolves around the intense but grand conviction of the honest administrator personified by Dilip Kumar. And the actor presents a superb performance. We have here a Dilip Kumar who eschews his normal penchant for hand gestures and other pet mannerisms. Instead Dilip Kumar turns out a marvellously intricate display of voice modulation and dialogue delivery. A performance that compares with the great actor's best and the barriers of age are easily undone by him ...

Source: The Indian Express, 29 October 1989.

Qila (1998) brought an aged Dilip Kumar once again on the silver screen after a gap of almost a decade. And the actor, opting for a double role and drawing diverse elements from many of his previous portrayals, appeared to be cashing on his earlier charisma. The film was intended to show allegorically the inevitable transition of society from its feudal moorings to a democratic form in which the decadent feudal order is sought to be corrected by a new worldview. Dilip Kumar portrays two brothers: one is a tyrannical feudal lord, an anti-hero, who has played havoc with the people in his domain, and the other is an upright professional, a judge, who is pained by the deeds of his evil brother. After the feudal lord is murdered, the democrat brother takes up a project for setting up a people's commune in the very palace of his brother to provide a life of compassion and care to his erstwhile victims. In his performance the actor looked rather tired, but managed to release a fairly large quantum of his patented histrionics. The rest of the cast, including the not-so-young Rekha, appeared to be awed by the presence of the thespian.

In four films out of the ten in this period – Subhash Ghai's *Vidhata* (1982), Yash Johar's *Duniya* (1984), Yash Chopra's *Mashaal* (1984) and K. Bapaiah's *Izzatdar* (1990) – Dilip Kumar emerged as the angry, ageing man replaying with a renewed vigour the dominant drama of vengeance initiated in Hindi cinema by him in films like *Ganga Jumna*. This genre could boast of many additions to its kitty by the younger contender, Amitabh Bachchan, mainly in the 1970s and the early 1980s. The idea perhaps was to tackle his successor on his own ground. These films depicted the transformation of an ordinary upright man into a vengeful dispenser of natural justice, beyond the purview of the institutionalized legal system.

Vidhata recounted on screen the tale of an ordinary individual's battle against the evil forces that have created havoc in his life. In the process, he becomes a ruthless mafia don seeking vengeance against his tormentors. Dilip Kumar starts off as a nondescript railway engine driver whose son (a police inspector) is killed by the villain (Amrish Puri). He then has to bring up his grandson. He entrusts this job to Sanjeev Kumar (a Good Samaritan) as he is preoccupied with writing his own destiny and that of his grandson. He becomes Vidhata (à la Godfather), and is sucked into many encounters with the villain. In the end, after a series of action-packed scenes and pithy dialogues, he is morally humbled by his grandson (Sanjay Dutt), who questions his grandfather's right to write his destiny. Shammi Kapoor also pitched in with an energetic performance, playing a happy-go-lucky engine driver friend of Dilip Kumar.

Mashaal essentially followed the plot structure of *Vidhata*. This time, the senior protagonist is a journalist committed to upholding the role of the media in exposing the sinister deeds of the anti-people forces. As he leads a spirited campaign against the local mafia don (Amrish Puri) through his small newspaper, the villain starts harrassing him, leading eventually to the death of his wife (Waheeda Rehman) under tragic circumstances. The wronged man is hit hard by the apathy of the justice delivery system and the indifference of the people around him and opts to become a powerful mafia don himself so that he can seek revenge against his tormentor. This anti-establishment stance is juxtaposed with the burning idealism of a young journalist (Anil Kapoor), whom the senior had earlier rescued from the ghettos of crime.

Duniya, designed in the same pattern as the above two films, presented Dilip Kumar again as a vengeful man with a high degree of intelligence. He has to settle scores with a trio of villains (Pran, Prem Chopra and Amrish Puri) who have destroyed his family life. Dilip Kumar's intensity of performance stands out in this movie.

Izzatdar was an attempt to capture the painful moral decline in society vis-à-vis the unshakeable ethics of a few strong-willed individuals. Recounted as a flashback by the protagonist, an upright judge, in the form of a book, the film depicts the upheaval caused in his life by a young unscrupulous upstart who has designed his success in life by trapping the judge's daughter in a love affair. Eventually, the judge himself becomes a powerful underworld don and enacts his drama of vengeance.

***

Two films in his senior actor phase, B. R. Chopra's *Mazdoor* (1983) and Subhash Ghai's *Saudagar* (1991), presented Dilip Kumar as the patriarch in two entirely different settings: one modern and the other feudal.

In *Mazdoor*, he plays an elderly foreman in a textile mill, who is greatly revered by his fellow-workers for his goodwill as well as his expertise in managing the technical operations in the mill. Inspired by an enlarged business vision much beyond his financial abilities and in collaboration with a struggling young textile engineer (Raj Babbar), he builds a modern industrial enterprise. He thus represents the grassroots entreprenurial capability of the country's working class. But eventually a family feud results, which has adverse repercussions. He faces serious problems on the professional and the domestic fronts: his workers go against him and his family members are upset with him.

Saudagar, hailed as the historical clash of two titans of Hindi cinema, Raaj Kumar and Dilip Kumar, basically focuses on the conflict between two ageing patriarchs. (Incidentally, these two actors came together after a gap of more than three decades; their previous venture together was *Paigham*, 1959.) Bir Singh (Dilip Kumar) and Thakur Rajeshwar Singh (Raaj Kumar) were close friends in their youth. Bir Singh, who was to marry his friend's sister, is compelled to marry another woman. Upon hearing this news, the *thakur*'s sister commits suicide, and the two friends become bitter enemies for life. Biru's eldest son Vishal (Jackie Shroff) takes up the initiative to make peace but is killed by the villain, Rajeshwar Singh's brother-in-law Chuniya (Amrish Puri). Eventually, it is the innocence of the love between Vishal's son Vasu (Vivek Mushran) and the *thakur*'s granddaughter Radha

(Manisha Koirala) that brings the warring families together. The patriarchs die in each other's arms while fighting the villain. The storyline of this film seems to have been inspired by Sunil Dutt's *Reshma Aur Shera* and H. S. Rawail's *Sunghursh*. However, unlike these two films, *Saudagar* failed to make much of an impact on the audience. The narrative was bogged down by excessive verbal clashes between the two giants. Dilip Kumar, in order to lend colloquial authenticity to his character, used the Haryanvi dialect, prompted apparently by Amitabh Bachchan's persona in *Namak Halal* (1982). However, the senior appeared somewhat stilted in his dialogue delivery.

***

In the films of this era, Dilip Kumar exhibited his formidable capacity to innovate and improvise. His portrayals, extremely credible and forceful, were executed with perfect timing and precision. His presence infused a certain gravitas to these films, which they badly needed. However, the minus point was that his characterizations tended to overshadow everything else. Also, except in three films, *Kranti, Saudagar* and *Dharm Adhikari*, Dilip Kumar's roles in this period were located in the fast-paced world of the metropolis, which must have greatly disappointed his highly faithful audience in rural areas and small towns.

Thus, none of the films in this phase of his career proved to be of any serious consequence even within the broad standards of commercial films, the sole exceptions being *Shakti* and, to a lesser extent, *Kanoon Apna Apna*. The film makers largely failed to offer to Dilip Kumar challenging roles and the actor virtually repeated himself in the aforementioned films, which were largely run-of-the-mill stuff, and lacked any serious purpose, except of course to keep the money coming in.

The Indigenous Hero's Personal Suffering and the Social Realities

Indian mainstream cinema in the classical period represented a synthesis of Indian tradition and the modernizing society, which formed the basis for the highly fascinating film spectacles set in the socio-political and cultural milieu of the times. These spectacles were created by drawing inspiration from a vast corpus of mythologies, folklore, religious beliefs and practices and integrating it with the realities of present-day rural/urban life. The two strands were often meticulously interwoven in the narration along with many vital contemporary issues.

In their films, masters like Mehboob Khan, Sohrab Modi, A. R. Kardar, Bimal Roy, Nitin Bose, Amiya Chakravarty and V. Shantaram reflected the entire gamut of problems afflicting the nation: widespread poverty and unemployment; large-scale alienation among the various strata; a growing sense of insecurity; a lack of women's empowerment; and the gradual loss of social and cultural identity. Their films were genuine, straight from the heart, and were imbued with a highly appealing aura. It is indeed ironical that *serious* cinema, which began to take shape during the late 1930s and 1940s, witnessed a huge expansion in the decade following independence. Although one would have expected the films of a recently independent nation to be joyful and jubilant, most of them were tragic, pessimistic and melancholic. Even big musical hits like *Barsaat, Baiju Bawra, Deedar, Anarkali* and *Udan Khatola* were laden with this kind of sadness.

Perhaps the recent memories of the country's traumatic Partition and its aftermath and the growing disillusionment of the people with the promises of a new prosperous life in the years after independence not being fulfilled affected the very content and orientation of all art forms. Cinema, with its mass appeal, was probably affected the most.

In this milieu, Dilip Kumar emerged as the fundamental protagonist and the main vehicle for many distinguished film makers of this era for depicting their cinematic vision on celluloid. His tragedies constituted the basic format of the film of this period and they reflected the immense suffering of the Indian psyche at that time. The grieving hero, who sometimes indulged in self-flagellation, portrayed how depressed society was during this period, lacking enthusiasm for even dreaming about a productive, prosperous and happy life. In fact, negativism had acquired a romantic charm of its own in this era. The artiste became the main metaphor for reflecting the agony and the growing disillusionment of the people both in real and abstract terms.

Thus, Dilip Kumar's cinema in this period (and also that of Guru Dutt) attempted to interpret the political philosophy, which was governing the process of nation building in the post-independence period, on an entirely different plane from the cinema of Mehboob Khan, V. Shantaram, K. A. Abbas and Raj Kapoor. These film makers showcased the ideas of the Nehruvian model of socialism: pro-poor, social reformist and anti-capitalist. The cinema of Dilip Kumar, with the suffering individual as its main focus, viewed the processes of social change with a lot of pessimism. Although this individual desired an undoing of the feudal past, this undoing only promised an unsure and bleak future. He, therefore, was caught in a cleft. Thus, either way, the suffering remained inevitable.

Therefore, Dilip Kumar's indigenous hero was built around two factors: first, the myth of the innocence of Indian rural society represented by docile peasantry believing in the dignity of labour and indigenous skills. The rural poor lived alongside the aristocracy, which appeared benevolent but kept strict control over traditional wealth through a brutally enforced patriarchal structure. Second, the felt need for a new prototype in the face of industrialization and urbanization. Our hero represented the individual awaiting social change amidst the conflicting forces of pre-industrial paternalistic social relations and the modernization being propelled by the state (for example, through heavy industry and big dams) and by the growing capitalist enterprise, as India emerged as a mixed economy after independence. But in his suffering, as the dislocated lover or the agonized rebel (often ending in death), he finally came to symbolize the upholder of tradition, but who is willing to accept change, whether social or economic or political, provided it has a 'human face'.

The foregoing aspects can be seen in films such as *Daag, Arzoo* and *Hulchal*, in which the protagonist breaks all familial bonds and goes to the town or city (where capital inflow is growing) in order to upgrade his status in the rigid traditional social structure with his newly acquired wealth and thus 'become worthy' of the woman he desperately loves. This indigenous hero, therefore, is not the 'new man' who challenges both the feudal/patriarchal social oppression as well as the capitalist exploitation. Only in four films – *Andaz, Madhumati, Leader* and *Sagina* – did Dilip Kumar's persona somewhat represent the 'new man'.

Thus, Dilip Kumar's protagonist became the main symbol of the typical 'ideological bargain' evolved by Indian cinema. The hero first challenges the prevailing social perceptions (often through socially unacceptable love for his woman) and becomes a rebel. The resulting conflict is developed with a clear-cut understanding of the ideologies involved – the 'status quoists' asserting the traditional values and maintenance of the prevailing social order on the one hand and the suffering renegade setting the agenda for upholding the basic human values of love, compassion, sacrifice and equality on the other. However, as the plot develops, this conflict is merely reduced to the evil designs of one or few individuals (the villain plus his minions), who paradoxically, are themselves rejecting the traditional values. The evil, in fact, is largely depicted as an individualistic aberration of greed and lust of the libidinous villain against the good old value system. In this whole process, the ideological stance of both sides is reduced to winning over the heroine; a simple commodification of the woman of desire. Often this bargain is rationalized through a moral justification preached by a saint-like figure towards the end of the film.

Certain male chauvinistic elements in Dilip Kumar's characters are seen in films like *Arzoo, Devdas, Shikast, Ganga Jumna, Mughal-e-Azam, Dil Diya Dard Liya* and *Sunghursh*. But the same hero would often also cry along with the heroine in times of distress (in *Ganga Jumna*, after Ganga is chased by the zamindar's men, he breaks down in the arms of Dhanno). Thus, unlike the infantile Raj Kapoor, who would seek emancipation through the security provided by the woman's lap, Dilip Kumar sought to seek the same through the suffering caused by love, and romanticizing this rejection in self-indulgence, while holding on to his male ego. For other heroes, the love interest of the heroine was easily assured. Dilip Kumar had to win over this support, if at all, through real hard work and a lot of suffering.

As seen earlier, in the post-classical period, Dilip Kumar's portrayals underwent a dramatic shift, reflecting the fundamental changes that were taking place in Indian cinema. The earlier pessimism and self-denial were gradually replaced by a positive carefree attitude, dynamism and a commitment to set right the wrong doers (as in *Leader, Ram Aur Shyam, Gopi* and *Sagina*).

In senior roles, Dilip Kumar represented (1) a formidable figure of parental authority, (2) a symbol of the power of the state or (3) an elderly angry and vengeful man. In all these roles, he appeared determinedly isolationist, convinced of his moral authority; he seemed determined to suppress anyone who refused to play the game according to the rules of morality and ethics set by him. And yet he appeared to play a reluctant hero, who was essentially a simple person but who had to draw upon his untested reserves of inner strength to tackle the various problems caused by adverse circumstances. The actor, however, continued to include in his characterizations the element of extreme vulnerability as exhibited by his deep concern for his wife in these roles (as seen in *Shakti, Mashaal* and *Karma*).

In his vigilante roles, the cutting edge of the patriarch's characterizations was marked by a complusive vengeance against those who have destroyed his personal and professional life; he bulldozes his way through the maze of evil and deceit. Amitabh Bachchan, Dharmendra, Vinod Khanna and virtually every other actor did the same but the forcefulness and intensity in the portrayals by the senior actor were far more devastating and earth-shattering.

Ironically, the short journey of Dilip Kumar to the high plateau of 'angry' cinema was an equally powerful appendage to the anti-establishment cinema of Amitabh Bachchan in the 1970s and 1980s. As shall be discussed in Volume 2, this cinema marked the transformation of Indian film's indigenous hero from an inward-looking suffering individual to an angry man externalizing his pain and striking with full force at the very social contradictions (if only symbolically) that had led to the failure of the social reconstruction agenda set for the nation since independence.

Dilip Kumar and Hindi Cinema

Dilip Kumar in the classical phase of Hindi cinema pioneered the development of the 'indigenous film hero' model and thus helped this cinema in establishing its true Indian identity. In contrast to Raj Kapoor and Dev Anand, who evolved for themselves completely urbane Westernized screen personalities, Dilip Kumar's persona was largely rooted in the wider Indian cultural ethos. No other male protagonist, except probably Sohrab Modi and V. Shantaram, has so remarkably contributed in developing the true cultural identity of the Hindi film.

Dilip Kumar also contributed in making the Hindi film completely hero-centric, in which its basic components – story, dialogues, treatment and the total imaging on the screen – were governed by the actor's style and screen personality. In fact, he completely subjugated the character he was playing with his own distinct histrionics. Thus, the personality of the hero became the personality of the film itself. (His larger-than-life portrayals, in fact, kept the viewers in great awe, dominating their faculties and leading to preconceived responses from them on the actor's handling of the character in a film.) Like the Hollywood giants Charlton Heston, Clark Gable, James Stewart, Cary Grant, Gregory Peck, Kirk Douglas, Marlon Brando and later Harrison Ford, Dilip Kumar could play a larger-than-life persona on the screen to perfection, that there was never a doubt about its authenticity. Only Raaj Kumar and later Amitabh Bachchan could claim to possess such ability.

In contrast with many of his contemporaries and the actors who came later, Dilip Kumar did not promote himself through films produced by him except in the case of *Ganga Jumna*. It goes to his credit that he reached the zenith as a result of his great sense of professionalism and creative use of talent.

In the potpourri of his films, Dilip Kumar exemplified originality through the vast range and depth of his talent in at least in twelve films: *Daag, Aan, Devdas, Azaad, Amar, Madhumati, Kohinoor, Mughal-e-Azam, Ganga Jumna, Ram Aur Shyam* and the latter-day *Shakti* and *Kanoon Apna Apna*. His portrayals in these films, in more ways than one, are the representative examples of his contribution in establishing the first-ever school of method acting in Indian cinema. This is the theme of the chapter that follows.

Notes and References

1. The film was based on the real story of an Indian doctor (Dwarkanath Kotnis) who lost his life in China while serving as a member of the medical mission sent by the Indian National Congress to serve the army of Mao Zedong fighting the Japanese forces.
2. Hordes of rural people in bullock carts would come from far-flung villages to nearby towns to witness on screen the great saga on the plight of rural peasantry depicted by Mehboob. No other Indian film since then has been able to touch the pulse of a nation on such a massive scale.
3. The major films of these directors were: Mahesh Kaul (*Gopinath* 1948, *Naujawan* 1951 and *Sautela Bhai* 1962); Vijay Bhatt (*Baiju Bawra* 1952, *Shri Chaitanya Mahaprabhu* 1953 and *Angulimaal* 1960); S. N. Tripathi (*Kavi*

Kalidas 1959, *Rani Roopmati* 1959 and *Sangeet Samraat Tansen* 1962); Raja Nawathe (*Basant Bahar* 1956 and *Sohni Mahiwal* 1958); M. Sadiq (*Shabab* 1954 and *Khota Paisa* 1958); R. C. Talwar (*Sangdil* 1952, *Ilzam* 1954 and *Mem Sahib*, 1956); P. L. Santoshi (*Barsaat Ki Raat* 1960); D. D. Kashyap (*Shama Parvana* 1954 and *Mera Salam* 1957); Raj Khosla (*Kala Pani* 1958, *Bombai Ka Babu* 1960 and *Ek Musafir Ek Hasina* 1962); Ramanand Sagar (*Ghunghat* 1960, *Zindagi* 1964 and *Arzoo* 1965); Nasir Hussain (*Tumsa Nahi Dekha* 1957 and *Dil Deke Dekho* 1959); and Shakti Samanta (*Howrah Bridge* 1958, *Insaan Jaag Utha* 1959 and *Jaali Note* 1960).

4.   The output of the comedians included films such as *Albela* (1951), *Asha* (1955), *Hum Sab Chor Hai* (1956), *New Delhi* (1956), *Chhoo Mantar* (1956), *Miss Mary* (1957), *Chalti Ka Naam Gadi* (1958), *Dili Ka Thug* (1958), *Khota Paisa* (1958), *Chacha Zindabad* (1959), *Shararat* (1959), *Jaalsaaz* (1959), *Ek Phool Char Kante* (1960) and *Bewaqoof* (1960).

5.   The film melody was evolved by a relative 'de-classicalization' of classical music. As pointed out by the noted film writer, Ashraf Aziz, its creators sacrificed the vocal gymnastics involved in classical rendering by eliminating the complex 'coloratura', and opted for harmony and tonal quality. The emphasis on a clear pronunciation of the lyrics made the film song a slight musical speech, so much so that in form it came closer to the folk song.

6.   *Shaheed* was among the few important films made on the country's freedom movement, the other notable ones being Bimal Roy's *Pehla Aadmi* (1950) and Ramesh Sehgal's *Samadhi* (1950). However, no big-budget spectacle was made on such a theme of great historical importance for modern India. The task was left to the British director, Sir Richard Attenborough, to re-create the saga of the freedom struggle when he made *Gandhi* (1982), some 35 years after the country achieved independence.

7.   Their body of work in the post-classical period is represented by: Hrishikesh Mukherjee's *Aashirwad* (1968), *Satyakam* (1969), *Anand* (1970), *Namak Haram* (1973), *Abhiman* (1973) and *Chupke Chupke* (1975); Basu Bhattacharya's *Teesri Kasam* (1966), *Anubhav* (1971) and *Avishkaar* (1973); Asit Sen's *Mamta* (1966, a remake of his Bengali classic *Uttar Falguni*), *Anokhi Raat* (1968), *Khamoshi* (1969, a remake of the Bengali film *Deep Jweley Jai*) and *Safar* (1970); Basu Chatterjee's *Sara Akash* (1969) and *Rajnigandha* (1974); and Gulzar's *Mere Apne* (1971), *Koshish* (1972), *Aandhi* (1975) and *Mausam* (1975).

8.   Bunny Reuben, *Dilip Kumar: Star Legend of Indian Cinema – The Definitive Biography*, New Delhi: HarperCollins, 2004, pp. 388–89.

Chapter 6

Dilip Kumar and
the Indian School of Method Acting

Dilip Kumar's 'school' represents a pioneering institution in cinematic acting and is indeed unique in world cinema. From an academic point of view, it symbolizes a case of an individual artiste building up, through his work, a great institution representing a creative art form. Not formally recognized in an academic sense, this institution presents a 'professor of dramatics' developing his theory through practical demonstration of the method in each of his films. The acting methodology pioneered by Dilip Kumar and the corresponding cinematic interpretation of the characterizations depicted by him became an essential reference compendium for future actors, directors and even some film critics and historians. By the late 1950s, this methodology, in fact, had become the benchmark for film acting.

For Dilip Kumar, the development of his school of acting must have been a painstaking process. The process seemed to have been facilitated by many factors. The foremost was the studio-based apprenticeship system prevailing at the time when Dilip Kumar and his contemporaries entered the film world. This apprenticeship was quite similar to the guru–*shishya* (guru–disciple) tradition in classical music and dance and the *ustad-shagird* (teacher–student) tradition in the unorganized sector where vocational skills are imparted to young artisans. Under this apprenticeship, the young artistes (and trainees in other departments of film making) were salaried employees of the studios. They were painstakingly taught the art by the directors, who polished the raw gems to make them into the glittering diamonds of the future.

Dilip Kumar also exploited, in a unique way, the ample opportunities provided by the great directors of his times. These directors, in turn, found in Dilip Kumar a highly promising actor who could not only improvise his talents in a wide range of roles, but also help them to create an overpowering cinematic persona of the protagonist who was well tuned with the themes of their films. The wide range of the characters built into well-conceived stories offered to Dilip Kumar immense possibilities to develop deeper insights into his style of acting. The complete evolution of the artiste took about four years after his arrival in 1944 with the film *Jwar Bhata*. As the actor soon mastered his method (as seen in *Shaheed*, 1948), he acquired a level of excellence that soon placed him in the top bracket along with stars at the international level.

The Dilip Kumar Method and Its Impact

The much-acclaimed method of Dilip Kumar is the outcome of the sustained efforts of the artiste towards founding an indigenous school of cinematic acting by carrying out a synthesis of the Western school of film acting and Oriental drama. In this venture, he created for Indian cinema a unique blending of the melodramatic tradition of Indian drama and the cinematic emphasis on visual imaging and underplay evolved in Western cinema.

The main Western influence seems to be the celebrated 'method' system pioneered by the Russian genius Konstantin Stanislavsky (1863–1938), undoubtedly the world's greatest theoretician of the dramatic arts. Defying the highly stylized theatrical conventions, going against the artificiality of stage dilettantism and opposing acting 'by instinct', the founder sought to introduce a natural state based on the laws of a human being's organic nature. According to him, in acting mere imitation of the gestures and intonations of the outer world are insufficient to create a human being's unique inner world. His method, therefore, is aimed at capturing the inner state of a performer and helping him or her translate it into an outer expression. This method, therefore, is a means for the performer, in his or her moment of 'inspiration', to command from his or her inner self the resources necessary for achieving the desired objective, i.e., enacting a scene cogently and perfectly.

In Hollywood, stalwarts like Paul Muni, Marlon Brando, Greta Garbo and later Al Pacino and Robert De Niro stand out as the most illustrious 'graduates' of the Stanislavsky School.

***

Dilip Kumar, apart from studying his senior and contemporary Western counterparts, seemed to have conducted a personal academic study of the Stanislavskian method to make it relevant to Indian cinema. In his acting pursuits, he engaged himself in elevating cinematic acting far above a mere external demonstration of emotions, as is found in what Stanislavsky had called the 'theatre of representation', to a truly 'living experience' that demanded spontaneous reproduction of authentic emotions.

However, Dilip Kumar did not merely remain a Stanislavskian realist method actor, but he harmonized his method with a vivid theatrical form of the Indian literary and drama tradition. In the creation of the living experience, the actor developed the ability to stir his inner being, that is, to awaken his own initiative in response to the needs of a characterization. For this, he very creatively adopted elements from the Indian romantic literary tradition, in which a protagonist uses the 'sense memory' to 'organize' emotions. As a result, the experiences and traumas of the past keep tugging at, and fuelling, his emotional make-up. This way the artiste could arouse at will the emotions implicit in a role.

The acting style evolved by Dilip Kumar made him very different from his contemporaries. Instead of simply becoming an Indian version of the Western peers, he became a pioneer himself. He soon moved beyond the realm of the dominant acting styles of his predecessors, K. L. Saigal, Prithviraj Kapoor and Sohrab Modi, and even the highly acclaimed natural actors Motilal, Ashok Kumar, Gope and Yakub. The whole process created, for the first time, a true identity of the cinematically mature 'modern' hero in Indian cinema; a feat that could not be accomplished fully by his illustrious senior, Ashok Kumar.

The Eisenteinian Emotive Mechanism

Through his method, Dilip Kumar laid the foundation of an extensive emotive experiment on celluloid aimed at delinking the audience members from what they are and facilitating their complete empathizing with the characters during the course of a film. In this interaction with the audience, the actor becomes a vehicle for portraying intense emotional experiences. Apart from the influences of the Stanislavskian theory, Dilip Kumar's method, advertently or inadvertently, exhibited many techniques similar to those articulated by the celebrated Russian film maker and theoretician, Sergi Eisentein in his *Film Theory* and other works.

In the manifestation of his romantic/serious scenes, Dilip Kumar is truly Eisenteinian. He appears to be articulating a dream in which the desire, the longing and the pain simply seem to transform themselves into a deep whisper from within. But soon the actor would consciously undermine this dream himself as it gets adversely affected by the outside milieu in which he is placed.

Such a dichotomy led to a sequence of events in which the actor would at times remain silent or suddenly erupt like a well-timed blast, resulting in an unexpected powerful outflow of negative emotions. Dilip Kumar adopted this duality, the conscious splitting of the positive and negative emotional fields, as the basic strategy in articulating the various aspects of his portrayals.

In-built in this method was yet another mechanism. Dilip Kumar also operated a two-way 'gestalt switch' with respect to his responses to his environment and their impact on the viewer. Through his subtle transitions even within a scene of very short duration, he conducts an interrogation of his inner self with outside reality, whereby the viewer gets closer to the reality through a visual interpretation of the self. Yet, in another situation, the artiste chooses to reach out to the reality but soon switches over to his inner self, indulging in self-defeating thoughts, and getting possessed with a strange sense of passivity while pushing the reality to the background. Thus, as the viewer views the reality in the narrative of the film, he or she perceives it as his or her own affected self and goes into a mood of self-indulgence on the pattern projected by the actor.

Another unique aspect of Dilip Kumar's method is conveying a myriad of emotions by brevity of style. It was largely the facial expressions and the eyes that did the talking. Equally important is the improvisation by which the artiste connects his expressions and body movements so as to gradually reveal the intended emotional plane. Thus, with these techniques devised by him, he could impart similar cinematic clarity in different roles.

The Essential Built-in Asynchronization

Dilip Kumar was the forerunner in establishing a highly appealing blending of acting and dialogue delivery and, in a sense, proving the thesis that good cinema is more visually powerful and relies less on the spoken word. The nuances of this blending, in fact, have elevated his style into an art. The strategy appears to be based on an innate sense of asynchronization in which the actor reveals the minute preparation of the facial expressions and selective body movements just before a build-up for taking up the dialogue and, during this delivery itself, begins to reveal the expression required for his act, which is to follow immediately. The actor would deliver the dialogue a few moments earlier and linger over it after the manifestation of a well-thought-out sequence of changes in the facial expressions.

In this underplay, the basic building block is silence. He plays with silence as well as with whispers and pauses. Within the domain of this silence he carries and regulates the amount and the timing of what is to be communicated in a few moments. And if the situation demands, there is sudden burst of a sort of high electric surge being accumulated from the prevalent silence, which takes the form of a dialogue and often with well-timed swift body movements. But as if that is not enough to overpower the viewer, there is often a complete collapse in the same scene, the artiste fumbles and gradually again takes refuge in the vast reservoir of his silence.

The pauses between the words are as important as the words. Though they are virtually unexpected, after a while, they become very rhythmic that the eventual synthesis is easily discernible by the audience. The thespian would also sound incoherent, a tactic, which itself is employed to depict the intensity of the turmoil within the soul of the character but unable to find a full expression. These attributes have made Dilip Kumar the master of the interplay between silence and articulation, in which silence often becomes even more expressive than the spoken words. He also resorts to this kind of asynchronization while intertwining the facial expressions with the physical gestures.

The Integration of Dialogue and Visual Presentation

Before Dilip Kumar's arrival on the scene, dialogue delivery was a rudimentary extension of the theatrical style, represented by the early actors like Master Vithal, Sohrab Modi and Prithviraj Kapoor. One genre of particular importance was the discourse between two characters based on dialogues and ripostes, used as an essential strategy in the narrative of a film.

Dilip Kumar emerged as the first actor in Indian cinema who carried out a unique integration of the dialogue with the visual presentation. This integration helped not only in the development of a truly cinematic approach to narration and treatment in commercial cinema, but also in liberating Indian films from the hangover of theatre. And yet this technique was not merely the subordination of the word to the visual as per the aesthetics of the parallel cinema that emerged later.

In this complex integration, Dilip Kumar introduced a remarkable differentiation between the 'visual personality' and the 'verbal personality' in the cinematic presentation of a character, locating the two in separate slots, which in an enactment, overlap in varying proportions as well as moving in different planes. Given the relative dynamics of these slots, the verbal personality sometimes slowly gets dissolved into the visual personality and then starts engulfing and overriding it. The result is a vivid manifestation of a mutual enrichment of the two through either their relative contraction or expansion. At the same time, their own distinctions are kept intact.

In his characteristic blending of underplay and overplay, the master often first gradually brings the visual personality to a desired plane as per the enactment on hand (through an initial sustenance of expressions and gestures) and then starts building up the verbal personality reluctantly, but this reluctant speaker either scuttles its formation, making it linger on, or develops it exponentially like a continuous series of explosions.

In the romantic scenes, the verbal and visual personalities are kept compatible with each other and the master literally treats his beloved as the beauty and the voice of Mother Nature.

In enacting comedies, the master develops another curious interplay between the verbal and visual personalities. He triggers a complete release of the visual personality, fully synergized, trying to appropriate the whole acting space in short, swift and humorous actions. He then immediately brings in the verbal to further expand the space of the desired humour so as to further build the oddity of the situation or action. And instead of doing a simplistic caricature, the actor creates a deep sense of humour. Like a cartoonist, he plays up the scene, distorting the verbal–visual attributes to reach a hilarious climax.

Another distinct feature of Dilip Kumar's presentation is his relationship with other characters in a film. As a typical isolationist, the master builds a wide space of autonomy for himself with respect to other characters. Either in the role of a passionate lover, as in his earlier films, or as a doting father in senior roles, he creates an impregnable layer around himself in which his grace and sensitivity appear vibrant.

Two Other Path-breaking Innovations

In the field of film acting, Dilip Kumar was also responsible for two path-breaking innovations, which helped develop a composite model of the Indian film hero.

First, in the picturization of songs, an essential component of most Indian films, Dilip Kumar evolved a cinematically matured style, providing immense dignity to the song and enhancing its appeal. Like K. L. Saigal, he too acquired the ability of interpreting the lyrics and the mood of the song through natural expressions and controlled movements.

Second, in films such as *Naya Daur*, *Ganga Jumna* and *Sunghursh*, Dilip Kumar brought in new features of choreography. Borrowing elements from the folk dances of Uttar Pradesh and Punjab, the actor used his ingenuity to improvise and presented a style not seen earlier in Indian cinema. Much later, it was Amitabh Bachchan, who further worked on this style, which became a hallmark of his screen image.

The Method and the Audience

The Indian method of film acting evolved by Dilip Kumar became the basis for the development of the archetype of Indian cinema's indigenous hero represented by the master. Apart from the strong socio-cultural settings of his characterizations, his path-breaking acting perceptions and unique dialogue delivery not only empowered this hero, but also made the Indian viewers adore him and empathize with him.

On one plane, he projected subtle and tender feelings: a poet-like character in pursuit of beauty and love. On another plane, he excelled in manifesting the pain of frustrated love and the impending downfall of his world.

This combination of duality in his characters made Dilip Kumar the dominant cult figure of his times, which had a tremendous impact on Indian people in general and the youth in particular. For them, he represented an ideal role model: not only did they adopt his style and mannerisms but, more importantly, they also empathized with his on-screen sorrow and despair. In other words, the thespian's rapport with the masses was phenomenal, which any of his contemporaries could hardly match.

This empathy that the viewer feels is not merely a direct outcome of the strong characterization of the actor, but also has elements of a preconceived interpretation. In this interpretation, Dilip Kumar, the actor, makes use of his personal insecurity, his despair and the resulting traumas to move the viewer away from his or her own emotional personality. The thespian becomes a rallying point for the viewer, who goes through a vicarious experience as he or she watches the scenes unfold on screen.

Many of Dilip Kumar's portrayals, in a sense, represented what some psychologists call the 'basic anxiety syndrome', a feeling of perpetual helplessness towards a potentially hostile world. In the case of this hero, it was nostalgia that offered solace and comfort. Therefore, in his method of acting, Dilip Kumar, appeared to be looking backwards and interpreting his actions in the context of the past.

For the audience, the prolonged emotional experience, so unexpected in the first viewing of a film, still remained intact on a repeat viewing. Each time, the basic intensity of the experience triggered among the audience a sense of renewed emotional unfulfilment. The first-time experience did not seem sufficient. It lingered on; the audience chose to 'relive' it again and again. Some people are reported to have seen the films of Dilip Kumar more than fifty times, and one aficionado saw *Mughal-e-Azam* more than 400 times! No actor except Dilip Kumar (apart from K. L. Saigal and Amitabh Bachchan) has scored so high on repeated viewing of films till date. Dilip Kumar's instant success in creating a mass following was also a result of the repeated viewing by the masses.

In his precise projection of emotions, the actor, in fact, began not only to educate the viewers to respond to the subtleties of human feeling, but also to equip them with an ability to articulate similar emotions in response to their own situations. That is why, in the classical phase of his career, Dilip Kumar became the role model for many youngsters. It indeed became fashionable for them to consciously fall in love and land up in situations where they cannot attain the girl whom they pine for. They become sad, melancholic and depressed, and like their hero, seek solace in suffering and pain and even resort to hitting the bottle.

* * *

Dilip Kumar, by synthesizing a perfect balance of underplay and overplay, laid the foundation of cinematic acting in Indian cinema. With his vast range of histrionics, he remained the basic model for those who followed him keenly as their ideal in building their careers in Indian cinema. If he had not become a formidable actor, the thespian would have indeed been an outstanding 'professor' in any prestigious film institution anywhere in the world.

Chapter 7

Film and Portrayal Diversity in Dilip Kumar's Cinema

Film Diversity

During his career that spanned more than five decades, Dilip Kumar appeared in fifty-nine films (excluding those films in which he appeared in a guest role and films that were shelved). As many as fifty-four of them belonged to social genre, four were costume dramas (*Aan, Udan Khatola, Yahudi* and *Kohinoor*) and one historical (*Mughal-e-Azam*).

One real test of the abilities of a cine artiste lies in his or her depiction of biographical roles. However, unlike his predecessor K. L. Saigal, he did not play any historical or real-life character, except that of Prince Salim (in *Mughal-e-Azam*, 1960), who later took on the title Jehangir. Apart from Saigal, some other actors also very ably portrayed biographical roles like V. Shantaram in *Dr Kotnis Ki Amar Kahani* (1946), Bharat Bhushan in *Mirza Ghalib* (1954) and Manoj Kumar in *Shaheed* (1965) as Bhagat Singh. In retrospect, one can conclude that Dilip Kumar's histrionics could have been deployed to re-create the personas of, say, Chanakya, Asoka the Great, Mirza Ghalib, Kabir and Birsa Munda (a leader who fought for tribal rights in the nineteenth century) among others.

During the course of his long innings, Dilip Kumar's most productive years were 1948 and 1955, followed by 1950, 1951, 1952, 1953 and 1986. The actor lost thirteen valuable years (1977–81 and 1990–97), as he did not take up any role during this period.

Unlike many other artistes, Dilip Kumar's formidable talent has remained underutilized, particularly after the classical phase. His annual output has been far less than that of other artistes; generally, only one film on an average per year. He also adopted too narrow an approach in his selection of roles. Even in the classical period, the actor exhibited strong adherence to one school of film making represented by Mehboob Khan, S. U. Sunny, Naushad and Shakeel Badayuni. But he also achieved tremendous gains when he worked with other highly creative and respected directors such as Bimal Roy, Amiya Chakravarty and Ramesh Sehgal.

Also, none of the directors of the 'parallel cinema' could get an opportunity to harness the thespian's stupendous potential, and thus a complete utilization of the actor in various streams of Indian cinema could not take place. Although Satyajit Ray acknowledged him as the finest artiste of his times and wanted to cast him in one of his films, this collaboration could not materialize and a great opportunity was indeed lost.

The lost opportunities are also equally glaring as far as the non-representation of our country's best actor in world cinema is concerned. David Lean's keen eye had identified Dilip Kumar as a potential artiste from the Orient for inclusion in the cinema of the West. In 1960, Lean offered him a stellar role in *Lawrence of Arabia* (released in 1962) with Peter O'Toole in the lead. But the actor refused the offer on the pretext of his apprehension that he would lose the patronage of his audience in India. The role finally went to Omar Sharif, the Egyptian actor, who soon became one of the legendary stars of Hollywood.

Dilip Kumar like his contemporaries – Raj Kapoor, Dev Anand and Raaj Kumar – never opted for the other mass medium, television. Perhaps these artistes thought that their larger-than-life images could not be properly depicted through the 'idiot box', which could have led to a lowering of their status. In contrast, Ashok Kumar, the seniormost artiste among them, had no qualms in appearing on television. He can be justifiably credited with breaking new ground for film artistes to switch over to television. Ashok Kumar played the title role in the 1986 TV serial *Zafar*, based on the life and times of the last Mughal emperor, Bahadur Shah Zafar (1775–1862). Also, his extremely spontaneous and friendly epilogue to each episode of the country's first soap opera, *Hum Log*, in the mid-1980s added much to its popularity.

Portrayal Diversity

Table 7.1 presents the profile of the roles played by Dilip Kumar in terms of the listed five attributes.

Table 7.1
A Profile of Roles by Dilip Kumar

Film	Portrayal	Social milieu	Character persona	Genesis of character	Final manifestation of character
I. Formative Period					
Jwar Bhata (1944)	Nautanki artiste	Urban/ rural	Romantic and caring	Upholder of love	Positive; reset on a happy course
Pratima (1945)	Aristocratic youth	Rural – aristocratic	Obsessed lover seeking gratification of unfulfilled love through idolizing the female figure	Upholder of love	Positive; reset on a happy course
Milan (1946)	Aristocratic youth	Rural – aristocratic	Romantic with strong moral bearing	Upholder of love	Positive; reset on a happy course
II. Classical Period					
Jugnu (1948)	College student	Urban	Flamboyant romantic turned obsessed lover	Upholder of love	Commits suicide after the heroine dies in a demented condition

(contd.)

Film	Portrayal	Social milieu	Character persona	Genesis of character	Final manifestation of character
Anokha Pyar (1948)	Struggling writer	Urban	Romantic/ idolized by two competing women / indecisive in conflict situation	Upholder of love	Positive; reset on a happy course
Ghar Ki Izzat (1948)	Educated youth	Urban upper class	Married / indecisive	Upholder of family ties	Positive; reset on a happy course
Nadiya Ke Paar (1948)	Landed aristocrat	Rural – aristocratic	Restless seeker of childhood love	Anti-establishment rebelling against social conventions	Dies with heroine in love pact
Mela (1948)	Poor village youth	Rural – poor	Restless seeker of childhood love	Upholder of love	Dies with heroine in love pact
Shaheed (1948)	Revolution-ary youth	Urban – upper class	Restless seeker of childhood love juxtaposed with commitment to society	People's hero – crusader for national liberation	Achieves martyrdom
Andaz (1949)	Estate manager	Urban upper class	Restless seeker of rejected love	Anti-hero	Gets killed on the altar of love
Shabnam (1949)	Nautanki artiste	Rural	Romantic – vengeful disposition in love	Upholder of love	Positive; reset on a happy course
Arzoo (1950)	Poor village youth turned aristocrat	Rural/ aristocratic	Restless seeker of childhood love/vengeful	Anti-hero	Loser in love; left alone
Babul (1950)	Postman turned musician	Rural/ aristocratic	Romantic/ indecisive, sought by two competing women/ self-obsessed social climber	Anti-hero	Loser in love; left alone
Jogan (1950)	Educated youth	Rural	Restless seeker of rejected love/ interpreter of love as path for emancipation	Upholder of love	Loser in love; left alone

(contd.)

Film	Portrayal	Social milieu	Character persona	Genesis of character	Final manifestation of character
Hulchal (1951)	Household servant turned circus man	Rural/ aristocratic/ urban	Restless seeker of childhood love	Anti-establishment – rebelling against social conventions	Invites death to validate his obsession
Tarana (1951)	Alien visitor (doctor)	Rural/ urban	Romantic/ suffering lover facing family and social opposition	Upholder of love	Positive; reset on a happy course
Deedar (1951)	Blind street singer	Rural / urban aristocratic	Restless seeker of childhood love	Upholder of love	Overcomes past through self-realization
Sangdil (1952)	Landed aristocrat	Rural – aristocratic	Romantic caught in sense of guilt	Anti-hero	Positive; reset on a happy course
Aan (1952)	Clan leader	Royal – rural	Upbeat romantic/ humorist/ tamer of shrew	People's hero – crusader against royal tyranny	Victorious; validating people's power
Daag (1952)	Village artisan	Rural poor	Sufferer due to social rejection, being an alcoholic	Anti-establishment – social deviant	Reformed; reset on a happy course
Footpath (1953)	Journalist	Urban poor/ urban rich	Unscrupulous social climber becoming neo-rich	Anti-hero	Reformed; reset on a happy course
Shikast (1953)	Landed aristocrat turned doctor	Rural – aristocratic	Suffering lover, trapped in the the past/ progressive – opposing feudal attitudes and lifestyle	People's hero – crusader for uplift of rural poor	Saves the life of his former beloved
Amar (1954)	Lawyer	Semi-urban – aristocratic	Romantic caught in a sense of guilt	Anti-hero	Overcomes past guilt through self-realization
Azaad (1955)	Social bandit / landed aristocrat	Rural/semi-urban aristocratic	Upbeat romantic/ humorist	People's hero – crusader for uplift and empowerment of poor	Victorious

(contd.)

Film	Portrayal	Social milieu	Character persona	Genesis of character	Final manifestation of character
Devdas (1955)	Landed aristocrat	Rural/ urban aristocratic	Indulgent, indecisive sufferer, trapped in the past	Anti-establishment – rebelling against family authority and social conventions	Chooses death as a silent protest against social order
Insaniyat (1955)	Clan leader	Medieval – rural poor	Sufferer due to rejection in love	People's hero – crusader against royal tyranny	Achieves martyrdom
Udan Khatola (1955)	Alien visitor	Tribal nobility	Romantic / musician	Upholder of love	Dies for upholding love pact with heroine
Musafir (1957)	Roadside destitute / violinist	Urban middle class	Suffering lover, trapped in the past	Upholder of lost love	Dies as a silent protest against misfortunes
Naya Daur (1957)	Tonga driver turned community leader	Rural poor	Upholder of collective community spirit	People's hero – crusader for people's economic rights	Victorious
Madhu-mati (1958)	Estate manager	Rural/ aristocratic	Sufferer seeking justice against feudal tyranny	Upholder of love	Dies for upholding love pact with heroine
Yahudi (1958)	Royal prince	Imperial	Indulgent obsessed lover	Anti-establishment – rebelling against parental/ state authority	Positive; reset on on a happy course
Paigham (1959)	Skilled industrial worker and union leader	Urban – poor	Talented technical innovator ready to sacrifice for a common cause	People's hero – crusader for workers' rights	Victorious
Mughal-e-Azam (1960)	Royal prince	Imperial	Indulgent obsessed lover	Anti-establishment – rebelling against parental/ state authority	Loser; victim of state power

(contd.)

Film	Portrayal	Social milieu	Character persona	Genesis of character	Final manifestation of character
Kohinoor (1960)	Royal prince	Royal	Upbeat romantic/ humorist/ proponent of music	Upholder of love	Victorious
Ganga Jumna (1961)	Rural worker turned dacoit	Rural poor	Sufferer due to lost dignity/ vengeful against feudal tyranny	Anti-establish-ment – rebelling against ineffective system of justice	Meets death for a just cause

III. Post-Classical Period

Film	Portrayal	Social milieu	Character persona	Genesis of character	Final manifestation of character
Leader (1964)	College youth	Urban/ aristocratic	Upbeat romantic/ humorist/ upstart, self-acclaimed politician exposing corruption in political system	Progressive, upholder of democratic values and modern attitudes	Victorious; highlighting role of youth as vanguard of democracy
Dil Diya Dard Liya (1966)	Household servant turned estate owner	Rural/ aristocratic	Restless seeker of childhood love/vengeful disposition in love	Anti-hero	Positive; reset on a happy course
Ram Aur Shyam (1967) (double role)	1. Aristocratic family youth 2. Rural youth	Urban aristocratic	1. Neurotic suffering due to family oppression 2. Upbeat romantic/ humorist	1. Victim of injustice 2. Dispenser of justice	Positive; reset on a happy course
Aadmi (1968)	Estate owner	Urban aristocratic	Egoist sufferer from guilt/ vengeful towards others	Anti-hero	Positive; reformed and reset on a happy course
Sunghursh (1968)	Clan heir	Medieval	Anti-violence pacifist/ striving for clan harmony	Anti-establish-ment – rebelling against family authority and tradition	Victorious

(contd.)

Film	Portrayal	Social milieu	Character persona	Genesis of character	Final manifestation of character
Gopi (1970)	Rural worker	Rural poor	Rustic hard-headed simpleton/ humorist	Upholder of family ties	Positive; reset on a happy course
Dastaan (1972)	1. Judge 2. High society rich youth	Urban aristocratic	1. Vengeful sufferer due to disillusionment in relationships 2. Upbeat romantic	Upholder of morality	Victorious over perpetrators
Sagina Mahato (1970) Sagina (1974)	Industrial worker/union leader	Rural – industrial	Rustic hard-headed indulgent/ humorist/ strong sense of a typical industrial worker	Representative of politically conscious working class	Victorious over capitalist forces and self-righteous radical leadership
Bairaag (1976) (triple role)	1. Business magnate 2. Household servant 3. High society rich youth	1. Urban aristocratic 2. Rural 3. Urban rich	1. Father figure tormented by past guilt and painful present 2. Rustic strong-headed rural youth 3. Indulgent, flamboyant, irresponsible youth	1. Seeker of family ties 2. Upholder of family ties 3. Anti-hero	Father is forced to disown blind son who gets his vision back

IV. Senior Roles

Film	Portrayal	Social milieu	Character persona	Genesis of character	Final manifestation of character
Kranti (1981)	Clan leader	Colonial period	Revolutionary father figure spearheading people's struggle	People's hero – crusader for national liberation	Achieves martyrdom
Shakti (1982)	Senior police officer	Metropolis	Upright father figure dedicated to profession; tormented by painful present	Upholder of state authority and justice system	Lives through personal grief
Vidhata (1982)	Engine driver turned mafia don	Urban – rich	Upright worker upholding belief in destiny/ vengeful; tormented by past injustice and painful present	Anti-establish-ment rebelling against ineffective system of justice	Dies, validating the punitive outcome for becoming rebel

(contd.)

Film	Portrayal	Social milieu	Character persona	Genesis of character	Final manifestation of character
Mazdoor (1983)	Industrial worker turned industrialist	Urban metropolis	Upright father figure, building modern industrial enterprise based on healthy owner–worker collaboration/ tormented by wrong-doers	People's hero – upholder of healthy owner– worker relationship	Positive; reset on happy course
Duniya (1984)	Ordinary family man	Urban metropolis	Vengeful, as tormented by three evil men men	Rebelling against ineffective system of justice	Dies after completing his vengeful mission
Mashaal (1984)	Journalist turned mafia don	Urban – metropolis	Upright professional committed to social role of media; tormented by evil-doers/ vengeful	Anti-establish- ment – rebelling against ineffective system of justice	Dies after completing his mission
Dharam Adhikari (1986)	Traditional rural judge	Rural aristocratic	Upright father figure dedicated to ancestral profession of justice giving	Upholder of traditional Indian justice system	Lives up to his his profession
Karma (1986)	Jail superintendent	Urban	Upright father figure dedicated to profession/ tormented by painful present/ dispenser of justice through vengeance	People's hero – crusader for nation's defence and security	Victorious
Kanoon Apna Apna (1989)	District magistrate	Urban	Law enforcer in conflict with the corrupt mob leader and radical activist	Upholder of law	Victorious
Izzatdar (1990)	Upright judge turned mafia don	Urban	Victim of an unscrupulous schemer and destroyer of his family life	Anti-establish- ment – rebelling against ineffective system of justice to destroy the evil man in his life	Victorious

(contd.)

Film	Portrayal	Social milieu	Character persona	Genesis of character	Final manifestation of character
Saudagar (1991)	Landed aristocrat	Rural rich	Vengeful patriarch/ upholder of family honour and friendship	Dispenser of justice	Dies after destroying the tormenter
Qila (1998) (double role)	1. Feudal lord 2. Judge	Rural aristocratic/ urban	1.Indulgent sadist/ tormenter 2.Compassionate and caring, fulfilling successfully his vision of a new social order	/1. Anti-hero 2. People's hero – upholder of anti-feudal attitudes and lifestyle	1. Murdered as outcome of natural justice 2. Victorious

Table 7.2 lists the directors who have worked with Dilip Kumar in his long career spanning over five decades.

Table 7.2
Directors of Dilip Kumar's Films

Director	Film/s
S. U. Sunny	Mela (1948), Babul (1950), Udan Khatola (1955), Kohinoor (1960)
Nitin Bose	Milan (1946), Deedar (1951), Ganga Jumna (1961)
Mehboob Khan	Andaz (1949), Aan (1952), Amar (1954)
Bimal Roy	Devdas (1955), Madhumati (1958), Yahudi (1958)
Subhash Ghai	Vidhata (1982), Karma (1986), Saudagar (1991)
Amiya Chakravarty	Jwar Bhata (1944), Daag (1952)
A. Bhimsingh	Aadmi (1968), Gopi (1970)
Ram Daryani	Ghar Ki Izzat (1948), Tarana (1951)
Ramesh Sehgal	Shaheed (1948), Shikast (1953)
B. R. Chopra	Naya Daur (1957), Dastaan (1972)
S. S. Vasan	Insaniyat (1955), Paigham (1959)
K. Asif	Mughal-e-Azam (1960)
Tapan Sinha	Sagina Mahato (1970, Bengali), Sagina (1974, Hindi)
P. Jairaj	Pratima (1945)
Shaukat Hussain Rizvi	Jugnu (1948)
M. I. Dharmsey	Anokha Pyar (1948)
Kishore Sahu	Nadiya Ke Paar (1948)
B. Mitra	Shabnam (1949)
Shahid Lateef	Arzoo (1950)
Kidar Sharma	Jogan (1950)
S. K. Ojha	Hulchal (1951)
R. C. Talwar	Sangdil (1952)
Zia Sarhadi	Footpath (1953)

(contd.)

Director	Film/s
S. M. S. Naidu	*Azaad* (1955)
Hrishikesh Mukherjee	*Musafir* (1957)
Ram Mukherji	*Leader* (1964)
A. R. Kardar	*Dil Diya Dard Liya* (1966)
Chanakya	*Ram Aur Shyam* (1967)
H. S. Rawail	*Sunghursh* (1968)
Asit Sen	*Bairaag* (1976)
Manoj Kumar	*Kranti* (1981)
Ramesh Sippy	*Shakti* (1982)
Ravi Chopra	*Mazdoor* (1983)
Yash Chopra	*Mashaal* (1984)
Ramesh Talwar	*Duniya* (1984)
K. Raghavendra Rao	*Dharm Adhikari* (1986)
B. Gopal	*Kanoon Apna Apna* (1989)
K. Bapaiah	*Izzatdar* (1990)
Umesh Mehra	*Qila* (1998)

Chapter 8

Two Other Indigenous Heroes:
Guru Dutt and Sanjeev Kumar

As the proponents of serious cinema, Dilip Kumar and Guru Dutt represented the two sides of the same coin. While Dilip Kumar remained preoccupied with a perpetually personalized sorrow, Guru Dutt depicted the same sorrow in a much wider social context. The brooding stance of Dilip Kumar in *Devdas* and *Amar* was specific to his sense of personal loss. Guru Dutt, on the other hand, developed his oeuvre by locating it right in the middle of the socio-political milieu and dissecting each human relationship to show the growing dehumanization of society. He was one the few 'actor-film makers' in mainstream cinema who attempted to employ the film medium as an interpreter of the day-to-day realities.

Guru Dutt and His Broad Canvas

Guru Dutt Padukone (9 July 1925 to 10 October 1964), who hailed from Karnataka (then known as Mysore), represented the cinema of despair in the later part of his life. As a thinker-craftsman, he had few peers in Indian cinematic history. And he is the only film maker who successfully mastered two entirely opposite genres.

In the first phase, he laid the foundation of Hindi cinema's first urban hero, presenting the first-ever realistic depiction of the life of the urban downtrodden – their daily joys and sorrows and the struggle for existence in the jungle of the metropolis. His films covered a wide spectrum, including conmen, hustlers, petty crooks, club dancers and musicians. The films in this phase were *Baazi* (1951), *Jaal* (1952), *Aar Paar* (1954) and *Mr and Mrs 55* (1955).

With the whole spectacle mounted on a high platform of song and dance and excellent imagery, these films had immense artistic and emotional appeal. The typical climax of a Hindi crime film, in which the hero, heroine, often their relatives and rest of the cast reach the den of the 'boss' where the final showdown takes place, is a unique contribution of his banners. His first film as hero was *Baaz* (1953), the only period film by the master, depicting the struggle against the Portuguese occupation of Goa, situated close to his native place.

Guru Dutt:
The master craftsman

In the second phase, which began in 1957, Guru Dutt made a permanent shift to serious cinema represented by his dark trilogy of *Pyaasa* (1957), *Kagaz Ke Phool* (1959) and *Sahib Bibi Aur Ghulam* (1962). In depicting the social decadence in terms of degeneration of human values and commercialization of social relations, these films regenerated the prevailing gloom and despair, which his protagonists tend to internalize within themselves. There is a persistent search for belonging and for wider social recognition, which the film maker hints is possible only in a new system, but like a true romantic, fails to delineate such a system.

The melancholic *Pyaasa* was written with Dilip Kumar in mind for the lead role. It appears that while Guru Dutt had evolved his light crime thrillers around Dev Anand's flamboyant persona, he was planning to build his serious cinema with Dilip Kumar in the role of his protagonist: the disillusioned brooder in search of his identity and love. Guru Dutt seemed to have been greatly influenced by Bimal Roy's presentation of Dilip Kumar as the internal sufferer in *Devdas*. In fact, in *Kagaz Ke Phool*, the director-protagonist is shown shooting a film on Devdas, and Waheeda Rehman, the chance discovery by the director, is cast in the role of Paro. According to knowledgeable sources, Dilip Kumar had apparently agreed to do the film and Guru Dutt and his team waited for the actor on the sets for quite a while. When Dilip Kumar did not turn up, Dutt's creative team, which included production chief S. Guruswamy, scriptwriter Abrar Alvi, cameraman V. K. Murthy, art directors M. R. Achrekar and L. G. Patil, after much discussion, decided that the film maker himself should now face the camera (see matter in screen below).

Guru Dutt Calls Crucial Meeting on the Casting of *Pyaasa*

Guru Dutt said, '*Abrar! Would you please call once all the members of the unit in my cabin. I want to hold an urgent meeting ...*

[After] everybody [had] collected in the cabin, Guru Dutt said, '*Dilip Kumar hasn't showed up today also. Never mind. Abrar! you can now cancel his contract. Professionally I do not consider anybody over and above me. Everyone comes to me as an artist. No body is indispensable ....*

He further said, '*I will not tolerate any obstacle or hindrance created by anybody. I shall request Raj Kapoor or someone else .... Dev Anand failed to turn up on the sets of* Baaz *so I decided to essay that role myself. Today Dilip Kumar has not showed up. I am ready to jump into the arena once again though I know my limitations. I also know that this is an audacity .... Whatever you all decide will be final and it has to be done now. Yes or no*'.

Abrar jumped up and said, '*Don't be foolish, Guru! Get up and get ready with your make-up. What do you say Murthy?*' Murthy got up enthusiastically in consent and was followed by others. They immediately set to work. The light man flooded the sets. Meanwhile Sahir Ludhianvi arrived. He came up and embraced Guru Dutt.

'Congratulations! I am sure you can do justice to this role yourself. Compose yourself, go ahead calmly and everything will be fine. You are too sentimental.'

Source: Translated from Anjan Kumar, *Shayara/Ameen*, two booklets on the lives of Meena Kumari and Guru Dutt (in Hindi) (Delhi: Raj Kamal, 1988).

In this memorable role, Dutt discovered in himself the serious actor and the immense ability to underplay the character, which was to become the basis of his screen persona in subsequent films. He also demonstrated how a film in its totality could serve its theme fully than simply basing it on the histrionics of its lead actors.

Pyaasa emerged as one of the country's landmark films in meaningful cinema and the first in a series of films addressing the state of nation and the growing alienation of the people in the post-independence period. Through the plight of an intensely emotional poet whom society has failed to recognize, the film depicted the transaction between the creativity of an artiste and the market in which the ruthless commodification of aesthetics muffles the voice of its creator.

Pyaasa was among the few commercial films, which were not literary adaptations, but were strongly rooted in the literary tradition. The poetic foundation of the film was inspired by Sahir's radical literary poetry as is evident from the title of the anthology, *Parchhaiyian* (which means shadows), published in the name of the poet in the film. (*Parchhaiyian* is, in fact, the title of a long poem penned by Sahir with the Second World War as the backdrop.) According to Guru Dutt, the idea for the plot came from a reference to the Greek philosopher Homer – 'Seven cities claimed Homer dead, while the living begged his bread.' The film also seemed to be inspired by Nitin Bose's *Lagan* (1941), in which the poor poet (K. L. Saigal) is in love with an upper-class girl (Kanan Devi) but she marries a rich man. To please her, the husband publishes the poet's work making him famous. (See Chapter 3 for details.) This film contributed towards developing the romantic stereotype of the suffering artiste in Indian cinema.

Kagaz Ke Phool followed the trend set by *Pyaasa*. This time Guru Dutt takes up another artiste, a visionary film director, to show once again the cruel transaction between art and the commercial world. A scathing attack on the functioning of commercial cinema, the film is the tale of a talented director who eventually takes recourse to self-destruction because of both family problems and his inability to succeed at the box office. Acclaimed as India's answer to *Citizen Kane* (1941), *Kagaz Ke Phool*[1] seems to be partly autobiographical, perhaps a subtle statement by Dutt on the complexities of his personal life and the growing meaninglessness of his existence. The film indeed is a rare attempt to be introspective about the suffering and the disillusionment of an individual much the same way as P. C. Barua and Bimal Roy achieved in *Devdas*, but in a larger framework. Ironically, like Raj Kapoor's *Mera Naam Jokar* (1970), also a quasi-autobiographical fantasy that flopped at the box office, so did *Kagaz Ke Phool*.

Dutt gave an epic dimension to the film: not only to his narrative, but also to the impending tragedy. The tragic refrain, *Bichde Sabhi Bari Bari* ... of the song *Dekhi Zamaane Ki Yari* ..., was skilfully blended into the theme of the movie to make a poignant impact. Sachin Dev Burman's evocative music, Kaifi Azmi's moving lyrics and Mohammed Rafi's exquisite rendition greatly enhanced the overall effect. Although *Kagaz Ke Phool* was critically acclaimed and was honoured with the President's Gold Medal for best film, its commercial failure was a serious setback to Guru Dutt. The highly sensitive multifaceted artiste now virtually refused to direct his films, appearing only as a hero in other directors' ventures.

Guru Dutt's deep sense of attachment to the rich Bengali cultural milieu (as also was the case with K. L. Saigal) inspired him to take up the highly acclaimed novel by Bimal Mitra as the third film of his famous trilogy. In sharp contrast with

Pyaasa and *Kagaz Ke Phool*, which dealt with the 'present', *Sahib Bibi Aur Ghulam* (1962), directed by Abrar Alvi, attempted to relate a painful past with a ray of hope for the future through an uneasy transition through the present. Compared to Satyajit Ray's *Jalsaghar* (1958), which deals with a similar theme, *Sahib Bibi Aur Ghulam* was a tragic commentary on Bengal's decaying feudalism in the nineteenth century. A tale told through the eyes of the servants, this film depicted a decadent society represented by a household of zamindars living in colonial Calcutta whose degenerate lifestyle cannot survive the onset of the modern age. If *Kagaz Ke Phool* was a tragedy about conflicting emotions and adverse circumstances, *Sahib Bibi Aur Ghulam* was essentially an enigmatic exposition of a variety of complex obsessions and of rampant debauchery among the aristocratic classes.

In between, with *Chaudhvin Ka Chand* (1960), Guru Dutt moved beyond his famous trilogy and masterfully handled a new genre for him: the Muslim social. A forerunner in capturing the traditional culture of Lucknow, this film broke fresh ground in interpreting the intricacies of a love triangle, wherein one friend sacrifices his life for the happiness of the other. In *Chaudhvin Ka Chand*, Dutt seemed to be pointing out that life was far less beautiful than a woman's face and its real beauty lies in a set of moral convictions and the stand one takes in human relationships. *Chaudhvin Ka Chand* was embellished by Shakeel Badayuni's fabulous poetry and by Ravi's (Ravi Shankar Sharma) mellifluous musical score. The film was directed by M. Sadiq.

Guru Dutt also gave a memorable performance in a less known film, *Sautela Bhai* (1962), directed by veteran Mahesh Kaul and based on Saratchandra's novel *Boikunther*. Here, he plays the otherworldly innocent and large-hearted elder brother, who not only supports the education of the spoilt younger stepbrother, but also wins him over in the eventual fight over the mother's and father's will.

Guru Dutt had a wonderful sense of comedy as seen in his earliest films, *Baaz, Aar Paar* and *Mr and Mrs 55*, particularly in his wistful liaison with the heroine. His comic persona in these films is characterized by sharp, witty one-liners, bohemian mannerisms, the excellent use of the local Bombay lingo and a comic friendship with his favourite comedian, Johnny Walker (whose real name was Badruddin Qazi).

As an actor, Dutt imbued his performances with tremendous intensity. On the basis of his oeuvre, he had begun to represent Hindi cinema's indigenous hero but with less diversity in portrayals. Unfortunately, he died under tragic circumstances in 1964, before he could realize his full potential.

Filmography (as hero)

Lakhrani (1945), *Baazi* (1951), *Jaal* (1952), *Baaz* (1953), *Aar Paar* (1954), *Mr and Mrs 55* (1955), *Sailaab* (1956), *Pyaasa* (1957), *Twelve O'clock* (1958), *Kaagaz Ke Phool* (1959), *Chaudhvin Ka Chand* (1960), *Sahib Bibi Aur Ghulam* (1962), *Sautela Bhai* (1962), *Bahurani* (1963), *Bharosa* (1963), *Sanjh Aur Savera* (1964) and *Suhagan* (1964).

The Social Basis of Guru Dutt's Cinema

Guru Dutt, whose work is often compared to his illustrious Bengali contemporary, Ritwik Ghatak, had no match in exploring the tragic idiom in Hindi cinema, besides the use of true-to-life characters, musical chorus for enhancing the aesthetic appeal as well as building up the emotional catastrophes in the narration. Far more than Mehboob Khan, V. Shantaram and Raj Kapoor, his work captured with great intensity the emotional and social complexities created by the large-scale modernization processes propelled by Nehruvian socialism and the accompanying industrialization and urbanization. These factors, in turn, generated immense dislocation of individuals as well as communities as far as their social milieu was concerned. While he was among the founders of neo-realism in Hindi cinema along with Bimal Roy, K. A. Abbas, Chetan Anand and Ramesh Sehgal, his realism was based on complex thematic layers, curious interweaving of relationships among his protagonists, intricate, richly stylized imagery and inlaying of very high-quality melodies in the narration. For Dutt, it was the creation of the cinematic environment as per the requirements of the theme that was important and its integration with characters was far more significant than the usual larger-than-life creation of the protagonists.

His last film, *Baharen Phir Bhi Aayengi*, was completed by his brother, Atma Ram in 1966, with Dharmendra[2] appearing in the role that was originally meant for Guru Dutt.

Sanjeev Kumar: A Talent Scouted by Dilip Kumar

The arrival of Sanjeev Kumar (whose real name was Harihar Jarivala and was born on 9 July 1938) in Hindi cinema in the mid-1960s marked the making of another 'other hero'. However, for this hero the journey towards stardom was along a difficult terrain. He started as a stage actor and soon made his mark in a variety of roles. In the Indian National Theatres' play, *Do Jahan Ke Beech* (a Hindi adaptation of Arthur Miller's *All My Sons*), he played an old man when he was merely 22 years old. Prithviraj Kapoor, the doyen of Indian stage and cinema, went out of his way to congratulate the young actor for his great performance.

Sanjeev Kumar made his debut as a hero in films with Homi Brothers' *Nishan* (1965), a costume drama, directed by the old-timer Aspi Irani. The struggling actor did a series of B-grade films such as *Husn aur Ishq* (1966), Homi Wadia's *Alibaba and 40 Thieves* (1966), *Smuggler* (1966) and *Gunehgar* (1967), starring often with the rugged Sheikh Mukhtar and danseuse Kum Kum. However, in these films his abundant talent was visible only to the discerning eye. Like many such actors who keep waiting on the sidelines in the hope of ultimately rising to the top rungs, he too would have soon gone into oblivion. But Sanjeev Kumar did not have to wait for long.

His 'discovery' was curiously facilitated by none other than Dilip Kumar. During the preparations for the multistarrer *Sunghursh* (released in 1968), the thespian and H. S. Rawail, the producer-director, were in search of a suitable actor to do the role of Dwarka, one of the powerful characters in the script. One night they went to see *Nishan* at a theatre in Bombay. They were greatly impressed by the hero's performance and the young actor was immediately signed for *Sunghursh*.

In *Sunghursh*, Sanjeev Kumar brought to the fore all his hidden histrionics. In one important scene, in which he plays a game of chess with the seasoned Dilip Kumar, he takes the senior actor head on, apparently slightly unnerving him. Dilip Kumar was all praise for the young actor and even predicted a great career for him in Indian cinema in the years ahead. Sanjeev Kumar once affirmed that the words of encouragement from the master was the fulfilment of a lifetime's dream and he treasured them throughout his life. Sanjeev Kumar faced his 'discoverer' once again in *Vidhata* (1982), exhibiting equal virtuosity as the thespian in many memorable scenes.

Sunghursh opened for Sanjeev Kumar the gateway to success and soon he became the most sought-after actor by the big-budget film makers as well as those pursuing serious cinema (for instance, Hrishikesh Mukherjee, Asit Sen, Rajender Singh Bedi, A. Bhimsingh, Atma Ram, Gulzar and even the pre-eminent Satyajit Ray). A slew of fairly successful films followed with the young actor in the lead role, such as *Anokhi Raat* (1968), *Khilona* (1970), *Dastak* (1970), *Anubhav* (1971), *Koshish* (1972), *Manchali* (1973), *Naya Din Nai Raat* (1974), *Mausam* (1975), *Aandhi* (1975), *Shatranj Ke Khiladi* (1977) and *Love and God* (1986).

Khilona proved a turning point in Sanjeev Kumar's career graph. Here, he essayed the role of a jilted poet who becomes insane and then regains his sanity. His depiction of the three phases of his characterization had the audiences clamouring for more!

In *Naya Din Nai Raat* (1974), directed by A. Bhimsingh, Sanjeev Kumar presented himself in as many as nine diverse roles representing the nine *rasas* or traits, each interpreted through a distinct personality (the near-real make-up for these roles was done by Sarosh Mody, the first Hollywood-trained make-up man in the Bombay film industry). The film, in fact, became a platform for the actor to provide a comprehensive presentation of his histrionics. (The film was the Hindi version of the Tamil movie *Navratri*, released in 1964, in which the legendary Sivaji Ganesan came up with nine spellbinding performances.) For the Hindi version, the role was first offered to Dilip Kumar, who declined but recommended the name of Sanjeev Kumar. As a goodwill gesture, in the beginning of the film, the senior actor introduced to the audience the film's theme and paid lavish tributes to the way in which Sanjeev Kumar interpreted each of the nine roles on the strength of his immense acting skills.

Sanjeev Kumar's linkages with the Guru Dutt school are far less direct than interpretative. His resemblance to the master as far as appearances and mannerisms were concerned was quite striking. In addition, like Guru Dutt, he projected a kind of sensitivity that would make an actor a class by himself. This resemblance, however, was not imitative but more of a coincidence. In this sense, Sanjeev Kumar represented a continuity of Guru Dutt's screen persona, and he was seen by many as filling up the void left by the great master.

A formal recognition as the true protégé of Guru Dutt was conferred upon Sanjeev Kumar by none other than the reigning movie mughal, K. Asif. After the premature death of Guru Dutt during the making of his magnum opus, *Love and God*, Asif found the best substitute in Sanjeev Kumar for the role of Majnu, which Dutt was doing.

The young actor, who played the character of Qais (who later is given the name Majnu) with his range of histrionics, captured the nuances of the character and his mystical obsession for Laila (the experienced Nimmi played the role of Laila). However, those who had the opportunity to see the footage in which Guru Dutt had acted found this brooder-actor simply transcending the boundaries of the film medium and enlivening the character's metamorphosis (particularly, the scene in which the crowd starts stoning the deranged lover). Sanjeev Kumar was also cast in the lead role in *Manchali* (1973), a rework of Guru Dutt's *Mr and Mrs 55*, apparently inspired by the resemblance of his screen persona with that of the master.

As in the case of Guru Dutt, one singular feature of Sanjeev Kumar's portrayals was their vast diversity. With his characteristic ease, he brought to life characters as diverse as an easy-going slick urban young man, passionate lover, indulgent drunkard, scheming business tycoon and the hot-headed patriarch. His style was unassuming and had a spontaneity and warmth reminiscent of Motilal, Ashok Kumar and Balraj Sahni.

Sanjeev Kumar, like many other credible actors, had a massive following among the viewers. There are two main reasons for his immense success. First, he arrived in the post-classical period of cinema as the antithesis of the prevailing macho, glamorous and stylized hero and thus he was easily recognizable as a down-to-earth character, among the people. He looked far more familiar, the man next door, who did not need an introduction. In this sense, Sanjeev Kumar was the first to challenge the typical hero-centred basis of Hindi cinema and introduce a definite qualitative improvement in characterizations.

Secondly, Sanjeev Kumar represented, in emotionally charged roles, an innate the strength of the Indian personality – outwardly vulnerable, yet inwardly strong enough to face the harsh realities of life. His characters were full of conviction and confidence, very positively oriented whether in romantic or action-oriented sequences. They rarely were obsessed with inner turmoil and agony. He displayed a natural subtle sense of humour; his comic characterizations were slick and elegant, not overdone, and left a lingering impact on the audience.

Sanjeev Kumar is yet another example of the underutilization of a great talent in Hindi cinema. Although he did as many as forty films during a short career of about twenty years, he could not get many opportunities to exhibit his potential in more meaningful roles. No film offers of the kind of *Devdas*, *Pyaasa* or *Sahib Bibi Aur Ghulam* came to him. In fact, Sanjeev Kumar would have achieved true greatness if he had arrived during the classical period.

Sanjeev Kumar:
An actor for all
seasons

Sanjeev Kumar's role as a deaf-and-dumb character in Gulzar's *Koshish* stands out as a unique one. He and the heroine (Jaya Bhaduri, also playing a deaf-and-dumb character) came up with very impressive performances. In fact, they seemed to just glide through the movie.

Sanjeev Kumar's role in the blockbuster *Sholay* (1975) pitted him against Dharmendra and Amitabh Bachchan. He managed to hold his own and, at times, surpass the other two heroes. In this film, his riveting performance is the stuff legends are made of.

In *Trishul* (1978), he played a ruthless building magnate with characteristic aplomb. Here again, he managed to hold his own against the formidable Amitabh Bachchan, who was then the 'reigning monarch' in Bollywood.

Sanjeev Kumar, a loner in his personal life, died on 6 November 1985 when he was merely forty-seven years old (Guru Dutt passed away at the age of thirty-nine). Like K. L. Saigal, Guru Dutt, Meena Kumari, music director Jaikishan and lyricist Shailendra and many others before him, he chose the path of self-destruction by trying to fight his loneliness by guzzling alcohol but to no avail. Noted film writer Bunny Reuben observes: '*Guru Dutt and Sanjeev Kumar. Both born on 9 July. Both unlucky in love. Both eating their hearts out in unuttered anguish. Both suffering introverts whose only sublimation lay in their work. Both died young. Both are immortal. Both will live forever in their works.*'[3]

Sanjeev Kumar's death left a void for the typical senior roles of the omnipotent patriarch in the violence-ridden films of 1980s and 1990s. This void was partly filled up by his illustrious seniors, Dilip Kumar and Raaj Kumar and later by Amitabh Bachchan.

Sanjeev Kumar: A Tribute by Dr Harindranath Chhatopadhyay*

The heave of your last breath was
  the first heave of a new ocean touching a new sky
It is sheer ignorance for us to grieve
  since deathless ones like you can never die!
Your memory in us keeps wide awake,
Master! With what simplicity you wrought
Rare historic magic for the sake
Of millions of your fans to whom you brought
Enormous entertainment unsurpassed...

Source: Cinema India-International, January–March 1986.

Some of Sanjeev Kumar's movies

Nishan (1965), *Husn Aur Ishq* (1966), *Alibaba and 40 Thieves* (1966), *Pati Patni* (1966), *Smuggler* (1966), *Aayega Aanewala* (1967), *Gunehgar* (1967), *Naunihal* (1967), *Sunghursh* (1968), *Anokhi Raat* (1968), *Aashirwad* (1968), *Gauri* (1968), *Raja Aur Rank* (1968), *Shikar* (1968), *Chanda Aur Bijli* (1969), *Dharti Kahe Pukarke* (1969), *Gustakhi Maaf* (1969), *Sachaai* (1969), *Satyakam* (1969), *Insaaf Ka Mandir* (1969), *Bachpan* (1970), *Devi* (1970), *Gunah Aur Kanoon* (1970), *Insaan Aur Shaitan* (1970), *Maa Ka Aanchal* (1970), *Night in Calcutta* (1970), *Priya* (1970), *Khilona* (1970), *Dastak* (1970), *Anubhav* (1971), *Koshish* (1972), *Manchali*

---

*A poet and a theatre and cinema personality. He was the brother of the famous poetess and freedom fighter Sarojini Naidu.

(1973), *Naya Din Nai Raat* (1974), *Charitraheen* (1974), *Aandhi* (1975), *Sholay* (1975), *Mausam* (1975), *Farar* (1975), *Shatranj Ke Khiladi* (1977), *Pati, Patni Aur Woh* (1978), *Trishul* (1978), *Naukar* (1979), *Silsila* (1981), *Vidhata* (1982), *Angoor* (1982), *Namkeen* (1982), *Qatl* (1986) and *Love And God* (1986).

Notes and References

1. Federico Fellini's 1963 world classic, *8 ½*, has a striking resemblance to *Kagaz Ke Phool* in capturing the disillusionment of a highly creative and successful film director. However, Fellini's film was far more complex in dealing with the psychological roots of the director's alienation and the meaninglessness he sees in his work and life. In this film, the grand celebration to honour the director ends when he shoots himself by going under the table kept on the dais.
2. Sometime in the early 1960s, it was Guru Dutt and Bimal Roy, as the two-member jury, who selected Dharmendra, a naïve youth from Punjab, in the annual *Filmfare* talent search contest from amongst many well-connected and influential candidates. The contest was organized by the United Producers, scouting for new faces for the film industry under the aegis of *Filmfare*.
3. Bunny Reuben, *Follywood Flashback – A Collection of Movie Memories*, New Delhi, Indus, 1993.

Chapter 9

'Disciples' of Dilip Kumar and 'The Phenomenon'

Like K. L. Saigal did in the pre-independence period, Dilip Kumar in the classical period inspired a whole generation in the art of film acting. As his 'method' reached perfection, the actor, through his films, initiated a unique 'cloning' process. He generated several protégés. This phenomenon was facilitated by the apparent possibilities of grooming one's rudimentary talents by imitation and also by a faint hope in the mind of a young aspirant to become another Dilip Kumar of the silver screen. These aspirants were highly motivated self-learners. They would earnestly view the films of their hero numerous times, keenly observe his style, discuss and dissect scenes threadbare and learn the dialogues and enact scenes. No other artiste in Indian cinema, not even the formidable Amitabh Bachchan, has inspired this kind of emulation.

The 'wannabes' would also change their dress code and hairstyle in keeping with the trends of their role model. For years they would dissipate their emotional and physical energies in trying to get into the mould of their 'guru'. And in order to provide extra vigour to their imitation, they would sometimes fall in love either with a Paro (as Devdas did) in their neighbourhood or with a school or a college classmate. They would also often seek to be reprimanded by their elders for this kind of indulgence so that they could get into the melancholic mood so often depicted by their idol on screen.

Let us try and analyse the reasons for such imitating tendencies. Two reasons are easily discernible. The first is that imitating the role model provides a highly self-satisfying sense of identity to the imitator and even helps form his personality, which could find appreciation in his peer group. The second reason seems to be that in the absence of adequate channels for expressing one's creative urges, a larger-than-life film personality prompts a young aspirant to see himself as 'the artiste' who can now participate vicariously in a perceived reality that is far more impressive and satisfying than the actual one.

In the case of Dilip Kumar, the prospective imitators were probably motivated by a self-conceived notion of a physical resemblance with the master and the apparent ease in imbibing his acting style. The patented style of the master had one unique characteristic: it seemed easy to copy. Such copying consists of reproducing faithfully Dilip Kumar's typical facial expressions and mannerisms and the stylized modulations in dialogue delivery. After years of regular practice, the imitators would feel they had come very close to the original and thus would be tempted to take this easy route in working out their possible film personality rather than developing their own individual styles. And yet, in the case of the impersonators, something always seemed amiss, as the master's nuances were not all that easily comprehensible even to his most dedicated followers. Only a few were able to refine the imitated style on the basis of their own talent.

The slew of aspirants over the last few decades, who were obsessed with their idea of becoming Dilip Kumar, met with different fates. Some reached Bombay to try their fortunes, but soon faded into oblivion. Many others had to be content with participating in college plays and joining local drama groups. For them, Dilip Kumar's cinema performed one important function: it provided them an in-depth exposure to film appreciation. They constituted a huge section of the film audience who flocked to see his movies.

Some disciples of the guru did make their mark in the film world and became successful in their own right, thanks to holding close affiliations with the Dilip Kumar school of acting throughout their career.

Products of the Dilip Kumar School of Acting

In the classical phase of Hindi cinema, Nasir Khan, the younger brother of Dilip Kumar, proved to be his true heir. He was a star in his own right and, in fact, arrived in the film world on his own. He made his debut with Nitin Bose's *Mazdoor* in 1945 made under Filmistan's banner, followed by P. L. Santoshi's *Shehnai* (1946) under the same banner. He worked with many top directors in the late 1940s and 1950s, appearing opposite nearly all the top heroines of this period: Ravindra Dave's *Nagina* (1951) and R. D. Mathur's *Aagosh* (1953) with Nutan; I. S. Johar's *Shrimatiji* (1952) with Shyama; Kamal Amrohi's *Daera* (1953) with Meena Kumari; *Angarey* (1954) with Nargis; M. I. Dharamsey's *Inaam* (1955) with Suraiya; and Shahid Lateef's *Society* (1955) with Nimmi. Nasir Khan was also the hero of Pakistan's first film *Teri Yaad*, directed by Daud Chand and released in 1948 in Lahore.

Nasir Khan, like his brother, had a sensitive face, and the ability to display a range of emotions was his main asset. But his ambit of portrayals was rather limited, excelling largely in serious roles depicted with a good sense of underplay. For instance, in Kamal Amrohi's masterpiece, *Daera*, his performance as the silent sufferer in a one-way ungratified love with the heroine (with whom he could not even exchange a word) won him critical acclaim. However, none of his other

Nasir Khan:
In his brother's
image

films could really promote him as a real superstar and the actor faded into oblivion till he was 'rediscovered' by Dilip Kumar, who cast him in the role of Jumna in *Ganga Jumna* (1961). In this movie, torn between his duty as a police officer as required by the state and the love and gratitude he has for his brother (Dilip Kumar), he exhibited some of the best moments of underplay and a kind of refinement seen in his brother's enactments.

***

One actor who made it really big by becoming an ardent disciple of Dilip Kumar during the classical and post-classical period was Rajendra Kumar (1929–99). He made his fortune merely by filling the space left by the thespian, who refused to do run-of-the-mill scripts. He was, as he admitted once, heavily influenced by the Dilip Kumar school of acting.

Rajendra Kumar also known as 'Jubilee Kumar'

Rajendra Kumar made his debut in Kidar Sharma's *Jogan* (1950), as Dilip Kumar's friend. Five years later he appeared in a character role as the heroine Geeta Bali's brother in Devendra Goel's *Vachan* (1955). He also did a role in V. Shantaram's *Toofan Aur Diya* (1956). Apparently, Mehboob Khan recognized the striking resemblance of his style and mannerisms with those of Dilip Kumar and cast him in *Awaaz* (1956, directed by Zia Sarhadi) and later in *Mother India* (1957). But the three films that took Rajendra Kumar to the top rungs of stardom were *Talaaq* (1958, with Kamini Kadam), *Chirag Kahan Roshni Kahan* (1959, with Meena Kumari) and *Dhool Ka Phool* (1959, with Mala Sinha and Nanda).

In his early films, despite the fact that Rajendra Kumar was used as a relief amidst the histrionics of the other lead actors, he left an indelible imprint: for example, vis-à-vis Sunil Dutt contesting familial authority along with feudal oppression in

Mother India; as the doctor who treats the cancer-affected husband (Raaj Kumar) of his former lover Meena Kumari in Sridhar's *Dil Ek Mandir* (1963); and the other lover in Raj Kapoor's love triangle *Sangam* (1964). However, it was Rajendra Kumar's cinema in its second highly glamorous Eastman colour phase that became the forerunner of the musical romances of the 1960s and early 1970s, such as *Mere Mehboob* (1963), *Arzoo* (1965) and *Jhuk Gaya Aasmaan* (1968).

Rajendra Kumar's screen persona had the trappings of the old-time classical soft heroes Prem Adib, Surendra and those of his contemporaries, Bharat Bhushan, Pradeep Kumar and Biswajit. He played second fiddle to Dilip Kumar as Surendra did to K. L. Saigal. In serious roles, his soft and subdued style contrasted with the intense histrionics of his leading ladies Meena Kumari, Mala Sinha and Vyjayanthimala. He created the image of the suffering lover in a modern setting but invariably failed to capture the intensity of the master. With his good looks, innate simplicity, a sense of decency and devoid of excessive histrionics, he represented the prototype of new 'simplified' film hero free from the agony of a painful past. He offered to Indian youth a new role model – educated, lovable, not vindictive, a pride of his parents and adored by his beloved and keen to get settled in life in a good profession. Like Manoj Kumar, and Rajesh Khanna later, he developed his screen image on excessive stylization.

***

Among the disciples of Dilip Kumar, Manoj Kumar (born on 24 July 1937) perhaps was the most faithful. A die-hard fan of the master since his college days in Delhi, Manoj Kumar entered the film world apparently through his strong family connections with the Congress Party and with the help of a distant uncle Mulkraj Bhakri. As soon as he reached Bombay in the mid-1950s, his first objective was to see Dilip Kumar in person. Bhakri took him to the shooting of *Yahudi*. With a pounding heart, Manoj saw Dilip Kumar perform in a long shot. He became extremely nervous and wanted to slip away – he didn't want Dilip Kumar to see him! The experience was more terrifying than fulfilling!

Manoj Kumar made his debut with *Fashion* (1957), followed by a series of inconsequential films like *Reshmi Rumal* (1961), *Banarasi Thug* (1962) and *Dr Vidhya* (1962). He got his first major break with Vijay Bhatt's *Hariyali Aur Raasta* (1962). On joining films, he gave up his real name, Harikrishan Goswami, and as a tribute to his master, he took the screen name after Dilip Kumar's name (Manoj Kumar) in *Shabnam* (1949).

Manoj Kumar might have remained one among the many good-looking actors without a distinct image of his own. But he was much more than an actor – he was multifaceted. Another *Shaheed* (released in 1965), the biographical film on the intrepid freedom fighter Bhagat Singh, dramatically changed the course of his career. The success of this film not only helped Manoj Kumar to discover his screen persona, but also inspired him to work for a new film genre. He became producer-director-writer and began an ambitious experiment on building nationalistic iconography within the framework of a formula film.

With *Upkar* (1967), Manoj Kumar launched himself as the idealist Indian hero, naming himself Bharat, and projecting himself as the ultimate icon of nationalism.[1] With the amazing success of his maiden venture, he soon produced, or acted in, a series of stridently nationalistic melodramas (*Yaadgaar* 1969, *Purab Aur Paschim* 1970, *Roti Kapda Aur Makaan* 1974 and *Kranti* 1981). In *Purab Aur Paschim*, he sought to emphasize the superiority of Indian culture over 'Western decadence', but he ensured that the film was suffused with glamour and sensuality – a box-office success strategy he perhaps learnt from 'the great showman' Raj Kapoor.

For most of his films, Manoj Kumar derived much of the inspiration from the contemporary political developments in the country. *Upkar* was the celebration on celluloid of peasant–soldier solidarity, embodied by Prime Minister Lal Bahadur Shastri's famous slogan *Jai Jawan Jai Kisan* in the wake of the Indo–Pakistan war of 1965.

The basis for *Purab Aur Paschim* can be attributed to the growing popularity of Prime Minister Indira Gandhi and her completely anti-West stance reflected in the foreign policy of the country. He also highlighted the negative impact of the dominance of the West on the economic, cultural and spiritual well-being of a developing society.

In *Roti Kapda Aur Makaan*, Manoj Kumar, evidently stimulated by Indira Gandhi's clarion call – '*Garibi Hatao*' (remove poverty) – brought to light on screen the anti-national activities of the trading class, black-marketeers and hoarders. Initially, in the film, he believes in lofty ideals and high principles, but is soon forced into a life of crime in order to provide the essential items for the survival of his family. In some ways, Manoj Kumar prepared the ideological ground for the anti-hero model of Amitabh Bachchan, which was to sweep Indian cinema in the 1970s and 1980s. (Bachchan appears as Manoj Kumar's brother in *Roti Kapda Aur Makaan*.)

On the basis of the stereotyped, hyperpatriotic protagonist, Manoj Kumar made a serious attempt towards proclaiming the status of the second-generation indigenous film hero, his model being Dilip Kumar's image. He modified the image to fit into the socio-political context of the 1970s. (This decade was marked by war, a huge influx of refugees, shortage of essential commodities, soaring prices, political turmoil and the 'quota raj'.) In spite of his dedicated efforts to incorporate the elements of the master's style in his acting, Manoj Kumar could not quite match the original. In the two films in which Dilip Kumar and Manoj Kumar worked together, *Aadmi* (1968) and *Kranti*, a self-conscious 'student' faced his 'teacher'. In these two movies, one could discern the master looking at his most-dedicated pupil with slight indifference. In fact, the shadow of the master eclipsed the screen persona of Manoj Kumar, so much so that the junior really could never discover his own acting potential independently.

***

Kadar Khan:
Character actor and
dialogue writer
par excellence

Kadar Khan is perhaps the only *character artiste* to have strong affiliations with Dilip Kumar's school of acting. He was born on 6 October 1925 at Pishin, now in the Balochistan province of Pakistan. He belonged to the Kakar tribe. He started in the 1970s as scenarist and dialogue writer, but soon started appearing in character roles. He played a small but memorable role in the Dilip Kumar starrer *Sagina* (1974) as the communist leader. Like his versatile contemporaries Amrish Puri (who, unfortunately passed away on 12 January 2005) and Anupam Kher, Kadar Khan has remained one of the most durable actors since the 1980s, specializing in a variety of roles including those of villain as well as comedian, making a comic pair with Govinda. In his style, Kadar Khan is a method actor, who would modulate his expressions and voice as per the requirements of the enactment on hand but according to a preconceived pattern. Some of his important films are: *Anari* (1975), *Adalat* (1975), *Mr Natwarlal* (1979), *Suhaag* (1979), *Raaz* (1981), *Inquilaab* (1984), *Kanoon Meri Mutthi Mein* (1984), *Dilwala* (1986), *Insaniyat Ke Dushman* (1987), *Ghar Ho To Aisa* (1990), *Karz Chukana Hai* (1991), *Sangdil Sanam* (1994), *Saajan Chale Sasural* (1996), *Judaai* (1997), *Rajaji* (1999), *Mujhse Shadi Karogi* (2004) and *Family Ties of Blood* (2005). He co-starred with Dilip Kumar in *Dharm Adhikari* (1986) and *Kanoon Apna Apna* (1989). For Amitabh Bachchan, he wrote dialogues in *Mr Natwarlal* (1979), *Lawaris* (1981) and *Naseeb* (1981). He also starred and introduced the TV show, *Hasnaa Mat*.

***

Acclaimed as the most talented disciple of Dilip Kumar after Manoj Kumar, Mukesh Khanna came into prominence with his role as Bheeshma Pitamah in the television serial *Mahabharat* in the late 1980s. With his overpowering presence and remarkable proficiency in underplay as well as in melodrama, he represented

Mukesh Khanna:
In the thespian's
mould

a possible new icon in cinematic acting. But the young actor soon got 'typed', mostly appearing in senior roles. He was cast as Dilip Kumar's son in *Saudagar* (1991). His other important film was *Tehelka* (1992), in which he appeared along with veterans Dharmendra and Naseeruddin Shah.

***

Shahrukh Khan represents the third-generation artiste who has evolved under the long shadow of Dilip Kumar. Formally announcing the immense influence of the master and also of Amitabh Bachchan on him, he arrived on the film scene in the early 1990s with a bang. He attempted to maintain renewed continuity with his two formidable seniors. He also took up the title role in Sanjay Leela Bhansali's *Devdas* (2002), apparently to re-create and relive the intense aura of the legend, as a kind of tribute to Dilip Kumar and thus the classical era. His screen persona and portrayals are discussed in Volume 2.

Disciples in Pakistan Cinema

On Pakistani cinema, Dilip Kumar's influence was profound. His prominent disciples include Nadeem (born Mirza Nazir Beg), Darpan, Habib, Yousuf Khan, Mohammed Ali and the famous comedian, Rangeela. Among them, Nadeem, considered to be the 'Amitabh Bachchan of Pakistani cinema', has emerged as the most successful disciple of the thespian. In a career span of more than three decades, Nadeem has acted in about 140 films, appearing in a variety of roles. The celebrated actor in a television interview, while recognizing the impact of the thespian on his style, declared: 'Dilip Saheb is an ocean of art; even possessing a drop out of that would be a big achievement for anyone.'

The Rise and the Fall of 'The Phenomenon'

If Dilip Kumar represented a transition from the pre-classical to the classical period, the arrival of Rajesh Khanna (who later came to be known as 'The Phenomenon') in the 1966 film *Raaz* marked the shift of Hindi cinema from its classical to the post-classical period.

Rajesh Khanna (born as Jatin Khanna on 29 December 1942), who entered films through his selection in the *Filmfare* talent

Rajesh Khana:
'The Phenomenon'

search contest, was by no means a student of the Dilip Kumar school of acting. Instead, he established his highly successful film persona by blending the diverse styles of the three top actors of the classical period – Dilip Kumar, Raj Kapoor and Dev Anand. He 'borrowed' certain elements from the flamboyant and romantic style of Dev Anand (as in *Do Raaste*, 1969 and *Aradhana*, 1969), the jovial bantering of Raj Kapoor (*Anand*, 1971 and *Bawarchi*, 1972) and the tragic histrionics of Dilip Kumar (*Safar*, 1970 and *Amar Prem*, 1972) as well as his liberated image in *Leader* (*Namak Haram*, 1973).

Rajesh Khanna's persona represented the synthesis of the main trends of Hindi cinema of the classical period. For instance, in *Anand* (the role first was offered to Raj Kapoor, who somehow could not do that film), ace director Hrishikesh Mukherjee presented Rajesh Khanna as the ailing hero, who suffers internally like the Dilip Kumar protagonist, but is jovial like Raj Kapoor's joker. Moreover, this new-age sufferer does not belong to the typical feudal milieu, but is a middle-class, city-bred commoner having a good support system to help him through his suffering. This character indicated the metamorphosis of the eternal sufferer who emerges as an individual who refuses to be overwhelmed by his suffering and instead faces the terminal illness (cancer) through positively interacting with the world around him.

With *Aradhana*, Rajesh Khanna launched the string of 1970s' romances. His impact as the eternal romantic was really astounding. The new actor was soon labelled 'The Phenomenon' and the first real superstar of Indian cinema. He not only displaced the seemingly unshakeable senior stars, but also put his contemporaries in the shade. He simply debunked all the old theories and introduced a new dynamism and glamour in the Indian hero's persona. He was the first-ever example of an actor marketing his image through well-designed and powerful media campaigns.

The romantic, flamboyant, suave and urbane image of Rajesh Khanna was also implicitly related to Dilip Kumar's persona in *Leader*. As discussed earlier, this film perhaps, for the first time, released the tragic Indian film hero from his traditional image, making it truly modern, upbeat and romantic. Dev Anand and Shammi Kapoor also projected this image, but it was representative of their respective trademark styles rather than the main trend.

In serious roles in films such as *Amar Prem, Safar* and *Khamoshi* (1969), Rajesh Khanna added to his deliberate stylization, distinct from Dilip Kumar's method of depiction of suffering and inner turmoil. Although he provided a continuity of the sorrowful image of the indigenous film hero in the post-classical period, giving him a new lease of life, the earlier aura of intensity was missing.

Rajesh Khanna's impact on cinema was far more than a reinvention of romance and a revision of its music syllabi. He initiated a complete transformation of the Indian film hero's persona, representing a big change from its old classical form to a new image as the hero of the middle class. He became the screen equivalent of the typical hero of a large variety of 'pulp fiction', which was being obsessively read by the middle classes. However, by the mid-1970s, his overstylization and somewhat unnatural mannerisms began undermining the image of an otherwise sensitive, delightfully subtle and highly watchable actor. He was soon overtaken by another superstar in the making, Amitabh Bachchan. The time had come for cinema to make a dramatic shift in its moorings, and the patrons, this time were the burgeoning working-class audience.

This shift was spearheaded by none other than the best student among the many disciples of Dilip Kumar: Amitabh Bachchan, who was soon to provide a highly creative and durable continuity to the senior actor's indigenous film hero. The second volume discusses the making of this hero, and analyses his films and portrayals in their specific social context.

Notes and References

1. In sharp contrast to the neo-realist film makers from the Indian People's Theatre Association (IPTA) in the classical period, Manoj Kumar interpreted nationalism in the context of strong anti-Western sentiments, glorifying India's past and occasionally touching upon the basic social contradictions within the society.

Chapter 10

Heroes' Gallery:
Dilip Kumar's Contemporaries

During the classical era, the dominant hero of Dilip Kumar shared the vast cinematic space with a large assembly of illustrious contemporaries. Many of them (some of whom we have met in the earlier chapters), with their charismatic presence and distinguished cinematic style, in their own way, infused life into a diversity of roles rooted in the socio-political and cultural milieu of their times.

A Director-Actor and a Thinker-Actor

V. Shantaram, one of the key founders of indigenous cinema, was also a highly spirited actor, though not in the conventional mould. As hero, he made his own acting statement that was fused with his thematic vision as director. Devoid of any melodramatic streaks and uncalled-for mannerisms, he infused into his portrayals a natural and down-to-earth simplicity, a style later displayed by two multifaceted individuals: Balraj Sahni (from the mid-1940s to the early 1970s) and Girish Karnad (from the mid-1970s onwards). Although Shantaram appeared as a hero in two silent films, namely, *Savkari Pash* (1925, which was about a poor peasant's plight as a mill worker after his land is usurped by a moneylender, à la *Dharti Ke Lal*) and *Udyakal* (1930) in the role of Chatrapati Shivaji, he developed his unique screen persona much later in his career through only four films: *Dr Kotnis Ki Amar Kahani*

(1946), *Parchhain* (1952), *Do Aankhen Barah Haath* (1957) and *Stree* (1961).

In *Dr Kotnis Ki Amar Kahani*, Shantaram virtually reincarnated the legendary Dr Dwarkanath Kotnis (even resembling him in looks), the Indian doctor who lost his life in China in 1942 while serving as a member of the medical mission sent by the Indian National Congress. The mission served the Eighth Route Army of Mao Zedong that was fighting the Japanese imperialist forces in China. Shantaram captured, with his typical resilience, the heroic dedication and suffering of this highly committed doctor as he struggled against tremendous odds to provide medical relief to the wounded. The hero, in his highly moving dying speech, describes how much love and warmth his Chinese wife would receive when she, in place of him, goes to join his family in India. In the realms of cinema and international relations in the post-Second World War period, this classic indeed became an important document.

Parchhain, a curious love tale, presented the interpretation of soulful love in an entirely different framework. In its entirety, this love sought by a seeker is an illusion, merely an image which always defies manifestation in the real world. The seeker is a blind singer who falls in love with his landlord's daughter (played by Jayashri) and as their relationship develops through sharing of music, he mentally conceives an image of hers but is never able to feel its manifestation as a human figure. When he recovers his eyesight, he comes to know that his beloved is no more in this world. In this movie, composer C. Ramchandra came up with some mellifluous melodies.

In *Do Aankhen Barah Haath*, one of the most remarkable pacifist works in Indian or world cinema hailing the Gandhian principles of non-violence and tolerance, Shantaram, as the visionary hero, transforms his spirited idealism into exemplary social activism. He is a far-sighted jailer who believes that instead of dumping criminals in the solitude of prisons, they should be enlightened to recover the basic human virtues of love and kindness, which lie buried in their hardened hearts. To validate this thesis in the eyes of the state, he embarks upon a difficult reform mission. He takes six hardened criminals, facing the death sentence, to a remote area, and through a long-drawn-out process of setting up an economically viable farming collective, he finally transforms them into virtuous men. The reformist hero dies the death of a martyr as he tries to stop the herd of cattle sent by the local trouble makers to destroy the standing crop that has been painstakingly cultivated by the hero and his 'brethren'. During the shooting of this difficult sequence, Shantaram suffered a serious eye injury, forcing him to delay his next film project (*Navrang*) by a couple of years. The song *Ay Malik Tere Bande Hum ...*' (from *Do Aankhen Barah Haath*) stands out as one of the most memorable bhajans ever in the annals of Indian cinema.

Stree, Shantaram's last film as hero, was a rework in colour of his superhit *Shakuntala* (1943; based on the legendary ancient Sanskrit poet Kalidasa's classic play *Abhiyan Shakuntam*), but failed to re-create the magic of the original. The director-actor appeared in the role of King Dushyant, while in the original, veteran Chandramohan portrayed this role much more convincingly.

***

Balraj Sahni (real name Yudhishthir Sahni), one of the most respected pioneers of the realist acting style in post-independence cinema, was perhaps the only intellectual-turned-actor of his times. Born on 1 May 1913 in Rawalpindi (now in Pakistan), he did his postgraduation in English literature from the famous Government College of Lahore. As a socially conscious youth, deeply troubled as he was by the turmoil and uprooting of millions during pre- and post-Partition

Balraj Sahni: One of Bollywood's most respected actors

India, he (as the actor revealed in his famous biography) underwent an acute existential crisis, forcing him to find for himself a socially productive role. This troubled conscience, in fact, was to later determine the content and ideological stance of his oeuvre, whether in literature, drama or films. Young Balraj started off by writing poetry in English. He then joined Rabindranath Tagore's Shantiniketan as a Hindi teacher for a brief stint. He next switched over to journalism and worked for a short period as a radio announcer for the BBC's Hindi service. Still unsettled, he started a magazine (called *Monday Morning*) in Delhi. In the mid-1940s, he reached Bombay and joined the Indian People's Theatre Association (IPTA), directing and acting in plays such as *Zubeida* and *The Inspector General*. Sahni, as many of his friends at IPTA (see Chapter 5 for more details) did, finally reached his destination, the film world, making his debut in Phani Majumdar's *Insaaf* (released in 1946).

Sahni, soon after his debut, became the foremost indigenous hero figure in the emerging *neo-realist cinema* being pursued earnestly by K. A. Abbas, Bimal Roy, Shambu Mitra, Chetan Anand, Zia Sarhadi, Hemen Gupta and Rajender Singh Bedi among others. The immediate outcome of this endeavour was Sahni's highly applauded trilogy of this period: Abbas's *Dharti Ke Lal* (1946), Zia Sarhadi's *Hum Log* (1951) and Bimal Roy's *Do Bigha Zameen* (1953). Sahni's true-to-life characterizations in these films reflected his own post-Partition trauma of being uprooted and the suffering and the ensuing agonies that this catastrophe caused.

Dharti Ke Lal, based on the well-known Bengali writer Bijon Bhattacharya's play *Nibanna* (1944), was set in the background of the 1943 Bengal famine, in which, according to some estimates, more than three million people perished. Film historians Ashish Rajdhyaksha and Paul Willemen hold the view that *Dharti Ke Lal* set the pattern for several films that depicted the moving of the destitute to escape deprivation in the village only to end up suffering in the city. The pathos-filled narrative presented Sahni in the role of Ramu, the restless and rebellious son of a poor farmer, who brings the hope of a better life in the city to fellow peasants reeling under abject poverty. After his debt-ridden father and other poor peasants lose their land to the wicked zamindar of the village, Ramu prompts his family along with thousands of similarly dispossessed families to move to Calcutta to escape the clutches of feudal oppression. But an indifferent and callous city makes life for these immigrants far more miserable. Ramu is unable to get any work and his wife is forced to become a prostitute to ensure survival of their family. In the end, the oppressed peasants refuse to be part of the alien city, make a return to their native roots and decide to enter into collective farming. This commune, however, refuses to take Ramu along in its venture for a new life, indicating perhaps a lack of sympathy for the fellow wrong-doers among the radical people's movements who have inadvertently misled them by raising their expectations to a high level and then delivering nothing.

In *Do Bigha Zameen*, set in a framework similar to *Dharti Ke Lal*, the protagonist once again stood at the exploitative rural–urban divide, eventually getting marginalized on both sides. Shambhu (played by Balraj Sahni), a poor, debt-ridden farmer, along with his wife and son, is forced to join the hordes of urban poor in Calcutta. By a certain date, he has to pay to the court a certain amount of money (enormous by his standards) in order to retrieve his land from a merciless moneylender. He takes up rickshaw pulling in order to accumulate the requisite amount. His son also chips in as a shoeshine boy. Shambu is seriously injured one day when he is goaded by the occupant of his rickshaw (a natty suitor pursuing his lady love) to catch up with another rickshaw puller. He runs so fast that he loses control of his rickshaw. Despite all their efforts and their immense sacrifices, they are not able to meet the deadline. Extremely disillusioned with the insensitive and harsh city life, he and his family return to their village only to find a factory being built on what was once their land. For the present times, this ending indeed echoed the fate of the peasants of Singur and Nandigram in West Bengal whose lands (in the form of special economic zones or SEZs) have recently been forcefully acquired by the state government for the construction of industrial units. Sahni's authentic portrayal of the archetype of Calcutta's ubiquitous rickshaw puller won him critical acclaim in the country as well as abroad. He had to haul the rickshaw himself, along with the passengers, through the lanes and bylanes of Calcutta; this was an era when computer animation was unknown.

Zia Sarhadi's *Hum Log* was a tragic tale about the miserable lives led by the marginalized class of people in the cities and how they are subjected to the cruel realities of urban existence. Sahni, the eldest son of a low-salaried bank employee, in desperation, steals money from his father's bank to pay for his sister's treatment (she is suffering from TB) and for his younger brother's education. After his father is sent to jail at the behest of his employer, the hero has to slog virtually ceaselessly to run the family. He is overworked and exhausted. He eventually falls dead in a courtroom where he is being tried for a murder that he did not commit.

In his second trilogy – *Seema* (1955), *Kathputli* (1957) and *Anuradha* (1960) – Sahni very ably captured the struggle of a professional striving to uphold his ideals despite intense emotional stress and other external pressures.

Amiya Chakravarty's *Seema* presented him as a committed social activist who runs a reform home for the destitute, where the distraught heroine (Nutan), an orphan, takes refuge. She is deeply perturbed as she has been wrongly accused of theft. She is prone to throwing tantrums and flinging objects around. Sahni manages to pacify her in a seemingly effortless manner and helps in apprehending the real culprit and brings about a seachange in her otherwise dormant life. In *Kathputli*, also started by Amiya Chakravarty (and later completed by Nitin Bose after Chakravarty passed away), Sahni appeared as a highly spirited stage director, seeking to express his creativity through the talent of a poor but ungroomed dancer (Vyjayanthimala). In Hrishikesh Mukherjee's masterpiece, *Anuradha*, Sahni excelled as a dedicated medical doctor. As stated in Chapter 5, *Anuradha* juxtaposed a husband's (Balraj Sahni) total devotion to philanthropic medicine with his wife's (Leela Naidu) complete dedication to the purity of music; an unusual theme in Hindi cinema. The wife gives up her music for her husband, but he is too preoccupied with his own problems to even notice her sacrifice. Sahni very vividly brought out the dilemma relating to the social responsibility of modern medicine vis-à-vis a doctor's domestic life.The sitar maestro Ravi Shankar composed the captivating music for this film, with most of the songs being based on ragas.

Apart from the foregoing films, Sahni's hero continued to cast his spell through a string of memorable works during this period.

In *Hulchal* (1951, produced by K. Asif and directed by S. K. Ojha), a tragic love triangle, the actor gave a memorable performance as the sympathetic jailer, who develops a rapport with the hero-prisoner (played by Dilip Kumar) and the former lover of his wife (played by Nargis). Paradoxically, Sahni used to come to the shooting of the film as a political detenu escorted by armed sentries. He and many other IPTA activists had been jailed as part of the Indian Government's efforts to contain the fallout of the Leftist uprising in Telangana (then a part of Hyderabad state).

In Rajender Singh Bedi's classic *Garam Coat* (1955), an adaption of Nikolai Gogol's famous story 'The Overcoat', Sahni, with a remarkable realism, depicted the existential anxieties of a common man in the face of growing economic hardships in post-independence India. He plays a low-paid clerk in a post office, who cannot afford to buy for himself a new woollen coat for winters. One day he loses a hundred-rupee note, resulting in acute hardship for his family. In his desperation, he starts visualizing his wife (Nirupa Roy) doing odd jobs to earn extra money; he even imagines that she has become a prostitute. In a fit of depression he decides to throw himself under a train, but discovers the lost note in the lining of his old coat.

Lal Batti (1957), Sahni's own directorial venture, set at the time of India's independence, depicted the traumatic experience of passengers when their train is stopped and they are forced to spend the night on a lonely railway platform. In *Kabuliwala* (1961, based on a short story by Rabindranath Tagore and directed by Hemen Gupta), Sahni gave a memorable performance as a simple-hearted Pathan (who had come to Calcutta to earn a livelihood by selling dry fruits so that he could pay his debts back home). He sees in a talkative little girl named Mini the image of his own daughter whom he has left behind in his native village in Afghanistan. Time rolls by. Only on the day of Mini's wedding does he realize that his daughter too must have become a young woman by now! In Shahid Lateef's *Sone Ki Chidiya* released in 1958, he played a radical poet and a defender of the rights of film extras. He saves the heroine, Nutan (who plays a famous actress in the movie) when she tries to commit suicide on coming to know that the man she loves (played by singer-actor Talat Mehmood) is after her wealth. Composer O. P. Nayyar's music in this film was almost divine.

Along with his remarkable contribution to the neo-realist cinema, Sahni appeared in innumerable sentimental family melodramas as the keeper of family values, often appearing as the magnanimous and sacrificing elder brother. Such portrayals were seen in *Bhabhi* (1957), *Devar Bhabhi* (1958), *Ghar Sansar* (1958), *Chhoti Behen* (1959), *Bhabhi Ki Chooriyan* (1961) and *Anpadh* (1962).

During the course of his career, Sahni occasionally departed from his usual track to employ his histrionics to portray a diverse range of roles. Hemen Gupta's *Taksal* (1956), following the pattern set by Zia Sarhadi's *Footpath*, moulded the prototype for the highly successful Amitabh Bachchan's angry cinema in the 1970s and beyond. *Taksal* brought on screen a wronged, vengeful man's acquiring wealth and power through criminal means. Sahni, an unsuccessful lawyer, is beset by disasters because of lack of money. After his son dies and his unmarried sister commits suicide (because she is raped

Jayashri and V. Shantaram in *Dr Kotnis Ki Amar Kahani* (1946).

Balraj Sahni (squatting) and Murad in *Do Bigha Zameen* (1953).

Guru Dutt in *Pyaasa* (1957).

Bharat Bhushan and Suraiya in *Mirza Ghalib* (1954).

Nanda, Rajendra Kumar and Mala Sinha in *Dhool Ka Phool* (1959).

Shashi Kapoor, Sunil Dutt, Achala Sachdev, Balraj Sahni
and Raaj Kumar in *Waqt* (1965).

Jaya Bhaduri and Sanjeev Kumar in *Koshish* (1972).

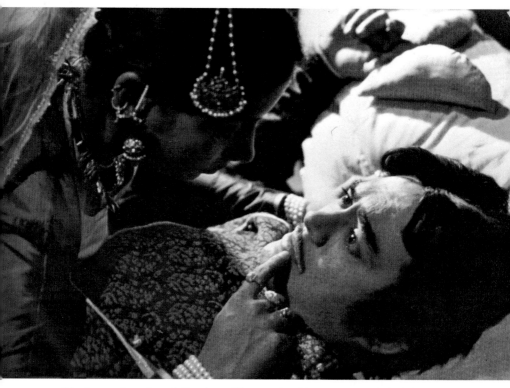

Shabana Azmi and Sanjeev Kumar in *Shatranj Ke Khiladi* (1977).

by her employer and can't bear the stigma), he proceeds to acquire riches through crime.

In *Dil Bhi Tera Hum Bhi Tere* (1960), Sahni played a warm-hearted, droll, street-smart toughie with a natural flair.

In *Punar Milan* (1964), a scathing attack on casteism, Sahni poignantly delineated the suffering of a doctor, who is born as an untouchable but raised by a Brahmin family. (During childhood he had left his village to escape the atrocities of the high-caste people there.) But just before his marriage to a Brahmin girl (Shashikala), his real identity is revealed and both his family (the one that has adopted him) and the high-caste community refuse to accept him. Only when, in an emergency, he saves the life of his fiancée's father, do the people around him realize the utter irrelevance of the casteist mindset and the beauty of judging others by their noble deeds.

Heera Moti (1959), a laudable film on man–animal relationships, was based on Munshi Premchand's famous short story 'Do Bailon Ki Katha'. In this film, Sahni, in the role of a poor farmer, very ably captured the way Indian peasants revere the pair of bullocks they keep for ploughing the land.

In *Suhag Sindoor* (1961), he brought out the agony and the subsequent simmering rage of an army officer who is deceived by someone he implicitly trusted.

In Kedar Kapoor's *Sapan Suhane* (1961), opposite Geeta Bali, he personified the typical hearty Punjabi truck driver (and his way of life) who has had to make sacrifices to reform his younger brother who has gone astray.

In *Haqeeqat* (1964), he epitomized the immense dignity and confidence of a major leading his men to defend the country's borders against the 1962 Chinese attack.

Apart from *Taksal*, Sahni also gave memorable performances as the anti-hero in *Baajuband* (1954), *Satta Bazaar* (1959), *Lajwanti* (1958), *Bindiya* (1960), *Pinjre Ke Panchhi* (1966) and *Sunghursh* (1968). In the first two films, he appeared as a compulsive gambler bent upon causing much suffering to his family. In both *Lajwanti* and

Bindiya (co-starring Nargis and Padmini, respectively), he displayed quite convincingly the sadistic streaks of a misled and suspicious husband. *Pinjre Ke Panchhi*, produced and directed by composer Salil Choudhury, enlisted Sahni in one of his best roles ever. The powerful narrative unravelled the transformation of two fugitives, a hardened Muslim criminal (Sahni) and his junior buddy (Mehmood), in the forced company of a pregnant woman (Meena Kumari). They are compelled to take refuge in the house rented by her husband who is undergoing medical treatment in another town. The two rediscover their true selves and their inner conscience as they serve the lady with utmost devotion. Eventually, the senior is shot dead by the police when the two are in the process of transporting the bed-ridden woman to the hospital. In *Sunghursh*, Sahni engaged the pacifist hero (none other than Dilip Kumar) in a long-drawn-out intrigue of hatred and vengeance (see Chapter 5 for details).

In senior roles, Sahni began to represent the archetype of elderly Good Samaritan whose presence is enlisted to boost the thematic thrust of the narrative. However, none of the films released in the mid to late 1960s and early 1970s – for instance, *Aman, Izzat, Duniya, Ek Phool Do Maali, Talash, Dharti, Do Raaste, Ghar Ghar Ki Kahani, Paraya Dhan, Hanste Zakhm* and *Amanat* – could offer him roles commensurate with his talent, the only exceptions being B. R. Chopra's *Waqt* (1965), Prabhat Mukharjee's *Shayar-e-Kashmir Mahjoor* (1972) and M. S. Sathyu's masterpiece *Garam Hawa* (1973).

In *Waqt* (the trendsetter for a slew of 'lost-and-found' movies), Sahni initially essayed the role of an affluent and overconfident merchant who wants to 'write' the destinies of his three sons. But *waqt* (time) has something else in store for him. An earthquake destroys his life and all his dreams. He is separated from his wife and children. Now a destitute, he begins searching for his wife and children. He is soon jailed for killing the man (played by the actor Jeevan) in charge of a remand home when he comes to know that Jeevan has ill-treated his son. He is eventually released from jail. By this time his sons (played by Raaj Kumar, Sunil Dutt and Shashi Kapoor) have grown up and are leading their own lives. Anyway, after a complex series of twists and turns, the family is reunited in the end.

The next film, produced by the Government of Jammu and Kashmir with Sahni in the lead role, was on the turbulent life of the radical Kashmiri poet Ghulam Ahmed Mahjoor (1885–1952). Mahjoor was declared the official national poet of Kashmir after his death.

In *Garam Hawa*, Sahni played, with a remarkable finesse, Salim Mirza, an aging, noble patriarch caught up in the undercurrents of post-Partition India. He is a successful footwear manufacturer in Agra who is beset by a series of misfortunes. He loses his ancestral property, which under new laws, is allocated to a Sindhi businessman; suffers serious losses in business due to the severe competition from a new class of migrant businessmen; and his daughter, seduced by her suitor, a scheming upstart, commits suicide. Mirza now decides to leave India and go over to Pakistan. En route to the railway station, he finds himself amidst a procession of dispossessed people (in which his son is also present) demanding their rights for a better life in what they consider their *watan* (homeland). Highly moved, Mirza abandons his plans to leave the country and joins the procession. Soon after finishing *Garam Hawa*, Sahni died on 13 April 1973, just short of his sixtieth birthday.

The Great Showman

Although Raj Kapoor in his early films donned the mantle of the tragedian, he soon discarded that image and moved on to become Hindi cinema's first full-fledged comic hero. His hero, in contrast with Dilip Kumar's hero's preoccupations with the agonized self, was a die-hard optimist, who prefered to foresee and await the arrival of an equitable and caring social order in a newly independent India. An irrepressible dreamer who wants to create an utopian world, his hero, instead of getting sucked into his own anguish, sets out, with honesty, innocence, resilience and missionary zeal as his weapons, to challenge the prevailing power structures (parental, feudal and societal). Celebrating the virtues of poverty (compassion, hard work and brotherhood), he cocks a snook at 'high society' and uses his films as the medium to expose the shenanigans and hypocrisies of the rich, thereby giving the hoi polloi a ground for empathizing with the theme of his films.

Raj Kapoor was born on 14 December 1924 in Peshawar (now in Pakistan). (Incidentally, Dilip Kumar too was born in the same place some two years earlier.) His full name was Ranbirraj Kapoor. After his family moved to Bombay, he started participating in the plays of Prithvi Theatres set up by his father Prithviraj Kapoor. As a child artiste, he appeared in *Inquilab* (1935). He next appeared in the 1946 movie *Balmiki* in a small role as Narad, who brings a change of heart in the powerful tribal chieftain Balmiki (played by his father) determined, in his vengeance, to annihilate his high-caste adversaries. The young actor made his debut as hero in Kidar Sharma's *Neel Kamal* (1947) in the role of an atheist sculptor, who strives to discover the social basis of his art and finds this when he falls in love with a young runaway princess (Madhubala), who has been adopted by a clan of untouchables. But later, the restless sculptor starts seeking his creative satisfaction in the love of the princess's sister, raised in the royal household. In the end, he discovers the soul of his art when a blue lotus (*neel kamal*) carved in stone emerges in the lake where the heart-broken princess has committed suicide. In a black-and-white film, the *neel kamal* appeared white.

Neel Kamal was followed by *Aag* (1948), the directorial debut film of Kapoor under his famous RK banner. An off-beat film presenting a discourse on creativity, aesthetics and social pressures faced by an artiste, it narrated the agonizing story of a drama enthusiast who is driven by a compulsive desire to become a theatre personality since his childhood. He keeps on dreaming about building his own theatre group, forcing his aristocrat father to disown him. He eventually succeeds but his face gets disfigured in a fire during the staging of a play. The heroine of his troupe (Nargis) becomes a star but she refuses to accept his love because of the ugly scar on his face. In the end, his newly wed wife (Nigar Sultana), after listening to his painful story, accepts him. In his second home production, *Barsaat* (1949), Raj Kapoor again appeared in a serious role, portraying very ably the agony of a city youth who falls in love with a poor Kashmiri *shikara* (a low-bottomed boat) girl (Nargis), juxtaposing in this off-beat narrative his classical interpretation of true love with the lustful attitude of his bosom pal (played by Premnath, his wife's brother in real life) towards women.

As observed in Chapter 5, after playing serious roles in his two in-house productions, Kapoor made a complete turnaround in his screen persona. In collaboration with K. A. Abbas, he evolved his own version of an Indian Charlie Chaplin. He thus replaced the brooding introvert in *Aag* and *Barsaat* by the Abbas-created image in *Awara* (1951), the first film of this genre, which marked a liberation for Raj Kapoor. The premise of *Awara* was that it is the social environment rather than heredity that determines the character and characteristics of a person. The hero Raju is a vagabond and a petty thief, nurtured by a criminal (K. N. Singh) who, as his revenge, had plotted against his (Raj Kapoor's) real father, a judge (Prithviraj Kapoor) to disown his pregnant mother (Leela Chitnis). Raj Kapoor makes his way into the world of the rich and mighty by wooing the daughter (Nargis) of an affluent lawyer. After a scuffle, he kills K. N. Singh. His sweetheart defends him in court, where the judge is none other than Prithviraj Kapoor. The magnificent musical score by Shankar Jaikishan was another highlight of the film. This film became very popular in the erstwhile Soviet Union after it was dubbed in Russian.

Raj Kapoor again switched tracks. *Aah* (1953) was a melancholic love triangle produced under the RK banner. Raj Kapoor lives with his well-to-do father in a small city. Upon his father's urging, he starts writing letters to a girl named Chandra (whom he proposes to marry) without actually seeing her or her photograph. She replies to his letters and the correspondence goes on. Chandra and Raj fall in love. Soon, a marriage proposal is put forth, but to Raj's consternation, Chandra rejects him. Subsequently, Raj finds out that the girl he had corresponded with was not Chandra (played by Vijayalaxmi), but her younger sister, Neelu (played by Nargis). After Raj's family physician, Dr Kailash (Pran), pronounces that that Raj is suffering from tuberculosis and will not live long, he tries to prove to Chandra that he loves her and tries to convince Neelu to marry Dr Kailash instead. *Aah* was studded with some melodious numbers composed by Shankar Jaikishan and sung soulfully by Lata Mangeshkar and Mukesh.

Shri 420 (1955) marked the apogee of Raj Kapoor's Chaplinesque vagabond. (The title relates to Section 420 of the Indian Penal Code, which deals with cheating and fraudulent activities.) This film, penned again by K. A. Abbas, depicted the adventures and escapades of a happy-go-lucky, educated country lad Raju, who travels to Bombay, the hub of opportunities, singing along the way, like a roaming bard, about his dreams and hopes. He initially stays amidst the residents of the footpaths of Bombay. He falls in love with an idealistic schoolteacher (played by Nargis). The narrative, packed with the comic antics of this jaunty hero, transports him to the filthy rich milieu of the metropolis through deceit and one-upmanship. He realizes that he has accumulated wealth through dubious means. A repentant Raju finally goes back to his people and his sweetheart. The stereotypical contrast shown between the corruption of the urban rich and the warm-hearted pavement dwellers soon became one of the most usable thematic elements for the film writers, a trend that is being followed even now. Once again, composers Shankar Jaikishan came up with a string of racy songs that became phenomenal hits, especially *Mera Joota Hai Japani* ...,

Pyaar Hua, Iqraar Hua Hai ..., *Mud Mud Ke Na Dekh ...* and *Ramiah Vastaviah ...*

In *Jagte Raho* (1956), directed by Sombhu Mitra and Amit Moitra, Kapoor's foray into the decadent city milieu was far more realistic. An innocent peasant, on a visit to a big city, wanders into the compound of a multistorey building in search of water to quench his thirst. Since it is nighttime, he is taken to be a thief. He seeks refuge in an apartment block, but is spotted and chased. He then keeps on going from one flat to another to dodge the crowd in his pursuit. In virtually every house he becomes a witness to the murky goings-on, including printing of counterfeit currency. In the end, he comes face to face with his tormenters on the roof and lashes out at the city folk for their utterly dishonest ways and inhuman attitude. As dawn breaks, he hears a moving melody and, in quest of the singer, he finds a woman (Nargis) in a compound nearby drawing water from a well, which she pours into his cupped hands from her pot. His thirst is finally quenched.

Apart from the aforementioned films, which were milestones, Kapoor also appeared in several memorable films made under different banners in the late 1940s and 1950s.

Mahesh Kaul's masterpiece, *Gopinath* (1948), presented Raj Kapoor as a glamour-struck youth desperately in pursuit of a film actress, but ignores Gopi (Tripti Mitra), the lower-caste girl adopted by his mother. The girl suffers as she secretly loves him. Eventually disillusioned, Gopi turns insane just when the hero, fed up with the star's whims and bizarre lifestyle, returns to her. The film is remembered for Tripti Mitra's remarkable performance, evoking the morbidity of a woman's suffering as brought out in the Bengali literary works of Saratchandra and other writers. In Satish Nigam's *Sunehre Din* (1949), the young actor appeared as a radio singer in love with a poor girl (Rehana) but who is also sought after by the daughter of a millionaire (Roop Komal).

Kidar Sharma's *Banwre Nain* (1950), a drama on celluloid denouncing discrimination in love on the basis of class and financial status, presented Kapoor as a city youth disowned by his family. He wanders into the countryside, where he falls in love with a haughty village belle (Geeta Bali), who drives a tonga. But soon he returns to the city and the girl, after waiting for a long time, goes to the city to find him. The timid hero is on the verge of marrying his scheming fiancée. The distraught heroine, upon hearing this news, joins the brass band in the marriage procession.

In Chandulal Shah's *Ambar* (1952), a comic costume drama, Kapoor appeared as the horse thief who tames the rajkumari (Nargis), the adopted daughter of the king (as was seen in Dilip Kumar's *Aan*). After the king's army commander usurps the throne, the hero kills the villain by mobilizing tribals disguised as dancers (à la S. S. Vasan's *Chandralekha*). The hero eventually turns out to be the lost son of the king.

Paapi (1953), also directed by Chandulal Shah and the only film in which Kapoor played a double role, he initially appears as a poor youth who does not believe in god and considers religiosity a curse. In a train accident, his lookalike, a highly revered swami, dies. The poor youth, while impersonating the swami, realizes the beauty of spiritual life and turns into a preacher.

In K. A Abbas's *Anhonee* (1952), starring Nargis in a remarkable double role, Raj Kapoor appeared as the lover who is contested by the heroine and her lost twin sister, a footloose and street-smart girl. *Chori Chori* (1956), a musical comedy based on Frank Capra's *It Happened One Night* (1934) and the last film Kapoor did with Nargis, presented him as an impoverished journalist, building a comic love relationship with a millionaire's runaway daughter. Other memorable films of the early 1950s in which Raj Kapoor displayed his upbeat romantic fervour included *Bhanwra* (1950: heroine Nimmi), *Dastaan* (1950: heroine Suraiya), *Jaan Pehchaan* (1950: heroine Nargis), *Pyar* (1950: heroine Nargis), *Sargam* (1950: heroine Rehana), *Bewaafa* (1952: heroine Nargis), *Ashiana* (1952: heroine Nargis) and *Dhun* (1953: heroine Nargis).

In the late 1950s and early 1960s, Raj Kapoor's hero exhibited a remarkable diversity in roles, thanks to films reinforced by powerful stories and competent direction, apart from great music. In *Sharda* (1957), the actor gave a memorable performance, first as the lover of a poor girl (Meena Kumari) and then as her stepson. In *Parvarish* (1958: heroine Mala Sinha), he is, in reality, the scion of an aristocratic family who is raised as a *sarangi* (a kind of bowed string instrument) player in a *kotha* (brothel). In *Main Nashe Mein Hoon* (1959), he plays an alcoholic reformed by his lady love (again Mala Sinha). *Do Ustad* (1959), one of the most successful and wholesome entertainment formulae worked out by Bollywood, presented Raj Kapoor as a free-wheeling, small-time comical pickpocket in intense competition with his separated elder brother (Sheikh Mukhtar) and a dreaded don, both of whom want to steal the jewellery of a millionaire's runaway daughter (Madhubala). The film was packed with foot-tapping numbers composed by O. P. Nayyar. It was Mohammed Rafi who sang for Raj Kapoor in this movie instead of Mukesh, his regular 'voice'.

Kanhaiya (1959, inspired perhaps by the 1950 Dilip Kumar–Nargis starrer *Jogan*), was about a village vagabond and inebriate (Raj Kapoor) who keeps on visualizing the Krishna-devotee heroine (Nutan) evoking her love for him in her songs and entices her to marry him. In *Chhalia* (1960), he appeared as a street-smart toughie, who makes a living by pickpocketing. He undergoes a transformation after he gives shelter to a distraught young bride (Nutan) who has been separated from her husband during the mayhem of Partition. *Nazrana* (1961) cast Raj Kapoor in a serious role. He plays a disappointed lover who has had to marry the sister (Usha Kiran) of the girl (Vyjayanthimala) he was in love with. When his wife suddenly dies, he rushes (along with his child) to meet his beloved, only to find her getting married to someone else. He presents his child as a marriage gift (*nazrana*) to the newly weds and walks away.

Through three highly emotive films of the late 1950s, Kapoor re-entered the sphere of neo-realist cinema: Ramesh Sehgal's *Phir Subah Hogi* (1958); K. A. Abbas's multistarrer *Char Dil Char Raahen* (1959); and Hrishikesh Mukherjee's *Anari* (1959).

In *Phir Subah Hogi*, based loosely on Fyodor Dostoevsky's classic *Crime and Punishment*, he portrayed a poor college student, who murders a vicious old moneylender who notices him (the hero) stealing money from his (the moneylender's) safe. The hero needs this amount to clear the debt incurred by his sweetheart's father, who had borrowed it from the villain. The police arrest the wrong man for the crime. Finally, one of the police detectives (who knows who the real murderer is) puts pressure on the hero to confess to his crime and save the innocent man from the gallows. He eventually does so and makes a moving plea on behalf of the dispossessed's rights to defend themselves against the real villains in society.

Char Dil Char Raahen presented the actor as an upper-caste Ahir youth who cannot marry his childhood sweetheart (Meena Kumari) because she is an untouchable. They finally meet (as other two separated lover-couples in the film) as construction workers, who have gone forth despite their oppressive past, to build together a road through a difficult terrain: metaphorically, a pathway to a better world.

In *Anari*, Kapoor once again (like in *Shri 420*) enters the world of the corrupt rich on a plank of compulsive honesty and truthfulness. He returns a lost wallet to an avaricious business magnate (Motilal), who is impressed with his rectitude and invites him home. There he meets his daughter, the heroine (Nutan). The naïve hero, unable to keep a job in the highly commercial environment of the metropolis driven by dishonesty and greed, finds shelter and love in the maternal, but quarrelsome, Mrs D'Sa, his landlady, played to perfection by Lalita Pawar. She, meanwhile, dies after taking spurious medicines made by a pharmaceutical company owned by his sweetheart's (Nutan) father. A distraught Raj Kapoor accuses him of killing ordinary people to amass wealth. The company owner gets him arrested for poisoning his landlady. In the end, the villain takes the responsibility for her death. Kapoor repeated this image of a truthful youth in *Shriman Satyavadi* (1960), but with far less appeal.

Aashiq (1962), a lacklustre affair despite being directed by Hrishikesh Mukherjee, presented Raj Kapoor as a singer who seeks fulfilment in the musical company of a tribal dancer (Padmini), causing much suffering to his wife (Nanda). The saving grace of the film was the appealing music by the duo of Shankar Jaikishan.

Kapoor returned to in-house productions after a gap of about five years with *Jis Desh Mein Ganga Behti Hai* (1960), directed by his cameraman Radhu Karmakar. As mentioned earlier, the film's theme was influenced by Jayprakash (JP) Narayan's famous crusade for eradicating the problem of dacoity in rural India. Raj Kapoor modelled the character of the protagonist simply on Jayprakash Narayan himself. A simple-hearted peace activist single-handedly disseminates his peace doctrine among the dacoit community settled in the ravines of Chambal valley and finally brings it back to the mainstream.

In *Sangam* (1964), his first colour venture, Kapoor played the role of a suspicious husband, as he had done earlier in Mehboob's *Andaz* (1949). *Sangam* carried definite lustful and erotic undertones. Sundar (Raj Kapoor), Gopal (Rajendra Kumar) and Radha (Vyjayanthimala) are childhood friends. As they enter adulthood, Radha and Gopal fall in love. Sundar too loves Radha, and when Gopal comes to know about this, he steps out of the way. But Sundar is rejected by Radha and her family as they feel he is an idler. To dispel such a view, Sundar joins the

Raj Kapoor (with an accordion in his hands) in a song sequence from *Sangam*

Indian Air Force as a pilot and undertakes a daredevil mission against the enemy. He is believed to have died while carrying out this mission. Now, Gopal and Radha begin their courtship. However, Sundar is not dead; he reappears and manages to marry Radha. But soon he starts doubting his wife. He suspects her of having an affair with another man, who he realizes, towards the end, is none other than Gopal. The climax shows his friend Gopal shooting himself.

As discussed in Chapter 5, while his earlier films of the 1950s highlighted socialist themes and rhetoric, Raj Kapoor, during the 1960s and beyond, adopted different means to maintain his image as 'the great showman'. He could not prolong his Chaplinesque image further and could not identify a new direction for his cinema in the changing socio-political milieu. He consequently translated his obsession with the female figure into cinema, but not always convincingly.

Raj Kapoor presented his autobiographical *Mera Naam Joker* (1970), a multistarrer mounted on a huge canvas, as a tribute to himself. Attempting to capture the grandeur of a Greek tragedy, and drawing inspiration from Charlie Chaplin's last personal statement film, *Limelight* (1952), about an ageing, washed-up clown, he projected the theme that suffering is one's own destiny, and even the woman one adores can remain elusive although she appears to be within grasp. The film could thus be seen as Raj Kapoor's response to Dilip Kumar's string of classical tragedies.

Kapoor's hero, in fact, had started losing his appeal by the mid-1960s. None of his films made under other banners – *Dil Hi To Hai* (1963: heroine Nutan), *Ek Dil Sau Afsane* (1963: heroine Waheeda Rehman), *Dulha Dulhan* (1964: heroine Sadhana), *Around the World* (1967: heroine Rajshree, Shantaram's daughter), *Diwana* (1968: heroine Saira Banu) and *Sapno Ka Saudgar* (1968: heroine Hema Malini, her first film) – could bring back his earlier magic. His last contribution to meaningful cinema was *Teesri Kasam* (1966), the dream project of lyricist Shailendra, and directed by Basu Bhattacharya, the son-in-law of the legendary Bimal Roy. In this memorable film, the actor virtually reincarnated on celluloid the Hindi writer Phaneshwarnath Renu's hero, Hiraman, of his short story *Mare Gaye Gulfam*. Raj Kapoor played a guileless bullock cart driver, who, in his naivety, seeks in vain the love of a dancer (Waheeda Rehman) who is part of a travelling *nautanki* (a kind of vaudeville show) troupe. *Teesri Kasam* exquisitely captured the essence of rural India, thanks to the splendid photography by Subrata Mitra and to the earthy musical score of none other than Shankar Jaikishan.

In senior roles too, he remained unimpressive as reflected in films like *Kal Aaj Aur Kal* (1971), *Do Jasus* (1975), *Khan Dost* (1976), *Gopichand Jasus* (1981), *Vakil Babu* (1982) and *Chor Mandili* (1982). Only in *Dharam Karam* (1975), made under his own banner, and in Sanjay Khan's *Abdullah* (1980), did he once again manage to evoke some of his earlier charisma. In *Dharam Karam* (directed by his son Randhir Kapoor, who was also the hero), the elder Kapoor appeared as a singer with a golden heart. In *Abdullah*, he made a great impact as an elderly secular Arab who raises a Hindu orphan as his own son (without changing his religion) despite the social ridicule heaped on him and the mayhem unleashed by a gang of desert dacoits.

Raj Kapoor died on 2 June 1988, when he was a few months short of 64; this was the day he received the Dadasaheb Phalke Award from the President of India.

The Urban Milieu Hero

In the 1950s, Dev Anand's hero, along with Guru Dutt's and Master Bhagwan's, 'moulded' Hindi cinema's 'proletarian' urban hero. Either as a small-time criminal or as an indigent unemployed youth, this hero lent a very realistic expression to the uncertainties and the turmoil of urban existence. He brought out the vulnerability of the lower strata of society amidst the hostile and callous environment of the metropolis. His protagonist would often strive to lead a respectable life but would get entangled in the city's crime network, finally taking the initiative on his own to work out

Dev Anand:
The suave and
debonair
urban hero

a life beyond the trappings of an evil and corrupt world. This hero was seen in his finest form in ten films: *Baazi* (1951), *Taxi Driver* (1954), *House Number 44* (1955), *Funtoosh* (1956), *Pocketmaar* (1956), *Baarish* (1957), *Nau Do Gyarah* (1957), *Solvan Saal* (1958), *Kala Pani* (1958) and *Kala Bazaar* (1960).

Dev Anand was born as Devdutt Pishorimal Anand on 26 September 1923 in Gurdaspur, Punjab. (He was also called Dharam Dev Anand.) After doing his graduation in English literature from Government College, Lahore (now in Pakistan), he joined his elder brother Chetan Anand in Bombay to participate in the activities of the Indian People's Theatre Association (IPTA). Like Raj Kapoor, he also started his career in serious roles, making his debut in P. L. Santoshi's *Hum Ek Hain* (1946), produced under the Prabhat banner. An inspiring parable on national unity, the film depicted him as the son of a rich widowed Hindu landlady. She is a virtuous matriarch who very zealously carries out an extremely innovative 'project' of raising in her household three orphans – a low-caste Hindu, a Muslim and a Christian – along with her own son.

Hum Ek Hain was followed by a slew of films in quick succession: *Aaghe Badho* in 1947; *Ziddi*, *Vidhya* and *Hum Bhi Insaan Hain* in 1948; *Jeet*, *Namoona* and *Shayar* in 1949; *Afsar*, *Khel*, *Nirala*, *Dilruba*, *Madhubala* and *Hindustan Hamara* in 1950; *Aaraam*, *Sanam* and *Sazaa* in 1951; and *Tamasha* in 1952.

In *Vidhya*, his first film with Suraiya, Dev Anand appeared as a campaigner for women's education and uplift. *Jeet*, a remarkable film for its message, presented Dev and his leading lady Suraiya as the two role models for imparting the Gandhian ideals in post-independence India. The two protagonists, defying their feudal background, give up their inheritance and launch the allround development of their village, facing the résistance offered by their opponents with the spirit of tolerance and non-violence.

In *Namoona*, set against the backdrop of post-Partition India, Dev Anand played a meek college student who falls in love with a rich girl (Kamini Kaushal) but her foster father refuses to accept him as he is a poor refugee without any social and financial security. In *Afsar*, he appeared as a journalist who exposes corrupt rural politicians who mistake him for a government official. In *Sanam*, the young actor portrayed with remarkable conviction the role of a runaway convict who takes refuge in the house of the police commissioner (K. N. Singh) whose daughter falls in love with him.

Fali Mistry's *Saza*, a tragic tale about childhood love (à la Dilip Kumar's *Nadiya Ke Paar*, *Deedar* and *Hulchal*) presented Dev Anand as a youth from a landed family who desperately longs to retrieve his childhood companion, the daughter (Nimmi) of a maidservant. The girl, since her childhood, has been suffering from a severe phobia caused by the terror unleashed by the hero's landlord father. The hero is once rescued after an accident by Shyama, who professes her love for him, but he is unable to shake off the memories of Nimmi. Composer Sachin Dev Burman's melodious music was a major factor in this movie. (In most of Dev Anand's films, it was Sachin Dev Burman who scored the music as Shankar Jaikishan did in most of Raj Kapoor's movies and Naushad in most of Dilip Kumar's films.)

In these early films, Dev Anand, on the basis of his handsome looks and irresistible smile, brought about a very refreshing change in the persona of the Hindi film hero. With his upbeat romantic and rather non-aggressive image, he stood out as a role model for a section of the Indian youth. For the urban male, his liberal modern image and uncomplicated mental make-up were plus points to be emulated. For the fairer sex, he became the most cherished dream lover, naughty, ever-smiling but doting, who would respect his woman in a natural and spontaneous way.

It was the 1951 film *Baazi*, directed by Guru Dutt, which announced the making of Dev Anand's urban hero, a small-time, street-smart gambler, struggling to come to terms with the pressures of day-to-day life. S. D. Burman's enthralling tunes and Sahir Ludhianvi's peppy lyrics added new zest to the film.

Three years later, elder brother Chetan Anand's masterpiece, *Taxi Driver*, projected younger brother Dev Anand as a true 'working-class' urban hero. He breathed life into his role as a Bombay cab driver, who is cynical about his lowly existence and the inhuman treatment he gets from arrogant passengers; yet his colleagues affectionately call him 'hero'. His ordinary routine life gets disturbed when he happens to rescue, from some hoodlums, a village girl (Kalpana Kartik), who has come to Bombay to become a playback singer. This act of bravery lands the hero in violent conflict with a criminal gang and now he has to prove himself to be a true hero by mobilizing his inner strength and meagre resources to erase the powerful anti-social forces from the crime-ridden metropolis. Here again, S. D. Burman and Sahir spun their magic with telling effect.

In *House Number 44*, Dev Anand played a pavement dweller (a pickpocket) who dreams about the girl living in the house outside which he sleeps at night. As the girl is forced to become a messenger by an underworld gang, he tries to break this gang operating from a house numbered 44.

In *Baarish*, Dev Anand appeared as an unwilling member of a Bombay mafia, a role inspired by Marlon Brando's character in Elia Kazan's masterpiece *On the Waterfront* (1954). *Funtoosh* marked one of the most memorable performances of Dev Anand as the poor but jovial scamp caught in the trap of the city's scheming rich. The villain (K. N. Singh) ensnares him by insuring his life for a hefty sum and later forcing him to end his life so that he becomes the beneficiary. In *Pocketmaar*, the actor went in for a complete transformation of his street-smart urban hero. The pickpocket nicks money from a poor lad, which he has earned (against tremendous odds) to send to his mother and sister who live in poverty in their village. His victim, completely shattered, commits suicide. Unable to come to terms with his guilt, Dev Anand goes to his victim's village home and starts taking care of the family. On his return to the city, he helps the police to bust a gang involved in crime.

In *Nau Do Gyarah*, Dev Anand churned out a different image of his hero: a carefree wanderer who dwells in a makeshift 'house' in his old truck and keeps on moving from place to place. When a runaway girl (Kalpana Kartik) takes refuge in his truck, he gets involved in solving a difficult crime. In *Solvan Saal*, his suave hero makes an aggressive, well-prepared entry into the heroine's (Waheeda Rehman) world of love, finally winning her from the deceitful character she is in love with. (She had eloped with her lover after her rich father refused to accept him but he disappears with her jewellery.) The hero now becomes a willing accomplice in her desperate search for the trickster. In both these films, Burmanda's lilting compositions and Majrooh Sultanpuri's lyrics remain etched in memory, especially *Hum Hai Rahi Pyar Ke ...* (*Nau Do Gyarah*) and *Hai Apna Dil To Awara ...* (*Solvan Saal*).

In Raj Khosla's *Kala Pani*, as the distraught son struggling to break the stranglehold of a corrupt legal system to rescue his father languishing in prison, Dev Anand's outstanding performance won him the coveted *Filmfare* award for the best actor. *Kala Bazaar*, a realistic depiction of the life of the urban poor, presented Dev Anand as a street-smart boss running a gang of touts engaged in selling film tickets in black. After he manages to break up the love affair of an upper-class girl (Waheeda Rehman) with Vijay Anand (his younger brother in real life) (as in *Solvan Saal*), he falls in love with her. He follows her to a hill station, which is the locale for the evergreen haunting melody *Khoya Khoya Chand ....* He soon realizes the stigma attached to his lowly profession and decides to reform himself and his associates. He starts a Safed Bazaar ('white' market) with his fellow-criminals to work out a respectful rehabilitation scheme. Nevertheless, he is convicted for his illegal activities and sent to jail.

In two films, *Maya* (1961, directed by D. D. Kashyap) and *Asli Naqli* (1962, directed by Hrishikesh Mukherjee), the manifestation of Anand's urban hero took place in an entirely different framework. He portrays a wealthy indulgent youth, in search of a meaningful and fulfilling life, which he cannot find amidst opulence and luxury. He joins the city's poor and underprivileged. He undergoes a transformation after facing the harsh realities of life, which the downtrodden do every day with a never-say-die attitude. He finds true love and affection there.

In two films – Raj Khosla's *CID* (1956) and Shakti Samanta's *Jali Note* (1960) – Dev Anand's hero was on the side of the law as a highly motivated cop in pursuit of the invisible underworld don. He played a similar kind of role, with much fanfare, flamboyance and style, later in *Jewel Thief* (1967), *Johny Mera Naam* (1970) and *Chhupa Rustam* (1973), all directed by his younger brother Vijay Anand.

In the 1950s, Dev Anand was associated with neo-realist cinema as well. He appeared as a committed revolutionary in K. A. Abbas's *Rahi* (1952, based on a short story by the renowned writer Mulk Raj Anand). Chetan Anand's *Aandhiyan* (1952) showed him as an upright lawyer who leads a campaign against a blackmailer businessman who wants to force marriage on a young girl (Nimmi), the daughter of his business rival. In Amiya Chakravarty's *Patita* (1953), he appears as the saviour of a poor rape victim and in Phani Majumdar's *Baadbaan* (1954), as a dedicated rural activist who sets up an ice factory and a workers' cooperative endeavour. In yet another Phani Majumdar film, *Faraar* (1955), set against the backdrop of the freedom struggle, Dev Anand showcased his talent in the role of a firebrand underground revolutionary who takes refuge in Goa (then under Portuguese rule) to escape the British police. He sets up a clandestine factory for making crude bombs, but is finally killed due to the treachery of his own men. Later, in Raj Rishi's *Sharabi* (1964), his portrayal – apparently inspired by Dilip Kumar's in *Daag* but set in a totally different ambience – depicted the loneliness of an alcoholic mine worker who is unable to give up the bottle despite the occupational hazards that he faces every day at work.

Dev Anand ventured into portraying the anti-hero with fairly remarkable élan. In this category fall Guru Dutt's *Jaal* (1953), Raj Rishi's *Dushman* (1957), Raj Khosla's *Bombai Ka Babu* (1960) and Shankar Mukherjee's *Sarhad* (1960). In *Jaal*, he was a small-time but sharply focused gold smuggler who does not care about love and who does not value human life. In *Dushman*, Dev Anand's negative character was built around the concept of irresponsible parenthood that instils wrong values and self-gratifying means to fulfil the desires of their children. A pampered and spoilt child grows up to become a notorious criminal hotly pursued in vain by the police. He marries an innocent girl but she leaves him along with their child when she comes to know his real identity. Repentant and disenchanted, he now wanders in the streets, occasionally visiting his wife so that he can meet their son. The way in which the tearful sufferer roamed about with a shabby beard and a worn-out blanket wrapped around him was seen later in *Guide* (1965).

In *Bombai Ka Babu*, the hero is a murderer on the run who impersonates his victim (whom he has killed in Bombay), the lost member of a rich family living in the hills (of what is now Himachal Pradesh). He flees from Bombay and takes refuge amdist his victim's family members. He falls in love with the victim's sister (Suchitra Sen, who played Paro to Dilip Kumar's *Devdas*), but cannot express his love for her because she thinks of him as her 'brother'. Eventually, the law catches up with him just as his 'sister' is getting married to somebody else. In *Sarhad*, Dev Anand played a sadistic landlord who lives as a recluse and does not allow anyone to peep into his personal life till the heroine (again Suchitra Sen) brings about a change of heart in him.

Apart from the foregoing films, Dev Anand's repertoire included several others, adding to the variety of his roles. In Raj Khosla's *Milap* (1955), he appears as a simpleton who inherits sudden wealth but falls into the trap of an unscrupulous and greedy lawyer. In the musical hit, *Amar Deep* (1958, directed by T. Prakash Rao), he depicts a poor youth in love with a millionaire's daughter (Vyjayanthimala), but loses his memory in an accident. In *Manzil* (1960, directed by Mandi Burman), the actor effectively portrayed a small-town musician who rebels against parental authority and goes over to Bombay to prove his merit in the world of music.

In *Hum Dono* (1961, directed by Amarjeet), an outstanding film that carried an inherent message of pacifism, Dev Anand's compelling double role presented a fascinating study in contrasts. In his first role he appeared as an army captain who has joined the forces in order to escape the trauma of his failed love affair with a rich girl (Sadhana). In his second role, he played a major (a lookalike of the captain), the archetype ramrod-straight soldier, glowing with utmost professional satisfaction. This officer has a loving, beautiful wife (Nanda), who is eagerly awaiting his return from the front. The two lookalikes meet in a military camp. Soon, war breaks out. The major gets seriously injured while fighting the enemy. He entrusts his junior with the delicate task of conveying this tragic news to his family. The major's mother and wife welcome him, mistaking him for the major. He is unable to tell them the truth, because he is fearful of the consequences. Soon, the real major returns and after a series of accusations and spats, he realizes the captain has not betrayed his trust. The musical score by Jaidev (who was once S. D. Burman's assistant) was a major highlight of the film. Dev Anand proposes to rerelease *Hum Dono* in colour in the wake of two other classics, namely, *Mughal-e-Azam* and *Naya Daur*.

Dev Anand just breezed through several lighthearted romances of this period, playing the ultraromantic hero to the hilt. These movies were marked by initial playful verbal skirmishes and then ardent wooing by the hero and finally the falling in love. In Subodh Mukerjee's *Paying Guest* (1957), he, disguised as an old man, played the troublesome tenant of the heroine (Nutan), with whom he soon falls in love. He appeared as a cricket star worshipped by the heroine (Mala Sinha) in *Love Marriage* (1959, also directed by Subodh Mukerjee). He clobbers several pace bowlers and scores runs at an unimaginably fast rate! He masqueraded as a wealthy man to win over a rich girl (Asha Parekh) in Nasir Hussain's *Jab Pyar Kisise Hota Hai* (1961). In *Tere Ghar Ke Samne* (1963, directed by Vijay Anand), Dev Anand appeared as an architect who is appointed by the heroine's

(Nutan) father to design a grand house, which has to be much more imposing than his adversary's located just opposite. The adversary is none other than Dev Anand's father! After a series of hilarious sequences and awesome verbal duels between the two fathers, everything is sorted out and peace is finally restored. In *Teen Deviyan* (1965, directed by Amarjeet), he carried on a courtship simultaneously with three heroines (Nanda, Kalpana and Simi) with different mindsets. The unique aspect of this film was that all the characters retained their original names: for instance, Dev Anand was called Dev and Nanda was called Nanda. All these movies were studded with catchy songs, many of which continue to be popular even today.

Another 1965 movie, Vijay Anand's *Guide* (based on the famous novel by R. K. Narayan), saw Dev Anand perhaps in the most outstanding role of his long career. *Guide* stands out as a saga of human transformation through sacrifice and renunciation amidst the overlapping complexities engendered by unbridled ambition, obsessive creativity, suppressed sexuality and the vagaries of destiny. The film narrates the story of a small-town tourist guide, Raju (Dev Anand), whose life gets transformed – first by sudden affluence and then by a kind of spiritual awakening when he meets two particular clients, a famous, but aging, archaeologist Marco (Kishore Sahu)

Dev Anand and Waheeda Rehman in a scene from *Guide*

and his unhappy and highly sensitive young wife Rosy (Waheeda Rehman). On the other hand, he himself becomes a stepping stone both for Rosy (whom he makes a dancing star) and for her husband (for whom he opens up an unexplored archaeological site). Marco is soon lost in his excavation work, least concerned about his fretting wife's demands for attention. Rosy soon falls in love with Raju, who taps her enormous potential as a dancer and she soon soars to dizzying heights of fame and fortune. Swayed by the sudden access to easy money, Raju starts indulging in a profligate lifestyle, spending Rosy's earnings in partying and gambling. Their relationship begins to go downhill. The growing mistrust between them finally leads to the inevitable – Raju is jailed for forging Rosy's signature on a bank cheque. After his release from jail, this disillusioned and broken man all of a sudden finds a new purpose in life when the people in a far-flung drought-hit area start revering him as a great sadhu who can bring rains by going on fast. As he takes an inward journey to find strength to uphold the belief of the poor people and the faith they have reposed in him, he finally overcomes the fear of death by submerging it in the cosmic truth of the immortality of the soul as enshrined in the Bhagavadgita. Composer S. D. Burman came up with what can probably be rated as his all-time great compositions, with each and every song honed to perfection. Overall, *Guide* was a masterpiece, a unique venture that remains etched in every film aficionado's memory. The film went on to bag several prestigious awards. However, its English version released in the West failed to impress the audience.

In another Vijay Anand directorial venture, *Tere Mere Sapne* (1971), Dev Anand again made his mark as an idealistic doctor who goes to a remote mining town to provide medical care to the people there. Here, he meets a renowned surgeon (played by Vijay Anand himself), who has become addicted to the bottle. The surgeon is bitter and cynical towards the medical profession and its role in improving the lives of ordinary people. But the newcomer is not affected by his attitude. He soon establishes himself there and seems to be performing medical 'miracles'. He snatches a newborn from the jaws of death through sheer perseverance. The local people begin looking upon him as a messiah. He meets a lively school teacher (Mumtaz) and they soon fall in love and get married. While she is pregnant, she is accidentally injured and her womb is affected adversely. She is told that a second child could endanger her life. Meanwhile, serious differences (over boarding and lodging and job functions) crop up between Dev Anand and the wife of the senior doctor who has appointed him. He soon gets disillusioned and starts losing faith in his idealism. He returns to the big city as a changed man who is determined to become rich and powerful. He does achieve fame and wealth, but at a price. He also gets involved with a famous singing star (Hema Malini), whom he cures of depression. His wife, who is carrying again, leaves him and goes back to the mining town as she feels that his avarice is getting the better of him. Finally, when Mumtaz and the child she is carrying dangle between life and death, Dev Anand persuades Vijay Anand to save their lives. *Tere Mere Sapne* was an adaptation of A. J. Cronin's celebrated 1937 novel, *The Citadel*.

Dev Anand made his directorial debut with *Prem Pujari* in 1970, a pacifist film denouncing the growing militarization of the human mind and the devastation caused by wars among nations. The protagonist (Dev Anand himself) is a soldier who gets disenchanted with his profession and is courtmartialled for 'dereliction of duty'. In disgrace, he abandons his family (his father is a highly decorated army officer) and his sweetheart (Waheeda Rehman). This pacifist, however, turns a nationalist as he gets embroiled in a spy ring that is obtaining crucial information on India's military secrets and passing it on to the enemy. He takes up arms to fight for the country in the 1965 war between India and Pakistan. This turnaround, however, somewhat undermined the film's initial message of peace.

In his second directorial venture, *Hare Rama Hare Krishna* (1971), Dev Anand sought to restore the spirit of Indianness among the alienated youth going astray under the influence of the hippy culture, caused, in turn, by irresponsible parenthood and emerging social tensions. The essential story was about a brother's (Dev Anand) long search for his lost sister (Zeenat Aman) who was separated from him in childhood when their estranged parents parted ways. The girl now has become a drug addict and moves around aimlessly with a bunch of hippies, smoking pot and singing songs in smoke-filled dens. The film proved to be a hit for its contemporary theme and its music (composed by Rahul Dev Burman, Sachin Dev Burman's son), especially the Asha Bhosle number *Dum Maro Dum* ..., which became a 'cult song'.

By the mid-1970s, Anand's hero began to lose his charm and appeal. He then started building, very diligently, a Westernized, transnational image for himself and his films (with a few exceptions). Yet many of his films of the 1970s and beyond somehow failed to impress the audiences. The fairly long list of such films includes *Chhupa Rustam* (1973), *Joshila* (1973), *Ishq Ishq Ishq* (1974), *Prem Shastra* (1974), *Amir Gharib* (1974), *Heera Panna* (1974), *Warrant* (1975), *Bullet* (1976), *Darling Darling* (1977), *Lootmaar* (1978), *Swami Dada* (1982), *Anand Aur Anand* (1984), *Hum Naujawan* (1985), *Sachche Ka Bol-Bala* (1989), *Lashkar* (1989), *Awwal Number* (1990), *Sau Crore* (1991), *Gangster* (1994), *Return of the Jewel Thief* (1996), *Main Solah Baras Ki* (1998), *Censor* (2001), *Aman Ke Farishtey* (2003), *Love at Times Square* (2003) and *Mr Prime Minister* (2005). Not deterred by such a setback, Dev Anand is currently in the process of making a new film titled *Chargesheet*.

Two films, *Des Pardes* (1978) and *Manpasand* (1980), briefly seemed to revive the old Dev Anand magic. *Des Pardes* was a revelatory commentary on the plight of Indian immigrants in the UK, many of whom have gained illegal entry. (This was the first film of Tina Munim, who later went on to marry the business tycoon Anil Ambani.) *Manpasand* was Bollywood's version of *My Fair Lady*, with Dev Anand essaying the role played by Rex Harrison and Tina Munim in the place of Audrey Hepburn.

Dev Anand's autobiography, *Romancing with Life* (Penguin, New Delhi), was released on his turning eighty-four (on 26 September 2007) by Prime Minister Manmohan Singh, whose birthday is the same as that of the actor but whose year of birth is 1932.

An Eccentric Allrounder

If there was one individual who was an actor, a singer, a composer, a lyricist, a scriptwriter, a producer and a director all rolled into one, it was Kishore Kumar, who stands out as unique in the annals

Kishore Kumar:
A unique
personality in
the film world

of Hindi cinema. He can easily be accredited as the first-ever modernizing force in Hindi cinema that provided an unprecedented dynamism to the Hindi film hero's persona. Like Raj Kapoor, he introduced a bubbling, jaunty and delightful comic idiom with his vagabondish attire, absurd antics and highly imaginative rendering of rib-tickling songs. He mastered in his own way the celebrated comedy genres of Hollywood's Jerry Lewis and Danny Kaye.

With the advantage of being a prolific and innovative singer, with little or no concern for the grammar of music, he packed his comic performances with offbeat and almost unpredictable vocal gymnastics, leading invariably to extremely hilarious outcomes. In fact, in the 1950s itself, he had laid the foundation of post-classical cinema, the prototypes of which were later built by Shammi Kapoor, Dev Anand and Rajesh Khanna in the 1960s and 1970s.

Kishore's hero, in most of his films, was a jovial, eccentric and apparently dull-headed youth, who appeared to be a caricature of the Westernized male. He often ridiculed, through his whacky actions and pithy dialogues, both the evil-hearted and the repressive social milieu. However, through this very caricature, he seemed to be making fun of himself as well as of the Westernized way of life, which, in India, was (and continues to be) a shoddy imitation of the original. In most of his films, he has portrayed himself as a non-conformist, whose attitude and behaviour run contrary to the traditional norms and customs, be they social or cultural. (These norms and customs are often upheld by the heroine in a grandiose manner.) Such was the pattern in films like *Mem Sahib* (1956), *New Delhi* (1956), *Asha* (1957) and *Chacha Zindabad* (1959). The impact was much more uproarious in *Padosan* (1968). In the lastmentioned film, Kishore Kumar, as the footloose and zany 'classical' singer, brings in extempore innovations in his music idiom to outwit the Carnatic music teacher (played by the ace comedian Mehmood) of the heroine in the across-the-window contest in the song *Ek Chatur Naar....* This song (in the vocals of Kishore Kumar, Manna Dey and Mehmood) stands out as one of the most hilarious comic sequences ever picturized.

Kishore Kumar was born on 4 August 1929 in Khandwa (now in Madhya Pradesh). His real name was Aabhas Kumar Ganguly. He was the younger brother of one of the all-time greats, Ashok Kumar, whom we have already met in earlier chapters. After the family moved to Bombay, Kishore Kumar started as a chorus singer for composer Saraswati Devi at Bombay Talkies. It was the legendary composer Khemchand Prakash who launched his career as a full-fledged singer in *Ziddi* (1948) and *Rimjhim* (1949). A diehard fan of K. L. Saigal, Kishore imitated him in his early songs with remarkable success (for instance: *Marne Ki Duanye Kyoon Mangu ...* in *Ziddi*, his first film song, and *Jagmag Karta Chand Poonam Ka ...* in *Rimjhim*). As a comedian, he carved a place for himself with Phani Majumdar's *Tamasha* (1952) as the jovial link between the egoist hero (Dev Anand) and indifferent heroine (Meena Kumari), finally paving the way for their union. Later, he played a similar role in *Ladki* (1953), *Paisa Hi Paisa* (1956), *Miss Mary* (1957) and, of course, *Padosan*.

Kishore announced the arrival of his comic hero with four films released in a row – *Ladki, Pehli Jhalak* (1954), *Baap Re Baap* (1955) and *Char Paise* (1955). While in *Ladki*, he was the confidant of the hero, in *Char Paise*, he appeared as an unconventional CID inspector who blended his natural comic streaks with his work responsibilities. After a series of funny situations, he brings to book a notorious cheat (Jayant) who swindles money with the help of his two comical but ambitious partners, Johnny Walker and Agha. *Baap Re Baap*, a comic treatment of socially forbidden love, presented him as the son of an aristocratic family who falls in love with a naïve garland-making girl (Chand Usmani). As the scenes go by, he builds up an extremely humorous critique that exposes the hypocrisy and arrogance of his own class.

Kishore further reinforced the persona of his eccentric hero through films such as *Paisa Hi Paisa* (1956), *New Delhi* (1956), *Bhai-Bhai* (1956), *Bhagam Bhag* (1956), *Delhi Ka Thug* (1958), *Jaal Saaz* (1959), *Chacha Zindabad* (1959), *Shararat* (1959) and *Apna Haath Jagannath* (1960).

In *Paisa Hi Paisa*, produced under Mehboob's banner and directed by Mehrish, Kishore Kumar was cast in one of his early comic roles. In this very well-crafted critique of the traditional moneyed class, the young actor appeared as the rebel son of an astute and avaricious stockbroker (played so very convincingly by the veteran Radhakishan). He marries a poor girl (Shakila), the daughter of his greedy father's debtor. When his father forces him to marry the daughter of his rival (Mala Sinha), to whom he owes a huge sum, Kishore gets a mask of his face prepared by a professional mask maker, and at the time of the marriage ceremony, makes her lover, a poor street dweller, his lookalike and presents him as the groom. The film thus underlined the rigid mindsets of the traditional rich class amidst the inevitable changes being triggered by rebellious young minds.

In *New Delhi*, a nationalist plea for 'unity in diversity', Kishore, with his trademark caricaturing, brought to the fore the deep sense of parochialism entrenched in the Indian mindset. He played a middle-class Punjabi youth, who after getting a job in New Delhi, frantically searches for a rented house. But the landlords insist that they would give their houses only to those belonging to their own community. In desperation, he disguises himself as a South Indian and falls in love with his Tamilian landlord's daughter (Vyjayanthimala), leading to a serious rift between the two families when the truth comes out. The lead pair invokes the slogan of 'national unity' and attempts to persuade the elders to agree to their marriage.

Bhai-Bhai presented our comedian as a street-smart poor youth who makes a living by pickpocketing and carries on a love affair with a street dancing girl (Nimmi). He is the separated younger brother of a millionaire (Ashok Kumar) who has left his wife (Nirupa Roy) and child (Daisy Irani) for a scheming seductress (Shyama). The hero finally saves his brother before he loses everything to the vamp.

Bhagam Bhag (1956) saw Kishore in the company of Bhagwan and, as the title implies, both of them keep on running from one adventure to another. They manage to keep the audience in splits virtually throughout the film. Composer O. P. Nayyar's fast-paced tunes added pep and vibrancy to the narrative.

Delhi Ka Thug presented Kishore as a goofy reporter in the equally crazy company of Nutan, an upper-class girl. In his stupidity, he is able to expose the drug blackmarket trade run by the heroine's father. His zany antics and capers left the audiences clamouring for more! In *Chacha Zindabad*, he appears as a Westernized 'freak' whom his parents want to get married to a traditional girl (Anita Guha), who is an exponent of classical dance and music. Both enter into a pact to display their disliking for each other to their parents, but eventually fall in love. In *Shararat* (1959), he was the desperate lover madly in love with a serious-minded neighbourhood girl (Meena Kumari) who refuses to be impressed by his unending jestering. He even stages his mock death procession to arouse her sentiments. And the irony is that he eventually commits suicide. In *Jaal Saaz* (1959), Kishore released his potential for comedy in full blast as a wayward youth, who keeps on making a fool of the deceitful villian (played by Pran). *Apna Haath Jagannath*, an offbeat film about the disdainful attitude of the upper and middle classes towards menial vocations, cast Kishore as the proponent of the dignity of labour. He starts a printing press against the wishes of his rich father and labours hard to get it going. His father disparages him. In the end, it is he who gives employment to his father, who had frittered away all his wealth in unproductive ways.

Amidst the plethora of the aforementioned comedies, which were set in some social context, Kishore also used his craft to build a genre of absurd cinema as seen in *Aasha* (1957), *Chalti Ka Naam Gadi* (1958), *Bewaqoof* (1960), *Jhumroo* (1961), *Half Ticket* (1962), *Mr X in Bombay* (1964), *Do Dooni Chaar* (1968), *Shrimanji* (1968), *Badti Ka Naam Daadi* (1974), *Shabash Daddy* (1978) and *Chalti Ka Naam Zindagi* (1981).

In *Aasha*, Kishore Kumar was in peak form, displaying his bizarre ingenuity in slapstick manoeuvring, singing and dancing, culminating in the immensely popular rambunctious rock-and-roll number *Ina Meena Deeka* ..., set to tune by C. Ramchandra. He appeared a crazy rich youth, who after being accused of murder, masquerades as an Arab theatre personality to woo the heroine (Vyjayanthimala) and stages a play in front of the villain to prove his innocence.

Satyen Bose's rib-tickling comedy *Chalti Ka Naam Gaadi* was an interesting study on mutually contrasting personalities in a family of three brothers. The trio run a garage. The eldest (Ashok Kumar) is a staunch misogynist and serious by nature. He keeps his two clumsy brothers in check and asks them to stay away from women. The second (Anoop Kumar) is a born romantic but extremely shy of women. The youngest (Kishore Kumar) is the upbeat, jovial jumping jack who falls in love with a rich girl (Madhubala), when she comes to the garage to get her car fixed on a rainy night. Almost each and every sequence was chockfull of humour and whacky antics.

I. S. Johar's masterpiece, *Bewaqoof*, is remembered for Kishore Kumar's outstanding performance as a winner in love, accomplishing this task by masquerading as a black American boxing champion with an equally hilarious Johar as his assistant.

Jhumroo (directed by Shankar Mukherjee) has been hailed as the zaniest expression of Kishore's comic persona. He played a whacky minstrel on the move (à la Raj Kapoor in *Jis Desh Mein Ganga Behti Hai*). He keeps on belting out one song after another in pursuit of his love for a rich girl (Madhubala), the daughter of an evil zamindar. In this movie, Kishore Kumar was himself the music director and he came up with a fabulous score. As Ashish Rajadhyaksha and Paul Willemen observe: 'The film proposes the craziest notions of tribal identity in Indian cinema: one song is a variant of "Tequila", another introduces rock into a Cossack dance, and the Kathmandu/Timbuctoo number sees the hero adopting a Fu Manchu look to rescue the heroine.'[1]

Half Ticket, directed by Kalidas, was about a rich youth, who works out his freedom from family oppression by running away from home. He dresses up as a schoolboy to obtain the half-price train ticket available to children. The villain (Pran) drops a stolen diamond into Kishore Kumar's pocket (without the latter being aware of it) and has to constantly chase him to retrieve the precious commodity! The film was dotted with several rollicking episodes. In *Do Dooni Chaar* (1968, directed by Debu Sen), an adaptation of William Shakespeare's play, *Comedy of Errors*, Kishore captured the nuances of the double role with his usual aplomb. In Ram Dayal's *Shrimanji* (1968), a robust comedy, Kishore, in the equally crazy company of I. S. Johar, portrayed a fashion consultant who turns his client (Johar), a diehard lover of Indian culture, into a completely Westernized man.

In sharp contrast with his immensely popular jester image, Kishore was also a master of tragedy and displayed amazing ingenuity in portraying serious roles. In *Andolan* (1949), a nationalistic story set against the background of India's freedom struggle, he appeared as a militant. One highlight of the film was footage showing Rabindranath Tagore singing his *Jana Gana Mana* .... In Bimal Roy's realist venture, *Naukri* (1954), he was a poor village youth, a diehard optimist who is sure of getting a good job in the city on his graduation so that he can free his family from the poverty trap. But his dreams fall flat, turning him into a cynic. In Mohan Segal's *Adhikar* (1954), a thought-provoking film advocating gender equality in matrimony, Kishore, a middle-class youth, marries the next-door girl (Usha Kiran) without revealing to her that he is a widower and has a daughter who is being taken care of by his parents in a village. The distraught wife leaves (upon hearing this news) him and finally returns home with his daughter presenting her as her child from her previous marriage. When the husband refuses to accept the child, she deplores him for his male chauvinist attitude demanding from him to accept her past the same way that he expects her to do.

Satyen Bose's *Bandi* (1957) also cast Kishore in a serious role as an illiterate sacrificing rural youth, who takes on the burden of supporting his elder brother's (Ashok Kumar) family after the latter is falsely jailed for murder. After his release, the vengeful ex-prisoner sets out to avenge himself and comes in violent conflict with his simple-hearted brother who has arranged the marriage of his daughter with the villain's son. In Hrishikesh Mukherjee's *Musafir* (1957), he appeared as a wayward youth, who turns desperate to find a job so that he can support his aged father and his widowed sister-in-law (Nirupa Roy).

Kishore, to the utter surprise of his fans and followers, all of a sudden made a complete turnaround to a serious 'new-wave' variety of cinema in his in-house productions, which he started in the 1960s. Conceived as a kind of personal experimental cinema, he sought to address the deeper issues of man's urge for freedom from his mundane existence. In the films of this genre – *Door Gagan Ki Chhaon Mein* (1964), *Door Ka Rahi* (1971), *Door Wadiyon Mein Kahin* (1982) and *Mamata Ki Chhaon Mein* (1989) – the actor very ably brought out his full potential for serious roles.

This legendary multifaceted genius died on 13 October 1987 of cardiac arrest at a time when he was the indisputable king of playback singing, his chief competitor, Mohammed Rafi, having left this world some seven years earlier (on 31 July 1980). His career as a singer is beyond the scope of this book.

A Poet-like Hero

Bharat Bhushan (1920–92), Hindi cinema's celebrated poetic hero, with several films located either in history or folk tales to his credit, was the foremost among the heroes of his times whose persona found fruition mostly in culture-specific or period-specific cinema. With his poet-like slightly effeminate good looks, simple but sophisticated demeanour and a pleasant disposition, Bhushan won much adulation from his female audience.

Bhushan was also the only actor whose career graph ran parallel to that of Dilip Kumar's *tragic hero* of the 1950s. A perfect

Bharat Bhushan
as Mirza Ghalib

fit in elaborate tragedies and period films that appeared in quick succession in the 1950s and the early 1960s (for example, *Baiju Bawra, Shabab, Basant Bahar, Mirza Ghalib, Rani Roopmati, Sohni Mahiwal, Sangeet Samrat Tansen* and *Jahanara*), he appeared to be an alter ego of his illustrious contemporary. Given the content and mood of the roles in the foregoing films, Dilip Kumar could have also easily portrayed them. Although Bharat Bhushan lacked the intensity and charisma of Dilip Kumar, he did possess the innate ability to portray the anguish of a sufferer in search of his destiny in a hostile world.

This poet-like hero, born in a well-to-do Vaishya (trader) family of Uttar Pradesh, was a discovery of Kidar Sharma, the writer-director who is also credited with launching the film careers of Raj Kapoor and Madhubala in his classic *Neel Kamal* (1947). Sharma cast Bhushan in a supporting role in his *Chitralekha* released in 1941. Seven years later, he presented him in the lead role in a tragic love story, *Suhaag Raat*, opposite Begum Para. This film also introduced the vivacious Geeta Bali, who soon was to become one of the most accomplished actresses of Hindi cinema. The success of *Suhaag Raat* opened the doors to several films in which Bhushan appeared as the hero: Bharat Vyas's *Rangila*

Rajasthan (1949), Nanabhai Bhatt's *Janmashtami* (1950), Ramesh Gupta's *Ram Darshan* (1950; Shashi Kapoor, Raj Kapoor's younger brother, appeared as a child artiste in this film), Devendra Goel's directorial debut *Aankhen* (1950) and *Ek Tha Ladka* (1951). None of these films could offer Bhushan a meaningful role except *Aankhen*. In this film, he played a self-sacrificing lover who commits suicide to ensure the happiness of his brother (Shekhar), who is also desperately in love with the heroine (Nalini Jaywant).

Bhushan was catapulted to stardom (along with his heroine Meena Kumari) by Vijay Bhatt's superhit musical *Baiju Bawra* (1952). Initially, Bhatt had planned the film with Dilip Kumar and Nargis in the lead roles, but an intuitive composer Naushad (despite being an ardent camp follower of Dilip Kumar) insisted on newcomers or, at least, not well-established actors. A very powerful presentation of the famous Bawra legend associated with the Mughal emperor Akbar's era, the film traced the painful journey that a classical singer has to undertake in order to fulfil his mission in life. Tansen, the court musician of Akbar, has prohibited singing around his palace. Baiju's father and his *bhajan mandali* (troupe) wander near the musician's palace, singing their traditional religious songs. Tansen's guards stop them and fatally injure his father. Baiju pledges to avenge the killing and finally defeats the musical genius in a *jugalbandi* (a classical musical performance by two soloists) held in the emperor's court. In the end, he and his childhood sweetheart Gauri (Meena Kumari) die together in the swirling waters of the river Jamuna. *Baiju Bawra* stands out as a landmark film for its incredible musical score. Naushad put his heart and soul into every composition, as did lyricist Shakeel Badayuni and the singers (Lata Mangeshkar, Mohammed Rafi and Shamshad Begum, apart from the highly respected classical musicians Khan Sahib Amir Khan and Pandit D. V. Paluskar).

The following year, Bharat Bhushan reached yet another high point as an actor with his stellar performance as the medieval

Vaishnav poet-saint in Vijay Bhatt's *Shri Chaitanya Mahaprabhu* (1953), for which he bagged the *Filmfare* best actor award.

The sudden success of *Baiju Bawra* greatly elevated Bhushan's stature. He was now the first preference of several top producers and directors for period films and costume dramas, a string of which soon hit the screen. Of course, there was the occasional 'social' film as well. In Sohrab Modi's classic biographical sketch, *Mirza Ghalib* (1954), Bhushan exquisitely internalized the restless persona of this Delhi-based legendary Persian and Urdu poet. Ghalib (1797–1869) was constantly striving to break new ground in poetry writing but failed to get due recognition and accolades from his peer group, which included the last Mughal emperor Bahadurshah Zafar. He finds inspirational love through Chaudhvi Begum (played by Suriaya), a dancing girl and a die-hard fan of his *shayari* (poetry). Finally, his complete disillusionment with the prevailing milieu (he was a witness to the 1857 rebellion) and his helpless concern for his suffering wife (played by Nigar Sultana, who loses many children due to miscarriage) result in the death of this genius, who was utterly lonely during his last days. In this film, the musical score by Ghulam Mohammed greatly enhanced the beauty of Ghalib's *ghazals*.

Shabab (1954), a hit musical enriched by Naushad's exceptionally soothing tunes, was the tragic love story of a poor musician (Bharat Bhushan) and a princess (Nutan).

Bhushan maintained his stride in the latter half of 1950s, sustaining the magic of his hero in a variety of roles. In Raja Nawathe's *Basant Bahar* (1956), set during the reign of the courageous ruler of Mysore, Tipu Sultan (1750–1799), he once again played a lovelorn classical singer, who 'sells' his voice to the villain in order to uphold the honour of his sweetheart (Nimmi). In this film, composers Shankar Jaikishan, for the first time, displayed their prowess in creating *pure classical music*, which was on par with Naushad's in *Baiju Bawra* and his other films of this period.

In G. P. Sippy's fanstasy venture, *Chandrakanta* (1956), based on the distinguished Hindi writer Devakinandan Khatri's widely read novel of the same name, the young actor is caught up in a long-drawn-out struggle to win over his love amidst a hair-raising, yet fascinating, milieu of mystery and intrigue.

In Filmistan's *Champakali* (1957) directed by Nandlal Jaswantlal, he co-starred with the reigning queen of Bengali cinema Suchitra Sen. Set against the backdrop of the nomadic life amidst the desert of Rajasthan, Bhushan appeared as a water diviner. He falls in love with a haughty woman (Suchitra Sen), while the daughter of the tribal chief, Champakali (Shubha Khote), desperately awaits acceptance as his wife. When the water in the area (where the nomads have pitched their camp) becomes scarce, Bhushan tracks down a traditional water resource hidden below the ruins of a fort, and, in this search, Champakali sacrifices her life.

Sakshi Gopal (1957, directed by Balchandra Shukla and Ramnik Vaidya) was a devotional film about the prosecution of a Lord Krishna devotee and *Mera Salam* (1957, directed by Harbans Singh), starring Bhushan opposite Bina Rai, a period film about the tragic life of a destitute singer.

Phagun (1958, directed by Bibhuti Mitra), a superhit musical fantasy (thanks to O. P. Nayyar's bewitching tunes) depicting the journey of two souls in search of each other in rebirths, portrayed Bhushan in the role of a flute player, the son of a landlord, in love with his soulmate, a *banjarin* or gypsy girl (Madhubala).

Raja Nawathe's *Sohni Mahiwal* (1958) once again brought Bharat Bhushan within the musical ambit of Naushad. Based on the famous love legend of Punjab, the film presented Bhushan in the role of Mahiwal, a traveller who seeks his emancipation in the soulful love of Sohni (played remarkably well by Nimmi). But the fulfilment of this forbidden love is marred by treachery and deceit. As in *Baiju Bawra*, the two lovers die together as they are drowned in the rising waters of the river Chenab. *Sohni Mahiwal* was the actor's last film with music by Naushad. Like Dilip

Kumar, he had also received immense musical support from this music director and from singer Mohammed Rafi who sang some great hits for the actor, including *O Duniya Ke Rakhwale* ... , *Man Tarpat Hari Darshan Ko Aaj*, *Tu Ganga Ki Mauj Main Jamuna Ka Dhara* (all three from *Baiju Bawra*) and *Aane Wale Ko Aana Hoga* ... (*Sohni Mahiwal*). In fact, it was Rafi who was, to a large extent, instrumental in boosting Bharat Bhushan's career. Apart from Naushad, Rafi sang for the hero under the baton of different composers. Other singers, such as Manna Dey (well versed in classical music), Talat Mehmood and Mukesh, also made their contribution to Bharat Bhushan's vocals.

During the late 1950s and the early 1960s, Bhushan collaborated with highly gifted composer-director-actor S. N. Tripathi to create three historical masterpieces: *Kavi Kalidas* (1959); *Rani Roopmati* (1959); and *Sangeet Samrat Tansen* (1962). Nirupa Roy was the heroine in first two films. (She had made her mark in Bimal Roy's *Do Bigha Zameen*, 1953, opposite Balraj Sahni.)

In *Kavi Kalidas*, Bhushan employed his eminently suited poetic persona to re-create on screen the personality of this remarkably prolific Sanskrit poet at the court of Emperor Chandragupta Vikramaditya (A. D. 375–414). Kalidas's oeuvre includes such masterpieces as *Abhigyaanashakuntalam*, *Meghadoot* and *Ritusamhaara*.

Rani Roopmati, a grand saga, replete with history, folklore and classical music, presented Bharat Bhushan in the role of Baaz Bahadur, the sultan of Mandu (1555 to 1562) during Akbar's reign. (Mandu is located in present-day Madhya Pradesh.) He was an accomplished exponent as well as a patron of classical music. The film brought on screen one of the most curious love affairs in Indian history – between Baaz Bahadur and Roopmati (Nirupa Roy), a damsel belonging to a Rajput clan and herself a renowned singer. (In the film, she even manages to defeat the formidable Tansen in a musical contest.) In this affair, the two develop an intimacy, not as man and woman, but as two souls in search of spiritual bliss through togetherness in music. One particular pathos-filled song (*Aa Lautke Aaja Mere Meet* ...), sung separately by Lata Mangeshkar and Mukesh, still casts a spell over the listener.

In *Sangeet Samrat Tansen* (1962), a remake of the K. L. Saigal starrer *Tansen* (1943), the actor subtly portrayed, with his own ingenuity and trademark softness, the legendary singer. The music was quite impressive, keeping in mind the theme of the movie.

Apart from the foregoing three films, Bharat Bhushan also appeared in the title role in Babubhai Mistri's historical *Samrat Chandragupta* (1958), again opposite Nirupa Roy.

Vinod Kumar's *Jahanara*, released in 1964, virtually marked the end of Bhushan's career as a period film hero. In this tragic tale of the Mughal emperor Shah Jahan's daughter, his only companion in his last days as a captive (he was imprisoned by his own son Aurangzeb), Bhushan once again essayed the role of an anguished lover-poet who keeps wandering around her palace to bring some solace to this lonely princess whose agony and anguish lead her to the verge of a breakdown. In this film, the ace composer Madan Mohan came up with a dazzling musical score.

Apart from building up a grand heritage of period films, Bharat Bhushan made his presence felt in several memorable social films as well. Unfortunately, the actor's contribution to the social genre has been less appreciated. The films in this category include Bimal Roy's *Maa* (1952), Ram Daryani's *Pehli Shadi* (1953), M. V. Raman's *Ladki* (1953), Chaturbhuj Doshi's *Aurat Teri Yahi Kahani* (1953), Hemen Gupta's *Meenar* (1954), S. K. Prabhakar's *Kal Hamara Hai* (1959), P. L. Santoshi's *Barsaat Ki Raat* (1960), Ramanand Sagar's *Ghunghat* (1960), R. Tiwari's *Mud Mud Ke Na Dekh* (1960), K. A. Abbas's *Gyarah Hazaar Ladkiyaan* (1962), Nitin Bose's *Dooj Ka Chand* (1964) and R. C. Talwar's *Naya Kanoon* (1965).

In *Ladki*, Bhushan, with the comic-friendly support of Kishore Kumar, negotiates his love affair with a girl, the daughter of a high-caste father and Harijan mother whom no one wants to marry. *Meenar*, made in memory of Bhushan's first wife Sarla, was an offbeat film that threw up an interesting debate between modern science and parapsychic phenomena. Bhushan is haunted by a candle-carrying spirit (Bina Rai) in search of her lost lover in her previous birth (the way Madhubala was seen in Kamal Amrohi's *Mahal*), but his buddy, the rationalist Pran, keeps rebuking him for taking his hallucinations as real.

The actor once again lent credibility to his role as a sensitive poet, but in a contemporary setting, in the superhit musical *Barsaat Ki Raat*. He used his poetry not only to express his love for his sweetheart (Madhubala) but also to enrich the great *qawwali*-singing tradition. His dramatic appearance as the singer in the *qawwali* competition, extolling the spiritual beauty of sublime love in *Na To Karwan Ki Talash Hai* ..., was the hallmark of the film.

In *Ghunghat*, a virtual remake of Dilip Kumar's *Milan* (1946), he excelled in depicting the predicament of the mistaken husband of a newly-wed veiled bride who gets separated from her groom in a train accident.

Gyarah Hazaar Ladkiyaan (1962), jointly written by K. A. Abbas and the noted Urdu poet Ali Sardar Jafri, presented Bhushan as a journalist who rebels against his millionaire father and joins a progressive journal that extols the rights of working women. In court, he defends his sweetheart (Mala Sinha), who is accused of killing a night club owner who tried to rape her sister, a cabaret dancer.

Dooj Ka Chand, a scathing attack on the commodification of women under the lecherous feudal order, projected the agony of a distraught brother whose foster sister has been married off to a very old landlord. As the brother is accused of murdering the landlord, it turns out that the bride was the latter's own illegitimate daughter.

Significantly, Bhushan, in sharp contrast with his recognition as an exemplary tragic hero, also exhibited a good sense of comedy. In Bimal Roy's *Maa* (1952), a touching family drama set in rural Bengal, he was a naughty youngster, playing pranks and soliciting the attention of his childhood sweetheart (Shyama). In a truly memorable scene, when his football team wins a match, he steals some fish along with his friends from a landlord's pond and sneaks into Shyama's kitchen, pleading with her to cook their 'catch' for them.

Mud Mud Ke Na Dekh, a caustic commentary against the dowry system, presented him as a jovial youth wooing a modern girl (Anita Guha) who has run away from home as her marriage has been arranged, without her consent, with a greedy bridegroom and a greedier family.

In Om Prakash's *Gateway of India* (1957), he makes a foray into the crime thriller genre in the small role of a poor but jovial poet who provides a helping hand to the heroine (Madhubala) in distress. She is a rich heiress who has run away from home to escape from the clutches of a scheming uncle, and like Raj Kapoor in *Jagte Raho*, she becomes instrumental in exposing a whole breed of evil men engaged in nefarious activities (Pradeep Kumar, Bhagwan, Johnny Walker, Chandrashekhar and Om Prakash). Only in the company of the poet does she find love and warmth. Despite the presence of so many male stars, it was the lissome Madhubala who stole the show.

In *Naya Kanoon*, he appeared again as a poet, who is jobless, whereas the woman he loves and marries (Vyjayanthimala) manages to find work as a singer in a radio station. He is not happy with this situation and begins thinking of separation. The plot had striking similarity with the earlier K. L. Saigal–Kanan Devi starrer *Street Singer* (1938) and later *Abhimaan* (1973) with Amitabh Bachchan and Jaya Bhaduri in the lead roles.

Bhushan's career went into sudden decline after 1965, when Hindi cinema began to acquire a compelling Western look. He shifted to playing senior roles with Rajshri's *Taqdeer* (1967) as the music teacher and Nasir Hussain's *Pyar Ka Mausam* (1969) as the estranged father of the hero. He continued to appear, off and on, in films such as *Kahani Kismet Ki* (1973), *Kasuati* (1974), *Yaarana* (1981) and *Sharabi* (1984).

Very sadly, he finally ended up doing small character roles and, in his old age, he virtually became a daily wage extra. Bhushan, however, took consolation in his second marriage to actress Ratna (she co-starred with him in *Barsaat Ki Raat* and *Dooj Ka Chand*) and in his huge collection of books till he passed away in 1992.

The Hero with the Royal Touch

Pradeep Kumar, truly the 'royal face' of Indian cinema, excelled in portraying both historical characters as well as the stereotypical liberal upper-middle-class youth. With a chiselled face, an aristocratic bearing and a fairly deep and resonant voice, he, like Bharat Bhushan, made his mark in several historicals and mythology-based movies.

Pradeep Kumar was born as Sital Batabyal in 1925 in what is now West Bengal. After studying fine arts, he entered the film world in 1944 as an assistant cameraman. The legendary film director Debaki Bose of New Theatres, impressed with his performance in a Bengali play, introduced him in *Aloknanda* in 1947. Bose also gave him his screen name. The young actor appeared in a string of New Theatres' Bengali productions. These films included

The 'royal' Pradeep Kumar

Grihadaha, Bishnupriya, Devi Chowdhurani, Bhooli Nai and *Chaitanya Mahaprabhu.* He won critical acclaim for his title role in *Chaitanya Mahaprabhu*, which the actor considered his most outstanding performance.

In the early 1950s, Pradeep Kumar moved to Bombay and joined Filmistan Studios. He made his debut in Hindi cinema with Hemen Gupta's *Anand Math* (1952), co-starring with Prithviraj Kapoor, Geeta Bali and Bharat Bhushan. He came into the limelight with the two of the biggest musical hits of all time: *Anarkali* (1953, music director C. Ramchandra) and *Nagin* (1954, music director Hemant Kumar), both under the Filmistan banner.

In the first film, opposite Bina Rai, he adeptly utilized his auric, regal persona in portraying the rebellious Prince Salim (who went on to become the Mughal emperor Jehangir). In *Nagin*, an offbeat love story set in a tribal milieu of snake venom collectors and sellers, he mesmerized the viewers as the *been*-playing snake charmer, who, with his enticing musical rendering, wins the heart of a damsel (played by Vyjayanthimala) belonging to a rival clan. His later films based on popular love legends – *Heer* (1956, heroine Nutan), *Shirin Farhad* (1956, heroine Madhubala) and *Yahudi Ki Ladki* (1957, heroine Madhubala again) – further enriched his image as a sufferer in pursuit of soulful love.

In Vijay Bhatt's lesser known costume drama *Patrani* (1956), set in the ancient period, he appeared as the royal prince of Pattan (in Gujarat) who hates ugliness and prefers to be always surrounded by beautiful women. He marries a princess (Vyjayanthimala) from South India but refuses to accept her as his wife because her complexion had turned dark after her long, hectic journey to reach Pattan. Eventually, the princess, in the guise of a court dancer, regains the love of her eclectic husband. Nandlal Jaswantlal's *Taj* (1954), like K. L. Saigal's *Tansen*, sought to extol the healing powers of music. This film presented Pradeep Kumar as a singer-hermit. He cures the paralytic princess (Vyjayanthimala), who had banned singing in her kingdom, with his music. His other films in the 1950s were Amiya Chakravarty's *Badshah* (1954, heroine Mala Sinha), *Sitara* (1955, heroine Vyjayanthimala), *Adl-e-Jehangir* (1955, heroine Meena Kumari) and *Durgesh Nandini* (1956, heroines Bina Rai and Nalini Jaywant).

In the social genre, he excelled equally well as the upper-class sophisticated and liberal aristocrat. He came up with a memorable performance in V. Shantaram's *Subah Ka Tara* (1954, heroine Jayashri), as the socially conscious youth who falls in love with a widow but eventually loses his mind in his pursuit of what was then considered forbidden love. In *Adalat* (1958), like *Mamta* released eight years later, the hero causes turmoil in the life of his beloved (Nargis) as he is unable to marry her. She becomes a nautch girl and finally when she kills the blackmailer villain, her lawyer-daughter (also Nargis) defends her in court. *Adalat* was studded with some phenomenal *ghazals* composed by Madan Mohan and rendered exquisitely by Lata Mangeshkar. In *Ghunghat* (1960), as the 'other' bridegroom, he complemented the brilliant performances by Bina Rai and Bharat Bhushan.

In the 1960s, Pradeep Kumar co-starred with veteran Ashok Kumar in *Aarti* (1962), *Rakhi* (1962), *Meri Surat Teri Aankhen* (1963), *Chitralekha* (1964), *Bheegi Raat* (1965), *Afsana* (1966) and *Bahu Begum* (1967). In all these films, except for *Rakhi* (heroine Waheeda Rehman), *Meri Surat Teri Aankhen* (heroine Asha Parekh) and *Afsana* (heroine Padmini), the leading lady was Meena Kumari. He blended well his natural stance with that of his senior. In Kidar Sharma's remake of *Chitralekha* with Meena Kumari in the title role, he appeared in the role of King Beejgupta. The film was based on the novel by the famous Hindi writer Bhagwati Charan Verma.

Pradeep Kumar ventured into other genres as well. For instance, he appeared in some crime thrillers such as *Hill Station* (1957), *Detective* (1958), *Taxi No. 555* (1958), *Police* (1958), *Ustadon Ke Ustad* (1963) and in N. A. Ansari's films such as *Mulzim* (1963) and *Zindagi Aur Maut* (1965).

Pradeep Kumar reached the high point in his career with the musical hit *Taj Mahal* (1963), in which he played the role of Mughal Emperor Shah Jahan. He also appeared in a less known sc-fi film, *Wahan Ke Log* (1967). He soon shifted to character roles with *Sambandh* in 1969 opposite his old-time companion Bina Rai. Like Bharat Bhushan, he continued doing minor roles, the last important one being that of King Balban in Kamal Amrohi's *Razia Sultan* (1983). He also put in brief, but impressive, appearances in films such as *Mehboob Ki Mehndi* (1971), *Hawas* (1974) and *Kranti* (1981). Pradeep Kumar died in Calcutta in October 2001 at the age of 76.

Two Super Heroes in Waiting

Shyam, another indigenous hero in the making, was one of the most promising actors of post-independence Hindi cinema. Like Dilip Kumar, his cinema too evoked the trauma of Partition and the agony of the protagonist to rediscover his identity amidst a seemingly never-changing oppressive social milieu. Tall and handsome, his persona reflected a curious mix of heroic strength and embedded sadness. The latter sought release through soulful love. Yet, he had a tremendous appeal in comic-romantic roles too. Had not tragedy struck, he would have been a serious contender for the top place, which was eventually filled up by Dilip Kumar.

Shyam and Suraiya
in *Dillagi*

Shyam was born as Shyam Sundar Chadha. His rise to stardom was phenomenal. He stormed the film world in 1948 with Shahid Lateef's *Shikayat* (co-starring Snehprabha Pradhan) and Bombay Talkies' superhit *Majboor* with Munawwar Sultana. *Majboor*, directed by Nazir Ajmeri, was among the first Indian films to depict the tragedy of socially forbidden interreligious love. Set in a village of North India, the film unfolds the turbulence caused by the daring love affair between a Muslim youth (Shyam) and a Hindu damsel (Munawwar Sultana). As the two communities in this village are caught up in deep hostility and mistrust created by Partition, the lovers are persecuted and separated. Eventually, the hero sacrifices his life to save the honour of his beloved. It is after this sacrifice that the repentant people finally realize the folly of their communal attitudes and pledge to live peacefully again.

In 1949, Shyam had as many as nine hit films to his credit, a rare phenomenon in the film world: M. Ehsan's *Chandni Raat* opposite Naseem Banu; A. R. Kardar's *Dillagi*, Ravindra Dave's *Naach* and M. Sadiq's *Char Din*, all opposite Suraiya; Krishan Kumar's *Kaneez*, Harish's *Dada* and Jagdish Sethi's *Raat Ki Rani*, all opposite Munawwar Sultana; and H. S. Rawail's *Patanga* and K. Amarnath's *Bazaar*, both opposite Nigar Sultana. The following year, the young actor again won acclaim for his sensitive performance in four films: Ravindra Dave's *Meena Bazaar* starring opposite Nargis; Raman Lal Desai's *Sangeeta* opposite Nigar Sultana; Najam Naqvi's *Nirdosh*; and O. P. Dutta's *Surajmukhi* both opposite Rehana. But sadly, Shyam's highly promising career abruptly ended in 1951 as he fell off a horse and died during the shooting of Filmistan's *Shabistan*, directed by B. Mitra. Both *Shabistan* and Anant Thakur's *Kale Badal* (1951) were released after his death.

***

Raaj Kumar, an acting icon in his own right and a strong contender for the status of indigenous hero, played a very significant role in enriching the Hindi film hero's persona in the 1950s and 1960s. Although he possessed immense abilities in depicting down-to-earth characters, his main specialization was larger-than-life portrayals relying heavily on slick, punchy oratory. His cinema at times presented two highly contradictory images: as a humble peasant falling prey to the feudal oppression (in films such as *Mother India* and *Godaan*) and as an arrogant, self-possessed feudal lord himself, in a violent confrontation with the world, seeking to keep up his somewhat infantile notions of honour and pride (in films such as *Kaajal*, *Lal Patthar*, *Dil Ka Raja* and *Saudagar*). Of course, there were many shades of characterization in between, as we shall soon see.

Raaj Kumar was born on 8 October 1926 as Kulbhushan Pandit in a Kashmiri Brahmin family in Balochistan (now in Pakistan). After his graduation, he moved to Bombay and joined the city's police force. As in the case of Dilip Kumar, his entry into cinema was marked by a curious play of chance and destiny. One day, a film producer came to the Mahim police station, where Raaj Kumar was posted, to make a complaint. He was impressed by the mannerisms, the style and the gravelly and sardonic voice of the young cop. Soon three films – Najam Naqvi's *Rangeeli* opposite Rehana, *Aabshar* opposite Nimmi and *Anmol Sahara*

Raaj Kumar:
A dominant actor

opposite Geeta and Jayashri, all released in 1952 – announced the arrival of a new hero in Bollywood. However, it was with Sohrab Modi's historical, *Nausherwan-e-Adil* (1957), embellished with an impressive musical score by C. Ramchandra, that the young actor found his foothold in Hindi cinema. The heroine in this film was Mala Sinha. But Raaj Kumar hit it off with Meena Kumari who was his co-star in several memorable films such as *Shararat* (1959), *Ardhangini* (1959), *Dil Apna Aur Preet Parayi* (1960), *Dil Ek Mandir* (1963), *Kaajal* (1965) and *Pakeezah* (1972). He, in fact, proved to be an ideal match for Hindi cinema's highly revered tragedy queen.

Raaj Kumar shot into the big league with Mehboob Khan's classic *Mother India* (1957). In his realistic portrayal of a poor farmer, he immortalized the suffering of the debt-ridden Indian peasantry trapped in the mesh of the age-old exploitative feudal traditions. He appeared as Nargis's husband, who, incessantly strives along with his wife, to grow sufficient crops so that the debts to the avaricious moneylender can be paid off. One day, while struggling to move a huge rock in his field, his arms are crushed and he becomes an invalid. Disgruntled and thoroughly defeated, he one day leaves his family and the cruel world for good. After winning accolades for his performance in this film, the actor remained on the top rung till the early 1970s with virtually two releases in a year. He went on to display his immense ability by appearing in diverse roles: as a street-smart toughie in *Ujala* (1959); the loving and caring husband in *Shararat*; the humble mill worker and elder brother of the trade union leader (Dilip Kumar) in *Paigham* (1959); and in *Dil Apna Aur Preet Parayi* as a doctor who loves the heroine, a nurse, but is enticed into marrying another woman, Nadira, who develops a neurosis and turns into an extremely jealous and suspicious wife.

As hero, he appeared in *Dulhan* (1958), *Swarg Se Sundar Desh Hamara* (1959), *Ardhangini* (1959), *Dil Apna Aur Preet Parayi* (1960), *Sautela Bhai* (1962), *Pyar Ka Bandhan* (1963), *Phool Bane Angarey* (1963), *Rishte Naate* (1965) and *Pakeezah* (1972). Unlike most top-rung actors of his days, Raaj Kumar also appeared in three mythological films: *Krishna Sudama* (1957), *Durga Mata* (1959) and *Maya Machhindra* (1960).

During the period from the late 1950s to the early 1970s, he also emerged as the most sought-after actor for playing 'supporting' roles, with his characters having a critical importance in the manifestation and resolution of the conflict with the hero in the ensuing love drama. In *Gharana* (1961), *Dil Ek Mandir* (1963) and *Zindagi* (1964), he had Rajendra Kumar for company. In *Waqt* (1965), *Hamraaz* (1967) and *Chhattis Ghante* (1974), he appeared alongside Sunil Dutt. In *Kaajal* (1965), his co-star was Dharmendra. In *Nai Roshni* (1967) and *Vaasna* (1968), he co-starred with Biswajit. In *Neel Kamal* (1968), Manoj Kumar was his co-star. In *Mere Huzoor* (1968) it was Jeetendra who shared the honours with him and in *Lal Patthar* (1971), it was Vinod Mehra.

Raaj Kumar was a master of tragedy in his own right, despite his trademark larger-than-life bearing and a dialogue delivery that apparently reflected an influence of the Sohrab Modi school of acting. With expressive eyes and a pent-up desperation, he would moan, expressing his grief with a breathless helplessness. This attribute has been manifested in full measure in *Mother India*, *Godaan*, *Dil Ek Mandir*, *Paigham*, *Kaajal* and *Lal Patthar*. In a memorable scene in *Kaajal* (1965), for instance, a repentant Raaj Kumar carries out a long tearful discourse with god, accusing him of turning him into an evil man.

In supporting roles too, Raaj Kumar exhibited his histrionics capably in portraying the agonized but dignified loser in love. He appeared as the formidable counterpoint to the dashing romantic hero, the love preference of the heroine. In the articulation of his passions for his love interest and the subsequent vengeful attendance towards her and her lover, he displayed immense talent in capturing the deep complexities of such roles. In such portrayals he would come virtually on par with Dilip Kumar, whom he personally considered as the only equal competitor in the field of film acting. In his career, he got an opportunity to test his skills in *Paigham* (1959) and when Subhash Ghai cast him opposite the thespian in *Saudagar* in 1991.

Among all these films, *Waqt* (released in 1965) marked the turning point in the career of Raaj Kumar. This film not only brought about a sudden transformation in his film image but also apparently in his behaviour and lifestyle in real life. In the mould of a suave, stylish and self-assured conman, who is determined to treat the world the way he was treated as a child left alone in the world, the actor, like Ashok Kumar in *Kismet*, carved the first prototype of Amitabh Bachchan's angry young man of the 1970s and 1980s. His majestic style of dialogue delivery and his powerful histrionics made a great impact on the audiences.

In Kamal Amrohi's masterpiece, *Pakeezah*, Raaj Kumar's pithy dialogue delivery and impressive performance stole the show. The protagonist is a modern youth who has broken away from his aristocratic background to join the Forest Service. In this transformation, he positions himself at the interface between the decadent feudal and the emerging modern milieu in order to rework the past to find a new future. In the process, he intervenes in the morbid life of a nautch girl Sahibjaan (Meena Kumari), who, despite her suffering, is anticipating her emancipation but is unable to foresee who would be her liberator. And this emancipation is epitomized in the message that the confident Raaj Kumar places at her feet in praise of their beauty and purity when he finds her sleeping in the ladies' compartment that he has boarded in his rush to catch the train. And every time the girl hears a train whistle, her hope of achieving freedom is rekindled, metaphorically reflecting the desire for liberation from the world to which she belongs. In the end, as the story reveals, the feudal values stand crumbled and the brave hero's marriage procession headed by his once-arrogant grandfather reaches the doorsteps of his beloved in the red-light area.

In Chetan Anand's *Heer Ranjha* (1970), Raaj Kumar underwent another metamorphosis in his image. Like Dilip Kumar and Bharat Bhushan, known for their tragic performances, Raaj Kumar adeptly transformed his larger-than-life image to play a distraught Ranjha caught in the web of forbidden love. Chetan Anand's *Heer Ranjha* was based on the famous love legend of Punjab and its unique feature was that virtually the entire dialogue was in poetry (penned by the renowned Urdu *shayar* Kaifi Azmi). Another highlight of this movie was the amazing musical score by Madan Mohan, with each song sculpted to perfection. It is said that Chetan Anand (who, as Raaj Kumar claimed, was his only friend in the film world), had planned a film on the Anarkali–Salim fable with an elderly Raaj Kumar in the role of Emperor Akbar. But when the actor insisted on playing the son, Prince Salim, an unhappy Chetan Anand shelved the project.

During the 1970s, Raaj Kumar's notable films (apart from those mentioned earlier) were *Maryada* (1971, with Rajesh Khanna as his co-star), *Dil Ka Raja* (1972, in a double role) and *Karmayogi* (1978, in the company of Jeetendra). Chetan Anand's patriotic extravaganza, *Hindustan Ki Kasam* released in 1973, marked the decline of the career as hero of this charismatic actor. *Hindustan Ki Kasam*, despite its authentic sets and impressive photography, lacked the human touch of the same director's earlier venture *Haqeeqat*. Set against the backdrop of 1971 Indo–Pak war in the western sector, the 1973 film projected Raaj Kumar as an Indian Air Force pilot, who leads a daredevil mission to destroy a Pakistani radar that picks up signals from IAF planes and alerts the enemy.

The 1980s and 1990s saw him in a variety of roles in films such as *Chambal Ki Kasam* (1980), *Bulandi* (1980), *Kudrat* (1981), *Sharara* (1984), *Raaj Tilak* (1984), *Marte Dam Tak* (1987), *Mohabbat Ke Dushman* (1988), *Surya* (1989), *Saudagar* (1991), *Tiranga* (1992) and *God and Gun* (1995).

He died on 3 July 1996, a few months short of his seventieth birthday, of throat cancer.

Heroes Turned Villains: Ajit and Premnath

Ajit, one of the most durable actors of Hindi cinema, was born as Hamid Ali Khan on 27 January 1922 at Golconda (on the outskirts of Hyderabad, now in Andhra Pradesh). With his tall, rugged and handsome presence, he took up the void left by the untimely death of the highly promising actor Shyam. After making an impressive entry with *Jeevan Saathi* (1949) followed by *Patanga* (1949), he soon became one of the most sought-after

Ajit:
A popular performer

heroes of the early and mid-1950s. His notable films during this period were *Beqasoor* (1950) and *Saiyan* (1951) both opposite Madhubala, *Dholak* (1951), *Anand Math* (1952), *Nastik* (1954), *Baradari* (1955), *Marine Drive* (1955), *Aaj Ki Baat* (1955), *Halaku* (1956), *Durgesh Nandini* (1956) and Ramesh Sehgal's *26 January* (1956).

In the beginning of his career, Ajit established his hero image by portraying two entirely different characterizations. In Roop K. Shorey's superhit, *Dholak*, he formed an extremely comic pair with Meena, one of less known but highly talented heroines of her times. The hilarious tale, penned by I. S. Johar (the plot was repeated later in several films), was about two fresh graduates who are in search of employment but they have to live as husband and wife to get jobs in a music and dance school, leading to a series of highly comic situations. The hallmark of the film was an enchanting music score by the legendary composer Shyam Sundar.

In Filmistan's *Nastik*, set against the backdrop of Partition, Ajit gave a brilliant performance in depicting the plight of a destitute youth, who reaches India with his grown-up sister and younger brother after their parents have been killed in riots. But in their own country, they fall prey to greed and lust. The priest of a temple takes away the ornaments they had, the younger brother dies of hunger and the sister commits suicide after she is forced to become a dancing girl by a wealthy lecherous man. With his faith in god shattered, the hero turns into an angry non-believer and a vengeful man. *Nastik* was also penned by I. S. Johar, who also made his debut as director with this film. Composer C. Ramchandra and poet Pradeep teamed up to come up with some fabulous songs.

In Ravindra Dave's *Guest House* (1959), a less known film, Ajit once again portrayed, with remarkable finesse, an idealistic but poor youth struggling against all odds to uphold the promise he made to his dying mother: never to tell lies. He refuses to save his buddy when he is arrested by the police. After he is thrown out by his guardian, he goes to Bombay where he, in the company of the warm-hearted heroine (Shakila), decides to reaffirm his idealism.

By the late 1950s, however, Ajit slowly began to lose his aura as a top star, as his films began to fail at the box office. These films included *Bada Bhai* (1957), *Kitna Badal Gaya Insaan* (1957), *Milan* (1958), *Mehndi* (1958), *Do Gunde* (1959) and *Baraat* (1960). In his last memorable film as hero, *Mehndi*, based on the courtesan Umrao Jaan's life, Ajit captured with immense dignity the complex role of the nawab, who is romantically involved with the dancing girl. However, it was Muzaffar Ali's 1981 film *Umrao Jaan* (with Rekha in the title role) that won wide acclaim from both the audiences and the critics.

In the 1960s, this robustly built but sensitive actor further went into oblivion, adding only some mid-budget crime thrillers to his earlier list of films: *Opera House* (1961), *Burmah Road* (1962), *Tower House* (1962) and *Shikari* (1963).

During the late 1950s and early 1960s, Ajit also excelled as a supporting actor in three films. In fact, he won almost as much kudos as the hero.

In *Naya Daur* (1957), as the carpenter buddy of the hero (Dilip Kumar), who is also his competitor for winning the love of the heroine (Vyjayanthimala), Ajit very ably juxtaposed his subdued but powerful style with Dilip Kumar's upbeat and boisterous performance.

K. A. Abbas's *Char Dil Char Raahen* (1959) presented Ajit in the role of a socially conscious Pathan chauffeur, who rescues a dancing girl (Nimmi) from the clutches of his boss, a villainous nawab.

In the monumental *Mughal-e-Azam* (1960), Ajit once again brought to the fore his histrionics while playing the role of Durjan Singh, the commander-in-waiting and a confidant of Prince Salim (Dilip Kumar). As a courageous, battle-scarred soldier, he prepares the helpless prince, caught in the turmoil of his love for Anarkali (Madhubala), for the revolt against royal tyranny represented by Emperor Akbar (Prithviraj Kapoor). When Salim asks him about the safety of Anarkali during the war, Durjan pledges to free her from the royal prison at any cost. He goes to the prison and, after a bitter fight with the guards, he frees her. Despite being seriously injured and his garments being blood-soaked, he brings her to the prince's camp. As he dies from his injuries, grief-stricken Anarkali, after completing her namaz, expresses her gratitude by spreading her white shawl over his body.

One of Ajit's most important films of the 1960s was *Nannha Farishta* (1969). He appears as Joseph, one of three dacoits (the other two are a Hindu played by Pran and a Muslim played by Anwar Hussain), who kidnap a child. However, they are deeply moved by the innocence of the little girl and they rediscover human virtues and give up their criminal ways.

In the 1970s and beyond, Ajit revived his sagging career by opting for villain roles, playing a suave don and punctuating his stylized performances with memorable catch phrases ('Mona darling', 'Lilly don't be silly' and '*Sara shahr mujhe "loin" ke naam se jaanta hai*'). During this phase of his career, the senior actor also gained popularity as a humorist by default with his highly popular brand of 'Ajit jokes'. Such jokes and their variations were regularly published in leading magazines and newspapers and relished by all sections of the readership. His noteworthy movies in this era include *Zanjeer* (1973), *Yaadon Ki Baraat* (1973), *Dharma* (1973), *Jugnu* (1973), *Pratigya* (1975), *Kalicharan* (1976), *Charas* (1976), *Hum Kisi Se Kam Nahin* (1977), *Mr Natwarlal* (1979, in which he played a positive role as a police officer), *Ram Balram* (1980), *Raaj Tilak* (1984) and *Criminal* (1995).

Ajit died of cardiac arrest on 22 October 1998 at Hyderabad.

***

In the 1950s, Premnath was the only actor who had the remarkable ability to play with equal ease both hero and villain. With a unique blending of masculinity and an unusual agility in his screen presence, as a hero, he projected a carefree disposition and a jovial, swashbuckling image. As a villain, he could appear sinister and menacing on the basis of his facial expressions and forceful dialogue delivery.

Premnath Malhotra was born on 21 November 1926, in Peshawar (the celebrated birthplace of Dilip Kumar and Raj Kapoor). After Partition, his family first moved to Jabalpur (now in Madhya Pradesh), and then to Bombay to join the Kapoor family (Premanth's sister Krishna was married to Raj Kapoor), which had made a name both in theatre and cinema.

Premnath's debut film was *Daulat Ke Liye* (1947). Raj Kapoor then cast him in a small role (as a committed but disillusioned man who is obsessed with the theatre) in his directorial debut *Aag* (1948), followed by a major role in his next film *Barsaat* (1949). In this film he stole the show as the debauched philanderer who views women as objects of a man's lust, while the hero believes in the beauty of true love. The young actor made his debut as hero in Mohan Bhavnani's last film *Rangeen Zamana* released in 1948, but it failed to make much of an impact.

The success of *Barsaat* greatly enhanced Premnath's stature in the 1950s. In D. D. Kashyap's *Aaram* (1951, hero Dev Anand),

Premnath:
Good man-cum-bad man

the young Premnath, with remarkable underplay, captured the anguish of a desperate lover who seeks solace in his adulation of the heroine (Madhubala), but is unable to express his feelings. In Mehboob Khan's colourful spectacle *Aan* (1952), in the role of the treacherous prince, Shamsher Singh, he brought about a complete revamping of Indian cinema's villain, hitherto dominated by stereotypes. Premnath's villain, on the other hand, was suave, sophisticated and dashing, virtually on the same footing as the hero.

The four films that set the persona of Premnath as hero were Amiya Chakravarty's box-office hit costume drama, *Badal*, Kidar Sharma's *Shokhiyan*, Mahesh Kaul's *Naujawan* and H. S. Rawail's *Sagaai*, all released in 1951.

In *Badal*, he appeared as the people's hero (à la Robin Hood) who leads a successful crusade against the royal tyranny unleashed by the benevolent king's ministers.

Shokhiyan, like Guru Dutt's *Baaz*, was set in the sixteenth century during the Portuguese annexation of Goa. This film presented Premnath as a highly spirited nationalist, who heads a movement against the onslaught by foreigners on his native land. Using his trademark symbolism of white clouds and a playful sea, Kidar Sharma beautifully juxtaposed his hero's nationalistic stance (and the freedom he yearned for) with the innocence of his sweetheart, a tribal girl (Suraiya).

In *Naujawan*, one of the most realistic depictions of love caught in the web of the rich–poor divide, Premnath perhaps came up with his career-best performance as hero. He portrayed a carefree, down-to-earth car mechanic, who storms into the life of a spoilt daughter (Nalini Jaywant) of a millionaire with his typical street humour and worldly wisdom. Finally, when he wins over the girl and also her snobbish class-conscious father, he refuses to be part of the rich class and settles down with his bride in his home located in a slum.

Some of Premnath's other movies in the 1950s were: O. P. Dutta's *Parbat* (1952) opposite Nutan, *Anjaam* (1952) opposite Vyjayanthimala, *Saqi* (1952), a costume drama opposite Madhubala, *Mehman* (1953) opposite Nimmi, and *Aab-e-Hayat* (1955) opposite Ameeta.

Among his leading ladies, Premnath formed the most popular pair with Bina Rai, that too in costume dramas, as seen in B. Verma's *Aurat* (1953), H. S. Rawail's *Shagufa* (1953), *Golkunda Ka Qaidi* (1954, directed by Premnath himself), Jayant Desai's *Hamara Vatan* (1956), *Samundar* (1957, directed by Premnath himself) and Kedar Kapoor's *Chengiz Khan* (1957). *Aurat*, based on the famous biblical legend of Solomon and Delilah, was about the tragic decline of man's prowess at the hands of a seductress. During the making of this film, the two stars fell in love and got married.

By the late 1950s, Premnath's hero image began to fade. He appeared now in run-off-the-mill productions of smaller banners. Such films included *24 Ghante* (1958), *40 Din* (1959), *Jagir* (1959) and *Apna Ghar* (1960). Only in Jag Mohan Matto's *Jagir* and Ram Pahwa's *Apna Ghar* was he able to re-create his earlier magic. *Jagir*, in which he co-starred with Meena Kumari, was a reform drama located at the feudal–modern divide. Like in *Awara*, the hero was the foster son of a benevolent *jagirdar* (landlord) who has given shelter to several poor families on his estate. The *jagirdar* had kidnapped him when his father, a rich medical doctor, refused to treat his (the *jagirdar*'s) injured son. He raises Premnath as a dreaded criminal but eventually implores him to return to a decent life. In *Apna Ghar*, he appeared as a spoilt rich man bent upon destroying his family life.

His last role as hero was that of Sohrab in Vishram Bedekar's *Rustam Sohrab* (1963), opposite Suraiya, a celebrated singer-actress. This was also her last screen appearance. The formidable Prithviraj Kapoor played Rustam in this film based on the famous Persian classic.

As a senior actor, Premnath hit the silver screen as a shrewd and scheming villain, an image installed by director Vijay Anand in *Teesri Manzil* (1966) and *Johny Mera Naam* (1970). However, he did not restrict himself to playing villain. He appeared in a wide variety of roles in movies such as *Amrapali* (1966), *Be-imaan* (1972), *Amir Gharib* (1974), *Sanyasi* (1975), *Aap Beeti* (1976), *Dus Numbri* (1976), *Darinda* (1977), *Heeralal Pannalal* (1978), *Jaani Dushman* (1979) and *Farz Ki Keemat* (1985).

In *Dharmatma* (1975), directed by Feroz Khan, Premnath sought to reinvent the Godfather in the Indian setting, based on the character of *matka* king Ratan Khatri, but without much success.

He appeared in Subhash Ghai's directorial debut *Kalicharan* (1976) and in his other productions: *Vishwanath* (1978), *Gautam Govinda* (1979), *Karz* (1980) and *Krodhi* (1981). He also made his presence felt in Sanjay Khan's *Chandi Sona* (1977).

Premnath, in this phase of his career, adopted the celebrated 'Pran model' of taking up the role of an elderly Good Samaritan. Like Pran, who underwent a dramatic shift in persona in Manoj Kumar's *Upkar* (1967), Premnath also made this change as a warm-hearted do-gooder under the same young director's initiative in *Shor* (1972) and *Roti Kapda Aur Makaan* (1974).

One of Premnath's unforgettable characters was that of a Goanese fisherman (Jack Braganza) in Raj Kapoor's runaway hit *Bobby* (1973). Premnath's boisterousness, bonhomie and zest for life were the highlights of this film. He also appeared in *Dharam Karam* (1976), directed by Randhir Kapoor (Raj Kapoor's eldest son).

His last film appearance was in *Hum Dono* (1985) after which he announced his retirement from films. Premnath was also an accomplished classical singer and had learnt music from Guru Jagannath. In the Punjabi film, *Gyaniji* (1977), he sang the Gurbani in his own voice. A true philanthropist, he did a lot of charity work for the poor throughout his life. He died of a heart attack on 3 November 1992.

The Actor with a Cause: Sunil Dutt

Sunil Dutt (real name Balraj Dutt), another indigenous hero in the reckoning for the top slot, was catapulted to fame in the late 1950s. He continued to enjoy great success in the 1960s and 1970s, after which he switched over to senior roles. He also turned producer-director in the mid-1960s. By nature, he was a philanthropist and was full of joie de vivre. He was tall, handsome and debonair, with a natural flair for acting.

Sunil Dutt:
An actor with a mission

During his first phase, he projected on celluloid two dramatically opposite screen personas. In the first category of films, he appeared as a liberal and a modern man. He attempted to tackle all problems – romantic, socio-economic or political – with equanimity and levelheadedness to the extent possible. This image was in sharp contrast with his excessively melodramatic persona of a wronged man, seething with vengeance in the second category of films.

Sunil Dutt was born in Khurd, in the Jhelum district of Punjab (now in Pakistan), on 6 May 1930. After working as an announcer on Radio Ceylon, he made his debut in 1955 in Ramesh Sehgal's *Railway Platform* as an unemployed youth. But it was the role of Birju, the renegade in *Mother India* (1957), which heralded his very dramatic arrival in Bollywood. (According to some sources, Mehboob Khan first offered this role to Dilip Kumar, but he refused to play the son of Nargis, his heroine in several films.) This powerful role of a bandit remained a fixation for Sunil Dutt as later seen in films such as *Mujhe Jeene Do* (1963) and *Pran Jaye Par Vachan Na Jaye* (1973). (Sunil Dutt saved Nargis from being engulfed in flames during the shooting of *Mother India*, and they fell in love and got married in March 1958.)

As a socially conscious youth, Dutt created his space through a number of films: B. R. Chopra's *Ek Hi Raasta* (1956) and *Sadhana* (1958), K. Narayan Kale's *Didi* (1959), Bimal Roy's *Sujata* (1959), Shakti Samanta's *Insaan Jaag Uttha* (1959) and Hrishikesh Mukherjee's *Chhaya* (1961).

In *Ek Hi Raasta*, he and the heroine (Meena Kumari), both orphans, get married and they have a son (played by Daisy Irani). They dedicate themselves to the welfare of other orphans. Unfortunately, Sunil Dutt is killed by a criminal as a form of revenge for sending him to jail. Meena Kumari then marries Ashok Kumar (Sunil Dutt's employer), but the child (who has been told that his father has been hospitalized) refuses to accept him as a 'father' and even threatens to kill him!

In *Sadhana*, a forerunner of Kamal Amrohi's *Pakeezah*, he portrayed an upper-class youth who is determined to rescue a courtesan (Vyjayanthimala) from the morass of her stigmatized existence. The creativity of a relatively unknown composer, N. Dutta, came to the fore in this movie, along with that of the radical poet Sahir Ludhianvi.

In *Didi*, an emotional tale of a brother–sister relationship, Dutt made his mark as a social activist who upholds his ideals against the whims of an overprotective elder sister always worrying about his well-being.

In *Sujata* he portrayed a somewhat timid youth (belonging

to an upper caste) desperately in love with a Harijan (read untouchable) girl (Nutan) raised by his mother. Such 'love' was considered scandalous, but the hero stuck to his guns, despite opposition from different sources.

In *Insaan Jaag Uttha*, he played a crane operator at a dam-building site. This film, shot when a large dam was actually being constructed, seemed to reflect Prime Minister Jawaharlal Nehru's vision. He had called dams and power plants 'modern temples'.

In *Chhaya*, Dutt's role was that of a poor poet in love with a millionaire's foster daughter. The film is remembered largely for Lata Mangeshkar's and Talat Mehmood's rendering of enticing melodies composed by Salil Choudhury and penned by Rajinder Kishen.

Dutt's hero left his imprint on several family melodramas of the 1960s and 1970s. For example: *Main Chup Rahungi* (1962), *Aaj Aur Kal* (1963), *Nartaki* (1963), *Ghazal* (1964), *Beti Bete* (1964), *Chirag* (1969), *Bhai Behan* (1969), *Meri Bhabhi* (1969), *Bhai Bhai* (1970), *Darpan* (1970) and *Zindagi Zindagi* (1972).

A hot favourite of B. R. Chopra, Sunil Dutt appeared as a doting lover in his three love triangles: *Gumraah* (1963, co-starring Ashok Kumar and Mala Sinha), *Waqt* (1965, co-starring Raaj Kumar and Sadhana) and *Humraaz* (1967, co-starring Raaj Kumar and Vimi).

His penchant for overtly sentimental roles was seen in Bimal Roy's *Usne Kaha Tha* (1960), apart from *Khandan* (1965), *Gaban* (1966), *Mehrbaan* (1967) and *Milan* (1967). In *Usne Kaha Tha*, based on the famous Hindi short story by Chandardhar Guleri and set against the backdrop of the Second World War, Sunil Dutt starred opposite Nanda. He played a self-sacrificing soldier who saves the life of the husband of the girl for whom he had nurtured a long-standing infatuation as a teenager. In *Khandan*, he appeared as a crippled farmer in a decadent feudal household torn apart by strife. *Gaban*, based on a famous novel by Munshi Premchand, was one of his best performances as a lower middle-class youth who steals money from the court's treasury to meet his wife's

(Sadhana) obsession with jewellery. In *Milan* he was the poor boatman with a heart of gold who provides solace to a grieving young widow (Nutan) belonging to a feudal family. In *Mehrbaan* he appeared as the adopted son of Ashok Kumar, who remains steadfast in his loyalty to his 'father', despite being humiliated and ridiculed by his foster brothers. (This theme was later taken up in Rajesh Khanna's *Avtaar*, 1983, and Amitabh Bachchan's *Baghbaan*, 2003.) For *Khandan*, he won *Filmfare*'s best actor award.

In sharp contrast with these roles, Dutt played, with the proficiency of a master comedian, hilarious roles in a couple of films: the bumbling lover in *Ek Phool Chaar Kante* (1960) and the love-smitten simpleton in *Padosan* (1968). This comic streak has evidently been inherited by his son, Sanjay Dutt. In *Ek Phool Chaar Kante*, he portrayed a zestful youth who had to please the four crazy possessive uncles of the heroine (Waheeda Rehman), each wanting her to marry a man with the attributes set by him. The Salman Khan–Karisma Kapoor starrer *Dulhan Hum Le Jayenge* (2000) was based on a similar plot.

Sunil Dutt, despite his distinct heroic and majestic demeanour, did not appear in many historical or costume dramas except in two: Lekh Tandon's *Amrapali* (1966) as King Ajatshatru of Magadh who is in love with the royal courtesan of Vaishali (Vyjayanthimala) ruled by his arch enemy, the Lachhvis, and in *Jwala* (1970, heroine Madhubala) as the runaway prince caught up in the turmoil engendered by a difficult love affair and also by enmity.

And to complete his share of film genres, he appeared in several suspense-cum-murder dramas such as Ravindra Dave's *Post Box 999* (1958), R. K. Nayyar's *Yeh Raaste Hai Pyar Ke* (1963), Raj Khosla's *Mera Saya* (1966) and Raj Tilak's *Chhattis Ghante* (1974).

In *Post Box 999*, based on Henry Hathaway's 1947 thriller *Call Northside 777*, Dutt played a journalist who carries out an investigation at the behest of a lady to establish the innocence of her son accused of murder.

Yeh Raaste Hai Pyar Ke was based on the infamous 1959 K. M. Nanavati murder case. (Nanavati was a naval officer who came to know about his wife's affair with another man during his long absences from home. He shot the paramour and surrendered to the police. During court proceedings, he was held 'not guilty' by the jury. As a consequence, trial by jury was abolished in Indian courts.)

In *Mera Saya*, a remake of the 1964 Marathi film *Pathlag*, the protagonist is a lawyer who is caught on the horns of a dilemma when a criminal woman, a lookalike of his dead wife (Sadhana), claims to be his spouse. Ace composer Madan Mohan's creativity was very much evident throughout the film, mainly because of the title song appearing as a refrain time and again.

In *Chhattis Ghante*, based on the 1955 Hollywood thriller *Desperate Hours* (starring Humphrey Bogart and Fredric March), Sunil Dutt appeared in a negative role. He played a gang leader who, along with his minions, enters Raaj Kumar's house (in his absence) and holds his family members hostage. He is eventually killed while trying to flee from the police, who have surrounded the house.

Dutt made his directorial debut in 1964 with *Yaadein*, the only single-actor film in Hindi cinema so far. *Yaadein* was an overtly experimental venture rarely seen in commercial cinema. The film depicted, in flashback, how a man deserted by his family gets trapped in an acute depressive state (caused by his inability to come to terms with his unhappy married life). He finally commits suicide. Unfortunately, this film failed at the box office.

His second directorial venture was *Reshma Aur Shera* (1971), a tragic Rajasthani folk tale set amidst the vast expanse of the Thar desert. Dutt came up with a memorable performance as Shera, who falls in love with Reshma (Waheeda Rehman) belonging to a rival clan. The unending feud between the clans, fuelled further by this love affair, leads to more bloodshed, finally culminating in the death of the lovers amidst the pristinely magnificent sand dunes. Sanjay Dutt, who was around twelve at that time, appeared briefly in the film as part of a *qawwali* chorus. In this film, the superb photography by S. Ramachandra and the soulful music by Jaidev brought alive the many hues and moods of the desert. However, his two other projects – *Dard Ka Rishta* (1982) about social support to cancer patients and *Yeh Aag Kab Bujhegi* (1991), highlighting the evils of dowry – failed to create much of an impact on the public at large.

In the 1970s, Dutt appeared in a few vengeance dramas (such as *Heera* 1973, *Zakhmi* 1975, *Darinda* 1977 and *Muqabla* 1979) and other assorted films (for example, *Geeta Mera Naam* 1974, *Umar Qaid* 1975, *Nehle Pe Dehla* 1976, *Nagin* 1976, *Paapi* 1977, *Daku Aur Jawan* 1978 and *Ahimsa* 1979) before venturing into senior roles. As a senior actor, he specialized in larger-than-life roles as in *Shaan* (1980, with a huge star cast including Amitabh

Sunil Dutt
as a dedicated
politician

Bachchan, Shashi Kapoor, Shatrughan Sinha and Kulbhushan Kharbanda), *Yari Dushmani* (1980), *Badle Ki Aag* (1982), *Raaj Tilak* (1984), *Dharmyudh* (1988) and *Parampara* (1993). His last screen appearance was in *Munnabhai MBBS* (2003) as the rustic but affectionate father of his own son, Sanjay Dutt.

Sunil Dutt was a committed social worker and peace activist in real life. He along with his wife Nargis worked tirelessly for the welfare of cancer patients. Ironically, Nargis fell victim to this dreaded disease and passed away on 3 May 1981. He was the sheriff of Bombay in 1982–83. Sunil Dutt and his family made strenuous efforts to help the victims of the 1992–93 Bombay riots. Sunil Dutt was a minister in Dr Manmohan Singh's Government till his untimely death on 25 May 2005.

Shammi Kapoor: The First 'Modernizing' Hero

Among the film heroes of the 1950s and 1960s, Shammi Kapoor (born as Shamsher Raj Kapoor on 21 October 1931) emerged as the most compelling cinematic figure for bringing about a sudden erosion of the classical cinema of the 1940s and 1950s and therefore of the image of its indigenous hero. His persona, groomed by a new class of directors – Nasir Hussain, Shakti Samanta and Subodh Mukerjee – led to a complete transformation of the Indian film into a culturally alien and highly Westernized prototype. With little concern for thematic strength and a viable story line, most of Shammi Kapoor's ventures were packed with glossy paraphernalia. They invariably contained fabulous oudoor locales (usually Kashmir), mandatory club scenes (where music and dance ruled the roost), exotic disguises for the hero and his sidekick and racy songs (with occasional melodies). A powerful force for the modernization of Hindi cinema, this hero set in motion the consumerist trend, which was expanded further in the 1970s and later by his elder brother Raj Kapoor as well as by Dev Anand. As a natural extension, Shammi Kapoor's prototypes of the 1960s were revived in a big way in the post-globalization years (1991 onwards), thanks to Yash Chopra and his camp followers.

'Yahoo'
Shammi Kapoor

Many other heroes (such as Joy Mukerji, Biswajit, Randhir Kapoor, Rishi Kapoor and Rajiv Kapoor, the last three being Raj Kapoor's sons) attempted to mould themselves in the Shammi Kapoor image, with varying degrees of success. Since Shammi Kapoor's cinema was targeted primarily at the emerging city-bred Westernized youth, who were heavily influenced by the 'rock'n roll' culture of the period, Hindi films, for the first time, witnessed a dramatic change in audience tastes. This development resulted in an uneasy distancing from Hindi cinema of those sections of viewers who, till then, had enjoyed the enchanting beauty of the classical film, of which soulful music was an integral part.

The two films that proclaimed the arrival of Shammi's loose-limbed, neck-twisting, body-jerking hero – an Indian version of Elvis Presley – were Nasir Hussain's directorial debut *Tumsa Nahin Dekha* (1957) and *Dil Deke Dekho* (1959, also directed by him). This highly stylized, freewheeling image reached its apogee in Subodh Mukerjee's *Junglee* (1961). The same pattern, with occasional variations, continued in Shakti Samanta's *China Town* (1962), Lekh Tandon's *Professor* (1962), Manmohan Desai's *Bluff Master* (1963), Shakti Samanta's *Kashmir Ki Kali* (1964), Bhappie Soni's *Janwar* (1965), Vijay Anand's *Teesri Manzil* (1966, produced by the aforementioned Nasir Hussain) and Shakti Samanta's *An Evening in Paris* (1967).

In most movies of this genre, the hero often would appear as a spoilt, self-indulgent and aimless brat belonging to a wealthy family. He would seek his identity in music (essentially he would start singing at the drop of a hat) and in wooing the 'ideal woman' he has all along been dreaming about. The flimsy plot or storyline merely provided a framework for the hero's antics and capers. Somewhere down the line, he would suddenly become 'responsible and mature', assert his authority, overcome the forces of evil and emerge triumphant.

In *Tumsa Nahi Dekha*, the film in which Shammi Kapoor introduced his trademark 'style', he appeared as a persistent lover who keeps alive his musical talents by belting out numerous songs to garner the attention of his lady love (Ameeta). Simultaneously, he is striving to be reunited with his lost father. Both he and Pran (the villain) claim to be the real son of one Sardar Rajpal. The ever-reliable O. P. Nayyar came up with some really breezy tunes in this movie.

In *Dil Deke Dekho*, a rework of the former film, Shammi Kapoor played a club singer, who again wants to bring together his separated parents. In between, he finds the time and the occasions for cavorting with the heroine (Asha Parekh) and for lip-syncing one song after another. This was the first film of composer Usha Khanna (one of the very few women in this field).

In *Junglee*, Shammi Kapoor emerged as a cult figure, thanks to his (rather singer Mohammed Rafi's) rambunctious YAHOO yell. (As shown in the film, this yell is powerful enough to send a boulder of snow rolling downhill!) He is initially portrayed as a rich, stern youth who refuses to smile or laugh as per his very strict mother's (Lalita Pawar) instructions. He is eventually healed of this malady by a Kashmiri damsel (Saira Banu) who helps him rediscover his true self with the warmth of her love.

In *Professor*, a hit musical comedy, Shammi Kapoor won critical acclaim for his impersonation of an elderly professor. He dons this disguise to gain entry into the household of his sweetheart (Kalpana), which is controlled by a strict spinster aunt (again Lalita Pawar) who does not allow the girls of the house to mingle with young males. But as the professor flirts with the girls, the aunt herself falls in love with him. Shankar Jaikishan's musical score in this film was studded with some exquisite melodies.

In *China Town*, Kapoor played a double role: twins separated at birth. He appears first as Shekhar, a musician in a Darjeeling club who is in love with a very wealthy heiress (Shakila). In the second role, he plays Mike, a gangster. Shekhar helps the police in nabbing Mike, whom he impersonates and befriends some members of his gang. (This technique was used in the hit film *Don*, released in 1978, with Amitabh Bachchan in the title role.) The catchy rock'n roll number *Baar Baar Dekho* ... was one of the highlights of *China Town*.

Kashmiri Ki Kali presented Shammi Kapoor as a rich bachelor in a perpetual search for ideal love, rejecting hordes of girls who have fallen for him. Eventually, his dream is fulfilled when he meets a poor flower-selling Kahmiri girl (Sharmila Tagore, who made her debut in Hindi cinema with this film). After the inevitable song-and-dance routines and after putting the villain (Pran) in his place, the hero and heroine emerge victorious. 'Rhythm king' O. P. Nayyar lived up to expectations and brought off some fabulous numbers.

In *Janwar*, set mainly in the beautiful locales of Kashmir (as also were *Junglee* and *Kashmir Ki Kali*), Shammi Kapoor (belonging to an affluent family) and the heroine (Rajshree), after a few initial spats, fall in love and seem to be heading for an idyllic paradise. But destiny intervenes and the hero is compelled to save his family honour that has been 'ruined' as a result of his elder brother (Rehman) having an affair with a poor girl (Shyama), who becomes pregnant.

In *Teesri Manzil* (a murder mystery with large dollops of humour and music thrown in), Shammi Kapoor appeared as a drummer-cum-singer in a hotel band whom the heroine (Asha Parekh) suspects to have killed her sister by forcing her to jump from the third floor (*teesri manzil*) of the hotel where he regularly performs. He eventually tracks down the real murderer on the basis of a vital clue provided by a coat button! In this film, it was composer Rahul Dev Burman who bedazzled the audiences with his boisterous numbers, belted out with verve and zest by Rafi and Asha Bhosle. *Teesri Manzil* went on to become a big hit and its songs are popular among the youth even today.

In *An Evening in Paris* (1967), a film chockfull of songs, he falls deeply in love with a rich girl (Sharmila Tagore) who has gone to France in search of 'true love', which she could not find in India. The hero pursues the heroine all over Paris, and also to Switzerland and Beirut, singing with full-throated glee. He eventually wins her love, busts a criminal gang (headed by K. N. Singh) and nabs the villain (Pran) in the climax, set amidst the awesome Niagra Falls.

Shammi Kapoor remained in the limelight in the 1960s and early 1970s through a string of films. For instance: *College Girl*

(1960, heroine Vyjayanthimala), *Singapore* (1960, heroine Padmini), *Boy Friend* (1961, heroine Madhubala), *Basant* (1962, heroine Nutan), *Dil Tera Diwana* (1962, heroine Mala Sinha), *Pyar Kiya To Darna Kya* (1963, heroine Saroja Devi), *Rajkumar* (1964, heroine Sadhana), *Badtameez* (1966, heroine Sadhana), *Laat Sahib* (1967, heroine Nutan), *Tum Se Achcha Kaun Hai* (1969, heroine Babita), *Prince* (1969, heroine Vyjayanthimala), *Sachchai* (1969, heroine Sadhana), *Pagla Kahin Ka* (1970, heroine Asha Parekh), *Jawan Mohabbat* (1971, heroine Asha Parekh), *Jane Anjane* (1971, heroine Leena Chandavarkar) and *Preetam* (1971, heroine Leena Chandavarkar).

However, during this period, two films revealed Shammi Kapoor at his sensitive best: Bhappie Sonie's *Brahmachari* (1968) and Ramesh Sippy's *Andaz* (1971). These films also proved that the actor possessed a huge reservoir of talent.

In *Brahmachari*, he appeared as a Good Samaritan who takes care of abandoned children (orphans). He is an orphan himself and knows what it is to be one. Despite facing serious financial problems, he somehow keeps up his good cheer and manages to feed, clothe, entertain and educate the large flock of children under his wing. He 'rescues' the heroine who is about to commit suicide by drowning in the sea. She has been rudely turned down by a highly affluent Pran (to whom she was betrothed during her childhood), as she comes from a poor family. The hero transforms her into a dazzling beauty and introduces her to Pran (at a ritzy restaurant), who is smitten by her (not knowing her real identity). The heroine eventually finds out that Pran is a philanderer and has had affairs with many women. The heroine gradually falls in love with the hero Shammi Kapoor. Finally, they are united and the children are thrilled. Shammi Kapoor performed magnificently, especially when he interacts with the children. The fabulous song sequences (especially the lullaby *Main Gaaoon Tum So Jaao ...*), the touching moments and the overall impact of the movie held the audiences spellbound. He bagged the *Filmfare* best actor award for this film.

In *Andaz*, Shammi Kapoor played a well-to-do widower with a schoolgoing daughter who is a student of the widowed heroine (Hema Malini), a school teacher. She has a son, a little younger than the hero's daughter. Her husband (Rajesh Khanna who appears in a cameo) has died in an accident. Shammi Kapoor and Hema Malini meet each other at a school function and are brought closer, ever so slowly, thanks to the constant efforts of the children. It was a greatly subdued Shammi Kapoor that was needed for the *Andaz* character, and he pulled off the role with finesse and underplay.

However, despite his dominant image as a 'modern' hero, Shammi Kapoor was also a major player in the classical cinema of the 1950s. He proved his mettle by convincingly playing the agonized lover in two love legends: *Laila Majnu* (1953) opposite Nutan and *Mirza Sahiban* (1957) opposite Shyama. He also brought about a refreshing change in the hero's persona in costume dramas as seen in Aspi Azad's *Gul Sanovar* (1953, his debut film opposite Shyama), *Chor Bazaar* (1954, opposite Suchitra) and *Shama Parvana* (1954, opposite Suraiya). His other films in this period included Mahesh Kaul's *Jeevan Jyoti* (1953, heroine Chand Usmani), P. N. Arora's *Rail Ka Dibba* (1954, heroine Madhubala) and actor-turned-director P. Jairaj's *Mohar* (1959, heroine Geeta Bali, his wife in real life).

In the neo-realist stream also, the young actor revealed his talent in films such as Lekhraj Bhakhri's *Thokar* (1953), Kidar Sharma's *Rangeen Raatein* (1956), K. A. Abbas's *Char Dil Char Raahen* (1959), Naresh Saigal's *Ujala* (1959) and K. N. Bansal's *Shaheed Bhagat Singh* (1963) in the title role. In *Thokar*, he was a disillusioned youth, singing the famous *nazm* penned by the legendary Urdu poet Majaaz Lucknawi (the maternal uncle of Javed Akhtar), *Aye Gham-e-dil Kya Karoon ...* sung by Talat Mehmood. In *Ujala*, a heart-rending depiction of the urban poor's miseries in the face of deprivation and street violence, he again portrayed an unemployed youth in search of his identity. In *Char Dil Char Raahen*, he made his mark as a Christian hotel chef who falls in love with a typist (Kum Kum) also coveted by the lecherous hotel owner. After the boss gets him jailed, he escapes and reaches the workers' commune where other separated Hindu and Muslim lovers have assembled to carve a new future for themselves.

***

After *Andaz*, Shammi Kapoor moved into the 'senior actor' phase. He emerged in a new avtaar as a director, his first venture being *Manoranjan* (1974). This movie was a virtual frame-by-frame remake of the rib-tickling Hollywood film *Irma La Douce* (1963), starring Jack Lemmon and Shirley MacLaine. In the Hindi version, Sanjeev Kumar was the hero (who appears as a policeman and a nawab) and Zeenat Aman the heroine (who plays a prostitute). Shammi Kapoor himself appeared in this movie as the effervescent owner of a restaurant where the women meet their prospective clients. This movie was unique in that there was no moralizing or preaching about prostitution: it was accepted for what it was (Shyam Benegal's 1983 film *Mandi* also adopted this trend).

In senior roles, Shammi Kapoor usually appeared as a bearded, paunchy, middle-aged and warm-hearted man, injecting into the narrative a touch of human concern and warmth, the way senior Balraj Sahni did in many films. He portrayed such characters in films such as *Zameer* (1975), *Parvarish* (1977), *Shalimar* (1978), *Prem Rog* (1982), *Vidhata* (1982), *Hukumat* (1987) and *Batwara* (1989). In Shammi Kapoor's 'second innings', his other notable films include *Mama Bhanja* (1977), *Betaab* (1983), *Ajooba* (1991), *Prem Granth* (1996), *Kareeb* (1998) and *Jaanam Samjha Karo* (1999).

Shammi Kapoor is one of the foremost Net users in India and is the chairman of Internet Users Community of India (IUCI).

Bharat Bhushan's Camp Followers

Mahipal (also known as Mahipal Singh), cast in the same mould as Bharat Bhushan, also had a poet-like persona and a face that looked like the archetype of Hindu gods and deities seen in calendar art. Apart from Hindu mythologies, he appeared in a number of costume dramas set in a medieval Muslim milieu, making the actor very popular in Gulf countries. His films in a way thus highlighted the ever-secular nature of our cinema.

Born in 1919 in Jodhpur (now in Rajasthan), Mahipal entered the film world in 1942 with G. P. Kapoor's *Nazrana*. He then acted in several films such as *Shankar Parvati* (1943), *Mali* (1944) and *Banwasi* (1948), which did not help him professionally. The veteran Sohrab Modi cast him in *Daulat* (1949) along with newcomer Madhubala, but this venture too failed to launch his career. It was Homi Wadia's 1950 hit *Ganesh Mahima* that changed his fortunes. Nanubhai Bhatt's *Laxmi Narayan* along with Homi Wadia's *Hanuman Patal Vijay*, both released in 1951, further helped him in consolidating his position as a key leading figure in mythologicals and costume dramas.

Mahipal – known for his roles in mythologicals and costume dramas

In these movies, he co-starred with none other than Meena Kumari, then herself a starlet. In the following year, he again paired with her in Babubhai Mistri's fantasy adventure, *Alladin Aur Jadui Chirag*. In his long career, he remained a hot favourite of Babubhai Mistri the undisputed master of the fantasy and mythological genres. The important films of this duo included *Nav Durga* (1953), *Maya Bazaar* (1958), *Sampurna Ramayan* (1961), *Kan Kan Mein Bhagwan* (1963), the musical hit *Parasmani* (1963) that launched the career of composers Laxmikant Pyarelal and *Shri Krishna Arjun Yuddha* (1971).

In Datta Dharmadhikari's *Sudarshan Chakra* (1956), *Maya Bazaar* and *Shri Krishna Arjun Yuddha*, he appeared as Lord Krishna, and in *Sampurna Ramayan*, he won critical acclaim for evoking the holy presence of Lord Rama on celluloid. He also appeared as Lord Rama in Manibhai Vyas's *Bajrang Bali* (1956). In *Tulsidas* (1954), on the other hand, he brought to life the legend of this medieval Rama devotee-poet and the creator of the epic

Ramcharitmanas. The film was jointly directed by Balachandra and Harsukh Bhatt.

Apart from these mythologicals, Mahipal also became a sought-after hero for Muslim fantasy fables. Apart from *Alladin Aur Jadui Chirag*, his other important films of this genre were Homi Wadia's *Husn Ka Chor* (1953) and *Zabak* (1961), Kedar Kapoor's *Lal Pari* (1954) and *Mast Qalandar* (1955), Rafiq Rizvi's *Karwaan* (1956) and Ramchandra Thakur's hit *Sheikh Chilli* (1956). In the last film, he gave a memorable performance as the jovial runaway prince who meets and falls in love with a princess (Shyama), also roaming in disguise to escape the treacherous army commander who has usurped her throne.

Mahipal's foray into the social genre was no less impressive. The celebrated director Ramchandra Thakur cast him in three runway hits: *Dharampatni* (1953), *Dr Z* (1956) and *Makkhee Choos* (1956). In these films the actor showcased his remarkable sense of comedy often in the crazy company of the then reigning comedy king Gope. In the hit comedy *Makkhee Choos*, Mahipal posted a very lively performance as the son of a miser (Gope), notorious in the city for his obsession for accumulating wealth and his disdain for giving money even in charity. Disgusted with his father's ways, he leaves home and becomes a theatre artiste. He joins hands with his sweetheart (Shyama) and his extremely clever but Good Samaritan maternal uncle (Jeevan) to reform his father, leading to a series of hilarious situations. Mahipal's other socials were Basant Bhatt's *Khoj* (1953) opposite Lalita Kumari and K. G. Punwani's *Madhur Milan* (1955) opposite Nigar Sultana.

The zenith of Mahipal's long career was marked by V. Shantaram's classic *Navrang* (1959), in which the heroine was Sandhya. The film was set in eighteenth-century India, when the country was witnessing the political upheaval caused by the annexation of Indian territories by the British. The film presented a twofold critique of the cultural orthodoxy that was prevalent among the Brahminical class for safeguarding purity in literature and other art forms and the emerging Western onslaught on the indigenous cultures. Divakar (Mahipal) is a poet who pens ornate, romantic poetry, fantasizing his quarrelsome wife (Sandhya) as his beloved. His verses are considered extremely vulgar by his wife, his father (a priest) and others. Despite his wife's utter disdain (who leaves him and moves to her parents' house), the poet keeps on evoking her in his love-laden poetry and songs. Eventually, he succeeds in establishing social acceptance of his 'radical poetry' when he wins the coveted title of court poet. The film is also remembered for the classical musical score by C. Ramchandra.*

By the late 1960s, Mahipal went into oblivion and, unlike many of his contemporaries, he did not appear in senior roles. He died of cardiac arrest at the ripe old age of 86 on 15 May 2005.

***

Talat Mehmood, the legendary singer, was also a worthwhile actor who appeared in as many as sixteen Bengali and Hindi films in the 1940s and 1950s. With his exceedingly good looks, aristocratic bearing and an uncanny simplicity, he looked all set to make it big as a hero. Born in Lucknow on 24 February 1924, he was a child prodigy, and started singing for All India Radio at the age of sixteen. He formally studied music at the famous Morris College in Lucknow, the

Talat Mehmood:
The silky voiced
singer-cum-actor

institution that had such alumni as fellow-singer Mukesh and music composers Roshan and Anil Biswas on its faculty. The

* There were some unique scenes in this movie. For instance, Sandhya appears as both a woman and a man in a Holi festival song sequence and in another song sequence she balances several pots (one on top of the other) on her head while performing a series of complex dance steps. This was an era when computer animation did not exist.

young singer became a national craze in 1944 with his maiden *ghazal*, *Tasveer Teri Dil Mera Behla Na Sakegi*. He then moved to Calcutta and acted (with the screen name Tapan Kumar) in several films, some of which were hits. In Bollywood, his big break as a singer came with the song *Ae Dil Mujhe Aisi Jagah Le Chal Jahan Koi Na Ho*, composed by Anil Biswas for *Arzoo* (1950, starring Dilip Kumar).

Talat made his debut in Hindi cinema with Amar Mallick's *Sampatti* (1949) in a supporting role.

A. R. Kardar introduced him as hero in *Dil-e-Nadaan* (1953). He very ably portrayed the long struggle of a talented singer striving to make a place in the world of recorded music, but his own life is devastated by an extremely neurotic wife (Shyama) who suspects him to be in love with her sister (Peace Kanwal). He starred in another eight films in the 1950s: Nitin Bose's *Waris* (1954), Lekhraj Bhakhri's *Dak Babu* (1954), Naqshab's *Raftar* (1955), Arjun Hingorani and Dharam Kumar's *Diwali Ki Raat* (1956), Dulal Guha's *Ek Gaon Ki Kahani* (1957), S. M. Yusuf's *Malik* (1958), Shahid Lateef's *Sone Ki Chidiya* (1958) and Akhtar Siraj's *Lala Rukh* (1958).

In *Waris*, Talat gave a memorable performance as the rebellious son of a zamindar who is disowned by his father for marrying a poor girl (Suraiya), forcing him to join the army during the Second World War. *Ek Gaon Ki Kahani* presented him in the role of a doctor who sets out to help the poor village folk. In *Sone Ki Chidiya*, Talat appeared in an unlikely role as an anti-hero. He plays a journalist who falls in love with a star (Nutan), an orphaned girl who makes it big in the film world. But he ditches her when he realizes that her wealth is controlled by her greedy relatives. In *Lala Rukh* (a costume drama), his last film as hero, he appeared as an indigent singer, pouring out his love for a princess (Shyama) through his heart-rending songs. This musical tragedy was based on the short story penned by the famous Hindi writer Acharya Chatursen Shastri. This film, however, was not commercially released.

By the late 1960s, Talat rapidly sank into oblivion both as singer and actor. He died on 9 May 1998. He was a recipient of the Padma Bhushan award.

**

Abhi Bhattacharya (1921–93), yet another durable actor, gained respect and admiration for his roles in both social and mythological films. While in social melodramas, like Pradeep Kumar, he evoked the stereotypical liberal upper-middle-class youth, in mythologicals, he joined the famous league of Shahu Modak, Prem Adib and Mahipal. A product of New Theatres, he made his debut as hero in 1946 with Nitin Bose's Bengali film *Nauka Dubi* (its Hindi version, *Milan* had Dilip Kumar in the lead). He arrived in Hindi cinema in 1952 with Debaki Bose's classic *Ratnadeep*, a trilingual film (Hindi/Bengali/Tamil), followed by Kartick Chattopadhyay's *Yatrik* (1952) in a supporting role. He won critical acclaim for his portrayal of the reformist school teacher in Satyen Bose's *Jagriti* and as the poor husband of an extremely beautiful wife in Bimal Roy's *Biraj Bahu*, both released in 1954. He also appeared as hero in Asit Sen's hit crime thriller *Apradhi Kaun?* (1957). His best-known performance was in Ritwik Ghatak's Bengali film *Subarnarekha* (1962), where he played the upright Ishwar Chakraborty, a refugee from East Pakistan, who seeks a new life in India after Partition.

By the mid-1950s, Bhattacharya's career moved towards mythologicals. He appeared in a plethora of films belonging to this genre, such as *Jagadguru Shankaracharya* (1955), *Ayodhyapati* (1955), *Mahabharat* (1965), *Badrinath Yatra* (1967), *Bhagwan Parshuram* (1970), *Har Har Mahadev* (1974) and *Maya Machhindra* (1975). The 1960s and 1970s saw him as one of the most durable supporting actors as seen in Hrishikesh Mukherjee's *Anuradha* (1960), Satyen Bose's *Dosti* (1964), Salil Choudhury's *Pinjre Ke Panchhi* (1966), Shakti Samanta's *Aradhana* (1969) and *Amanush* (1974) and Dulal Guha's *Dost* (1974) and *Pratiggya* (1975).

Forgotten Heroes

During its formative and classical phases, Hindi cinema enclosed in its fold many relatively unknown heroes, whose names have virtually faded from memory.

Karan Diwan (1917–79), a once-celebrated hero, stormed into the film world with two superhit films in 1944: M. Sadiq's *Ratan* and R. S. Choudhary's *Gaali*. (*Ratan* also greatly boosted the career of composer Naushad.) In *Ratan*, he won accolades for portraying the agony of a destitute lover and, in *Gaali*, he was greatly appreciated as an educated modern landlord who chooses to marry a blind young widow. His other memorable films of the 1940s include S. F. Hasnain's *Duniya* (1949), M. L. Anand's *Lahore* (1949), Kidar Sharma's *Thes* (1949), M. Sadiq's *Anmol Ratan* (1950) and AVM's *Bahar* (1951).

In the 1950s, Diwan collaborated with V. Shantaram in producing *Dahej* (1950) (opposite Jayashri) and *Teen Batti Char Raaste* (1953) (opposite Sandhya). In the first film, the protagonist leads a crusade against his greedy and cruel parents (Jayant and Lalita Pawar) as they are ill-treating his wife for not bringing enough dowry. In the second film, the hero falls in love with a poor, dark-complexioned girl who eventually becomes a singing star. It is said that the film was inspired by the early struggling years of Lata Mangeshkar. His other major movies of the 1950s were *Jalianwala Baagh Ki Jyoti* (1953), *Musafir Khana* (1955), *Jalwa* (1955), *Taqdeer* (1958) and *Madhu* (1959). He appeared fleetingly in a few films in the next two decades such as Suraj Prakash's *Aamne Saamne* (1967, hero Shashi Kapoor) and K. Shankar's *Shehzada* (1972, hero Rajesh Khanna).

Shekhar, one of the least appreciated lead actors of the 1940s and 1950s, was a master of realistic portrayal in his own right. Devoid of any extraneous histrionics, his low-key performances, often as a virtuous next-door youth, displayed an extraordinary simplicity. Being a highly reliable actor, several well-known film makers cast him in mid-budget socials. The meaningful films in his highly impressive inventory were Shobhna Samarth's *Hamari Beti* (1950) opposite Nutan, B. R. Chopra's *Chandni Chowk* (1954) opposite Meena Kumari, S. Bhagat's *Hamdard* (1953) opposite Nimmi, Shahid Lateef's *Darwaza* (1954) opposite Shyama, P. L. Santoshi's *Ha Ha Hi Hi Hu Hu* (1955), Harsukh Bhutt's *Chhote Babu* (1957) opposite Nimmi, Hrishikesh Mukherjee's *Musafir* (1957) opposite Suchitra Sen, Mahesh Bhutt's *Aakhri Dao* (1958) opposite Nutan and Rakhan's *Bank Manager* (1959) opposite Kamini Kaushal.

Another less-known hero of the 1940s and 1950s, who displayed a fairly long durability, was Suresh. Tall and handsome, he remained in the limelight for many years, collaborating with nearly all the top-notch directors and leading ladies. His films include Mohan Sinha's *1857* (1946) opposite Munawwar Sultana, A. R. Kardar's *Dulari* (1949) opposite Madhubala, Phani Majumdar's *Goonj* (1952) opposite Suraiya, A. R. Kardar's *Yasmin* (1955) opposite Vyjayanthimala and the same director's superhit *Jaadu* (1957) opposite Nalini Jaywant and Mohammed Hussain's *Aji Bas Shukriya* (1958) opposite Geeta Bali.

Rehman, one of the most durable supporting actors in Hindi cinema, was also a celebrated hero of his times. However, his contribution as hero has been less appreciated, given his high visibility in supporting roles in the latter part of his career. His major films as hero include *Nargis* (1946) and *Roomal* (1949), both opposite Nargis, *Badi Bahen* (1949) opposite Suraiya, *Paras* (1949) and *Pardes* (1950), both opposite Madhubala, *Pyar Ki Manzil* (1950) opposite Munawwar Sultana and *Pyase Nain* (1954) opposite Nimmi.

Sheikh Mukhtar, the tall and towering actor with a rough-hewn face and an epitome of sheer physical strength combined with large-heartedness, made his presence felt in several films of the formative and classical periods of Hindi cinema. A talent scouted by none other than Mehboob Khan during his stint at Sagar Movietone in the 1930s, Sheikh Mukhtar appeared in the master's two highly acclaimed works: *Bahen* (1941) and *Roti*

(1942). In the first film, he made his mark as an overpossessive brother and in the second as the innocent tribal, who, along with Sitara (the heroine), ventures into the decadent urban milieu of the filthy rich. He also made his mark in S. Khalil's *Nai Zindagi* (1943), Wajahat Mirza Changezi's classic *Shahenshah Babar* (1944), Safdar Mirza's *Bhukh* (1947) and Harish's *Toote Tare* (1948) and *Dada* (1949).

In the 1950s and 1960s, Mukhtar appeared in small-budget films, with his trademark image as a good-hearted toughie. These films include *Ustad Pedro* (1951), *Mangu* (1954), *Do Mastane* (1958), *Qaidi No. 911* (1959), *Bada Admi* (1961), *Tel Malish Boot Polish* (1962), *Ustadon Ke Ustad* (1963), *Hum Sab Ustad Hain* (1965), *Thakar Jarnail Singh* (1966) and *Raat Andheri Thi* (1967). His comic pairing with the short-statured Mukhri was very popular in the 1950s.

In the 1950s, Mukhtar turned producer with the superhit *Do Ustad* (1959, hero Raj Kapoor) in which he came up with a powerful performance as an anti-hero. In *Noorjehan* (1968), also produced by him, he appeared in the role of Sher Khan, the first husband of the Mughal queen (played by Meena Kumari) before her marriage to Emperor Jehangir.

Sajjan, the celebrated mimic artist and 'thinker' actor, was also a strong contender for top-notch stardom in the 1950s, but his career as hero could not attain its full glory. He appeared in the lead in many noteworthy films of the classical era such as *Muqaddar* (1950) opposite Nalini Jaywant, *Sheesha* (1952) opposite Nargis, *Toofan* (1954) opposite Pratima Devi and Munawwar Sultana, *Kasturi* (1954) opposite Nimmi, *Do Dulhe* (1955) opposite Shyama, *Lagan* (1955) opposite Nalini Jaywant and *Bahana* (1960) opposite Meena Kumari. He then seamlessly switched over to playing a character actor, or, at times, a villain. In this avtaar he acted in numerous films, the major ones being *Kabuliwala* (1961), *Ashirwaad* (1968), *Johny Mera Naam* (1970), *Pagla Kahin Ka* (1970) and *Dostana* (1980).

Manohar Desai was another actor whose forte was mythological films and fantasy movies. His prominent ventures include *Gunasundari* (1948), *Sati Ansuya* (1956), *Janam Janam Ke Phere* (1957) and *Chandramukhi* (1960).

Chandrashekhar (born in 1922) is another one of the most enduring Bollywood actors. His career, spaning over five decades, makes for fascinating reading. He is perhaps the only cine personality who has been a hero of some standing and a highly respected character artiste who has readily opted for minor roles (even during his best years). He has ventured into other fields as well. He has variously been a producer-director and has also worked as an assistant director, an assistant editor and even as a production assistant and a visual effects specialist. He is also an exponent of Western dance. Above all, he has been associated with the cine artistes' movement, leading a lifelong crusade for their rights.

Chandrashekhar made his debut in a stellar role in Chaturbhuj Doshi's 1954 film *Aurat Teri Yehi Kahani*. He made his mark as hero in Tara Harish's musical hit (Chitragupta was the composer) *Kali Topi Lal Rumal* (1959) as a street-smart toughie who plays a mouth organ to woo the haughty heroine (Shakila). He was also in the lead in the same director's *Nachhe Nagin Baaje Been* (1960), Mohammed Hussain's *Main Hoon Aladdin* (1965) and Daljit Krishna's *Namaste Ji* (1965). In *Sapan Suhane* (1961), he appeared as the spoilt younger brother of Balraj Sahni and in *Tel Malish Boot Polish* (1961) as the younger brother of the low-caste Sheikh Mukhtar who provides him college education by taking up shoe polishing and massaging in the streets.

Chandrashekhar ventured into film direction with two musicals *Cha Cha Cha* (1964) and *Street Singer* (1966), co-starring with Helen and Sarita, respectively.

Cha Cha Cha, a musical, set a new trend in Indian cinema as the first film to showcase the arrival of the emerging Western dance genre. Both Chandrashekhar and Helen exhibited their acumen in capturing the essence of this dance style. The phenomenal music score was by a relatively obscure composer Iqbal Qureshi, who utilized Mohammed Rafi's vocal range to the maximum. *Street Singer*, unfortunately, did not make any waves.

Apart from his occasional casting as hero, Chandrashekhar in the 1950s and 1960s made his presence felt in a variety of supporting roles as well as villainous roles as in *Baradari* (1955), *Basant Bahar* (1956), *Baghi Sipahi* (1958), *Barsaat Ki Raat* (1960), *Angulimal* (1960) and *Dooj Ka Chand* (1964). However, from the 1970s onwards, he kept appearing only in minor roles in films like *Kati Patang* (1970), *Anamika* (1973), *Karamyogi* (1978), *Shakti* (1982), *Disco Dancer* (1983), *Sharabi* (1984), *Dance Dance* (1987), *Gharwali Baharwali* (1988), *Krodh* (1990), *Ghar Ki Izzat* (1994) and *Qahar* (1997). He announced his retirement from films in 2000 after appearing in *Khauff*.

As a member of film crews, the veteran actor was the assistant director for all Gulzar's 1970s films: *Koshish* (1972), *Parichay* (1972), *Achanak* (1973), *Aandhi* (1975) and *Mausam* (1975). In Sunil Dutt's *Reshma Aur Shera* (1971), he worked as the assistant editor and for *Khakee* (2004) as the visual effects compositing artist. Recently the Cine and TV Artistes' Association (CINTAA) has urged the Indian Government to honour him with the Dadasaheb Phalke Award.

From the south came Ranjan, the most favourite hero of director S. S. Vasan. He enthralled the Hindi film audiences as the swashbuckling hero in *Nishan* (1949) and *Mangala* (1950), and as the scheming villian in *Chandralekha* (1948), all directed by his mentor. In Babubhai Mistri's *Madari* (1959), he again donned the hero's mantle.

Gemini Ganesan, the father of actress Rekha, in contrast, introduced in the Hindi film hero's persona a refreshing touch of a well-groomed sophisticated South Indian youth as seen in superhits such as *Devta* (1956), *Miss Mary* (1957) and *Raaj Tilak* (1958).

Notes and References

1.   Ashish Rajadhyaksha and Paul Willemen, *Encyclopedia of Indian Cinema*, London: British Film Institute and New Delhi: Oxford University Press, 1994.

Appendix 1

K. L. Saigal: Select Filmography

1. **1932: Mohabbat Ke Ansu**
   B: New Theatres, Calcutta
   D: Premankur Atorthy
   M: Rai Chand Boral
   C: K. L. Saigal, Akhatri Moradabadi, Hussain Sadiqi, Ansari, Mahjabeen

2. **1932: Zinda Lash**
   B: New Theatres, Calcutta
   D: Premankur Atorthy
   M: Rai Chand Boral
   C: K. L. Saigal, Hafizji, Hussain Sadiqi, Ansari, Mahjabeen, Rani, Ali Mir, Kapoor

3. **1932: Subah Ka Sitara**
   B: New Theatres, Calcutta
   D: Nitin Bose
   M: Rai Chand Boral
   C: K. L. Saigal, Ratanbai, Izhaar Hussain Sadiqi, Hamid, Ansari, Ali Mir

4. **1933: Puran Bhakt**
   B: New Theatres, Calcutta
   D: Debaki Bose
   M: Rai Chand Boral
   C: Kumar, Anwari, K. C. Dey, Tara, Uma Devi, K. L. Saigal, Hussain Sadiqi

B: Banner   D: Director   M: Music director/s   C: Cast   L: Lyricist (given wherever available)

5. **1933: Rajrani Meera**
    B: New Theatres, Calcutta
    D: Debaki Bose
    M: Rai Chand Boral
    C: Durga Khote, Prithviraj Kapoor, Pahadi Sanyal, Rattanbai,
        K. L. Saigal, Hussain Sadiqi, Ansari

6. **1934: Chandidas**
    B: New Theatres, Calcutta
    D: Nitin Bose
    M: Rai Chand Boral
    C: K. L. Saigal, Uma Shashi, Pahadi Sanyal, M. Nawab,
        Ansari, Ansaribai
    L: Aga Hashr Kashmiri

7. **1934: Daku Mansoor**
    B: New Theatres, Calcutta
    D: Nitin Bose
    M: Rai Chand Boral
    C: Prithviraj Kapoor, Pahadi Sanyal, K. L. Saigal, Uma Shashi,
        Husn Bano

8. **1934: Rooplekha**
    B: New Theatres, Calcutta
    D: P. C. Barua
    M: Rai Chand Boral
    C: Rattanbai, Pahadi Sanyal, Noor Mohammed, K. L. Saigal
    L: Bani Kumar

9. **1935: Devdas**
    B: New Theatres, Calcutta
    D: P. C. Barua
    M: Rai Chand Boral
    C: K. L. Saigal, Jamuna, K. C. Dey, Kshertrabala, Rajkumari,
        Kidar Sharma
    L: Kidar Sharma

10. **1935: Kaarwaan-e-Hayat**
    B: New Theatres, Calcutta
    D: Premankur Atorthy and Hemchandra Chunder
    M: Mihirkiran Bhattacharya
    C: K. L. Saigal, Rajkumari, Pahadi Sanyal, Rattanbai, Shyama
        Zutshi, M. Nawab, Hamid

11. **1936: Pujarin**
    B: International Filmcraft, Calcutta
    D: Prafulla Roy
    M: Timir Baran
    C: K. L. Saigal, Chandra, Pahadi Sanyal, Rajkumari,
        M. Nawab, K. C. Dey, Kidar Sharma

12. **1936: Crorepati**
    B: New Theatres, Calcutta
    D: Hemchandra Chunder
    M: Rai Chand Boral and Pankaj Mullick
    C: K. L. Saigal, Molina, Pahadi Sanyal, M. Nawab, Kidar
        Sharma, Jagdish Sethi, Rajkumari, Amar Mullick, Nemo,
        Sardar Akhtar, Trilok Kapoor
    L: Kidar Sharma

13. **1937: President/Didi**
    B: New Theatres, Calcutta
    D: Nitin Bose
    M: Rai Chand Boral and Pankaj Mullick
    C: K. L. Saigal, Leela Desai, Kamlesh Kumari, Devbala,
        Prithviraj Kapoor, Prabha, Jagdish Sethi

14. **1938: Dharti Mata/Desher Mati**
    B: New Theatres, Calcutta
    D: Nitin Bose
    M: Pankaj Mullick
    C: K. L. Saigal, K. C. Dey, Uma Shashi, Pankaj Mullick,
        Shyam Laha, Durga Das, Prithviraj Kapoor
    L: Pandit Sudarshan

15. **1938: Street Singer/Saathi**
    B: New Theatres, Calcutta
    D: Phani Majumdar
    M: Rai Chand Boral
    C: K. L. Saigal, Kanan Devi, Boken Chatto, Rekha, Jagdish, Bikram Kapoor
    L: Arzoo Lucknavi

16. **1938: Dushman/Jiban Maran**
    B: New Theatres, Calcutta
    D: Nitin Bose
    M: Pankaj Mullick
    C: K. L. Saigal, Leela Desai, Najam, Shiraz Farooque, Nemo, Devbala
    L: Arzoo Lucknavi

17. **1940: Zindagi**
    B: New Theatres, Calcutta
    D: P. C. Barua
    M: Pankaj Mullick
    C: K. L. Saigal, Pahadi Sanyal, Ashalata, Jamuna, Shyam Laha, Nemo, Sitara Devi
    L: Kidar Sharma, Arzoo Lucknavi

18. **1941: Lagan/Parichay**
    B: New Theatres, Calcutta
    D: Nitin Bose
    M: Rai Chand Boral
    C: K. L. Saigal, Kanan Devi, Naresh Bose, Nawab, Jagdish
    L: Arzoo Lucknavi

19. **1942: Bhakta Surdas**
    B: Ranjit Movietone, Bombay
    D: Chaturbhuj Doshi
    M: Gyan Dutt
    C: K. L. Saigal, Khurshid, Monika Desai, Kesarbai, Narendra
    L: D. N. Madhok

20. **1943: Tansen**
    B: Ranjit Movietone, Bombay
    D: Jayant Desai
    M: Khemchand Prakash
    C: K. L. Saigal, Khurshid, Mubarak, Nagendra, Kamladevi
        Chatterjee, Kesari, Bhagvan Das
    L: Pandit Indra, D. N. Madhok

21. **1944: Bhanwra**
    B: Ranjit Movietone, Bombay
    D: Kidar Sharma
    M: Khemchand Prakash
    C: K. L. Saigal, Arun, Kamladevi Chatterjee, Monika Desai,
        Kesari, Yakub
    L: Pandit Indra, Kidar Sharma, Swami Ramanand

22. **1944: Meri Bahen/My Sister**
    B: New Theatres, Calcutta
    D: Hemchandra Chunder
    M: Pankaj Mullick
    C: K. L. Saigal, Sumitra Devi, Nawab, Akhtar Jahan, Heeralal,
        Chandrawati
    L: Pandit Bhushan

23. **1945: Kurukshetra**
    B: Unity Productions, Calcutta
    D: Rameshwar Sharma
    M: Pandit Ganpat Rao
    C: K. L. Saigal, Shamali, Nawab, Kashmiri, Radharani, Ajit, Tara
    L: Jamil Mazhari

24. **1945: Tadbir**
    B: Jayant Desai Productions, Bombay
    D: Jayant Desai
    M: Lal Mahomed
    C: K. L. Saigal, Suraiya, Mubarak, Jillo, Rehana,
        Rewashankar Marwadi, Shashi Kapoor
    L: Swami Ramanand

25. **1946: Omar Khayyam**
    B: Murari Pictures, Bombay
    D: Mohan Sinha
    M: Lal Mahomed
    C: K. L. Saigal, Suraiya, Wasti, Madan Puri, Benjemin
    L: Dr Safdar 'Aah'

23. **1946: Shahjehan**
    B: Kardar Productions, Bombay
    D: A. R. Kardar
    M: Naushad Ali
    C: K. L. Saigal, Kanwar, Ragini, Jairaj, Nasreen, Anwari,
        Kesarbai
    L: Majrooh Sultanpuri, Khumar Barabankavi

27. **1947: Parwana**
    B: Jeet Productions, Bombay
    D: J. K. Nanda
    M: Khurshid Anwar
    C: K. L. Saigal, Suraiya, Najma, K. N. Singh
    L: D. N. Madhok

Source: Compiled from (1) Har Mandir Singh 'Hamraaz', *Hindi Film Geet Kosh*, Vol. I (1931–40), Vol. II (1941–50), Vol. III (1951–60) and Vol. IV (1961–70), Kanpur: published by Satinder Kaur, 1980 and (2) Ashish Rajadhyaksha and Paul Willemen, *Encyclopedia of Indian Cinema*, London: British Film Institute, and New Delhi: Oxford University Press, 1994.

Dilip Kumar: Filmography

1. Jwar Bhata (1944)

Type of film:	Social, B&W
Banner:	Bombay Talkies
Cast:	Mridula, Shamim, Agha Jaan, Dilip Kumar, P. F. Pithawala, K. N. Singh, Arun Kumar, Bikram Kapoor, Jagannath Arora, Naseem Lodhi, C. J. Pande, Khalil, Mumtaz Ali
Director:	Amiya Chakravarty
Story/script/ dialogues:	Amiya Chakravarty (story), Bhagwati Charan Verma (dialogues)
Music director:	Anil Biswas
Lyricist:	Narendra Sharma
Cinematographer:	R. D. Mathur

2. Pratima (1945)

Type of film:	Social, B&W
Banner:	Bombay Talkies
Cast:	Dilip Kumar, Swarnalata, Jyoti, Mumtaz Ali, Mukhri, Zebunissa, Shah Nawaz
Director:	P. Jairaj
Music director:	Arun Kumar
Lyricist:	Narendra Sharma

3. Milan/Nauka Dubi (1946)

Type of film:	Social, B&W
Banner:	Bombay Talkies
Cast:	Dilip Kumar, Ranjana, Meera Misra, Pahadi Sanyal, Moni Chatterjee, Shyam Laha
Director:	Nitin Bose

Story/script/ dialogues:	Based on Rabindranath Tagore's novel, *Nauka Dubi*, Sadhanakanta Das (script), Bhagwati Charan Verma (dialogues)
Music director:	Anil Biswas
Lyricists:	Arzoo Lucknavi , P. L. Santoshi
Cinematographer:	Radhu Karmakar

4. Jugnu (1947)

Type of flm:	Social, B&W
Banner:	Shaukat Art Productions
Cast:	Noorjehan, Dilip Kumar, Ghulam Mohammed, Sulochana, Latika, Praveen, Shashikala, Mohammed Rafi
Director:	Shaukat Hussain Rizvi
Music director:	Firoz Nizami
Lyricists:	M. G. Adib, Asghar Sarhadi, Shakeel Badayuni

5. Anokha Pyar (1948)

Type of film:	Social, B&W
Banner:	Ambika Films
Cast:	Dilip Kumar, Nargis, Nalini Jaywant, Sankatha Prasad, Mukhri, Kesarbai, Uma Dutt, Habib, Shiekh, Munshi Munakka
Director:	M. I. Dharamsey
Music director:	Anil Biswas
Lyricists:	Zia Sarhadi, Bahzaad Lucknawi, Gopal Singh Nepali, Shams Azimabadi

6. Ghar Ki Izzat (1948)

Type of film:	Social, B&W
Banner:	Murli Movietone
Cast:	Mumtaz Shanti, Dilip Kumar, Manorama, Jeevan, Dixit, Suleman, Gulab, Gope
Director:	Ram Daryani
Story/script/ dialogues:	K. S. Daryani (story), I. C. Kapoor (dialogues)
Music director:	Pandit Gobindram
Lyricist:	I. C. Kapoor
Cinematographer:	Kumar Jaywant

7. Nadiya Ke Paar (1948)

Type of film:	Social, B&W
Banner:	Filmistan
Cast:	Kamini Kaushal, Dilip Kumar, Sushila Sahu, Ramesh Gupta, David, Maya Bannerji, Gulab, S. L. Puri, Hari Shivdasani, Samson, Kanta Kumari, Satyanarayana, Tiwari, Ranibala, Anant Prabhu
Director:	Kishore Sahu
Music director:	C. Ramachandra
Lyricist:	Moti

8. Mela (1948)

Type of film:	Social, B&W
Banner:	Wadia Films Ltd
Cast:	Nargis, Dilip Kumar, Jeevan, Amar, Roop Kamal, Abbas, Allauddin, Chandabai, Khalil, Noorjehan, Baby Zubeida
Director:	S. U. Sunny
Music director:	Naushad
Lyricist:	Shakeel Badayuni

9. Shaheed (1948)

Type of film:	Social/patriotic, B&W
Banner:	Filmistan
Cast:	Kamini Kaushal, Dilip Kumar, Chandramohan, Leela Chitnis, V. H. Desai, S. L Puri, Ram Singh, Prabhu Dayal, Raj Adib, Shashi Kapoor
Director:	Ramesh Sehgal
Story/script/ dialogues:	Azm Bazidpuri
Music director:	Ghulam Haider
Lyricists:	Raja Mehdi Ali Khan, Qamar Jalalabadi

10. Andaz (1949)

Type of film:	Social, B&W
Banner:	Mehboob Productions
Cast:	Dilip Kumar, Nargis, Raj Kapoor, Cuckoo, V. H. Desai, Sapru, Murad, Anwaribai, Amir Banu, Jamshedji

Director: Mehboob Khan
Story/script/   Shams Lucknawi (story)
   dialogues: S. Ali Raza (script)
Music director: Naushad
Lyricist: Majrooh Sultanpuri
Cinematographer: Fardoon Irani

11. Shabnam (1949)

Type of film: Social, B&W
Banner: Filmistan
Cast: Dillip Kumar, Kamini Kaushal, Jeevan, Paro,
                       Mubarak, Rajender Singh, Haroon, Shyama,
                       Cuckoo
Director: Bibhuti Mitra
Story/script/   Helen Devi (story), Bibhuti Mitra (script), Qamar
   dialogues: Jalalabadi (dialogues)
Music director: Sachin Dev Burman
Lyricist: Qamar Jalalabadi
Cinematographer: Marshall Braganza

12. Arzoo (1950)

Type of film: Social, B&W
Banner: Indian National Pictures
Cast: Dilip Kumar, Kamini Kaushal, Gope, Cuckoo,
                       Arif, Shashikala, Seeta Bose, Neelam, Khan,
                       Chandabai, Ram Shastri, Hamid, Kamalakar
Director: Shahid Lateef
Story/script/
   dialogues: Shahid Lateef
Music director: Anil Biswas
Lyricists: Prem Dhawan, Majrooh Sultanpuri, Jan Nisaar
                       Akhtar

13. Babul (1950)

Type of film: Social, B&W
Banner: S. U. Sunny Art Productions
Cast: Nargis, Dilip Kumar, Munawwar Sultana, Amar,
                       A. Shah, Janakidas, H. Pahadi, Vinod Ismail,
                       Jugnu, Chandabala, Seema, Meher, Rajbala,
                       Khurshid

Director:	S. U. Sunny
Story/script/ dialogues:	Azm Bazidpuri (story)
Music director:	Naushad
Lyricist:	Shakeel Badayuni
Cinematographer:	Fali Mistry

14. Jogan (1950)

Type of film	Social, B&W
Banner:	Ranjit Movietone
Cast:	Nargis, Dilip Kumar, Pratima Devi, Pesi Patel, Purnima, Baby Tabassum, Anwari, Ramesh Thakur, Darpan, Rajendra Kumar
Director:	Kidar Sharma
Story/script/ dialogues:	Kidar Sharma
Music director:	Bulo C. Rani
Lyricists:	Meerabai, Kidar Sharma, Pandit Indra, Butaram Sharma, Himmatrai Sharma
Cinematographer:	D. C. Mehta

15. Hulchal (1951)

Type of film:	Social, B&W
Banner:	K. Asif Productions
Cast:	Dilip Kumar, Nargis, Yakub, Jeevan, Sitara Devi, K. N. Singh, Balraj Sahni, Cuckoo, Geeta Nizami, Faizee
Director:	S. K. Ojha
Music directors:	Sajjad Husain and Mohammed Shafi
Lyricist:	Khumar Barabankvi

16. Tarana (1951)

Type of film:	Social, B&W
Banner:	Krishan Movietone
Cast:	Madhubala, Dilip Kumar, Shyama, Kumar, Jeevan, Gulab, Devaskar, Bikram Kapoor, Girdhari, Chandu, Gope
Director:	Ram Daryani
Music director:	Anil Biswas
Lyricists:	Prem Dhawan, Kaif Irfani, D. N. Madhok

17. Deedar (1951)

Type of Film:	Social, B&W
Banner:	Filmkar Productions
Cast:	Dilip Kumar, Nargis, Ashok Kumar, Nimmi, Baby Tabassum, Murad, Jal Merchant, Parikhit, Baby Anwari, Niharika Devi, Uma Shashi, Surender, Agha Mehraj, Yakub
Director:	Nitin Bose
Story/script/ dialogues:	Azm Bazidpuri
Music director:	Naushad
Lyricist:	Shakeel Badayuni
Cinematographer:	Dilip Gupta

18. Sangdil (1952)

Type of film:	Social, B&W
Banner:	Talwar Films Ltd
Cast:	Dilip Kumar, Madhubala, Leela Chitnis, Pratima Devi, Shammi
Director:	R. C. Talwar
Music director:	Sajjad Husain
Lyricist:	Rajinder Kishen

19. Aan (1952)

Type of film:	Costume drama, colour
Banner:	Mehboob Productions
Cast:	Dilip Kumar, Nimmi, Nadira, Premnath, Mukhri, Sheela Naik, Murad, Cuckoo, Abdul, Agha Mehraj, Nilambi, Amirbano
Director:	Mehboob Khan
Story/script/ dialogues:	R. S. Choudhary (script), S. Ali Raza (dialogues)
Music director:	Naushad
Lyricist:	Shakeel Badayuni
Cinematographer:	Fardoon Irani

20. Daag (1952)

Type of film:	Social, B&W
Banner:	Mars and Movies
Cast:	Dilip Kumar, Nimmi, Usha Kiron, Lalita Pawar,

	Kanahiyalal, Jawahar Kaul, Leela Mishra,
	Chandrashekhar, Krishankant
Director:	Amiya Chakravarty
Story/script/	
dialogues:	Amiya Chakravarty and Rajendra Shankar (story),
	Rajender Singh Bedi (dialogues)
Music directors:	Shankar Jaikishan
Lyricists:	Shailendra, Hasrat Jaipuri
Cinematographer:	V. Baba Saheb

21. Footpath (1953)

Type of film:	Social, B&W
Banner:	Ranjit Movietone
Cast:	Dilip Kumar, Meena Kumari, Anwar Hussain, Ramesh Thapar, Kuldip Kaur, Achala Sachdev, Ramesh Thakur, Akhtar, P. Kailash, Janakidas, Maruti, Sumati Lajmi
Director:	Zia Sarhadi
Story/script/	
dialogues:	Zia Sarhadi
Music director:	Khayyam
Lyricists:	Majrooh Sultanpuri and Ali Sardar Jafri

22. Shikast (1953)

Type of film:	Social, B&W
Banner:	Asha Deep
Cast:	Dilip Kumar, Nalini Jaywant, Master Kapoor, Om Prakash, Durga Khote, K. N. Singh, Leela Mishra, Shamlal, Hemawati, Shambu Mitra
Director:	Ramesh Sehgal
Music directors:	Shankar Jaikishan
Lyricists:	Shailendra, Hasrat Jaipuri

23. Amar (1954)

Type of film:	Social, B&W
Banner:	Mehboob Productions
Cast:	Madhubala, Nimmi, Dilip Kumar, Jayant, Ulhas, Mukhri, Husn Bano, Murad, Shakeel Nomani
Director:	Mehboob Khan

Story/script/
  dialogues: S. Ali Raza, Mehrish, S. K. Kalla, B. S. W. Ramaiah
                     (story)
                     S. Ali Raza, Mehrish, S. K. Kalla, B. S. W.
                     Ramaiah, Agha Jani Kashmiri (dialogues)
Music director: Naushad
Lyricist: Shakeel Badayuni
Cinematographer: Fardoon Irani

24. Azaad (1955)
Type of Film: Costume drama, B&W
Banner: Pakshiraja Studios
Cast: Dilip Kumar, Meena Kumari, Pran, Om Prakash,
                    S. Nazir, Badri Prasad, Raj Mehra, Randhir,
                    Achala Sachdev, Murad, Shammi, Deepa, Sai,
                    Subbalakshmi
Director: S. M. S. Naidu
Story/script/
  dialogues: Namakkal (story), Rajinder Kishen (dialogues)
Music director: C. Ramchandra
Lyricist: Rajinder Kishen
Cinematographer: Sailen Bose

25. Devdas (1955)
Type of film: Social, B&W
Banner: Bimal Roy Productions
Cast: Dilip Kumar, Vyjayanthimala, Suchitra Sen,
                    Motilal, Nazir Hussain, Kanhaiyalal, Pran
Director: Bimal Roy
Story/script/
  dialogues: Based on Saratchandra Chatterjee's novel
                     Nabendu Ghosh (script)
                     Rajender Singh Bedi (dialogues)
Music director: Sachin Dev Burman
Lyricist: Sahir Ludhianvi
Cinematographer: Kamal Bose

26. Insaniyat (1955)
Type of film: Costume drama, B&W
Banner: Gemini Pictures

Cast: Dilip Kumar, Dev Anand, Bina Rai, Vijayalakshmi,
                          Jayant, Jairaj, Shobhna Samarth, Kumar, Badri
                          Prasad, Agha, Zippy (chimpanzee), Mohana,
                          Ishwar Lal
Director: S. S. Vasan
Story/script/
  dialogues: Gemini Story Department
Music director: C. Ramchandra
Lyricist: Rajinder Kishen

27. Udan Khatola (1955)

Type of film: Costume drama, B&W
Banner: Sunny Art Productions
Cast: Dilip Kumar, Nimmi, Jeevan, Surya Kumari, Agha,
                          Nawab, Roopmala, Tuntun
Director: S. U. Sunny
Story/script/
  dialogues: Azm Bazidpuri
Music director: Naushad (also producer)
Lyricist: Shakeel Badayuni
Cinematographer: Jal Mistry

28. Musafir (1957)

Type of film: Social, B&W
Banner: Film Group
Cast: Suchitra Sen, Dilip Kumar, Kishore Kumar,
                          Shekhar, Usha Kiron, Durga Khote, Baby Naaz,
                          David, Daisy Irani, Bipin Gupta, Rashid Khan,
                          Nazir Hussian, Rajlakshmi, Mohan Choti, Nirupa
                          Roy
Director: Hrishikesh Mukherjee
Story/script/
  dialogues: Hrishikesh Mukherjee (story)
                          Hrishikesh Mukherjee and Ritwik Ghatak
                          (script)
                          Rajender Singh Bedi (dialogues)
Music director: Salil Choudhury
Lyricist: Shailendra
Cinematographer: Kamal Bose

29. Naya Daur (1957)

Type of film:	Social, B&W (the film was rereleased in colour after 50 years, i.e., on 3 August 2007)
Banner:	B. R. Films, Bombay
Cast:	Dilip Kumar, Vyjayanthimala, Ajit, Chand Usmani, Jeevan, Manmohan Krishna, Nazir Hussain, Leela Chitnis, Johnny Walker, Partima Devi, Daisy Irani, S. N. Bannerji, S. Nazir, Radhakishan, Kum Kum, Minoo Mumtaz
Director:	B. R. Chopra
Story/script/ dialogues:	Akhtar Mirza (story), Kamil Rashid (dialogues)
Music director:	O. P. Nayyar
Lyricist:	Sahir Ludhianvi
Cinematographer:	M. N. Malhotra

30. Madhumati (1958)

Type of film:	Social, B&W
Banner:	Bimal Roy Productions
Cast:	Dilip Kumar, Vyjayanthimala, Johnny Walker, Pran, Jayant, Tarun Bose, Tiwari, Mishra, Baij Sharma, Bhudo Advani
Director:	Bimal Roy
Story/script/ dialogues:	Ritwik Ghatak (story), Rajender Singh Bedi (dialogues)
Music director:	Salil Choudhury
Lyricist:	Shailendra
Cinematographer:	Dilip Gupta

31. Yahudi (1958)

Type of film:	Costume drama, B&W
Banner:	Bombay Films
Cast:	Sohrab Modi, Dilip Kumar, Meena Kumari, Nigar Sultana, Nazir Hussain, Murad, Anwar Hussain, Minoo Mumtaz, Tiwari, Bikram Kapoor, Baby Naaz, Romi, Helen, Cuckoo, Kamala Laxman
Director:	Bimal Roy

Story/script/   Based on Aga Hashr Kashmiri's play *Yahudi Ki*
  dialogues: *Ladki*
                 Nabendu Ghosh (script),
                 Wajahat Mirza (dialogues)
Music directors: Shankar Jaikishan
Lyricists: Shailendra, Hasrat Jaipuri
Cinematographer: Dilip Gupta

32. Paigham (1959)

Type of film: Social, B&W
Banner: Gemini Films
Cast: Dilip Kumar, Vyjayanthimala, Raaj Kumar,
                 B. Saroja Devi, Pandari Bai, Motilal, Johnny
                 Walker, Minoo Mumtaz, Vasundhra Devi,
                 Pratima Devi, Banerjee, Shivraj, Ishwar Lal, Amar
Director: S. S. Vasan
Story/script/
  dialogues: Gemini Story Department
Music director: C. Ramchandra
Lyricist: Pradeep

33. Mughal-e-Azam (1960)

Type of film: Historical, partly in B&W and partly in colour
                 (the film was rereleased fully in colour in late
                 2004)
Banner: Sterling Investment Corporation
Cast: Prithviraj Kapoor, Dilip Kumar, Madhubala,
                 Durga Khote, Nigar Sultana, Ajit, Kumar, Murad,
                 Jilloo, Vijayalakshmi, S. Nazir, Surendra, Gopi
                 Krishna, Jalal Agha, Tabassum, Johnny Walker
Director: K. Asif
Story/script/
  dialogues: K. Asif and Amanullah (script), Amanullah,
                 Kamal Amrohi, Ehsan Rizvi, Wajahat Mirza
                 (dialogues)
Music director: Naushad
Lyricist: Shakeel Badayuni
Cinematographer: R. D. Mathur

34. Kohinoor (1960)

Type of film:	Costume drama, B&W
Banner:	Republic Films Corporation
Cast:	Dilip Kumar, Meena Kumari, Jeevan, Kum Kum, Mukhri, Kumar, Leela Chitnis, S. Nazir, Wasi Khan, Azim, Master Nissar, Tuntun, Rajan Kapoor
Director:	S. U. Sunny
Music director:	Naushad
Lyricist:	Shakeel Badayuni
Cinematographer:	V. Baba Saheb

35. Ganga Jumna (1961)

Type of film:	Social, colour
Banner:	Citizen's Films
Cast:	Dilip Kumar, Vyjayanthimala, Nasir Khan, Azra, Kanhaiyalal, Anwar Hussain, Nazir Hussain, S. Nazir, Leela Chitnis, Praveen Paul, Helen, Husn Bano, Ranjit Sud, Khwaja Sabir, Amar, Bihari, Haroon, Narbada Shankar, Fazlu, Ram Kumar, Akashdeep, Baby Aruna, Baby Naaz
Director:	Nitin Bose
Story/script/ dialogues:	Dilip Kumar (story) Wajahat Mirza (dialogue)
Music director:	Naushad
Lyricist:	Shakeel Badayuni
Cinematographer:	V. Baba Saheb

36. Leader (1964)

Type of film:	Social, colour
Banner:	S.M.F. Syndicate, Bombay
Cast:	Dilip Kumar, Vyjayanthimala, Jayant, Motilal, Nazir Hussain, Sapru, Hiralal, Amar, Janakidas, P. Kailash, Jagdish Sethi, Leela Mishra, Marlin, Madhumati
Director:	Ram Mukherji
Story/script/ dialogues:	Dilip Kumar (story)
Music director:	Naushad
Lyricist:	Shakeel Badayuni

37. Dil Diya Dard Liya (1966)
Type of film: Social, colour
Banner: Kay Productions
Cast: Dilip Kumar, Waheeda Rehman, Pran, Johnny
                      Walker, Rehman, Shyama, Sajjan, Rani, S. Nazir,
                      Sapru, Amar, Dulari
Director: A. R. Kardar
Story/script/
  dialogues: Kay Productions Story Department
                      Kaushal Bharti (dialogues)
Music director: Naushad
Lyricist: Shakeel Badayuni
Cinematographer: Dwarka Divecha

38. Paari (1966) (Bengali)/Anokha Milan (1972) (Hindi)
Type of film: Social
Cast: Dilip Kumar, Pranoti, Abhi Bhattacharya, Dilip
                      Roy, Keshto Mukherjee, Dharmendra (guest
                      appearance)
Director: Jagannath Chatterjee
Music director: Salil Choudhury
Lyricist: Shailendra

39. Ram Aur Shyam (1967) (double role)
Type of film: Social, colour
Banner: Vijaya International, Madras
Cast: Dilip Kumar, Waheeda Rehman, Mumtaz, Pran,
                      Nirupa Roy, Kanhaiyalal, Nazir Hussain,
                      Zebunissa, Baby Farida
Director: Chanakya
Story/script/
  dialogues: D. V. Narasaraju (story)
Music director: Naushad
Lyricist: Shakeel Badayuni
Cinematographer: Marcus Bartley

40. Aadmi (1968)
Type of film: Social, colour
Banner: P. S. V. Films

Cast:`	Dilip Kumar, Waheeda Rehman, Manoj Kumar, Simi, Pran, Sulochana, Ulhas, Padma Chauhan, Mohan Choti, Agha, Shivraj
Director:	A. Bhimsingh
Music director:	Naushad
Lyricist:	Shakeel Badayuni

41. Sunghursh (1968)

Type of film:	Costume drama, colour
Banner:	Rahul Theatres
Cast:	Dilip Kumar, Vyjayanthimala, Balraj Sahni, Sanjeev Kumar, Jayant, Durga Khote, Sulochana, Sunder, Ulhas, Iftekhar, Sapru, Mumtaz Begam, Padma, Urmila, Padmarani, Mehmood Junior, Master Arun, Kamaldeep, Jagdish Raj, Master Lebi, Ram Mohan, Rajesh Kumar, Paro, Devdutt, Snehalata, Rani, Rirku, Devan Verma, Ramlal, Lata Sinha, Sadhu Singh, Munshi, Prince Arjun, Anju Mahendru, Dilip Dewan, Ranu
Director:	H. S. Rawail
Story/script/ dialogues:	Based on Mahashweta Devi's story H. S. Rawail and Anjana Rawail (script)
Music director:	Naushad
Lyricist:	Shakeel Badayuni
Cinematographer:	R. D. Mathur

42. Gopi (1970)

Type of Film:	Social, colour
Banner:	Prosperity Pictures
Cast:	Dilip Kumar, Saira Banu, Pran, Johnny Walker, Sudesh Kumar, Shyamlal, Mukhri, Om Prakash, Nirupa Roy, Lalita Pawar, Farida Jalal, Durga Khote, Aruna Irani
Director:	A. Bhimsingh
Music directors:	Kalyanji Anandji
Lyricist:	Rajinder Kishen

43. Dastaan (1972) (double role)

Type of film: Social, colour
Banner: B. R. Films
Cast: Dilip Kumar, Sharmila Tagore, Bindu, Prem Chopra, I. S. Johar, Padma Khanna
Director: B. R. Chopra
Story/script/
  dialogues: I. S. Johar
Music directors: Laxmikant Pyarelal
Lyricist: Sahir Ludhianvi

44. Sagina (1974)

Type of film: Social, colour
Banner: Roop Shree International
Cast: Dilip Kumar, Saira Banu, Anil Chatterjee, Om Prakash, Aparna Sen, Swaroop Dutt, K. N. Singh
Director: Tapan Sinha
Music director: Sachin Dev Burman
Lyricist: Majrooh Sultanpuri

45. Bairaag (1976) (triple role)

Type of film: Social, colour
Banner: M. R. (Mushir Riaz) Productions
Cast: Dilip Kumar, Saira Banu, Leena Chandavarkar, Nasir Khan, Prem Chopra, Nazir Hussain, Leela Mishra, Mukhri
Director: Asit Sen
Music directors: Kalyanji Anandji
Lyricist: Anand Bakshi

46. Kranti (1981)

Type of film: Costume drama, colour
Banner: Vishal Pictures
Cast: Dilip Kumar, Manoj Kumar, Hema Malini, Shashi Kapoor, Shatrughan Sinha, Parveen Babi, Nirupa Roy, Prem Chopra, Pradeep Kumar, Madan Puri, Sarika, Master Kunal
Director: Manoj Kumar
Story/script/
  dialogues: Manoj Kumar

Music directors: Laxmikant Pyarelal
Lyricists: Santosh Anand, Manoj Kumar

47. Shakti (1982)

Type of film: Social, colour
Banner: M. R. Productions
Cast: Dilip Kumar, Amitabh Bachchan, Smita Patil, Raakhee, Amrish Puri, Kulbhushan Kharbanda
Director: Ramesh Sippy
Story/script/ dialogues: Salim-Javed
Music director: Rahul Dev Burman
Lyricist: Anand Bakshi

48. Vidhata (1982)

Type of film: Social, colour
Banner: Trimurti Films
Cast: Dilip Kumar, Shammi Kapoor, Sanjay Dutt, Sanjeev Kumar, Amrish Puri, Padmini Kolhapure, Sarika, Madan Puri, Suresh Oberoi
Director: Subhash Ghai
Music directors: Kalyanji Anandji
Lyricist: Anand Bakshi

49. Mazdoor (1983)

Type of film: Social, colour
Banner: B. R. Films
Cast: Dilip Kumar, Nanda, Raj Kiran, Raj Babbar, Padmini Kolhapure, Rati Agnihotri, Suresh Oberoi, Madan Puri, Johnny Walker
Director: Ravi Chopra
Music director: Rahul Dev Burman
Lyricist: Hasan Kamaal

50. Mashaal (1984)

Type of film: Social, colour
Banner: Yash Raj Films
Cast: Dilip Kumar, Waheeda Rehman, Anil Kapoor, Amrish Puri, Rati Agnihotri, Nilu Phule, Madan Puri, Saeed Jaffrey
Director: Yash Chopra

Music director:	Hridayanath Mangeshkar
Lyricist:	Javed Akhtar

51. Duniya (1984)

Type of film:	Social, colour
Banner:	Dharma Productions
Cast:	Ashok Kumar, Dilip Kumar, Rishi Kapoor, Amrita Singh, Amrish Puri, Prem Chopra, Pran, Saira Banu, Pradeep Kumar, Kulbhushan Kharbanda
Director:	Ramesh Talwar
Music director:	Rahul Dev Burman
Lyricist:	Javed Akhtar

52. Karma (1986)

Type of film:	Social, colour
Banner:	Mukta Arts
Cast:	Dilip Kumar, Nutan, Dara Singh, Anupam Kher, Jackie Shroff, Anil Kapoor, Naseeruddin Shah, Tom Alter, Poonam Dhillon, Sridevi, Shakti Kapoor, Satyanarayan
Director:	Subhash Ghai
Music directors:	Laxmikant Pyarelal
Lyricist:	Anand Bakshi

53. Dharm Adhikari (1986)

Type of film:	Social, colour
Banner:	Gopikrishna Movies
Cast:	Dilip Kumar, Jeetendra, Pran, Kadar Khan, Shakti Kapoor, Asrani, Sridevi, Preeti Sapru, Rohini Hattangadi, Anuradha Patel, Geeta Siddharth
Director:	K. Raghavendra Rao
Music director:	Bappi Lahiri
Lyricist:	Indivar

54. Kanoon Apna Apna (1989)

Type of film:	Social, colour
Banner:	Madhavi Productions
Cast:	Dilip Kumar, Nutan, Sanjay Dutt, Madhuri Dixit, Kadar Khan, Anupam Kher, Gulshan Grover, Tej Sapru, Satyen Kappu
Director:	B. Gopal

Music director: Bappi Lahiri
Lyricist: Indivar

55. Izzatdar (1990)

Type of film: Social, colour
Banner: Divya Films International
Cast: Dilip Kumar, Govinda, Madhuri Dixit, Bharati,
                   Shafi Inamdar, Shakti Kapoor, Anupam Kher,
                   Raghuvaran, Asrani
Director: K. Bapaiah
Music directors: Laxmikant Pyarelal
Lyricist: Anand Bakshi

56. Saudagar (1991)

Type of film: Social, colour
Banner: Mukta Arts
Cast: Dilip Kumar, Raaj Kumar, Vivek Mushran,
                   Manisha Koirala, Anupam Kher, Gulshan Grover,
                   Dina Pathak, Jackie Shroff, Deepti Naval, Dalip
                   Tahil, Mukesh Khanna, Anand Balraj, Amrish Puri
Director: Subhash Ghai
Story/script/   Subhash Ghai, Sachin Bhowmick, Kamlesh
  dialogues: Pandey (dialogues)
Music directors: Laxmikant Pyarelal
Lyricist: Anand Bakshi
Cinematographer: Ashok Mehta

57. Qila (1998) (double role)

Type of film: Social, colour
Banner: Eagle Films
Cast: Dilip Kumar, Rekha, Smita Jayakar, Mamta
                   Kullkarni, Mukul Dev, Gulshan Grover, Satish
                   Kaushik, Avtar Gill
Director: Umesh Mehra
Music director: Anand Raj Anand
Lyricists: Anand Raj Anand and Dev Kohli

Note: There were several film projects of Dilip Kumar that remained incomplete: for instance, *Shikwa*, *Mera Watan*, *Chanakya Chandragupt* and *Kalinga*.

Index

Abbas, Khwaja Ahmad, 28, 35, 68, 74, 125, 132, 133, 135, 140-41, 169, 178-79, 200, 228, 264, 286, 295-96, 298-99, 308, 327-28, 341, 357

Acharya, Gunwantrai, 22

Acharya, N. R., 72, 74, 125

Achrekar, M. R., 259

Adib, Prem, 39, 60, 61, 275, 363

Advani, Bhudo, 21

Advani, J. P., 44, 48, 49, 62

Agha (Agha Jaan), 126, 139, 317

Ahmed, W. Z., 68

Ajanta Cinetone, 62

Ajanta Movietone, 21, 29, 48, 119

Ajit (Hamid Ali Khan), 145, 146, 186, 339-42

Ajmeri, Nazir, 333

Akhtar, Begum (Akhtari Faizabadi), 177

'Akhtar', Gauri Shankarlal, 28

Akhtar, Javed, 217, 357

Akhtar, Sardar, 177

Ali, Mohammed, 279

Ali, Muzaffar, 341

Ali, Naushad, 21, 24, 88, 108, 115, 141, 142-43, 151, 161, 170, 175, 192, 197, 198, 209, 246, 305, 323, 324, 325, 326, 364

Altekar, Parshwanath Yeshwant, 16, 52, 62

Alvi, Abrar, 28, 259, 262

Amanat, Agha Hasan, 44

Aman, Zeenat, 202-03, 313, 358

Amarjeet, 310-11

Amarnath, K., 334

Ambani, Anil, 314

Ameeta, 344, 353

Amrohi, Kamal, 17-18, 27-28, 75, 138, 141, 178, 273, 328, 332, 337, 347

Anand, Chetan, 32, 68, 132, 135, 137, 179, 200, 203, 264, 286, 304-05, 308, 338

Anand, Dev, 1, 27, 65, 76, 132, 145, 159, 178, 200, 203, 205, 210, 231, 246, 258, 280, 303-16, 343, 352

Anand, Inder Raj, 68, 126, 141

Anand, M. L., 76, 364

Anand, Mulk Raj, 135-36, 308

Anand, Vijay, 76, 137, 203, 307-08, 310-13, 345, 353

Anjaan, 144

Annapurna, 135

Ansari, N. A., 332

'Anuj', Sambha Lal Shrivastava, 29

Anwar, Khurshid, 142

Apte, Baburao, 15, 62

Apte, Shanta, 1, 60, 90

Arora, P. N., 357
Arun, 63
Arya Subodh Natya Mandali, 17
'Ashant', Pandit Mukhram Sharma, 29, 141
Asif, K., 17, 18, 67, 68, 138, 143, 156-58, 168, 254, 266, 289
Asoka the Great, 245
Asrani, G., 205
Atma, C. H., 112
Atorthy, Premankur, 20, 55, 57, 82, 95, 128
Atre, Acharya, 115
Atre, P. K., 15, 29, 59
Avadhoot, V., 140
Azad, Aspi, 357
'Aziz', Munshi A. Shah, 28
Azmi, Kaifi, 28, 144, 261, 338

Babbar, Raj, 225
Babi, Parveen, 203, 217
Babita, 203, 356
Bachchan, Amitabh, 1, 2, 3, 4, 182, 191, 204, 205, 218, 219, 223, 226, 231-32, 242, 244, 268, 269, 271, 277-79, 282, 290, 329, 337, 349, 351, 354
Badami, Sarvotam, 23, 48, 49, 68-70, 72, 115
Badayuni, Shakeel, 144, 151, 198, 246, 262, 323
Bahl, Hansraj, 141
Balchandra, 360
Bali, Geeta, 274, 291, 298, 322, 330, 357, 365
Bannerji, Jyotish, 13
Bansal, K. N., 357
Banu, Naseem, 17, 40, 115, 334
Banu Saira, 17, 203, 213, 302, 354
Bapaiah, K., 223, 255
Barabankavi, Khumar, 144
Baran, Timir, 82, 89, 90, 95, 96
Barrymore, John, 46
Barua Pictures, 20

Barua, P. C., 19-20, 68, 81, 82, 95-96, 100, 112-13, 165, 188, 189, 261
Batish, S. D., 142
Bedekar, Vishram, 15, 345
Bedi, Rajender Singh, 28, 135, 141, 265, 286, 289
Begum, Shamshad, 24, 142, 323
Bengal School, 18-20
'Betaab', Narayan Prasad, 22, 28
Bhagat, S., 365
Bhagwan, Master, 139, 303, 329
Bhakhri, Lekhraj, 357, 362
Bhakri, Mulkraj, 275
Bhansali, Sanjay Leela, 72, 279
Bhatawadekar, Sakharam, 11
Bhatt, Balwant, 24, 48, 68
Bhatt, Basant, 360
Bhatt, H., 55
Bhatt, Harsukh, 360
Bhatt, Nanubhai, 359
Bhatt, Vijay, 24, 35, 49, 52, 61, 63, 67, 84, 139, 143, 276, 323, 324, 331
Bhattacharya, Abhi, 363
Bhattacharya, Basu, 204, 302
Bhattacharya, Bijon, 286
Bhattacharya, Rinki, 165
Bhave, K. P., 45
Bhavnani, Mohan, 8, 21, 23, 29, 33, 40, 43, 44, 46, 49, 54, 62, 65, 72, 97, 178, 343
Bhimsingh, A., 211, 212, 254, 265-66
Bhole, Keshavrao, 90
Bhopali, Asad, 144
Bhosle, Asha, 142, 314, 355
Bhushan, Bharat, 50, 145, 146, 246, 275, 322-30, 358
Bhushan, Pandit, 28
Bhutt, Mahesh, 365
Bibbo, 21, 40, 48, 49, 114, 177
Billimoria, Dinshaw, 39, 45, 46, 48
Billimoria, Eddie, 39, 45, 47, 54-55
Bindu, 215
Biswajit, 203, 275, 336, 352
Biswas, Anil, 90, 141, 142, 361, 362

Biswas, Smriti, 24
Bogart, Humphrey, 3, 350
Bokhari, Ali, 80
Bombay Talkies, 14, 33, 64, 73, 119,
    124, 125, 128, 138, 180, 182, 316
    legacy of, 25-27
Boral, Rai Chand, 81, 82, 89, 90, 94,
    108
Bose, Debaki, 19, 31, 49, 52, 66, 68, 84,
    93, 113, 155, 330, 363
Bose, Hemendra Mohan, 128
Bose, Kamal, 140
Bose, Madhu, 23, 67
Bose, Nitin, 19-20, 24, 27, 35, 68, 75,
    76, 82, 84, 93, 96, 97, 101, 108, 114,
    119, 127, 128, 132, 155, 179, 188,
    190, 227, 260, 273, 288, 327, 363
Bose, Sadhana, 40
Bose, Satyen, 76, 138, 319, 321, 363
Bose, Subhash Chandra, 20, 23, 76,
    188
Bow, Clara, 41
Brando, Marlon, 232, 237, 306
Buck, Pearl S., 140
Burman, Mandi, 309
Burman, Rahul Dev, 314, 355
Burman, Sachin Dev, 141-42, 164, 261,
    305-06, 310, 312, 314

Capra, Frank, 15, 161, 298
Chakravarty, Amiya, 26, 35, 64, 119,
    125, 132, 135, 138, 179, 181-83, 227,
    246, 288, 308, 331, 343
Chanakya, 210, 255
Chandavarkar, Leena, 203, 356
Chand, Daud, 273
Chander, Krishan, 28
Chandra, 96
Chandramohan, 39, 51-53, 181, 285
Chandra, Navin, 62
Chandrashekhar, 329, 367, 368
Chandravarkar, Bhaskar, 91
Changezi, Wajahat Mirza, 366
Chaplin, Charlie, 32, 72, 295, 302

Chatterjee, Anil, 213
Chatterjee, Bankimchandra, 29, 75
Chatterjee, Basu, 204
Chatterjee, Partho, 103, 183
Chatterjee, Saratchandra, 19, 29, 81,
    95-96, 113, 147, 161, 166, 183, 262,
    297
Chattopadhyay, Harindranath, 59,
    269
Chattopadhyay, Kartick, 363
Chekhov, Anton, 59
Chishti, Khwaja Salim, 169
Chitnis, Leela, 1, 40, 49, 74, 295
Chitragupta, 142
Chitre, N. G., 11
Chopra, B. R., 73, 75, 76, 137, 185, 225,
    292, 347, 348, 365
Chopra, Prem, 215, 217, 224
Chopra, Ravi, 255
Chopra, Yash, 138, 223, 255, 352
Choudhary, R. S., 13, 22, 23, 46, 48,
    55, 70, 115, 141, 364
Choudhury, Colonel N., 123
Choudhury, Salil, 141, 143, 168, 188,
    292, 348, 363
Chugtai, Ismat, 28
Chunder, Hemchandra, 20, 61, 63, 95,
    97, 105
Chunnilal, Rai Bahadur, 27
Cooper, Patience, 40
Cronin, A. J., 204, 313

Damle, Fatehlal, 84
Damle, Master V., 15
Damle, Vishnupant, 14,
Darpan, 279
Daryani, Ram, 114, 128, 254, 327
Dasgupta, Baradaprasanna, 94
Dave, Ravindra, 24, 273, 334, 340, 349
Dayal, Ram, 320
Deitrich, Marlene, 123
DeMille, Cecil B., 18, 159, 177
De Niro, Robert, 237
Desai, Chimanlal, 23

Desai, Dhirubhai, 41, 61, 84
Desai, Jayant, 22, 47, 54-55, 72, 82, 84, 102, 104, 106, 180, 344
Desai, Leela, 93, 97, 99
Desai, Manmohan, 203, 353
Desai, Manohar, 366-67
Desai, Raman Lal, 334
Desai, Ramnik, 67
Desai, V. C., 115
Desai, Vasant, 142, 143
Desai, Virendra, 61
De Sica, Vittorio, 189
Devi, B. Saroja, 190, 356
Devi, Chandrbati, 104
Devi, Kanan, 1, 40, 48, 86, 90, 93, 99, 260, 329
Devi, Mahashweta, 210
Devi, Pratima, 366
Devi, Sabita, 40, 48, 70
Devi, Saraswati, 90, 316
Devi, Seeta, 40
Devi, Sitara, 177, 198
Devi, Sumitra, 104
Dey, K. C., 96, 98
Dey, Manna, 142, 316, 326
Dhaibar, K. R., 14
Dharamsey, M. I., 49, 152, 273
Dharmadhikari, Datta, 359
Dharmendra, 98, 203, 270, 279, 336
Dhawan, Prem, 144
Dhumal, 139
Dil, Munshi, 27-28
Divakar, V. P., 11
Divecha, Dwarka, 140
Diwan, Karan, 145, 146, 364
Doshi, Chaturbhuj, 22, 54, 67, 72, 82, 102, 327, 367
Dostoevsky, Fyodor, 180, 300
Douglas, Kirk, 232
Dovzhenko, Alexander, 98
Dungan, Ellis R., 31, 159
Dutt, Bimal, 189
Dutt, Geeta, 142

Dutt, Guru, 1, 97, 101, 132, 133, 137, 138, 142, 143, 145, 173, 179, 198, 200, 201, 228, 257-64, 266-68, 270, 303, 305, 308, 336, 343
Dutt, Sanjay, 224, 349, 351
Dutt, Sunil (Balraj Dutt), 1, 76, 145, 146, 180, 191, 204, 226, 274, 293, 346-51, 368
Dutt, Swaroop, 214
Dutta, O. P., 61, 334, 344

East India Film Company, 19
East India Films, 41, 54, 185
Edison, Thomas, 11
Einsenstein, Sergei, 32, 98
Eliot, George, 111
Elwin, Verrier, 31

Fairbanks, Douglas, 22, 45
Faiz, Faiz Ahmed, 144
Famous Pictures, 51
Fatehlal, S., 14, 15
Fearless Nadia (Mary Evans Wadia), 22, 23
Fellini, Federico, 270
Filmistan, 27, 64, 119
Ford, Harrison, 3, 232

Gable, Clark, 3, 232
Gandharva, Bal, 52, 53
Gandhi, Indira, 277
Gandhi, Mahatma, 19, 35, 71, 85
Gandhi, Naval, 45
Ganesan, Gemini, 368
Ganesan, Sivaji, 212, 266
Ganguly, Aabhas Kumar (see under Kumar, Kishore)
Ganguly, Dhiren, 19
Ganguly, Kumudlal Kunjilal (see under Kumar, Ashok)
Ganguly, Ram, 69, 116
Garbo, Greta, 49, 237
Geeta, 335
Gemini (banner), 18, 159-60

Ghai, Subhash, 220, 223, 225, 254, 337, 345
Ghalib, Mirza, 92, 94, 245, 324
Ghariali, Nariman, 62
Ghatak, Ritwik, 96, 168, 186, 263, 363
Ghaznavi, Rafiq, 90
Ghosh, Gourkishor, 213
Ghosh, Kaliprasad, 69, 70, 112
Ghosh, Kirit, 88
Ghosh, Prafulla, 23, 48, 65
Gidwani, Moti, 13, 24, 28, 41, 44, 55, 56
Gilbert, John, 49
Goel, Devendra, 274, 323
Gogol, Nikolai, 289
Gohar, 22, 40, 42, 47
Gopal, B., 220, 222, 255
Gope, 139, 238, 360
Goswami, Harikrishan (*see under* Kumar, Manoj)
Grant Anderson Theatre, 66
Grant, Cary, 3, 232
Griffith, D. W., 32
Guha, Anita, 318, 329
Guha, Dulal, 362, 363
Guleri, Chandardhar, 135, 348
Gulzar (Sampooran Singh), 189, 204, 265, 268, 368
Gunjal, Dada, 28, 48, 49, 55, 62
Gupta, Dilip, 140, 188
Gupta, Hemen, 68, 135, 189, 286, 290, 327, 330
Gupta, Ramesh, 64, 323
Guruswamy, G., 259

Habib, 279
Hafis, I. A., 55
Haider, Ghulam, 24, 141, 142
Hamid, Gul, 39, 63
Harish, 334, 366
Harish, Tara, 367
Harrison, Rex, 314
Hasnain, S. F., 364
Hassan, Najmal, 39

Hathaway, Henry, 349
Helen, 367
Henry, O., 167
Hepburn, Audrey, 314
Heston, Charlton, 232
Hingorani, Arjun, 203, 362
Hiralal, 198
Hitchcock, Alfred, 215
Hitler, Adolf, 32, 123
Hollywood, 3, 12, 13, 16, 40, 41, 45, 49, 69, 93, 120, 140, 145, 157, 196, 215, 220, 232, 237, 246, 266, 315, 350, 358
Homer, 156, 260
Homi Brothers, 264
Hoogan, B. S., 21, 90
Hope, Anthony, 50
Husain, Sajjad, 142
Husnlal Bhagatram, 142
Hussain, Anwar, 190
Hussain, Mohammed, 365, 367
Hussain, Najmul, 63
Hussain, Nasir, 139, 310, 329, 352, 353
Hussain, Nazir, 167, 186, 203

Iman, Akhtar-ul, 28
Imperial Theatres, 12-13, 21, 45, 55, 66, 177
Indian Art Production, 21
Indian cinema
  as a medium of education, 34
  Bengal School in, 18-20
  classical period of, 3, 283
    post, 199-216
  early innovators in, 11-12
  first four icons of, 65-78
  formative period of, 2-3, 7-36
  four distinctive phases of, 4
  inventors of grand spectacle in, 16-18
  influence of literature on, 27-29
  international recognition for, 30-32
  invention of melodies in, 141-44

Indian cinema contd...

landmarks in, 134-41
leading ladies of the pioneering era
in, 40
mythological, 33
nationalist sentiments and, 33
sensuality in, 34
spiritual, 84-88
silent era in, 8
study of various categories of, 1-2
talkie era of, 12-13
first talkie film of, 12-13
Indian National Army, 20, 76, 188
Indian National Congress, 284
Indivar, 144
Indra, Pandit, 28
Irani, Ardeshir, 8, 12-13, 21
Irani, Aspi, 22, 56, 264
Irani, Daisy, 167, 318, 347
Irani, Fardoon, 13, 41, 140, 198
Irfani, Kaif, 144
Ishwarlal, 39, 48, 53, 54, 122
Islam, Qazi Nazrul, 29, 92

Jafri, Ali Sardar, 144, 328
Jagirdar, Gajanan, 15, 53, 56, 58-60,
62, 84
Jaidev, 69, 141, 142, 143, 310, 351
Jaikishan (*see also* Shankar
Jaikishan), 268, 295, 296, 301,
303, 305, 324, 354
Jain, Ravindra, 205
Jaipuri, Hasrat, 144
Jairaj, P., 21, 39, 48-51, 107, 122, 126,
128, 254, 357
Jalal, Farida, 213
Jalalabadi, Qamar, 144
Jamuna, 93, 95, 100
Jaswantlal, Nandlal, 22, 42, 43, 46,
115, 138, 325, 331
Jayant (Zakaria Khan), 63, 158, 175,
210
Jayashri, 284, 331, 335, 364

Jaywant, Nalini, 152, 180, 323, 331,
344, 365, 366
Jeetendra, 203, 336, 338
Jeevan, 152, 161, 186, 198, 292, 360
Jehan, Akhtar, 104
Jinnah, Mohammed Ali, 176
Johar, I. S., 50, 71, 138, 139, 205, 215,
273, 319, 320, 340
Johar, Yash, 223
Joshi, Manilal, 41, 42
Jullunduri, Hafiz, 92

Kabir, 245
Kadam, Kamini, 274
Kaiser, Farookh, 144
Kale, Keshav Narayan, 29, 51, 64, 347
Kale, Madhav, 39, 50, 62
Kalidas, 76, 320
Kalpana, 311, 354
Kamalahasan, 159
Kanwal, Peace, 362
Kapoor, A. P., 21, 48, 49, 62
Kapoor, Anil, 221, 224
Kapoor, G. P., 359
Kapoor, Karisma, 349
Kapoor, Kedar, 291, 344, 360
Kapoor, Raj, 1, 68, 69, 72, 76, 132, 136,
137, 139, 145, 172, 178, 191, 194,
200, 201, 205, 210, 212, 228, 236,
231, 246, 261, 263, 275, 280, 281,
293-303, 304, 305, 315, 320, 322,
323, 342, 346, 366
as the great showman, 293-303
Kapoor, Rajiv, 352
Kapoor, Randhir, 68, 303, 346, 352
Kapoor, Rishi, 352
Kapoor, Shammi, 69, 146, 203, 205,
224, 315, 352-58
Kapoor, Shashi, 69, 203, 217, 293, 323,
351, 364
Karandikar, A. P., 11
Karani, Paysi, 13, 36
Karani, Pesi, 41, 54

Kardar, A. R. (Abul Rashid), 22, 24, 35, 54, 56, 63, 67, 82, 107, 119, 137, 143, 151, 208, 227, 255, 334, 362, 365
Kardar Studio, 24
Karmakar, Radhu, 140, 301
Karnad, Girish, 283
Karnataki, Vasudev, 56
Kartik, Kalpana, 306, 307
Kashmiri, Aga Hashr, 17, 28
Kashyap, D. D., 307, 343
Kashyap, D. S., 61, 72, 139, 307, 343
Kashyap, J. S., 29
Kaul, Mahesh, 132, 139, 262, 297, 343, 357
Kaur, Kuldip, 71, 175
Kaushal, Kamini, 151-52, 173, 179, 304, 365
Kaushik, R., 140
Kaye, Danny, 315
Kazan, Elia, 306
Kesar, 79
Khalil, 39, 40, 41, 42
Khalil, S., 366
Khan, Amjad, 63, 168
Khan, Feroze, 203
Khan, Kadar, 278
Khan, Khan Sahib Amir, 323
Khan, Mazhar, 53-54, 59
Khan, Mehboob, 17, 23, 33, 35, 51, 52, 60, 61, 64, 71, 76, 114, 115, 119, 132, 135, 136, 143, 155, 168, 172, 176-79, 185, 189, 195, 200, 227, 228, 245, 263, 274, 335, 343, 347, 365
Khan, Nasir, 124, 190, 218, 273
Khan, Raja Mehdi Ali, 28, 144
Khan, Salim, 217
Khan, Salman, 349
Khan, Sanjay, 203, 303, 345
Khan, Shahrukh, 2, 279
Khan, Ustad Faiyaz, 110, 111
Khan, Ustad, Zande, 90
Khan, Yousuf, 279
Khandekar, V. S., 15, 29

Khanna, Mukesh, 278-79
Khanna, Rajbans, 140
Khanna, Rajesh, 1, 167, 203, 208, 280-82, 315, 338, 349, 357, 364
Khanna, Usha, 354
Khanna, Vinod, 203
Kharbanda, Kulbhushan, 351
Khatri, Devakinandan, 325
Khayyam, 141, 205
Kher, Anupam, 220, 278
Khosla, Dwarka, 54, 68
Khosla, Raj, 139, 203, 233, 307, 308, 309, 349
Khote, Durga, 1, 14, 21, 40, 49, 66, 169, 211
Khote, Shubha, 325
Khurshid, 49, 93, 102, 103, 104
Kinikar, Shashikant, 51
Kiran, Usha, 167, 299, 321
Kishen, Rajinder, 141, 144, 348
Kohinoor Films, 40, 41
Koirala, Manisha, 226
Komal, Roop, 297
Kotnis, Dr Dwarkanath, 284
Krishnarao, Master, 90
Krishna, Daljit, 367
Kulkarni, Sitarambapu, 14
Kumar, 39, 64
Kumar, Anand, 76
Kumar, Anjan, 260
Kumar, Anoop, 139, 319
Kumar, Ashok, 1, 26, 27, 39, 44, 65, 73-78, 83, 122, 124, 125, 156, 178, 215, 220, 238, 267, 316, 318, 332, 337, 348, 349
  filmography of, 78
Kumar, Dharam, 362
Kumar, Dilip (Yusuf Khan), 1, 2, 3, 17, 52, 60, 72, 76, 97, 116, 119-30, 131-234, 257, 258, 259, 266, 269, 289, 292, 298, 299, 305, 308, 309, 322, 323, 325-26, 328, 333, 335, 336, 337, 341, 342, 362, 363
  and Hindi cinema, 231-32

Dilip Kumar contd.

and Indian school of method
  acting, 235-44
and Pakistani cinema, 279-80
as numero uno, 131-234
contemporaries of, 283-368
death scenes enacted by, 192-93
directors of films by, 254-55
disciples of, 271-82
films and portrayal diversity in
  cinema of, 245-56
films and portrayals in post-
  classical era, 205-16
personal sufferings and social
  realities and, 227-31
profile of roles by, 247-54
towards liberation of the tragic
  image by, 193-99
Kumar, Hemant, 141, 142, 143, 330
Kumar, Kishore, 2, 112, 139, 142, 167,
  205, 315-21
Kumar, Krishan, 334
Kumar, Manoj, 203, 204, 212, 216, 217,
  245, 255, 275-78, 282, 336, 345
Kumar, Pandit Shiv, 28
Kumar, Pradeep (Sital Batabyal), 76,
  145, 146, 217, 275, 329, 330-32,
  363
Kumar, Raaj (Kulbhushan Pandit),
  75, 93, 95, 145, 182, 190, 225, 232,
  246, 269, 275, 293, 334-39, 348,
  350
Kumar, Rajendra, 76, 115, 146, 202,
  203, 274-75, 301, 336
Kumar, Sanjeev, 52, 203, 205, 210,
  224, 257, 264-70, 358
movies of, 269-70
Kumar, Surya, 115
Kumar, Vinod, 327
Kumari, 98
Kumari, Kamlesh, 97
Kumari, Lalita, 360

Kumari, Meena, 27, 76, 138, 184, 193,
  194, 196, 203, 260, 268, 273, 274,
  275, 292, 299, 300, 316, 318, 323,
  335, 337, 344, 347, 365, 366
Kumari, Raj, 40, 93, 95, 102
Kum Kum, 264, 358

Lall, K. B., 115
Lang, Fritz, 123
Lateef, Shahid, 64, 173, 255, 273, 290,
  333, 362, 365
Laxmikant Pyarelal, 359
Lean, David, 246
Lemmon, Jack, 358
Lenin, Vladimir, 32
Lewis, Jerry, 315
Linlithgow, Lady, 99
Lohar, Chimanlal, 61, 70, 72, 141
Lohar, C. M., 115
Lubitsch, Ernst, 59
Lukhnavi, Arzoo, 28, 92
Lucknawi, Majaaz, 357
Ludhianvi, Sahir, 144, 164, 180, 259,
  260, 305-06, 347
Lumière Brothers, 11

MacLaine, Shirley, 358
Madan Theatres, 13, 31, 41, 43, 44
Madan, Jamshedji Framji, 8, 12-13, 21
Madhok, Dinanath, 22, 49, 55, 62
Madhubala, 1, 64, 75, 170, 175, 294,
  299, 319, 322, 325, 328, 329,
  331, 341, 344, 349, 356, 357,
  359, 365
Madhuri, 49
Maharashtra Film Company, 14
Maheshwari, Ram, 68
Mahipal, 358-61, 363
Mahjoor, Ghulam Ahmed, 293
Majumdar, Nagendra, 50
Majumdar, Phani, 20, 27, 50, 62, 63,
  76, 82, 96, 99, 119, 286, 308, 316,
  365

Majumdar, Sushil, 114, 182
Majumdar, Tarun, 114
Malhotra, M. N., 140
Malini, Hema, 203, 217, 302, 313, 357
Mangeshkar, Hridyanath, 205
Mangeshkar, Lata, 1, 142, 168, 296, 323, 327, 332, 348, 364
Manto, Sadat Hasan, 25, 28, 51, 141
Mao Zedong, 284
March, Fredric, 350
Master, Homi, 13, 40, 41, 42, 46, 48
Mathur, R. D., 140, 273
Meena, 71
Mehboob Productions, 23
Mehmood (Mehmood Ali), 139, 205, 292, 316
Mehmood, Talat, 112, 116, 142, 175, 290, 326, 348, 357, 361-63
Mehra, Raj, 197
Mehra, Umesh, 220, 255
Mehtab, 40, 49
Menon, Raghava R., 86, 92, 103, 110, 112
Merchant, Jal, 39, 48
Minerva Movietone, 17, 18, 20, 59, 61, 119, 134
Mir, Izra, 13, 23, 31, 41, 48, 54
Mirza, Safdar, 366
Mirza, Sultan, 116
Mirza, Wajahat, 28, 141, 198, 200
Mishra, B. P., 40, 66
Mishra, B. R., 45
Mistri, Babubhai, 327, 359, 368
Mistry, Fali, 140, 305
Mitra, Bibhuti, 27, 138, 152, 255, 325, 334
Mitra, Bimal, 261
Mitra, Joytendra, 135
Mitra, Shambhu, 135, 286
Mitra, Sombhu, 72, 297
Mitra, Subrata, 303
Mitra, Tripti, 297
Modak, Shahu, 39, 60-61, 122, 363

Modi, K. M., 17
Modi, Rustam, 17
Modi, Sohrab, 8, 17, 18, 21, 33, 35, 39, 51, 56, 59, 61, 65, 67, 83, 115, 132, 134, 157, 158, 227, 238, 324, 336
filmography of, 77
Mody, Sarosh, 266
Mohammed, Ghulam (actor), 53, 55, 122
Mohammed, Ghulam (music director), 141, 324
Mohammed, Master, 63
Mohan, Madan (Madan Mohan Kohli), 142, 143, 144, 327, 332, 338, 350
Mohinder, S., 142
Moitra, Amit, 72, 297
Motilal, 39, 52, 65, 69-73, 83, 114, 122, 125, 139, 162, 190, 207, 238, 267, 300
filmography of, 77-78
Mridula, 123, 126
Mubarak, 64, 103
Mukerjee, Gyan, 26, 27, 74, 75, 119
Mukerjee, Subodh, 138, 202, 310, 352, 353
Mukerji, Joy, 203, 352
Mukerji, Rono Deb, 204
Mukerji, Shashdhar, 27, 73
Mukesh (Mukesh Chand Mathur), 112, 142, 296, 299, 326, 327, 361
Mukharjee, Prabhat, 292
Mukherjee, Hrishikesh, 72, 76, 139, 166, 167, 168, 188, 189, 204, 255, 265, 281, 288, 299, 301, 307, 321, 347, 363, 365
Mukherjee, Keshto, 205
Mukherjee, Shankar, 308, 319
Mukherji, Ram, 207, 255
Mukhri, 139, 198, 366
Mukhtar, Sheikh, 177, 182, 264, 299, 365, 366, 367
Mullick, Amar, 20, 84, 113, 188

Mullick, Pankaj, 82, 89, 90, 96, 99
Mumtaz, 203, 312, 313
Munda, Birsa, 245
Muni, Paul, 237
Munim, Tina, 314
Munshi, K. M., 29, 41, 70
Murad, 195, 196
Murthy, V. K., 140, 259
Mushran, Vivek, 225

Nadeem (Mirza Nazir Beg), 279-80
Nadira, 195, 336
Nagalingam, P. K., 41
Nagar, Amritlal, 29
Naidu, Leela, 139, 289
Naidu, Sarojini, 26, 106, 269
Naidu, S. M. S., 196, 255
Najam, 99
Nakshab, 28
Nanavati, K. M., 350
Nanda, 58, 203, 274, 301, 310, 311, 348
Nanda, J. K., 28, 68, 82
Naqvi, Najam, 27, 61, 67, 183, 334, 335
Naqvi, Nazim, 49
Narayan, Jayprakash, 191, 301
Narayan, R. K., 72, 134, 311
Narayan, Satya, 198
Narayan, Udit, 144
Narendra, 28
Nargis, 1, 49, 50, 71, 140, 150, 152, 153, 156, 172, 174, 177, 210, 218, 273, 289, 292, 295, 296, 298, 299, 331, 334, 347, 365, 366
National Studio, 23
Naushad (see under Ali, Naushad)
Navketan Films, 137, 142, 201, 203
Nawab, 101
Nawathe, Raja, 84, 132, 139, 324, 325
Nayampalli, S. B., 21, 62
Nayyar, O. P., 24, 141, 143, 290, 299, 318, 325, 353, 355
Nayyar, R. K., 72-73, 349
Nazir, 64, 196
Nehru, Jawaharlal, 23, 26, 35, 136, 348

Nepali, Gopal Singh, 29
New Theatres, 14, 19, 20, 68, 81, 82, 84, 87, 90, 96, 99, 113, 124, 128, 155, 163, 168, 188, 189, 330, 363
Nigam, Satish, 297
Nimmi, 60, 156, 161, 181, 195, 266, 273, 298, 305, 308, 318, 324, 325, 335, 341, 344, 365, 366
Nissar, Master, 21, 39, 43, 116
Noorjehan, 24, 56, 65, 115, 150
Nutan, 203, 221, 273, 299, 300, 302, 310, 311, 318, 344, 347, 356, 357, 365

Ojha, S. K., 156, 255, 289
Osten, Franz, 26, 49, 63, 64, 73, 74, 123
O'Toole, Peter, 246

Pabst, G. W., 123
Pacino, Al, 237
Padmini, 72, 292, 301, 332, 356
Pagnis, Vishnupant, 15
Paintal, Kawarjit, 205
Painter, Baburao, 8, 10, 14, 30, 45, 53
Pakshiraja Studio, 196
Paluskar, D. V., 89, 111, 323
Pancholi Art Pictures, 24
Pancholi, Dalsukh M., 24, 56, 142
Paranjape, Raja, 15
Paranjpye, R. P., 11
Parekh, Asha, 203, 310, 332, 354, 355, 356
Paro, 152
Patankar, S. N., 11, 41
Patel, Ambalal, 23
Patel, Vallabhbhai, 71
Pathare, Jaywant, 140
Patil, Dinkar D., 58
Patil, L. G., 259
Patwardhan, Vinayak Rao, 111
Pawar, G. P., 62
Pawar, Lalita, 300, 354, 364
Pawar, Vasant, 143

Peck, Gregory, 145, 232
Pendharkar, Baburao, 15, 56, 58
Pendharkar, Bhalji, 15, 16, 45, 57, 59, 60, 67, 68
Peshwa, Madhavrao, 60
Phalke, Dhundiraj Govind (Dadasaheb), 7-10, 12, 14, 30
    number of films by, 9
'Phani', Pandit, 28
Pillai, Jai Gopal, 20
Pithawala, 126
Pope, Alexander, 183
Prabhakar, S. K., 327
Prabhat Film Company, 14, 15, 16, 31, 33, 51, 53, 54, 56, 59, 84, 119, 304
    films made by, 14-15
Pradeep (Ramachandra Narayanji Dwivedi), 29, 125, 144, 340
Prakash Pictures, 24
Prakash, J. Om, 203
Prakash, Khemchand, 90, 103, 116, 141, 142, 316
Prakash, Om, 24, 197, 212, 329
Prakash, Suraj, 364
Pran, 1, 24, 187, 196, 209, 212, 224, 296, 318, 320, 328, 342, 345, 353, 355, 356
Prasad, Badri, 21
Premchand, Munshi, 21, 29, 35, 97, 291, 348
'Prem', Dr Dhaniram, 29
Premnath (Premnath Malhotra), 52, 145, 195, 295, 339, 342-46
Presley, Elvis, 202, 353
Prithvi Theatres, 68, 69
Pronin, V., 140
Punwani, K. G., 360
Puri, Amrish, 218, 224, 225, 278

Qadir, Kozhikode Abdul, 112
Qureshi, Iqbal, 142, 367

Raakhee, 203, 219
Radhakishan, 317

Rafi, Mohammed, 24, 142, 150, 261, 299, 321, 323, 326, 354, 355, 367
Rai, Bina, 159, 325, 328, 331, 332, 344
Rai, Himanshu, 8, 21, 25, 26, 31, 123
Rajadhyaksha, Ashish, 286, 320
Rajkamal Kalamandir, 16
Rajshree, 302, 355
Rakhan, 365
Ram, Atma, 265
Ramachandran, M. G., 196
Ramachandra, S., 350
Raman, M. V., 76, 327
Raman, Sir C. V., 13
Ramchandra, C., 142, 143, 197, 284, 319, 330, 335, 340, 361
Ramola, 24
Rangeela, 280
Rani, Bulo C., 155
Rani, Devika, 26, 27, 40, 49, 63, 64, 73, 74, 122, 123, 124, 125, 129, 182
Ranjan, 368
Ranjit Studio, 22, 24, 46, 47, 54, 119, 180, 185
Rao, Anant, 10
Rao, K. Raghavendra, 220, 255
Rao, T. Prakash, 309
Ratan, D. K., 115
Rathor, Kanjibhai, 40
Ratna, 330
Ratra, V., 140
Rattanbai, 93
Ravi (Ravi Shankar Sharma), 142, 262
Rawail, H. S., 72, 76, 210, 226, 255, 265, 334, 343, 344
Ray, Satyajit, 10, 15, 114, 246, 262, 265
Raza, Ali, 141
Raza, S., 200
Rehana, 297, 298, 334, 335
Rehman, 355, 365
Rehman, Waheeda, 140, 203, 209, 211, 212, 224, 259, 302, 307, 311, 313, 332, 349, 350
Reinhardt, Max, 123

Rekha, 203, 223, 341, 368
Rekha, Swarna, 105-06
Renu, Phaneshwarnath, 302
Reuben, Bunny, 124, 268
Rishi, Raj, 308
Rizvi, Ehsan, 28
Rizvi, Rafiq, 360
Rizvi, Shaukat Hussain, 24, 51, 56, 150
RK banner, 294, 295
Robson, Mark, 50
Romani, Akhtar, 144
Roshan (Roshanlal Nagrath), 142, 143-44, 361
Roy, Bimal, 19, 20, 27, 35, 72, 76, 96, 119, 125, 132, 135, 137, 139, 140, 142, 143, 161, 164-66, 168, 179, 183, 186, 188, 189, 200, 227, 246, 258, 261, 270, 286, 320, 327, 328, 347, 348, 363
Roy, Jamini, 87
Roy, M. N., 22
Roy, Nirupa, 167, 212, 289, 318, 321, 326, 327
Roy, Prafulla, 67
Roy, Sudhendu, 140

Sadhana, 203, 302, 310, 348, 349, 350, 356
Sadiq, M., 76, 139, 151, 262, 334, 364
Sagar Movietone, 17, 23, 24, 69, 114, 119, 176, 185, 365
Sagar, Ramanand, 69, 139, 141, 203, 327
Saheb, V. Baba, 140, 190
Saheb, Wali, 56
Sahib, Mir, 90
Sahni, Balraj, 1, 135, 139, 157, 179, 189, 211, 267, 283, 285-93, 326, 358, 367
Sahu, Kishore, 27, 64, 122, 138, 150, 255, 311
Saigal, Amar Chand, 79

Saigal, Kundal Lal, 1, 2, 3, 19, 39, 44, 78-112, 113, 114, 125, 128, 144, 146, 148, 156, 163, 165, 166, 168, 189, 209, 238, 242, 244, 245, 260, 261, 268, 271, 275, 316, 327, 329, 330, 331
Saigal, Naresh, 357
Samanta, Shakti, 76, 114, 139, 203, 308, 347, 352, 353, 363
Samarth, Kumarsen, 67
Samarth, Shobhna, 40, 57, 70, 355
Sandhya, 361
Sandow, Raja, 39, 41-43, 46-48
Santoshi, Pyare Lal, 27, 139, 273, 327, 304, 365
Sanyal, Pahari (Narendranath), 39, 90, 112-14
Sanyal, Prabodh, 100
Sapru, 172
Sarhadi, Zia, 23, 35, 49, 119, 133, 135, 141, 179, 184, 185, 255, 274, 286, 288, 290
Sarika, 217
Sarita, 367
Sarkar, Jyotish, 12
Sarla, 327
Sarpotdar, Narayanrao, 16
Sarpotdar, Narayanrao Damodar, 29, 46
Sathyu, M. S., 204, 292
'Seemab', Mukand Lal, 21, 28, 92
Segal, Mohan, 320
Sehgal, Ramesh, 27, 28, 52, 69, 75, 132, 133, 138, 179, 180, 183, 246, 254, 264, 299, 339, 347
Sen, Aparna, 214
Sen, Asit, 76, 114, 189, 204, 212, 217, 255, 265, 363
Sen, Heeralal, 11
Sen, Mrinal, 128
Sen, Suchitra, 162, 167, 309, 325, 365
Sen, Sudhir, 114
Serajuddin, 79

Seth, Chiman, 198
Sethi, Jagdish, 98, 334
Shah, Chandulal, 8, 22, 42, 46, 47, 55, 71, 298
Shah, Dayaram, 22
Shah, Naseeruddin, 221, 279
Shailendra, 144, 168, 205, 268, 302
Shakespeare, William, 17, 66, 320
Shakila, 317, 340, 354, 367
Shamali, 93
Shammi, 126
Shams, Munshi, 28
Shankar Jaikishan, 69, 141, 142, 143, 295, 296, 301, 303, 305, 324, 354
Shankar, K., 212, 364
Shankar, Ravi, 135, 289
Shankar, Uday, 135
Shantaram, V., 1, 8, 10, 14, 15-17, 21, 35, 51-53, 56, 59-60, 68, 84, 119, 132, 134, 135, 143, 221, 227, 228, 245, 263, 274, 283, 284, 285, 302, 331, 360, 364
Shanti, Mumtaz, 56, 129
Sharif, Omar, 246
Sharma, Kidar, 22, 51, 64, 68, 71, 76, 82, 84, 95, 101, 104, 115, 119, 132, 137, 140, 152, 154, 155, 170, 255, 274, 294, 297, 322, 343, 357, 364
Sharma, Pandit Mukhram (see under Ashant)
Sharma, Rameshwar, 105
Shashi, Uma, 93, 94, 98, 99
Shashikala, 174, 291
Shastri, Acharya Chatursen, 362
Shastri, Lal Bahadur, 276
Shekhar, 145, 167, 323, 364
Shivaji, Chatrapati, 33, 45, 46, 283
Shorey, Roop K., 71, 339
Shroff, Jackie, 72, 221, 225
Shukla, B., 55
Shukla, Balchandra, 325
Shyam (Shyam Sundar Chadha), 76, 333-34, 339

Shyama, 273, 305, 318, 329, 355, 357, 360, 362, 365, 366
Simi, 311
Singh, Bhagat, 276
Singh, Dr Manmohan, 314, 351
Singh, K. N., 295, 305, 306, 355
Singh, Neetu, 203
Sinha, Mala, 203, 274, 275, 299, 310, 317, 328, 331, 335, 348, 356
Sinha, Mohan, 61, 67, 107, 115, 116, 365
Sinha, Shatrughan, 217, 351
Sinha, Tapan, 179, 204, 212, 213, 254
Sippy, G. P., 203, 325
Sippy, Ramesh, 217, 255, 356
Sircar, B. N., 8, 19-20, 21, 81, 124, 155
Sitara, 40, 366
Soni, Bhappie, 353, 356
Sridhar, 275
Stanislavsky, Konstantin, 60, 236-37
Sternberg, Josef von, 123
Stewart, James, 232
Subbulakshmi, M. S., 31, 85
Subramanyam, K., 43
Suchitra, 357
Sudarshan, Pandit, 28
Suharwardis, 79
Sulochana (Ruby Myers), 40, 42, 45, 46, 54, 55
Sultan, Tipu, 324
Sultana, Munawwar, 115, 174, 333, 334, 365, 366
Sultana, Nigar, 49, 295, 324, 334, 360
Sultanpuri, Majrooh, 28, 108, 144, 307
Sunder, Shyam, 24, 141, 142, 340
Sunny, S. U., 137, 143, 150, 151, 152, 161, 174, 197, 246, 254
Suraiya, 49, 93, 106, 108, 142, 157, 273, 298, 304, 324, 334, 344, 345, 357, 362, 365
Surdas, 102
Surendra, 39, 112, 114-16, 125, 275
Suresh, 145, 146, 365

Suryakumari, 161
Swaranlata, 126

Tagore, Rabindranath, 25, 29, 45, 89, 92, 112, 123, 127, 129, 188, 286, 290, 320
Tagore, Sharmila, 203, 355
Talwar, Ramesh, 255
Talwar, R. C., 139, 175, 255, 327
Tandon, Lekh, 349, 353
Tembe, Govindrao, 14, 51, 53, 90
Tennyson, Lord Alfred, 50
Thakur, Anant, 334
Thakur, Mahendra, 61
Thakur, Ramchandra, 23, 49, 115, 360
Thapar, Ramesh, 184
Tiwari, R., 327
Torne, Dadasaheb, 11
Tripathi, S. N., 84, 139, 141, 326

Ulhas, 63-64
Usmani, Chand, 317, 357

Vacha, Savak, 27
Vaidya, Ramnik, 325
Vakil, Nanu Bhai, 23, 48, 62
Vasan, S. S., 17, 18, 72, 97, 132, 134, 158, 159-60, 189, 254, 298, 368
Veena, 76, 157
Verma, B., 344
Verma, Bhagwati Charan, 29, 35, 124, 332
Vijayalaxmi, 296
Vikramaditya, Chandragupta, 326
Vimi, 348
Vinayak, Master (Vinayak Damodar Karnataki), 14, 15, 51, 56-58, 59, 61

Vithal, Master, 39, 43, 44-45, 55, 176, 240
Vyas, Bharat, 29, 144, 322
Vyas, Manibhai, 54, 359
Vyas, Narayan Rao, 111
Vyas, Narotam, 28
Vyas, V. M., 48, 49, 55, 61, 84
Vyjayanthimala, 1, 162, 186, 190, 202, 203, 210, 275, 299, 301, 309, 317, 319, 329, 331, 341, 344, 347, 349, 356, 365

Wadia, Homi, 22, 43, 63, 264, 359, 360
Wadia, J. B. H., 1, 22, 31, 63
Wadia Movietone, 22-23, 151
Wadkar, Hansa, 40
Wali, Wali Mohammed, 28
Walker, Clint, 50
Walker, Johnny (Badruddin Qazi), 139, 186, 205, 263, 317, 329
Warerkar, Mama, 15, 29, 62
Warner Brothers, 30
Willemen, Paul, 286, 320

Yagnik, Alka, 144
Yagnik, Navin, 62
Yakub, 55, 156, 177, 238
Yesevi sect, 79
Yussuf, Salman, 79
Yusuf, S. M., 362

Zafar, Bahadurshah, 77, 247, 324
Zebunissa, 49
Zils, Paul, 68
Zubeida, 40, 42, 48